A HISTORY OF
GREEK POLITICAL THOUGHT

A HISTORY
OF
GREEK POLITICAL THOUGHT

by

T. A. SINCLAIR

Professor of Greek in the Queen's University
of Belfast

ROUTLEDGE & KEGAN PAUL LTD
Broadway House, 68-74 Carter Lane
London

First published in 1951
by Routledge & Kegan Paul Limited
Broadway House, 68-74 Carter Lane
London, E.C.4
Printed in Great Britain
by Robert Cunningham & Sons Limited
Alva, Clackmannanshire

*Owing to production delays
this book was not published
until 1952*

CONTENTS

PREFACE

I wish to thank those friends and colleagues with whom I have discussed various parts of this book—K. M. T. Chrimes (Mrs Atkinson), E. D. Phillips and W. H. Porter (Cork); to thank also Frances Hume and others who typed it, and D. R. Bradley and D. A. McAlindon for help in proof-reading.

The notes at the end of each chapter are intended primarily to indicate the ancient sources for that chapter; for the book should be read as it was written with these at elbow. They also serve to supplement the footnotes and to give a *small selection* of modern works. It would have been easy to compile an extended bibliography for the whole work, but it would have been misleading and of no practical value. There are many well-known histories of philosophy, books on political science, books about the Greek authors here utilised, but there are very few that deal with the development of Greek Political Thought. I mention here: (1) Ernest Barker, *Greek Political Theory: Plato and his Predecessors* (1918, 1925, 1947)—a book so well known that I thought it advisable not to consult it too often when writing my own; (2) Hans von Arnim, *Die politischen Theorien des Altertums* (1910)—six very fine lectures; (3) A. von Verdross-Drossberg, *Grundlinien der antiken Rechts- und Staatsphilosophie*, Vienna, 1946, 1948—mainly concerned with Plato. To these I add, though it only reached me just as this book was going to press, and is less general in its scope, (4) Heinrich Ryffel, *ΜΕΤΑΒΟΛΗ ΠΟΛΙΤΕΙΩΝ*, *Der Wandel der Staatsverfassungen*, Bern, 1949 (Noctes Romanae Nr. 2).

The translations from the Greek are my own except for one quotation from Philo on page 299. For it I have to thank Messrs W. Heinemann & Co. for permission to use the Colson-Whittaker translation in the Loeb Library.

While this book was being printed, died Martin P. Charles-worth, Robert Mitchell Henry and John McC. Loewenthal—three friends to whose critical judgment I had hoped to submit my finished work. Let it therefore be dedicated to their memory.

July 1951

INTRODUCTORY

Sitôt que quelqu'un dit des affaires de l'état Que m'importe?, on doit compter que l'état est perdu.—ROUSSEAU.

AMONG the causes of the various events which make up human history not the least is Political Thought. Even when it does not immediately result in political action, the thinking of political philosophers is often found to lie behind great social and political changes. Of course, not all human actions in politics can be so traced; apart from the complex motives of all human activity there are the feelings and passions of the multitude, the greed and ambition of the individual or the group; and in such may be read the causes of many political events no less than in the writings of philosophers. But the mere fact that political thought does play and has played in European history a very large part in the causation of political action is due to the Greeks, and to that extent at any rate Greek Political Thought has a bearing upon life in Europe to-day. It was the Greeks who first consciously applied political thought to action and attempted to construct a state and order its life in accordance with a set of principles. Needless to say they did not always succeed and in the history of the world their practical achievements were short-lived. Too often the power was lacking to make effective the theory, both the material power, that is to say, the technical resources or Applied Science, and the political power, the opportunity of imposing, by force or persuasion, a political framework. Their supreme creation, the City-State, insignificant, selfish and quarrelsome, is not their chief legacy to us, remarkable achievement though it was. Our debt is chiefly to the men who created Political Science. For them it was a practical science aiming at finding out how to construct a state and how best to live in it. For us the gap between theory and action is wider and we thank them

I

not for practical advice, sensible though it may sometimes be, but because they created the habit which our civilisation has never either wholly lost or wholly mastered, of thinking things out beforehand.[1]

That important action should be preceded by information and discussion and not be based on the passing moods or intuitions of a despot is one of the principles of civilisation, and the best minds among the Greeks aimed always at establishing it. They saw this as part of the whole problem of creating order out of chaos, of establishing civilisation instead of barbarism. This is a problem, as the twentieth century has proved beyond a doubt, which cannot be solved once and for all and then put aside; every generation of mankind, every people and nation has to attempt it afresh and every individual ignores it at his peril. Not that earlier efforts at solving it are irrelevant; on the contrary, every other effort may help our own, especially that effort which lay nearest to the early stages of the historical process of the building of western civilisation.

There is indeed little danger that the primacy and importance of the Greeks in political thought will be forgotten. The outstanding qualities of Plato and Aristotle will see to that. Certainly in the past political thinkers have on the whole recognised their greatness, often making a foe of one and a friend of the other. But there is perhaps a danger that the greatness of the giants may obscure our vision of the lesser folk and may even create among some students a vague impression that Greek Political Thought began with Plato and ended with Aristotle. In the chapters which follow the reader will be asked to view the subject more largely, to consider political thinkers before Plato and after Aristotle. The fact that Socrates wrote nothing and Protagoras and Solon little that has survived makes the former task difficult and hazardous; and the loss of Dicaearchus and other Hellenistic prose-writers does the same for the latter. But if the saving of our civilisation partly depends, as it surely must, on each generation understanding the basis of the heritage which it receives, then there can be no doubt that the task is worth attempting, if need be, again and again.

The Greeks themselves, as we have seen, were disposed to

---

[1] προδιδαχθῆναι λόγῳ πρότερον ἢ ἐπὶ ἃ δεῖ ἔργῳ ἐλθεῖν, *Thucydides* II 40 (Pericles).

view civilisation as the antithesis of barbarian despotism, the marks of which were Slavery for all, No legal redress and Political domination. The wealth and refinement of Lydia under Croesus, the organisation of the Persian and Median empire were as naught in the absence of personal freedom and the rule of law. Of course they knew very well that the oriental monarchs had no monopoly of the vices of despotism, that Greeks too might and did violate the principles of Law and Freedom. Indeed it was just because the lust for wealth and power was so strong among them that they knew its dangers and feared its consequences. The able and unscrupulous popular leader who made himself sole ruler ($\tau \acute{v} \rho a \nu \nu o s$, tyrant) was both abhorred and admired, and Thrasymachus spoke no more than the truth about his fellow countrymen when he said (Plato *Repub.* I 344) that their detestation of a tyrant's injustice was due not to fear of committing his crimes but to fear of suffering them. Their passion for equality, too, where it existed at all, was largely due to envy, to the dislike of seeing another man, no better than oneself, winning wealth and honour. 'To get more than one's share' was readily condemned in a neighbour but was each man's secret hope for himself; for it was one of their besetting sins and was expressed in one word ($\pi \lambda \epsilon o \nu \epsilon \kappa \tau \epsilon \hat{\imath} \nu$). Thus Greek political thinkers were well aware of some of the powerful factors in human nature which run counter to civilisation and to the ideals of order and harmony which the Greeks associated with it. There was little danger of their forgetting the connection between psychology and politics or of expecting too much of human nature. Long before Plato's searching analysis of the evils of contemporary society they knew that bad characters mean bad politics, as surely as bad husbandry means little to eat, that a good constitution, as it helps a body to resist disease, helps a state to counter its foes within and without. They thus early found that civilised society rests on three bases—maintenance of adequate subsistence, character ($\mathring{\eta} \theta o s$) of the people, and political institutions or constitution ($\pi o \lambda \iota \tau \epsilon \acute{\iota} a$). We tend to separate the study of these three into Economics, Ethics and Politics, but Greek thinkers kept them together. The study of behaviour and of goods and supplies were as much part of $\pi o \lambda \iota \tau \iota \kappa \acute{\eta}$ as questions of forms of government. The emphasis shifted from one to the other; only Aristotle, perhaps, did justice to all three. In the earlier half of the fifth century the emphasis was on constitutions;

3

Socrates shifted it towards character. Plato kept both these well in mind but tended to pass lightly over economics, although his contemporaries, witness the *Ways and Means* of Xenophon and the *Plutus* of Aristophanes, were becoming well aware of its importance.

On the other hand all were agreed that a really civilised life could only be lived in connection with a city (πόλις). This was not the huge urban agglomeration of modern times, but a town of moderate size together with its own piece of territory, in any part of which a citizen might have his home. The three chief external marks of the polis were thus (1) Size: it must be large enough to provide for its own administration, but not so large that its members are unknown to each other. (2) Economic Independence (αὐτάρκεια self-sufficiency): the territory should be large enough to feed the population. Needless to say this was a perpetual difficulty. Bad harvests and growing populations played havoc with such a precarious economy, and this had serious political consequences; even the larger communities lived under the shadow of starvation. The suppression of piracy in the Aegean had helped little, for imports had to be paid for and only distant lands, Scythia and Egypt, had food to export. Exchange of commodities was generally on a small scale. Corinth, it is true, could manufacture large quantities of pottery for export and Athens could exchange surplus olive-oil for grain from the Black Sea but most cities were not so fortunate. (3) Political Independence (αὐτονομία): this was the most important of the three. Though it was doomed to gradual extinction after the war which was fought to save it, this principle received an almost fanatical devotion from earlier Greeks. It was the mark of a true polis not to owe any allegiance to any other city or overlord or 'foreign power'. To be forced into such a position was a mark of disgrace, and loss of autonomy was as keenly felt as loss of personal freedom and was indeed called by the name 'enslavement'. Internally the government might be of any form; that did not affect the status of the city. But the right to choose or change that government was fought for, always strenuously but not always successfully, by Greek cities in the Aegean islands and on the coast of Asia Minor.

It should, however, be remembered that not all the communities of ancient Greece answered to this threefold description. In large areas of the mainland such as the interior of the Peloponnese, the plain of Thessaly and the hinterland of north-west Greece, people lived for the most part not in cities, but in loosely knit groups of tribes and villages. Outside the mainland, in the islands and in the colonised areas of Sicily, South Italy and elsewhere, the city communities predominated and in the life and activity of the Mediterranean region it is the city-state that really matters. They were exceedingly numerous; even a comparatively small island like Rhodes contained two. They differed greatly from each other in size and power and in other ways, but the majority were small and weak, so that it is hardly possible to pick out *typical* examples. In actual fact we tend to think first of Athens and Sparta because we know a good deal about them. But neither of these could be described as typical. Athens-Attica was well above the average in size and could not maintain her population on home produce alone. Sparta with its rigid conservatism and militarised society had no counterpart anywhere but in Crete. But where none is a typical example, all are good and Aristotle thought it worth while to examine the government of 158 of them in detail. We can only form a general impression, which is one of countless cities and islands of minute size but each one an independent sovran state.

The sovran state—this notion is a joint legacy bequeathed, for good or evil, by these innumerable and insignificant cities. The civilised life which they designed to live in them never achieved either stability or permanence and their absolute sovranty was fated to disappear, but no one has ever disputed the fact that the ancient Greek polis was the progenitor and forerunner of the modern State, both in practice and, more significantly, in theory. The idea of 'The State' round which centres much of modern political thought is a development of the Greek city, and it was partly to remind us of this fact that the word 'city-state' was coined. The Greeks had but one word πόλις to denote both *city* and *state* and the allied words πολίτης, dweller in a polis, and the adjective πολιτικός could not properly be applied to the affairs of those people, Greek or Barbarian, who did not live in a city-state. On the other hand a Greek πόλις could well be a predominantly agrarian community with most of its citizens engaged in farming.

It may be disputed whether this limitation of scope was advantageous or not to the development of political thought, but it is probably true to say that but for this limitation political thinking among the Greeks would have developed much less rapidly.

Whatever be the ultimate origin of the city-state, the fact that so many of them were founded means that great attention must early have been given to political problems, both the invention of political institutions and their proper working. This gave to Greek political philosophy two marked characteristics which it never wholly lost, first, a strongly practical bent and second, a tendency always to be looking for the ideal or perfect State. Now modern political thought has veered away from the former of these, has tended to become divorced from active politics and to call itself Political Theory. It has concerned itself much with the State as an entity, sometimes carrying the notion to absurd lengths, and with such questions as 'What is the State?' This is not the sort of question which a Greek would take for a starting point. As time went on and he began to reflect upon what earlier generations had built, he did begin to ask such questions as 'What is the origin of the State?' and 'What is its purpose?' but the problems of political thought remained all the while chiefly practical. The constantly recurring questions were 'What is the best kind of State, the best size and place? What kind of government or constitution is the best? Who are to have control and how many of them should there be? Who are to be citizens and what rules should be made for their conduct and for their admission to that body?' The antitheses of rulers and ruled, οἱ ἄρχοντες and οἱ ἀρχόμενοι, and of the Few and the Many meet us constantly, not our familiar antithesis of State and Individual. This would have been tantamount to opposing the πόλις and the πολίτης, which would be slightly absurd, as if one were to make an antithesis of the hen and the egg.

Not all these questions were clearly formulated in the minds of the early framers of constitutions, but when a city was being set up or a colony founded, such questions had to be asked and some sort of answers had to be found, so that the questions were never merely theoretical. Even after the great eras of city-founding, after the second wave of colonisation had begun to spend itself, there still remained opportunity for the political adviser. Constitutions were often short-lived; a new generation, a newly-dominant party demanded new answers to the questions. The scanty remains of the literature of the sixth and seventh centuries B.C. reflect all too clearly the instability of political life in the Greek states, the frequent exiles, the bitter feuds and the resort to dictatorship to restore order. Yet in spite of it the Greeks never lost faith in the value of the city-state and in its superiority over barbarian or semi-barbarian ways of life.

The search for the Ideal State, which might at first sight appear incompatible with the strong practical bent, was in fact part of it and had its origin in the same circumstances. Most of the cities founded in the eighth and seventh centuries B.C. were 'colonies', for so we translate the Greek ἀποικία. Overcrowding, underfeeding, political animosity or frustrated ambition often caused a section of the people in one State to band themselves together under a leader (οἰκιστής) and go forth to found a new and quite independent city. When a site was found and any existing inhabitants dispossessed and driven inland or elsewhere, it remained to enlist the aid of an expert in city-states, who should frame a constitution and draw up a code of laws. The wisdom of the so-called Seven Wise Men was largely political and some of them were said to be much in demand as Lawgivers (νομοθέτης). Having commissioned some such expert, the leader could but say to him 'make us the best State you can'. Thus the situation was not unusual of being able to build a State *de novo*, and it is not really surprising that Greek political thought moved towards the construction of Ideal States. There was always a chance that the opportunity might occur of setting up an actual State.

The period of history preceding the outburst of colonisation in the seventh century B.C. is most obscure. But it must have been the period when city-state ideas were first formed and put into action. We know not even the name of any lawgiver earlier than Zaleucus in the seventh century so we can say nothing of those whose thinking led to the idea of the polis. We know only of a process of change, not of any minds behind it. We know that there was a weakening of the power of the family and of the tribe, whenever the new city-organisation was set up, but we do not know how early this process began. The surprising, even disturbing, thing is that we have rather more information about a still earlier epoch, that is, before the coming of the Dorians about 1000 B.C. This invasion marked the end of a previous civilisation, in which the best known historical event is the Trojan War. This war was well known to the Greeks; Thucydides used τὰ Τρωικά as a chronological landmark. The fall of Troy according to one system of chronology took place in 1184 B.C. Now both ancient

poets and modern archaeologists testify that this was not a period
of scattered tribal life everywhere, but of a civilisation largely
urban, in which there were cities but not city-states. A fifth-
century tragedian, dramatising some ancient myth would naturally
project into early Corinth or Argos many features of the life of
his own day, but he was not necessarily wrong when he pictured
ancient magnificence of city and palace. Archaeology has revealed
the existence of great cities, much wealth, good roads and much
other evidence of a prosperous urban civilisation before the end
of the second millenium before Christ. Now, as will be shown in
Chapter I, the royal city of 'mythical' times was something
very different from the city-state of the next millenium, though it
was called by the same name—πόλις. It may therefore be argued
that the centuries that preceded the city-state have little or no
importance in Greek political thought. Admittedly we are without
any information which would enable us to trace the development
of thought in that era. Nevertheless there is a particular reason
why we should take some notice of the pre-city-state era and
the reason is the unique position of the Homeric poems in the
education of the Greeks.

A man's thinking on political matters is largely conditioned by
three factors—his early upbringing and environment, the contemporary political scene and his knowledge of past history. For
those political thinkers with whom this book will deal we have
in most cases scanty information as to the first of these, though
we can see, for example, how different must have been the background of Plato and Polybius. We are in a better position to know
something of the contemporary situation, though its actual influence in any one case is often a matter of conjecture. Moreover we
know that many took pains to acquaint themselves with contemporary conditions in other cities than their own. The earliest lawgivers found it extremely useful to compare one city with another
and see how their constitutions worked, and Solon was doing
quite a common thing when he set out on his travels to make
observations.[1] The travels, too, of Herodotus and Plato were important, each in their way; and to compare different forms of

---

[1] κατὰ θεωρίης πρόφασιν, Herod. I 29. The word θεωρία (*observation*) came later
to be associated with a life of contemplation and reflexion rather than of
travel and seeing for oneself. It finally gave the English word *theory* as something opposed to *practice*.

government was at all times part of the stock material of political thought. It is when we consider the knowledge of the past as a formative influence in political thinking that we begin to see the necessity for beginning with Homer. The politicians of the fourth century B.C. were in varying degrees influenced by what they thought they knew about the Persian Wars a century before, but the influence of the past as embodied in the Homeric poems was not only more universal and more continuous, but was strongest in the earlier and more formative epochs. Those 'wise men' who were called on to make laws for cities, from 'Lycurgus' at Sparta to Protagoras at Thurii, had all been brought up on Homer, their chief, if not their only, school-book. They had learned to look to the *Iliad* and the *Odyssey* not merely for historical facts but for ethical principles, to seek in the great men of the past the standard for good men of the present. As time went on some reacted violently and rejected the inadequate ethic of the heroic age, but history and myth remained a strong influence. From Homer they had learned of a state of society very different from that of their own day yet not quite unfamiliar, described by Homer partly in old-fashioned poetical language but sometimes also in 'modern' words such as πόλις itself. The picture of society given in the Homeric poems is neither wholly coherent nor wholly consistent but there is a certain superficial unity about it which, while it does not bear close examination, served well enough as an account of the political conditions of the heroic age. To it therefore we now turn.

CHAPTER I

HOMER

THE events described in the Homeric poems, so far as they are historical, took place for the most part round about 1200 B.C. The poems themselves were probably written considerably later than that,[1] but they preserve traditions going back not merely to the Trojan war but a great deal earlier. As much as half a millenium may have elapsed between the earliest features mentioned in the poems and the date of their composition. During this period there took place a decline of the Mycenean civilisation, the Trojan war, the Dorian invasion and we know not how many other upheavals. The changes, social, political and linguistic, caused by these upheavals are reflected in the Homeric poems, but only very incoherently and not in such a way that we can form a connected piece of social, still less of literary history. We can, however, say that, while the whole long period is, as it were, telescoped, the emphasis is on the earlier part, say before 1000 B.C.; the period between 1000 and 800 is one of the most obscure in all ancient history. Thus the poet consciously archaises without, of course, being completely successful or consistent—a common feature of Epic poetry. On the political side this archaising tendency is strong, with the result that we get a picture not of the immediate but of the remote antecedents of the city-state. In this respect our position does not differ greatly from that of a Greek of the Classical era; the Homeric poems and the traditional myths made up most of his knowledge of his early history. We have, however, the advantage of knowing that the period was a long one and of knowing, thanks to archaeology, considerably more about Mycenean civilisation than the classical

[1] It need hardly be said that their date is still a matter of great dispute.

Greek. We are therefore on our guard against telescoping five centuries into one.

What chiefly concerns us, however, is not the chronology of pre-history but the political notions which the Greeks derived from their early and intimate acquaintance with the Homeric poems. We find four examples of something like a political organisation, two in the *Iliad* and two in the *Odyssey*. Those in the latter are less detailed and less instructive. The four are: (1) the kingdom of Ithaca, (2) the mythical kingdom of Scheria, (3) the city of Troy, (4) the overlordship of Agamemnon. No two of these are exactly alike. There is much similarity between the first two which come from the *Odyssey* and belong to the far west and not to the Aegean. The city of Troy is more Asiatic than Greek, but it is seen through Greek eyes and a poet's eyes too; little can be affirmed of its political organisation. What is common to all is a generally accepted division into King (ἄναξ, βασιλεύς), Nobles (ἀριστῆες, ἥρωες but also βασιλῆες) and People (λαός, λαοί, *v. infra*). This looks like a foretaste of the future, the *One*, the *Few* and the *Many*. But in the Homeric poems there is no clear picture of the *political power* actually wielded. In the island of the Phaeacians (Scheria), visited by Odysseus, Alcinous is king, but he has not much power, being largely dependent on the goodwill of his 'leaders and counsellors' and they also may be called kings (βασιλῆες). The position of Odysseus as King of Ithaca is very curious.[1] His father Laertes had long since retired; neither he nor any one else acted as deputy during the absence of Odysseus. It seems likely that if the faithful Penelope had given way to one of the importunate suitors, her new husband would have become king. Odysseus' son Telemachus based his claim on heredity, yet admitted that that conferred on him no absolute right, since there were many other βασιλῆες in Ithaca who might have a claim.[2] In Troy Priam's kingship is both more absolute and more secure, but as the city was at war, Hector's power is more conspicuous than his father's.

On the Greek side too there is the difficulty of knowing whether the organisation is simply that of an army in the field or a faithful picture of a political organisation. The military organisation, if it can be so called, is Commander-in-chief, heroes, who fought in

[1] See G. Finsler, *Homer*³ 1 2, 134 ff.
[2] *Odyssey* 1 394 ff.

chariots, and rank and file (λαοί), who fought with club and bow. But this, as we have seen, is a social distinction first and only incidentally a military one. Nestor's attempt to improve the organisation by arranging that troops should fight in tribes and brotherhoods passed unheeded. Numerous and oft-quoted passages, on the other hand, show that the power of Agamemnon was not merely that of a commander in the field, but rested also on his kingship. He may, like the Spartan kings in historical times, have acquired further powers in war than belonged to him in peace, but in the *Iliad* his claim to obedience is based, both by himself and by others, not on military necessity but on his 'constitutional' position as holder of the symbol of sovranty, the staff or σκῆπτρον; he was a sceptre-bearing (σκηπτοῦχος) king, whose wide dominion over mainland and islands entitled him to greater honour than the rest. On the other hand the rest, Nestor, Achilles, Odysseus and others, were kings too, each with his own territory, though we cannot say for certain whence he derived his title to it. The relation of these kings or princes to Agamemnon was not that of subject and monarch; each was a monarch in his own right, a monarch of Aristotle's fourth or Heroic class,[1] each exercising military, religious and judicial authority. On the other hand they were bound by some kind of allegiance to him; for his mere summons (ὀτρύνειν) obliged them to assist him in war. They might be made to pay a fine (θωή) if they refused, but the service might, if we may judge by a single instance,[2] take the form of provision of equipment. We cannot say what obligations towards Agamemnon lay upon these princes when they were at peace but, having kingdoms of their own to rule, they can hardly have formed the great king's immediate retinue. There was indeed such a retinue round Agamemnon, even as there was round Philip of Macedon in the fourth century, but it was not composed of independent princes. Nor were they the same as the counsellors and advisers of good king Alcinous, but a band of companions and henchmen, who fed at Agamemnon's table and formed his personal bodyguard. The lesser kings too had such companions, perhaps fewer of them, for such was Patroclus to Achilles. Similar puzzles confront us when we consider Agamemnon in relation to the whole host, the contingents brought by the various princes as well as

---

[1] Aristotle, *Politics* III 1285 b. See Chap. XI.
[2] *Iliad* XXIII 297.

his own subjects. His speeches to the assembled army are not simply those of a commander before a battle. Others are invited to express opinions and an envoy from the foe is received in the presence of the assembly. But the envoy addresses himself not to the whole host or to Agamemnon but to the champions (ἀριστῆες), that is, presumably, the nobles.

Like many other problems connected with Homer those which have just been mentioned have been the subject of much controversy among both historians and Homeric scholars. But for the student of political thought what emerges from all this is the fact that a young Greek of the classical age early learned to know this composite political picture as part of the history of the Hellenic race. He would thus gain acquaintance with social and political conditions very different from his own, yet quite clearly related. Sceptre-bearing kings with wide-spread dominions had long disappeared from the Greek world of the sixth century B.C., and most of the lesser monarchies too. Troy and Mycenae were buried in ruins but Argos, Athens, Sparta, Ithaca were all still there, though greatly changed; and when he travels among the cities and islands of his own day his mind is already well prepared for the study of comparative politics. Again, when he makes his first acquaintance with legal and judicial matters, he will recall the eighteenth book of the *Iliad*, the famous Trial Scene depicted on the shield which Hephaestus made for Achilles. He will be as puzzled as we are to know the exact significance of the procedure and may wonder why here no king takes part in the administration of justice.[1] But he will recognise the gathering in the market-place and note the changes that had taken place in the customs relating to homicide. Though the city-states of his own day were so different from the cities of heroic times, yet both belonged to him and not to the Barbarian. The essentials of civilisation were secured by the one no less than the other. Poets, as he had been taught to believe, were the great teachers and civilisers and it was from Homer that he had learned the first rudiments. The savage and gigantic Cyclops and his kindred had been depicted by Homer as typically

---

[1] For Aristotle (*Pol.* III 1285 b 10) thought it part of a king's duty in heroic times. But he may have been wrong; most of the evidence suggests a body of men, not an individual. See G. Finsler, *Homer*[3] I 2, p. 138, and M. P. Nilsson, *Homer and Mycenae*, pp. 223-224. And on the trial scene in the shield of Achilles see R. J. Bonner and Gertrude Smith, *Administration of Justice from Homer to Aristotle* (1930) Vol. I, pp. 31-41.

uncivilised; they did not know how to till the land, they had no regard for the gods or for each other. Civilised men came together, the Cyclopes shunned each other. There was no law, no rule but the arbitrary domination over wife and family. They had neither meeting places for discussion nor any proper ways of behaviour or of doing anything—τοῖσιν δ' οὔτ' ἀγοραὶ βουληφόροι οὔτε θέμιστες (*Odyssey* IX 112).

The Homeric poems, like the great gods and myths, were part of the common heritage of all Greek peoples in the smallest island no less than the large city. Though the language of the Greeks had many dialects, the differences between them were not such as to hinder ordinary intercourse. Greeks understood each other and were aware of the unity in diversity which made the Hellenic tongue one and sharply distinguished it from the meaningless 'bar-bar' chatter which gave foreigners their name βάρβαροι. The language of Homer was the same for all, whatever its origin, and this strengthened the one-ness of Hellenic speech. But it was not a dead language, though nobody spoke it that we know of; it was the normal means of literary expression before the days of prose[1] or dramatic poetry and for Epic verse it continued to be used for over a thousand years. Its importance for our subject is not negligible. Thought is coloured by words and their associations, and the earliest Greek thinkers made their first acquaintance with political terminology and political history in the poems of Homer. We shall therefore now consider some of the more important political terms in the *Iliad* and the *Odyssey*. Of these the most striking is πόλις itself. In Homer the word signifies City but not State. When Aristotle remarked that the relationship between rulers and ruled came naturally into being for the purpose of securing their common safety, he was using the language of his own day, but he was preserving a fact well-known to Thucydides; the earliest polis was a place of defence, a strong point, sometimes fortified, sometimes, as Homeric epithets show, relying more on natural defences and steepness of approach. Other Homeric epithets, as well as archaeological discoveries, show that the Homeric city was laid out with streets and buildings and was a place of residence as well as of defence. The residents were πολῖται, who shared with the king both the privilege of living in it and the duty of defending it. That this was the first duty of a citizen of

---

[1] That is, written prose.

a state was thus self-evident and the connection between the right to citizenship and the ability to bear arms long continued in Greek ways of thinking. In Homeric society this class is small; it is composed only of nobles or champions; the aged Priam was accompanied by some of his πολῖται when he visited Achilles. Here again this restricted use of πολίτης, where the English 'citizen' gives a quite erroneous impression, was never quite forgotten and helps to explain both the great reluctance of city-states, oligarchic and democratic, to add to the number of their πολῖται, and the constant preoccupation of Greek political thought with the problem how citizenship is to be determined. The Homeric language distinguished πόλις from ἄστυ, the latter being the place of residence of those who were not πολῖται. We translate both words by 'city' or 'town' and the distinction was not usually drawn in classical times. But it was not lost altogether, for πόλις was often used to mean the central, elevated, fortified part or ἀκρό-πολις. It may be inferred, though not certainly demonstrated, that the term λαός or λαοί 'people' means the residents out in the ἄστυ, as opposed to the nobles who lived in the πόλις, but the word has no importance as a term in political philosophy.

It is far otherwise with δῆμος, which we also translate by 'people'. Like πόλις it would seem to denote primarily place, for such expressions as δήμῳ ἐνὶ Τρώων can only mean in the *land* of the Trojans. The combination therefore, πόλις καὶ δῆμος, does not mean the city and its people but the city and the country, the territory outside the walled πόλις, and beyond, or perhaps including, the ἄστυ. Since *dēmos* meant the land outside the πόλις, it came easily to be used to denote the people living there. So though in Homer πόλις is rarely used as a collective noun for the dwellers in it, δῆμος was often so used and δήμου ἀνήρ soon passed from 'man of the countryside' to 'man of the people', and its course is set for its stormy history. In this case little survives of the original meaning except the Attic and Elean use of *deme* to denote a district. Unlike πόλις and δῆμος and somewhat unexpectedly, the word ἀγορά did not originally denote place but assembly (ἀγείρω, collect) and then 'place of assembly'. It was an essential part of a city and its proper use, as we have seen, one of the marks of civilised society. Even in classical times men gathered in the *agora*, not merely to do their marketing (ἀγοράζειν), but to talk (ἀγορεύειν). In war no less than peace it was essential

to hold an assembly (ἀγορὰν θέσθαι). Its importance in the social
life of the Greek city-state needs no emphasis. It may be mentioned here that cognate words for the tribes and brotherhoods
of the Athenian state had a place in the Epic dialect. They may
have had some social importance in time of peace but little of
this appears in the *Iliad*. And, though the Athenians found it convenient to use this ancient way of organising and classifying the
population of Attica, which was large for a single polis, the terms
'tribe' and 'phratry' were of no importance in Greek political
thinking. But it is worth noting here at the outset, since the institutions of ancient society are not the subject of this book, that
even Athens, the most finished of city-states, the quickest to respond to new political ideas, retained much of a social organisation
of great antiquity and never ceased to view with alarm any proposal that appeared to run counter to her ancestral laws and
customs.

No less instructive than the words for city and people are those
which show us that in the Homeric poems the Greek citizen first
learned the notion of justice, the words δίκη and θέμις. The former,
both in itself and through its derivatives (δίκαιος is Homeric),
played an important part in the development of both legal and
political terms. The word Dikè was more concrete than the English 'justice' or 'right' would suggest. Its original meaning was
perhaps 'way' or rather an 'indication of the way', the way to go,
the way to do or the way to deal with a situation or a person.
So, whether the question was simply how something should be
done or the more difficult one of settling a dispute fairly, the
answer was δίκη. And those people, whether kings or nobles, who
could be relied upon to give good 'indications' were highly esteemed. This early association with a pronouncement of a verdict
was greatly extended in classical times to cover suit, case, penalty
and so on. But at the same time the notion developed that behind
the decisions of the law lay justice, and we shall see in the next
chapter something of the importance of δίκη as a basis of political
morality as well as of judicial procedure. It should however be
noticed that Homer no less than Hesiod realised that the right
way of doing things was not the way of violence (βία); deeds of
wickedness (σχέτλια ἔργα) and lawlessness (ὕβρις) are often contrasted with δίκη. On the other hand δίκη need not have any moral
or juridical force; it may be simply the way, habit or custom of a

person or class of persons. The translation of what is habitually done into what ought always to be done was never complete and can never be complete. It goes on continually and much of a man's political behaviour will depend on how far he believes in the validity of making such a transference.

Now Dikè and Themis are often coupled; a knowledge of them is the mark of a civilised man. Both imply that the established way is the right way, but there are differences between them. Not only is δίκη a less solemn word than θέμις; it is also less authoritative, or rather it derives its authority differently. It depends partly on its general acceptance as being the way, and partly on the prestige of the ruler or noble or elder who pronounces the δίκη. What is θέμις, on the other hand, is right because it has behind it the weight of divine authority. Among men this authority might, as we saw, be wielded by a king, βασιλεὺς σκηπτοῦχος. So either a god or a king was capable of θεμιστεύειν, laying down what is θέμις, pronouncing θέμιστες. Only while holding the staff or sceptre could a king so pronounce, for the σκῆπτρον conferred the divine authority. This distinction became blurred, as the assembled nobles gained in power at the expense of the king, since this was to their advantage; and there was no incongruity felt when Homer wrote δικασπόλοι, οἵ τε θέμιστας πρὸς Διὸς εἰρύαται, for the dealers of δίκη felt that they too were maintaining the ordinances that came from Zeus.[1] Yet the distinction was a real one. For in Homer Themis is personified; she is a goddess, the embodiment of divine authority. Dikè is not yet a goddess, not until Hesiod. To do those things which were θέμις, such as honouring parents, and to refrain from those which were οὐ θέμις, such as abuse of strangers and suppliants, were duties imposed from above with divine sanction behind them. Hesiod attempted to exalt Δίκη to a similar status and to show that earthly rulers in disregarding Δίκη were themselves guilty in the eyes of the gods. He did not degrade Themis, who was for him the mother of political virtues, but extended and amplified the notion of Right and brought it into association with the πόλις. Themis on the other hand did not develop into a political idea but declined as royal and patriarchal authority declined. The ordinances of the new polis are not the θέμιστες of kings but the θεσμοί and νόμοι laid down by θεσμοθέται and νομοθέται (lawgivers).

[1] *Iliad* I 238-9.

Such were the chief features of the political heritage which Greek pre-history had bequeathed to the Greek philosophers of the future. For all its historical inconsistencies and its mingling of discrepant elements Homer's picture of heroic society, heroic ideals and heroic speech remained firmly fixed in men's minds as something philosophical as well as historical. Later generations remembered the guiding principle of a Homeric hero's life, the advice given by Phoenix to Achilles, αἰὲν ἀριστεύειν καὶ ὑπείροχον ἔμμεναι ἄλλων, 'Always aim at excellence and be superior to the rest'; and without difficulty, though with unhappy consequences, transferred it from military to civilian life (see Chap. V). It was not of course from Homer that the Greek acquired his passion for independence, his fear of tyranny, his belief in ordered freedom or any of the characteristic ideas of the city-state; still less does modern political thought owe anything directly to Homer. But to the Greek political thinker the Homeric poems meant a great deal. This is especially true of the early stages of political thought, but even Plato and Aristotle, who quote Homer freely, do not do so as a literary embellishment but because, whether quoted with approval or disapproval, the Homeric poems were part of what we would nowadays call 'the literature of the subject'.

FURTHER NOTES AND REFERENCES
CHAPTER I

The material for the chapter is of course the *Iliad* and the *Odyssey*; but it should be remembered that the interpretation of these two epics and their relation to constitutional and literary history are matters of dispute and difficulty with which the above brief account of a literary and linguistic background is not intended to deal. The chapter owes much to M. P. Nilsson, *Homer and Mycenae* (1933), Chap. VI, G. Finsler, *Homer* (3rd edit. rev. E. Tièche, 1924) I 2, 132-150, J. L. Myres, *Political Ideas of the Greeks* (1927) Lectures II and IV.

CHAPTER II

FROM HESIOD TO HERACLITUS

WHATEVER be the value of the Homeric poems for the history of Greek Political Thought, there can hardly be any question about the two genuine Hesiodic poems, the *Works and Days* and the *Theogony*. They are not of course political literature any more than the *Iliad* and the *Odyssey*, but the former at any rate does contain the earliest written record of the conscious application of human thinking to the problems of living together. Hesiod, it is true, was a poet, a singer who, he tells us, learned his craft from the Muses. His metre and diction are still those of the Homeric hexameter—a medium not always well adapted to the ideas which he was trying to express. Moreover he conveys his meaning partly in precept and partly in myth. But it is not difficult to peer through these conventions and see the rudiments of moral and therefore of political philosophy shaping themselves. When for example in the *Theogony* he says that Zeus wed Themis, who gave birth to Eunomia, Dikè and Eirenè, we see at once that he is laying down Good Order, Right and Peace as principles of human society. Again, to illustrate the difference between the rule of Force and the rule of Right he tells a fable of the nightingale and the hawk; and when, some three hundred years later Thrasymachus was defining Justice as the rule of the stronger, he was repeating in effect what the hawk said to the nightingale: 'He is a fool who seeks to resist the mighty.' It is against such a doctrine and the conduct to which it leads that Hesiod protests. It was all too readily accepted in international affairs (see Chap. VI), and internally too, as Hesiod found, society was too much based on violence and ὕβρις: the rulers and judges of his land, though called by the good old name βασιλῆες, had no longer the kingly virtues of the princes of heroic times, and bribery and perjury were rife. To these unjust judges and to his idle brother Perses are addressed many precepts, moral and agricultural. The poet gives in the *Works and Days* a vivid picture of the hard life of a small farmer on a Boeotian hillside, so that we know something of his social and economic conditions. He uses the word πόλις frequently and in such a way as to suggest that it was the normal political unit. And though he has nothing to tell us of problems of government, he leaves us in no doubt about the principle on which government should be based—the now familiar principle of Δίκη. Though nowhere defined, Dikè is personified, deified, illustrated as becomes a poet. It is, above all, that which distinguished human society from animals, birds and fishes, for there is no δίκη among them. It is the Right Way or Justice, opposed to lawlessness and violence and to 'taking the law into one's own hands'. For this, as Hesiod saw, is the very negation of justice and such people (he calls them χειροδίκαι[1]) would, as we say, strike at the very root of all political association. It is true that people of rank and power, especially when acting together, can often succeed in getting their way contrary to justice, but sooner or later, says Hesiod, they must fail, for the gods mark wicked deeds and punish them; and, in words prophetic of the Just and the Unjust Arguments in Aristophanes' *Clouds*, 'It will be a black day for the Just Man if the Unjust gets the greater δίκη.' Besides, Justice is a positive boon to a city; without it there can be no prosperity. In a community, therefore, in which judicial and administrative power both rest with an aristocracy, the rulers have a very great responsibility, since the whole people will suffer for their mistakes. And if the aristocrat (ἐσθλός) adheres to his supposed right to do as he likes, while requiring the common people (δειλὸς βροτός) to behave in an orderly way, there never will be any Right Way or Justice established for all. Such a sense of responsibility Hesiod found nowhere among the 'bribe-devouring' rulers of his time nor was he hopeful of finding better. Good rulers, as he says in the *Theogony*, are a gift from Zeus, as a good poet is a gift of Apollo. Both need to be blessed and taught by the Muses, for as skill in music and song are necessary to a poet, so skill in speech is necessary for a ruling prince: 'From his lips come honeyed words and all the people look to him as he gives judgments righteously.' This goes farther than the Homeric hero's need 'to

---

[1] In a misplaced line *W.D.* 189.

be a speaker of words'. It is the earliest indication of the close connection between eloquence and justice, which many had cause to deplore in the fifth and fourth centuries.

After Hesiod's death (before 700 B.C.) the idea of Justice as a deity ready to help a just God continued to inspire the poets, until in Aeschylus' hands it became a theological rather than a political concept. But those who during the next two centuries were endeavouring to put it into practice and make it the basis of a constitution had their own thinking to do and little opportunity of doing it. The seventh and sixth centuries were marked by social and political upheaval in nearly every state, and it was in the school of necessity that men of those times learned to think politically. Colonies were still being founded by exiled or discontented groups, so that there was much opportunity for action, if little for thought. The need was everywhere felt for Good Order (εὐνομία) and Good Behaviour (εὐκοσμία). Now the quickest way to secure good order has always been held to be *the strong arm*: and most of the Greek states were at one time or another ruled by a dictator[1] or tyrant (τύραννος). He was sometimes one who had risen to power by championing the poorer classes against a corrupt nobility, but his power was gained by force and maintained by force, so that corruption and deterioration almost inevitably followed. Pisistratus of Athens, who undoubtedly did much good, died with his reputation intact. Periander of Corinth attempted to rule within a constitutional framework. But however well tyrants might rule, tyranny, with its implications of usurpation and violence, was never *right* and was not regarded as a political principle at all. Other forms of rule by one man, monarch or chief magistrate, find their place in political thought, but tyranny in the strict sense was at best a temporary expedient for securing order, a transitory and dearly-bought benefit. In fifth-century Athens men of opposing political views could all congratulate themselves that they no longer lived under the tyranny of Hippias son of Pisistratus. Aristotle indeed included tyranny in his survey of constitutions but only, he says, for the sake of completeness, 'not because there is much worth saying about it.'[2] In short the Greeks knew very

---

[1] It was only in the political context that τύραννος carried the implication of violence. It is often, especially in poetry, indistinguishable from βασιλεύς. The word μόναρχος carries rather more derogatory flavour.

[2] οὐχ ὡς ἐνούσης πολυλογίας περὶ αὐτήν, *Politics* IV 1295 a.

well that, however successful tyranny might be in securing obedience, it was in itself ἀνομία, the very antithesis of εὐνομία, which is a condition of respect for νόμοι, of both Law *and* Order.[1] The need was not for the strong arm, but for men of wisdom and understanding, who should act as lawgivers and draw up constitutions. There was need too for the codification and publication of existing laws, but the demand for this was not always successful.

Of the writers who made Good Order the theme of their verses we have some knowledge of two—Tyrtaeus and Solon. Tyrtaeus was the seventh-century elegiac poet who inspired the Spartans with courage against their Messenian foes. The war contributed to the consolidation of the city, and the surviving fragments of the *Eunomia* of Tyrtaeus show us something of the process. But their bearing on Spartan history and their relation to that Lycurgus for whom Herodotus claimed the credit of having turned the Spartans from bad government to good, remain more than obscure. However, there are among the poet's warlike exhortations two passages of political interest. The first claims the approval of the Delphic Oracle[2] for a Spartan constitution with kings at the head, a body of elders, and men of the people, whose duty it is to respond to the legal enactments (of their superiors[3]). There is no mention of Lycurgus or of Ephors, but what is of interest is that here we have an outline of a new kind of constitution, a new way of securing good order by a combination of kingship and aristocracy with a body, perhaps not a large one, of citizens. The other passage is one of many in which the poet praises courage on the battlefield as the highest virtue, but he also disparages by comparison those other virtues, so much prized by the aristocracy, which had no patriotic value; athletic prowess, personal beauty, good birth, wealth and even eloquence—none of these can be compared with courage in war. The old ideals must be made to subserve the interests of the πόλις. The uselessness of athletic skill for securing Eunomia or any national good is also stressed by Xenophanes.

[1] See note at the end of the chapter.

[2] Delphic Apollo did not legislate for states except on the sacral side, though he did sometimes appoint a lawgiver. But the divine approval was obviously useful and was often sought.

[3] Interpretation very uncertain. See H. T. Wade-Gery in *Class. Quart.* XXXVIII 1944, p. 6.

A generation or so later than Tyrtaeus the Athenian Solon combined in himself the roles of lawgiver and poet. Already an important step had been taken in the search for εὐνομία by the codification and making public of existing laws by Draco. But it was Solon not Draco whom later Athenians regarded as the founder of their liberties. Whether all the political improvements which were believed to be the work of Solon are rightly attributed to him is very doubtful. But these doubts do not deprive Solon of his place in the history of political thought. This is secure and does not chiefly rest on his reforms. Legislation does not always produce the effects intended by its sponsors, and when Aristotle,[1] writing more than two centuries after Solon's death, points out those features of Solon's work which he found most favourable to the people (δημοτικώτατα)—the prohibition of loans on the security of the person, the right to go to law on another's behalf and the right of appeal to a popularly constituted court—he also warns us against assuming that Solon foresaw or intended all the political consequences. In spite of his unique position as ruler as well as philosopher-poet we must estimate his importance in political thought by his writings rather than by the effects of his political work, or by Plutarch's or some other's account of it. And though we have as usual to deplore the loss of most of his poems, we have enough to show us that that importance is very great.

As a poet and a moralist he goes back to Hesiod and takes up again the idea of divine Justice, which he links with Eunomia. He shares with Hesiod the belief in a just Zeus who punishes violence and outrage and holds men responsible for their sins. Good Order can only be secured if all are agreed that the right way is the way of Justice, not of lawlessness, δίκη not ὕβρις. All must unite against the disorderly elements, whether they be high or low in society. These are not now the χειροδίκαι of the *Works and Days* but the disaffected (δυσμενεῖς), who did not wish the polis to function. The first requirement of what it is now legitimate to call the State is that all its members should believe in it and be convinced of the need for it. Its enemies were those who did not believe in it, who found its control irksome and preferred the scramble for ill-gotten wealth. Solon sought to convince rich and poor alike that disorder (δυσνομία) was the enemy of them

---

[1] *Ath. Pol.* IX I.

all and the punishment of them all, that it inevitably led to disruption (στάσις) and to the subjugation (δουλοσύνη) of the whole people to a tyrant. In short, disorder, far from being an opportunity for unlimited profit-making, was a national disaster (δημόσιον κακόν). The State is thus something common to all and all alike have an interest in maintaining it. A party victory resulting, as such victories often did, in large-scale banishment of opponents was likewise a national disaster, a fact which Solon found it difficult to bring home to the victors. Indeed the Greeks, for all their political ability, were slow to learn this salutary lesson; and one of the causes of the many failures among city-states was this tendency to identify the state with the group in power, and the common good, τὸ κοινόν, with party advantage. Equally antisocial and likely to weaken even a great city was the thoughtless folly of those who make the accumulation of wealth their chief object and are quite unscrupulous in their methods. The acquisition of moderate wealth by honest labour was encouraged. Such remarks were clearly prompted by the rise of the rich merchants. Solon saw that their rise created a social and political problem, but he had no solution to offer beyond the general precept of moderation. For him there were but two classes, the nobles, ἐσθλοί, and the people, δῆμος. The demands of the latter were legitimate up to a point, but there could be no ἰσομοιρία, equal-sharing between them and the nobles. Tyranny he abhorred and feared; for him freedom meant freedom from δουλοσύνη, subjection to a tyrant, and freedom from debt or subjection to the land-owning class. Yet force was necessary to keep warring factions apart; and so βία and δίκη are not irreconcilable opposites, as Hesiod thought; they must be made to work together in the cause of Good Order.

Of the other elegiac and iambic poets of the seventh and sixth centuries little needs to be said. They reflect the strong patriotism of the city-state as well as its violent upheavals and social discontent. They survive, if at all, only in fragments, with the one exception of Theognis about the end of the sixth century. About 1400 lines of elegiac verse have survived under his name. It is more than doubtful whether all the verses are by Theognis and they contain no important contribution to political thought, yet they are worth mentioning here for two reasons. They illustrate a certain attitude of mind towards political problems, and they reflect social and economic changes which did have an influence on future thought. The connection between goodness, good birth and good breeding easily develops into the use of *good* (ἐσθλοί, ἀγαθοί, *optimi, optimates,* the *best people*) to describe the highest social class and thence also the aristocratic party. Conversely the common people could be termed the *bad,* the *poor* (κακοί, δειλοί). The moral content of the words was not forgotten when used by Theognis, who claimed (148) that Justice belonged to the Good, or by Pindar, a strong believer in heredity. And Theognis' advice (31-38) 'Do not associate with the lower classes but always cultivate the right people' was intended to be both sound morality and a recipe for political stability. Elsewhere (105) he remarks that there is no point in showing kindness to the poor; you might as well sow seed on the sea for all the return you will get for your pains. Other examples of a similar attitude might be quoted, for it is not uncommon, and certainly not confined to the sixth century B.C. Its interest for our subject is merely negative, for it acted, as confusions of terms often do, as a drag and a hindrance to clear political thinking.

The sixth century B.C. was a period of social and economic revolution, caused by expanding commerce, more metal coinage, increased slave-labour and greater mobility of wealth. It was the impact of this revolution on the affairs of his city Megara that fired Theognis to write his bitter verses. Many of his associates, for example, were marrying the daughters of wealthy upstarts, a confounding of 'good' and 'bad' which shocked him even more than the rise to political power of the commercial middle class. While Theognis was deploring these changes at Megara, Athens not far away first went through the tyranny of the Pisistratids and then underwent the reforming process associated with the name of Cleisthenes, with its strengthening of the middle class and consequential weakening of the distinction between old rich and new rich. All this had an effect on future political thinking. The political reformer with practical ends in view looks at the material conditions about him, since these may well be the deciding factor in determining the steps which it will be possible to take. These, in turn, may be unexpectedly altered. Wars and disasters, the discovery of a new source of wealth, such as the silver mines at Mt. Laurion, of a new invention, like coinage, may create new problems while solving an old.[1] The Spartans took fright at the idea of coined money, as Hesiod had taken fright at overseas trade, when it first began; but both had come to stay; and though contemporaries cannot see their effects, the next generation has to reckon with the material conditions, just as much as with the ideas, bequeathed to it by its predecessors.

But, it may be said, was it only poets and lawgivers who contributed to the formation of political thought? Had not philosophy herself something to say? The sixth century saw the beginnings of Greek scientific thought and it might be expected that this would lead to more scientific thinking about political problems. But the cosmological theories of early philosophers are termed 'scientific' because they are not founded on ancient myth or supernatural agency, not because of any new instrument of thought which could be applied in other fields. It can of course be pointed out that $\dot{a}\rho\chi\dot{\eta}$, beginning, First Cause, which early science was seeking to identify, became also the word for authority, office of state. But however interesting the semantic changes of $\dot{a}\rho\chi\dot{\eta}$, $\ddot{a}\rho\chi$-$\epsilon\sigma\theta\alpha\iota$ and the rest may be, they give us no clue to any connection between physical and political. On the other hand towards the end of the sixth century at least two of the philosophers of the time did think about the problems of *political* living and must therefore take their places along with Solon and the other Wise Men and poets as purveyors of political thought. They are Pythagoras and Heraclitus (Herakleitos). Whether the mathematics and harmonics of the former and the physics of the latter had any effect on their political theories matters but little. In themselves neither the Arithmetical Mean of the one nor the Perpetual Flux of the other supports any political theory.

Pythagoras of Samos was the elder of the two. He left his native island for South Italy and Sicily soon after the advent to power of the tyrant Polycrates, that is about 530 B.C. Heraclitus, justifiably nicknamed the Obscure, was in his prime about 25 years later. Our knowledge of both is scanty. Of Heraclitus we have numerous short fragments and those of political import must be pieced together as best we may. We know little or nothing of his life. Of Pythagoras on the other hand we have a not very trustworthy *Life* tradition but no fragments that we can be sure of. Not only did he leave no written works but even in his lifetime,

[1] Even Plato came to realise this. *Laws* 709 A.

so anecdote tells us, he did not talk much. When he did open his lips, his disciples hung upon his words but regarded them as secret. Later generations in Italy could but say αὐτὸς ἔφα or *ipse dixit* in support of what they wished to be considered Pythagorean doctrine, and an entirely spurious set of 'golden verses' of Pythagoras was long current in antiquity. Thus in the absence of attested fragments it has always been a puzzle to know how much of so-called Pythagoreanism is due to Pythagoras himself and how much to his followers and disciples in the centuries which followed—Philolaus, a contemporary of Socrates, Archytas of Tarentum, whom Plato met, and others even later. Aristotle generally speaks of 'the Pythagoreans' or even 'those who call themselves Pythagoreans'; he mentions some by name but gives us no information about Pythagoras himself. It is not therefore surprising that attempts to reconstruct a Pythagorean political theory have had different and even contradictory results.[1]

The story of his life was often told, though not till long after his death. Finding, so Aristoxenus[2] says, conditions under Polycrates intolerable for a free man, he migrated to the newer cities of Magna Graecia and here succeeded in creating for himself in the city of Croton an opportunity to put political ideas into practice; and although his régime collapsed even before his death, the political influence of the Pythagoreans long continued in South Italy, and in Plato's time Tarentum was actually ruled by Archytas the Pythagorean. Already famous throughout the Greek-speaking world as a man of most extraordinary powers, both mental and spiritual, Pythagoras soon found himself with a large body of followers in Croton. These he organised as a kind of religious community, the members of which lived together and shared their goods. Presumably they had in common an intense admiration for their master, his moral earnestness, his uncanny power with numbers and his dietary rules; presumably they shared his belief in the soul and its immortality and migrations. But what bond of political ideas first united them we do not know. It does, however, seem certain that this group of 300 devoted

---

[1] See note at the end of this chapter.
[2] Of Tarentum, a pupil of Aristotle, famed as a writer on music. His work on the life and sayings of Pythagoras is only known to us by excerpts and references. He was deliberately trying to exalt the Pythagoreans and humble the followers of Plato.

followers very soon became not only a political group, but the ruling party in the city. A hundred and fifty years later Plato was imagining an Ideal Commonwealth in which the supreme power should rest with just such a community of philosophers, having all things in common and no private ownership among them. But as for Croton in 529 B.C., it is disputed whether the Pythagorean party stood for the old landed aristocracy, which was still strong in agricultural Croton, or caught the rising tide of commercial wealth and established a middle class ascendancy. In any case it was the rule of the Few not the Many; and for the time at any rate politics takes its place along with religion, diet, music and mathematics as marks of the Pythagorean fraternities. Croton was not the only place where they obtained political influence. Their activities were described by Aristoxenus as 'inspiring the cities with a spirit of freedom'. But was this true? At Locri, the story goes, the people refused to have anything to do with such a clever and dangerous person as Pythagoras, who might upset the laws and customs of their fathers. Pythagoras' reply is not recorded but it ought to have been 'Quite right'. For it was Pythagoras, according to his fourth century supporters, who said 'Hold fast to the habits and laws of your fathers, even if they are much worse than others'. It seems indeed that the political theory of Pythagoras himself must have been something very different from the tenets of Pythagoreanism as retailed for us by Aristoxenus, Dicaearchus and others, in whose hands the Pythagorean polity becomes a model of harmony between ruler and ruled, and who cited as a Pythagorean saying 'There is no greater evil than anarchy', which we know as a tag from Sophocles.[1] Of Pythagoras himself we may perhaps say that he demonstrated that successful government may be carried on for a time by an intellectual élite bound together by ties of a common philosophy and way of life rather than ties of race or social status. But even that was of short duration. In 509 the house of the brotherhood was burned to the ground and its members perished or fled. This was presumably the work of an angry mob who could stand government by cranks no longer; but here again Aristoxenus tells a different tale and makes the attack out to be an act of personal vengeance on the part of a violent and unpleasant but influential Crotoniate

---

[1] ἀναρχίας δὲ μεῖζον οὐκ ἔστιν κακόν, Soph. *Antig.* 672. Creon, of course, speaks.

who had been refused admission to the Pythagorean circle. But we hear of further attacks on Pythagoreans in the next century.

One of the greatest losses which the history of ancient philosophy has met is that of the book which Heraclitus is said to have deposited in the temple of Artemis in his native Ephesus. His contemporaries found his work almost impossible to understand and the author had neither the faculty nor the desire for popular exposition. His surviving fragments are numerous, but they are short and disjointed and this seems to have been his normal style of utterance. His contemporaries were thus as liable to misunderstand him as we are. Yet many subsequent thinkers, Stoic, Christian and Hegelian[1] have drawn something from Heraclitus, and the collection of pungent and paradoxical sayings which has come down to us has been much studied. There is, however, little in the fragments which is directly political, although one of the three parts of his book was said to have dealt with τὸ πολιτικόν.

Heraclitus was both an intellectualist and an individualist. Intelligence, he found (113), was common to all men, a part of the human heritage, but in practice few made any use of it. A man with brains is worth ten thousand (49), but it must be brains, not memorised information (40). Intelligence is also something above and beyond man; some call it Zeus(?), which is to confine it falsely (32). Though he was arrogant and proud of his own intelligence, he says (50): 'Hear not me but the Logos'. The man of brain has the power that brains give, but he is not free to do as he pleases; he must be self-controlled and not give way to pleasure, for there is nothing so inimical to intelligence as self-indulgence, which causes the mind to become wet and flabby instead of firm and dry (117-118). The individual, moreover, is responsible for his actions; he cannot blame God for the defects of his own character (119). With such an ethical standpoint it is not surprising to find (121) Heraclitus pouring contempt on his fellow citizens for banishing a certain Hermodorus, a man of outstanding ability and public service. Such a procedure seemed to Heraclitus incredibly foolish. Yet at Athens ostracism often worked out in some such

---

[1] e.g. Ferdinand Lassalle, who in 1858 published his *Die Philosophie Herakleitos des Dunklen*. But there have been many different estimates and interpretations of ὁ σκοτεινός.

way; the problem of the outstanding individual in an egali-
tarian society was a very real one in a small state and Aristotle[1]
finds it worthy of discussion. The theory in Heraclitean philosophy of Strife between Opposites may have a political bearing,
but it is by no means clear what it is. The saying (53) 'War is
both father of all and king of all; it makes some gods, others
men, some slaves, others free' looks to be descriptive not ad-
visory; but he does appear to have held (80) that strife or rivalry
is a healthy condition, a right usage, a δίκη, which is going a step
further than Hesiod's approval of the good Ἔρις. This notion
of free competition as a basis of society agrees well with his views
as to men of ability. On the other hand no state could allow a
citizen to rise to the top by other than lawful means, and for
Heraclitus Law, like Intelligence and Strife, was a universal principle of divine origin. Human laws are fed by it and Law is to
the polis what Intelligence is to Man (114). 'Even the sun must
not leave his appointed path, else the Erinyes, champions of Δίκη,
will find him out' (94). So too a people should fight for its law
as for its city-wall (44). To the question 'Can that be Law which
is ordained by a single man?' Heraclitus' reply, if we may be
certain of the context, would be 'Yes, it is νόμος also to obey the
counsel of one man' (33). Here again the question was one of
importance for the Greeks, and while hatred of tyranny (see Introduction and next chapter) led most of them to regard it as
incompatible with Law, not all one-man rule was necessarily
illegal. It is forcibly argued in a speech in Sophocles' *Antigone*,[2]
to which reference was made above, that where the power of
one man is legitimately derived, he must be obeyed in all things
great and small, just and unjust; and in an imaginary conversation,[3] composed in the following century, even the official acts of
a tyrant are stated to be Law or to be accepted as such. But for
Heraclitus the important thing would seem to be that Law takes
its place along with Intelligence and Rivalry as one of the three
cosmic principles to which the structure of the πόλις must con-

---

[1] *Politics* III 1284 and V 1302b 18 and 1308b 17. See Chap. XI.
[2] 639-680 esp.

> ἀλλ᾽ ὃν πόλις στήσειε, τοῦδε χρὴ κλύειν
> καὶ σμικρὰ καὶ δίκαια καὶ τἀναντία.

[3] Xenophon, *Memorab.* I 2, 43 where the words ὅσα τύραννος ἄρχων γράφει,
καὶ ταῦτα νόμος καλεῖται are put into the mouth of Pericles.

form. To approve of 'taking the counsel of one man' is not to show favour of monarchical government or indeed to express any opinion about it.

FURTHER NOTES AND REFERENCES

CHAPTER II

Hesiod, *Works and Days* 174-285, *Theogony* 75-97, 902.

Tyrtaeus, Fragments 3 and 9; Solon Frr. 1, 3, 5, 8, 10, 16, 23, 24 and Xenophanes Fr. 2, as in Diehl *Anthol. Lyr.* I.

Theognis; the reff. in the text are to lines consecutively numbered.

Pythagoras; Fragments of Aristoxenus ed. F. Wehrli (1944) nos. 16, 17, 18, 33, 34, 35. For divergent interpretations of the political theories of Pythagoras see E. L. Minar, *Early Pythagorean Politics* (1942), A. Delatte, *Essai sur la politique pythagoricienne* (1922), and G. Thomson, *Aeschylus and Athens* (1941) p. 213.

Heraclitus; the reff. are to fragments in Diels-Kranz *Vorsokratiker*[5]I, but any political interpretation is very hazardous. I find general support for the views above expressed in Gregory Vlastos, 'Equality and Justice in Early Greek Cosmologies', *Class. Philol.* XLII 1947.

Eunomia and Eukosmia

Homer once (*Od.* XVII 487) uses εὐνομίη but not personified, as in Hesiod's *Theogony*, and not in relation to the πόλις, simply as opposed to ὕβρις. Politically it meant first, a condition of law, where laws are observed; second, a condition where the laws are good. Both senses are noted by Aristotle *Politics* IV 1294a. But the connection between νόμος and νέμειν was not forgotten and those who spoke of εὐνομία (or of ἰσονομία) in politics often were thinking of *distribution* of good things. Opposed to εὐνομία were both ἀνομία, a condition of no law, and δυσνομία, a condition where there is law but it is not observed, or where in the speaker's view the laws are bad or the distribution faulty. For full discussion and different views see H. Stier in *Philologus* LXXXIII (1928); A. Andrewes in *Class. Quart.* XXXII, 1938; V. Ehrenberg in his *Rechtsidee im frühen Griechentum*, and more recently in *Aspects of the Ancient World* (1946) ch. VI; J. L. Myres in *Class. Review* LXI, 1947, p. 81.

Unlike εὐνομία, εὐκοσμία never became a political slogan. It meant orderly and decent conduct and it kept its emphasis on personal rather than on political behaviour. But under the influence perhaps of Pythagoras and certainly of Damon the musician it came to denote not the mere outward conformity, but the inward order of the soul, the orderly and harmonious frame of mind. Damon (early fifth century) was a σοφιστής who in teaching music stressed its importance as a means of securing this mental harmony and consequently the political importance of education in μουσική. See Heinrich Ryffel in *Museum Helveticum* IV, 1947, p. 23.

CHAPTER III

THE NEW FREEDOM

A T the beginning of the sixth century, as we saw in the last chapter, political thought was dominated by the search for good order, εὐνομία. Before the end of the century that had given way, at any rate at Athens, to ἰσονομία, which it was the aim of Cleisthenes' constitution to establish. The equality implied in ἰσονομία is not absolute equality, but equal rights for all under a lawful constitution. Eunomia did not always imply that the laws were good, only that they were respected.[1] Isonomia implies both equality before the law and 'fair play for all'.[2] The two ideals are thus different but not necessarily incompatible; both were directly opposed to tyranny. At Athens the belief in ἰσονομία was greatly strengthened by the success of her citizens in both military and naval warfare against the Persians at the beginning of the next century (491-479 B.C.), and the existence of tyranny was widely held to be a source of military weakness in a state. That a city not hitherto famed for skill in warfare should have fought with such courage and success against greatly superior numbers, first at Marathon and then at Salamis, provided apparently certain proof that the free institutions of the Athenian πόλις were superior to any other kind of state organisation. The previous generation (509 B.C.) had thrown off the oppressive yoke of the tyrant Hippias; now the generation of Aeschylus, who himself fought at Marathon, has repelled the Persian invasion and a second liberation, this time of the whole of Greece, has taken

[1] See note at end of Chap. II.

[2] Hence, though primarily associated in Herodotus with democracy, it was also appropriated by oligarchs. Cp. the remarks of J. A. O. Larsen in the first of the *Essays in Political Theory presented to Geo. H. Sabine* (Cornell U.P. 1948).

place. This was an age of earnest optimism, of serious thinking and increased hope. The intense feeling aroused by the liberation is nowhere better illustrated than in the play entitled *The Persians* which Aeschylus produced in 472 B.C. It is true that Aeschylus' fame as a thinker, apart from his poetic and dramatic fame, must always rest more on his theology than on his political ideas, which centre round a poet's conception of δίκη and a belief that Zeus will punish the wicked and not allow the righteous to perish. But the note struck by the *Persae* was re-echoed by all Greeks of the time. The poet puts these words into the mouths of Greek naval leaders at Salamis: 'Come, sons of Hellas, set free your land, set free too children, wives, temples of your fathers' gods and the tombs of your ancestors. We fight for our all.' For these were indeed the prizes which were won by the victory and which the Greeks most cherished—the chance to go on living where a man feels that he belongs, among his own people, his own gods, in the land where his fathers lie buried; and to be personally free, not like the Persians, whose relation to their king was that of slave to master, to live in a régime which took some care, and had regard to the common weal.

The Persian menace had called forth the co-operation of Athens and Sparta and others. But there were those who did not see that the invasion was a threat to the whole notion of free and independent cities. Or if they did see it, they did not care. There were many who disliked the whole idea of the State, impartially just to all its members and utterly regardless of ancient privilege. This feeling was strong at Thebes and the Thebans did not fight; they 'medised' (μηδίζειν). They were of course not allowed to forget this defection and their enemies often reminded them of it. Half a century after the final victory over the Persians in Greece and almost on the very site of that battle at Plataea we find the Thebans still making their traditional defence on the charge of μηδισμός. They urged, so Thucydides tells us, that they were not to blame for their submission to the invader, because they had not proper independent government, only a 'power-group', a δυναστεία ὀλίγων ἀνδρῶν. It was not an oligarchy in the accepted sense and it could not be described as ἰσόνομος, that is to say no one had any rights under it. Thus the people were living without any νόμοι, not under a lawful constitution at all. It was only, they said, after the Persian War was over that their city really became mistress in her own house (αὐτοκράτωρ ἑαυτῆς) and acquired laws (νόμους ἔλαβε). Now whether this defence is valid or not, it is most instructive. It shows us the reverse side of the picture painted by Aeschylus and demonstrates the growing importance in Greek political thought of the idea of a *Constitution*, a πολιτεία based upon, and almost identical with, its own *Laws*, νόμοι. The analysis and synthesis, the classification and imaginary construction of the various possible forms of constitution for a πόλις was from now on one of the chief concerns of Greek political philosophers; and Plato's two great political books are entitled, one Πολιτεία, the other Νόμοι.

Thus the right to have one's own laws and the chance to have a constitution for one's own city were regarded as one of the greatest prizes of the victory over the Persians. We may find it easier to recapture some of the enthusiasm which the very idea of having a constitution aroused, if we think of the laws of a city as a charter rather than a set of rules, a charter not granted by some superior power but won by the citizens' valour. For to each citizen his city's laws were his charter of freedom, his safeguard against oppression by a tyrant or by a privileged class and his guarantee of future liberty.[1] Every city's own laws were as much part of its defences as its wall, and the old tag of Heraclitus (Fr. 44) was well matched with that of Phocylides 'Better a tiny and orderly city set high upon a rock than the senseless disorder of Nineveh'. Changes in constitution were therefore regarded with suspicion; if they went far, they would change the whole character of the city and of the citizens too. If a constitution is changed to oligarchy, the ways (τρόποι) of the citizens change in the same way. It did not seem strange to a Greek to talk of a man's character as oligarchical; Plato uses δημοκρατικός and even ἰσονομικός to sum up the character of a changeable and pleasure-seeking kind of man. For the kind of man who lived under a particular régime would be different from one living under some other. This notion continued while free institutions lasted; Isocrates never tires of calling the constitution the very *mind* (ψυχή) of a city; Aristotle speaks of it as the *life* of the state; Demosthenes says that a city's laws are its *character*. Thus the notion that it is comparatively unimportant what system of government you have,

---

[1] This is not to say that no law operated under Greek tyrants; many of these tried to rule 'constitutionally'.

provided that the public services are carried on efficiently, would have been quite meaningless to a Greek, just as meaningless as Plato's 'isonomic kind of man' in English. It was a matter of the greatest importance to an individual whether he lived under a democracy or an oligarchy; he would be useless, as well as despised and unhappy, in the wrong kind of state.

It is not therefore difficult to see why the question, what is the best form of constitution? became and long remained the prime concern of Greek political thought. Its earliest extant discussion[1] occurs in the third book of the *Histories* of Herodotus (*c.* 485-425 B.C.). Like much of Greek philosophical literature it is in the form of a reported dialogue, not of course a Platonic dialogue of questions and answers, but one following the Protagorean method of a series of statements of the case for and against. The occasion, which Herodotus avers to be historical, is a discussion by Persian leaders as to what form of government they should adopt after they had rid themselves of the Magian usurper in 522 B.C. It is not inconceivable that such a discussion should have taken place, but most of what we read in the passage in Herodotus cannot be a report of what Persian nobles said in 522 B.C., but a dialogue, composed some seventy years later, after the manner of fifth century Greek philosophers.

The first speaker, Otanes, moved the abolition of the Persian monarchy, which, he said, had proved bad and irksome under Cambyses and the Magian. The objections to it on principle are: (1) the sole ruler can do as he likes and is ἀνυπεύθυνος, *not answerable to anyone*, and (2) however excellent his disposition, he is bound to acquire a different way of looking at things from that of the ordinary man. A two-fold deterioration of character sets in; he becomes swollen with insolence and pride by the abundance of wealth and power, and at the same time jealous and suspicious of those around him. This causes him to do many senseless and cruel things; if these meet with no approval, he is angry; if they are praised, he suspects insincerity. Those of his subjects who are of the highest character and integrity are most hated and feared. Worst of all, he breaks down old ways of living, violates women and puts men to death without trial. The alternative proposed is that the sovran power should pass into the hands of τὸ πλῆθος, that is the full complement of adult male

---

[1] Unless we count Hippodamus. See p. 63.

citizens. Such an arrangement is marked by that 'lovely word, equality', κάλλιστον οὔνομα ἰσονομίη. The personnel of the government is chosen by lot and every person appointed to office has to render an account of it to the people. Resolutions likewise are subject to the authority of the whole people. In this speech we have on the one hand the first of many attempts at analysing and appraising the position of a τύραννος from a Greek point of view; it was a subject which had all the fascination of the forbidden, but it was one of great practical importance so long as the danger of tyranny remained. On the other hand we have what may be described as a few notes on democracy. The word δημοκρατία, rule of the people, is not used on this occasion, though Herodotus knows it (VI 43), but the marks are those traditionally associated with Athenian democracy—namely equality[1], the use of the lot in elections, the εὔθυνα or scrutiny at the end of a term of office and the sovranty of the people.

The next speaker, Megabyzus, agrees with Otanes about the vices of tyranny but he finds *hybris* also in the rule of the people. He urges that the tyrant does at least know what he is about, while the mob does not, being without knowledge or education. He accordingly presses for rule by the few, oligarchy. The arguments in its favour are, first, the theoretically quite irrelevant one that the three speakers as Persian nobles are sure to obtain high office in it, and second, that only men of knowledge and education are fit to govern. 'It stands to reason that you will get the best advice from the best men' (ἀρίστων ἀνδρῶν οἰκὸς ἄριστα βουλεύματα γίνεσθαι). Protagoras, as we shall see later, regarded this as an argument in favour of better education; but for the moment it is one of the stock arguments in favour of aristocracy and it is, as Socrates saw, quite worthless unless you know the meaning of *best*. But as it stands it is based on the idea that the aim of government is εὐβουλία, good counsel. This now takes the place of the older εὐκοσμία and εὐνομία as a catchword of aristocracy. In itself the word has of course no constitutional significance and Sophocles in his *Antigone* (c. 440 B.C.) makes Creon, a sole ruler, profess to regard it as a guiding principle of government, while Protagoras claimed to teach it.

As a matter of history neither of these proposals was adopted, and the Persian monarchy was re-established under Darius, who

---

[1] ἰσονομία, ἰσοκρατία, ἰσηγορία, ἰσοτέλεια denote various aspects of it.

appears as the third speaker. He does not expressly reply to the charge of ὕβρις made against tyranny, a charge which Megabyzus had laid against democracy, as many others did after him. But he was clearly aware that any government might behave in a 'hybristic' and tyrannical manner. For he is made to preface his statement with the proviso that in any discussion of the three forms, demos, oligarchy and monarchy, we must consider only the best in each case. This foreshadows the six-fold classification of constitutions, three good of their kind and three deviations or bad forms, which is familiar to us from Plato onwards.[1] Moreover the conclusion put into the mouth of Darius is one to which in a large degree and with their own reservations both Plato and Aristotle would have assented—that the rule of the single *best* man is best. On the other hand the arguments used are those of the time and the occasion and are drawn from practical experience of absolute rulership: a sole ruler can get rid of disaffected persons (δυσμενεῖς, Solon's word) without undue publicity; he can keep a firm hand on the nobles, who would otherwise be scrambling for leadership; from this civil war would result and the need for a single strong arm to restore order, so that monarchy becomes inevitable. This inevitability is held to prove its excellence—a way of interpreting history not unknown in our own day. Similarly it is asserted that democracy inevitably leads to the degradation of government; for government falls into the hands of the second-rate persons and these are eventually displaced by a single first-rate person who has won the support of the people and becomes sole ruler. Thus again monarchy is proved to be the best, especially for the Persians, since it was traditional among them and it was a good principle not to abolish ancestral ways when they were working well.

Thus concluded what Protagoras might have called the ἀντιλογικοὶ λόγοι[2]; but Otanes, who had unsuccessfully urged the claims of equality, now asks for and obtains special exemptions for himself and his family under the new monarchy. 'I will neither rule nor be ruled', he says, οὔτε γὰρ ἄρχειν οὔτε ἄρχεσθαι ἐθέλω. This is just the reverse of later political theory which made it a mark of a good citizen that he should be able and willing both

[1] See below Chap. IX.

[2] The debt of Herodotus to Protagoras probably goes much deeper than the form; but the source of this dialogue is unknown.

to rule and to be ruled. In general, however, these chapters of Herodotus present us with a blend of the traditional Greek notions of the sixth century and the philosophical outlook of the fifth. The objections to the absolute rule of a single monarch, though they may well have been made by Persians who had suffered under it, are typically Greek and already old-fashioned, though widely held, when Herodotus wrote; so too the extolling of the ἄριστοι. But much of the argumentation reflects the current discussions of the fifth century, when Herodotus lived, wrote and travelled and made long sojourns at Athens.

This mixture of the old and the new in political thought is a feature of Herodotus' work as a whole. He does not obtrude his own opinions but he often lets his sympathies be seen. He stands for freedom and equality. He is the relentless foe of tyranny and oppression and dwells with pleasure on the stories of the downfalls of great tyrant houses; for he had himself fled from tyranny at home. Such an attitude does not make for clear thinking and Herodotus' many admirers do not claim that he is a political thinker; yet his work taken along with the *Persae* of Aeschylus would be a much better introduction to Greek political thought than Plato's *Republic* with which so many students begin. His history is an account of the opposition between East and West, which culminated in the liberation of Greece and the Aegean from the Persian menace in 478. He goes back to mythical times and in rambling fashion tells us of the antitheses, the pairs of opposites, such as Barbarian and Greek, ὕβρις and σωφροσύνη, slave and free, tyranny and liberty. He uses his terms loosely; tyranny is 'an uncertain thing', equality 'a good thing'. His favourite word for equality is ἰσηγορίη, equality of speech. So strongly was any restriction of free speech resented that Herodotus uses the word almost as if it meant 'absence of tyranny' (v 78). For him free speech is the first requisite of a state. It creates a condition of life which makes men ready to face death and strong to overcome a foe many times more numerous. The barbarian was quite incapable of seeing why the Greeks should fight if no master forced them, or why they would not simply come to terms with the invader. At Sparta and Athens answers to these two questions were clear and oft-repeated. For the former there is the famous remark of Demaratus, which might be taken to epitomise Herodotus' view of the relations between citizens and their city: 'Though

free they are not entirely free; for they have a master—Law.'
For the latter there is the retort of the Spartans to Hydarnes the
Persian—that there can be no common ground between lovers
of freedom and those who know nothing of it, being all from the
lowest to the highest slaves of a master. Now the Theban excuse
for submission, as we have seen, was exactly this, that they had
no Law, nothing, that is, to fight for. For Law meant Freedom.

But already in Herodotus' own day the pleasing simplicity of
this doctrine was becoming old-fashioned. The meaning of the
word νόμος, *law*, was being much discussed and it was obvious
that it was also the regular word for what we call *custom*.[1] Demaratus had proudly said ἔπεστι γὰρ δεσπότης *NOMOΣ*. Perhaps
Nomos was really now becoming a despotic ruler with all the
uncertainty and fickleness of the traditional τύραννος. At any rate
Herodotus has another tale to tell which, like the story of Demaratus, ends with the emphasis on νόμος, but the point of the story
is quite different. The following is a translation of most of the
passage: it keeps the word νόμος where it occurs and makes
no attempt to reproduce in English the interplay of νόμος and
νομίζειν. 'If one were to offer to all men the choice of the best
nomoi in the world, they would all after a good look around
choose their own. . . . There are many indications that men do
in fact adopt this attitude towards nomoi. This story will serve
for one: King Darius during his reign summoned Greeks who
were present at his court and asked them for what sum of money
they would agree to eat their fathers at death. They replied that
they would not do so on any account. Darius after that summoned members of a tribe of Indians who do eat their parents
and asked them in the presence of the Greeks, who followed
what was said through an interpreter, what sum of money they
would take to consume their fathers with fire. They cried out in
horror at the very mention of such a thing. Both these are practices established by Nomos (νενόμισται) and I think Pindar was
quite right in that poem in which he said that Nomos was king
of all.'

This passage of Herodotus (III 38) appears to us to illustrate
both the power and the variety of national *customs* but to tell us

---

[1] It will not do to try and unite the two ideas in 'customary law'; such
an expression restricts the meaning of law, instead of widening it so as to
include custom.

40

nothing about *laws*. Yet Plato, who quotes the Pindaric fragment more fully, shows that in its context Pindar had in mind something more than custom.[1] The word νόμος, however, was one, not two, and the Greek notion of Law was in fact very closely allied to the Greek notion of Custom. Just as for Hesiod δίκη was the way things are done, and therefore the right way of doing them, so νόμοι are those things which are and have been habitually done (ἃ νενόμισται) and therefore rightly done. But at the time when Herodotus was writing the inadequacy of such a conception of law in relation to a state was becoming apparent and, for all its approval of νόμος, the passage shows unmistakable doubts. So once again Herodotus appears to stand with one foot on the political ground of the period of the Persian wars and the other among the critics and sceptics of his own time. For while the Greeks of the liberation hailed Nomos as their Charter, setting them free from the arbitrary rule of a despot and the disordered social life which that entailed, a new generation sprang up and began to see that Nomos may itself be a tyranny—a series of customs and conventions imposed upon men who might not always wish to conform to them. The 'good look around', which the theorising of Herodotus allowed to each man, might result, if not in a preference for others' ways, at least in a lack of conviction about the validity and importance of one's own. Thus the conception of νόμος as a liberating force fades away when the liberation is won, and that which was seen as freedom's safeguard begins to appear as its negation. It is too soon yet to say that such a fundamental problem of political philosophy as the reconciliation of Law with Liberty has emerged, but the seeds are there. Already even in Aeschylus' earliest extant play, the *Suppliants*, the plot turns on the opposition between two different νόμοι, one which permits and one which forbids marriage between first cousins. But the dramatist-theologian himself believed firmly in the validity, divinely derived, of Law. He saw it on the one hand setting man free from oppression and despotism, on the other saving him from anarchy. Law might be a stern master and

---

[1] Pindar, as Callicles saw (Plato, *Gorgias* 484 B), was referring to the right of the stronger. But there is another fragment of Pindar (215 Schr., 203 Bowra) which does say: 'Different people have different customs; every man prefers his own right way, δίκη.' On the whole subject of *Nomos-Basileus* see H. E. Stier in *Philologus* LXXXIII 1928.

men need sometimes to be frightened into obedience to it. But respect for law is the best protection for the land and a bulwark of the State. The *Eumenides* of Aeschylus is perhaps the most eloquent statement of his belief in the congruence of divine and human institutions.

FURTHER NOTES AND REFERENCES

CHAPTER III

Tyranny a source of military weakness. Herodotus v 66, 78, 91-92. cp. Hippocrates *A.W.P.* xvi.

AESCHYLUS, *Persae* 402-405, 241-242; *Supplices* 700, προμαθὶς εὐκοινόμητις ἀρχά.

Thebans' defence. Thucydides III 62.

ἰσονομικός τις ἀνήρ. Plato, *Repub.* VIII 561 E.

The 'Persian' dialogue on constitutions. Herod. III 80-82.

εὐβουλία, ἄριστα βουλεύματα. Sophocles, *Antigone* 178-183; Plato, *Protagoras* 318 E.

ἄρχειν καὶ ἄρχεσθαι. Herod. III 83; Soph. *Antig.* 669; Plato, *Laws* 643 E; Aristotle, *Politics* III 1277a. See Chap. XI.

ἰσηγορίη. Herod. v 78.

νόμος. Herod. III 38, VII 102-104, (Demaratus) 135-6, (Hydarnes) VIII 143-144; Plato, *Gorgias* 484 B.

AESCHYLUS, *Eumenides* 511-526, 681-699.

J. L. Myres, *Political Ideas of the Greeks* (1927) Lecture V and F. Heinimann, *Nomos und Physis* (see note at end of Chap. IV) which is particularly good on the Demaratus episode (pp. 29-36).

CHAPTER IV

PROTAGORAS AND OTHERS

Dire qu'il n'y a rien de juste ni d'injuste que ce qu'ordonnent les lois positives, c'est dire qu'avant qu'on eût tracé de cercle, tous les rayons n'étoient pas égaux.—MONTESQUIEU.

De tous les gouvernements le plus mauvais est celui où la richesse et les capacités se partagent le pouvoir.—G. SOREL.

I T is generally agreed that the fifth century B.C. is one of the most important periods in the history of the world and that we are inadequately equipped to give an account of it either historically or intellectually. Especially would we know more of the two decades (460-440) when Protagoras and Herodotus visited Athens, some of the finest Greek tragedies were produced, and Socrates was a young and eager enquirer. Many of the men who contributed most to the intellectual development of the age, and of succeeding ages, exerted their influence through the spoken as well as the written word and of their written words few have survived. We count it good fortune that the fame of Attic drama caused copies to be made, so that at least some small fraction of fifth-century tragedy and comedy has come down to us. We have the histories of Herodotus, whose bearing on political thought was discussed in the last chapter and we have the inestimable boon of the work of Thucydides (see Chap. VI). But much of the material for writing an account of the intellectual development of fifth-century Greece is a confused, meagre and sometimes inconsistent blend of tradition and fragment, anecdote and imitation. We have numerous fragments of Empedocles and others, whose importance does not lie in political philosophy. The outstanding men for our purpose are Protagoras and Socrates his younger contemporary. Of these the former wrote much but none of it survived; the latter wrote nothing. And for our knowledge of the two in relation to each other we have to depend largely on the writings of Plato, who made no pretence of giving an unbiassed historical account of either of them. Only of Gorgias among the professed educators have we extensive remains and these are of greater stylistic interest than political. When the evidence is so meagre, interpretation is hazardous and subjective and it is not surprising that even in antiquity conflicting opinions were held and conflicting traditions current. Modern scholars have reduced the material to order[1] and eliminated some absurdities, but there are inevitably many unsolved problems and much difference of opinion. Was the age predominantly one of Enlightenment, in which thinkers and teachers set men free from superstition or from the shackles of conventional morality? Was it a scientific age or was it one of revolt against the barrenness and uselessness of the science of the time? Was it a conflict between Religion and Science, or between Science and Humanity, or between Humanity and Religion?

Whatever answers may be given to these questions, there can be no doubt that it was an age of great intellectual activity and that nowhere was this activity more stimulated and fostered than at Athens. The many causes of Athenian intellectual predominance cannot here be analysed, but the connection between political thought and political conditions and opportunities makes it desirable to give a brief account of its background in fifth-century Athens. The success of the Athenian navy at Salamis had been followed by a rapid expansion of naval power and this in turn had greatly increased Athenian political power in the Aegean Sea. In return for naval protection against possible Persian attack many cities and islands were ready to pay tribute to Athens. With naval power maritime trade also expanded, and the material prosperity thus acquired added to the city's magnificence and supplies of imported food. The intense national pride and sense of achievement which, as we saw in the last chapter, were both reflected in and stimulated by the plays of Aeschylus, now surveyed a wider field, and a new generation was eager to embrace larger opportunities. To take part in this great expansion, to be one of the leading men in Hellas' leading Naval Power was a not unworthy

---

[1] Notably H. Diels: *Die Fragmente der Vorsokratiker*, 5th edition revised by W. Kranz, 3 vols., Weidmann, Berlin, 1934-1939.

ambition, and fathers who had fought at Salamis were ready to give their sons a chance by equipping them with 'the best education that money could buy'. Now the Athenian State, while carefully providing for the defence and even the nutrition of the people, made no provision, save through theatres and festivals, for their education, yet at the same time required a very high degree of education in its citizens, if they were to discharge their duties. This raised a new problem, but it was not immediately seen as a problem, least of all by the ever-changing officials of the State. Yet the political importance is clear enough of the question 'What kind of education will best fit a man to take his share[1] in the life of the πόλις ?' If one surveyed the whole field of Hellenic civilisation, the answers could not fail to be numerous; for, since each city has its own πολιτεία and therefore its own life,[2] each will require something different of its citizens. In some cities the Few will play a larger and indeed quite a different part from the Many. But at Athens under the constitution of Cleisthenes, now already widened and made more democratic, there was a part for every adult male except the very poor and a big part for those who were able and ambitious. And the path to power now lay not by way of the armed bands of a Pisistratus; it lay open to the man whose speech carried conviction and who could claim expert knowledge. Such an education would certainly fit a man for political life at Athens. So if any man, citizen or stranger, was able to provide such an education, he would find in Athens a splendid and lucrative field for his lectures and demonstrations and an audience eager to learn and willing to pay. To political power and material prosperity is added a demand for political education, and in this triple combination we have the soil in which much of fifth century political thought grew.

Now political thought springing from such a soil will differ from that of the previous century in the importance attaching to the individual citizen. In Athens before Solon the individual had counted for nothing and after Solon for little enough till the Persian wars. The tribe, the clan, the brotherhood—all these had been gradually rendered less potent and their political importance

---

[1] The equivocal expression is not inappropriate. As time went on the emphasis was less on the duty to be done and more on the reward. The Athenian expected the city to 'pay a dividend'.

[2] βίος = way of life. See p. 161 n. 2.

reduced to nothing. But for the fetters thus removed from the feet of the individual there had been substituted the over-all and binding authority of the Athenian state. The lesser loyalties had been swallowed up in the greater but the individual still counted for little. He was, however, content to do so for the moment. He had great personal freedom, little or no state-interference with his private life or with his efforts to make money for himself and his family or even with his plans to dispose of his gains. He had no reason to resent the paramount authority of a city which so provided for his needs, and of which he felt himself to be a part. When therefore we speak of individualism as manifesting itself about the middle of the fifth century, it is not associated with any assertion of the rights of man, still less an attack on the rights of the πόλις. Indeed the self-assertiveness of the individual and eagerness for better education were indications of a desire to serve the city, as well as to win honour and distinction for oneself in doing so. Whatever be the form of the constitution, and no Greek was likely to underestimate that, there would always be the need for men of energy and ability; and in an expanding and vigorous Athenian empire there seemed to be endless scope. Energy and ability, all-round goodness, ἀρετή—in democratic Athens this was no longer regarded as the hereditary privilege of noble families.[1] Many no doubt still clung to Pindar's[2] belief that inborn goodness was superior to that acquired by learning, but few maintained that it could not be taught at all. This came about the more easily because ἀρετή was both the sum total of the qualities that make a real man and the ability to do something really well. In the latter case training was clearly both possible and desirable, so the question whether general goodness, including good conduct, could also be taught was not asked until Socrates, according to Plato, put it to Protagoras. The answer was too obvious; the laws and customs of a city could be learned and these were in themselves an education in good behaviour.[3] But the individualist of the fifth century asked for more than this; he asked for an education for himself, for which he was ready to pay. In response

[1] Yet the principle of heredity still held; free-born Athenian descent was a condition of citizenship. W. Jaeger, *Paideia*, Eng. trans., I, p. 284.

[2] e.g. *Nem.* III 40-42; *Olymp.* II 86-88.

[3] 'To establish a legal standard by written law was for the Greeks an *educational* act.' Jaeger, *Paideia* I, p. 107.

to this demand and attracted by the prospects, expert teachers, σοφισταί, came to Athens from other cities and stayed for longer or shorter periods.

Some of these resident or visiting lecturers[1] had a contribution to make to political thought, others had not. They differed widely in their methods, doctrine and subject-matter, but their presence in Athens and their educational activity there demonstrated the connection between politics and culture, the profound influence of the education of the citizens on the nature and value of the State. What that influence *ought* to be they hardly asked. The Athenian state was taken for granted, and in various ways they sought to fit young men for a successful career there in politics or in 'the professions', so far as these were differentiated. They did not feel the need to ask what effect the wider distribution of knowledge and ability would have on the State itself, but they created conditions which would inevitably raise such questions. The problem of the relations between Science and Society, the place of a growing body of specialists in a community, has a modern sound about it, but it is not essentially different from the problem created by the expansion of knowledge and education in the age of Pericles. The nature and existence of the problem were not then apparent, any more than the present-day problem was in 1870. But Plato in the next century was conscious of the difficulty and in his *Republic* the search for social justice is found to be closely linked with the study of the relations between Knowledge and Power. In 450 B.C. there appeared to be no problem except, so to speak, one of production—more energy and ability, more knowledge. It was of course easier to instil the knowledge of a craft than knowledge of a subject, easier to teach 'how' than to teach 'why', let alone teaching an ultimate purpose. And among the pupils many were able to acquire a knack of doing things for one who could grasp the basis of a subject.

The liberation of the Aegean from the power of Persia not only

---

[1] Protagoras was proud to call himself a *Sophist*, a teacher of mankind like the poets of old (Plato, *Protag.* 316 D - 317 C), but their subsequent unpopularity, in which Socrates shared, and the writings of Plato, in which Socrates is differentiated from the sophists, set the word σοφιστής on a pejorative course. The distinguishing marks of the older, fifth-century sophist were his claims (1) to expert knowledge, (2) to ability to teach, (3) to a fee for his teaching. Socrates made none of these claims; but in other respects may be reckoned among them. See Chap. V.

increased the intercourse of the Greek cities and islands with each other, but improved and extended foreign travel generally. If there were few who travelled for themselves, the travel-books of Hecataeus and Herodotus were read by many. We saw in the last chapter how Herodotus' survey of the laws and customs of many lands had weakened the notion of Νόμος as something liberating and inspiring and showed how it might become irksome and restrictive. But a far more serious challenge was at hand. If Law differed so much from place to place, if that which was forbidden in one country was permitted and even enjoined in another, surely Heraclitus must have been wrong when he said 'All human laws are nourished by one divine law'. If he looked back to the earlier poets, as the Greek instinctively did in search for moral and political guidance, he would find the Homeric and Hesiodic conception of Δίκη, the Right Way, and its divine authority. But δίκη, too, was not everywhere the same. The right way to make a plough or handle an ox can be found out by watching other people, but can you infer from observing the behaviour of men what is the right way to behave? Was there nothing that was common to all men all over the known world? It was pointed out by some of the σοφισταί of the fifth century that the one universal feature was that everywhere men were born, grew up and died. The process of growth was in Greek φύσις, habitually[1] translated by the Latin *natura* and the English *nature*. This discovery, that the 'physis' of man is everywhere the same, had the merit of being based on observation[2] and had important consequences, but did it really answer the question What is Man?—a question to which Ethics and Politics must have an answer? The process of growth is one which man shares with all animals and if we ask the old teachers, the poets, what it is that distinguishes men from beasts, we learn again that it is just that notion of δίκη.[3] The new teachers, as we shall see, had other answers; the essential at this stage is to note the *actualité* of the question.[4]

[1] But in the first instance incorrectly, since *natura* is not a process. But φύσις gradually approximated to *natura*. See below.

[2] Opinions about the use of observation, the value of the evidence of the senses, lie outside the scope of this book. It is the preoccupation of this age with the φύσις of Man rather than that of the Universe that is striking.

[3] Hesiod, *W.D.* 278-279.

[4] One possible answer may be mentioned here, because there is no thinker to whom it can be ascribed, although developments of it are to be found

48

Now, if Nomos is considered in the light of these enquiries there are four possible lines of thought: first, to make φύσις dependent on νόμος and νόμος on the gods. That is virtually to go back to the old position where Hesiod describes as νόμος the assigning (νέμειν) by Zeus of δίκη to Man. This position was now impossible; νόμος, as we saw, had become far too closely attached to the πόλις and would be quite inappropriate to describe that which initiates or controls the growth of the animal or vegetable world. In the one place where the expression 'law of nature' is used[1] it is intended to be paradoxical and it means not a law obeyed by nature but a law derived from it. It belongs in fact to the fourth line of thought (see below). The second possibility is to dissociate nomos from physis, that is from the growth-process, making both separately dependent on a higher power. Thus, while it is part of φύσις to grow old and die, νόμος is immortal and unageing. This is the theme of a fine poem in Sophocles,[2] in which the chorus sing of the laws which all our words and all our deeds must obey: 'They walk on high, born in heaven above; their only begetter is Olympus and no φύσις of mortal men engendered them. Never shall forgetfulness send them to sleep; there is a mighty god in them and he grows not old.' This view is not new, it is essentially that of Heraclitus again. But, though old-fashioned, it was by no means dead. It was popularly summed up in the idea of the Unwritten Laws which were felt to be binding on all men, at any rate on all Greek men, whatever be the variation in local νόμοι. The exact connotation of the phrase ἄγραφοι νόμοι varied with the speaker and the context, but they generally included the two precepts θεοὺς σέβειν and γονέας τιμᾶν. Now both religious

---

among the Cynics. It is that there is no difference at all between man and beast, that one is not more savage than the other and that there should be no education, no courts of justice, no laws, no compulsion of any kind to practise ἀρετή. This 'back to nature' school of thought had in the latter part of the century sufficient vogue to be satirised in the comic stage. The *Wild Men* (ἄγριοι) of Pherecrates was produced in 420 B.C. We know no more than the passing reference in Plato, *Protag.* 327 D. This theory must be distinguished from that of Callicles. In Aristophanes' *Birds*, too, part of the comic effect is based on the fun of being a bird and behaving like one.

[1] Plato, *Gorgias* 483 E, κατὰ νόμον τῆς φύσεως. The Greek for 'law of nature' was ἀνάγκη τῆς φύσεως, e.g., laws which could not be broken with impunity. See Chap. V (Antiphon).

[2] *Oed. Tyr.*, 863-873.

observances and, still more, duty to parents were often made the subject of legal enactment and so were no longer unwritten. This may have strengthened them in practice, but it weakened the claim, always made on their behalf, that they came from the gods. But apart from the separate precepts the idea of an unwritten but generally accepted Law had a big future in Jurisprudence especially in the foundations of Equity.[1]

The third line differs from the second only in taking a more anthropocentric view. Putting aside, but not denying, the unwritten laws and considering only man-made νόμοι, some came to the conclusion that, while human laws owe nothing to a mere growth-process, it was natural for man to order his life by νόμοι. This view was in the long run the most fruitful in political thought but it was for a time obscured by the immense popularity of the fourth line of thought.

This was to make right and wrong dependent on φύσις. Early science, making use of direct observation, had shown that in everything there appeared to be a normal or right condition. This might be disturbed or corrupted, as winds disturb the φύσις of the sea (Herod. VII 16) or lack of rain the normal level (φύσις) of a river (Herod. IV 50). Medical writers spoke constantly of δικαία φύσις as the normal, healthy condition of the human body. So, if one may describe as right by nature (δίκαιον φύσει) that which is in a right condition, why not describe human conduct in the same terms? Let those actions be right which are so by nature, not because man-made law or custom has decided. The rules by which men regulate their conduct have no validity that can be derived from the order of nature: men call them νόμοι and act upon them as believing in them (νομίζειν); but of all the existing laws, conventions and customs there is no trace in τὰ φυσικά, the natural things, only in τὰ νόμιμα, the conventional things. Thus νόμος and φύσις turn out to be mutually exclusive and directly opposed to each other. Whatever in all the universe, be it act or fact or name, is not found to be derived from φύσις can only be said to exist νόμῳ, that is, in virtue of some agreed opinion or convention of men.

All these conflicting views and different interpretations[2] appear

---

[1] See Aristotle, *Rhetoric* I, ch. 13; Andocides *de Myst.* 85. Further on unwritten laws in Sophocles in Chap. V.

[2] See last note at the end of this chapter.

confusing and unsatisfying and must indeed have been so to the older people, already unsettled by a changing outlook. But the majority found it all very stimulating and exciting, and it is typical of the intellectual ferment of the time and a good sample, so to speak, of the newly-dug soil. The most immediately fruitful line of thought was the antithesis of φύσις and νόμος, nature and convention; it could be applied to everything under the sun and could be made to yield interesting and surprising results. It requires no general illustration here: the literature of the century is filled with it almost *ad nauseam*. What use was made of it by political thinkers will become apparent as we examine them, but it will be an advantage to give here its supposed[1] earliest formulation and earliest ethical application. It came not from any of the new σοφισταί but from Archelaus surnamed ὁ φυσικός. He was particularly interested in biology, in birth, growth and decay, which he associated with the principles of hot and cold. In all his studies of the growth of man he found no trace of right and wrong; these, therefore, had no existence in nature but only by custom or convention of man—τὸ δίκαιον εἶναι καὶ τὸ αἰσχρὸν οὐ φύσει ἀλλὰ νόμῳ. We do not know how the 'physicist' worked out the implications of this, but there were many[2] who took it to imply that apart from the varying opinions of men there is no standard of morality. 'If therefore we say "this is right" or "this is wrong", the only *fact* expressed is the existence of some feelings in ourselves or in others or in both.' Again, 'Was not he who laid down νόμος in the beginning a man like you or me?' So says Pheidippides in the *Clouds* (1421), claiming the right to make a new νόμος by which sons may beat their fathers.

Protagoras was a native of Abdera in Thrace, a town which gave birth to more than one famous philosopher but was otherwise noteworthy for the folly of its sailors. The year of his birth is unknown, probably between 490 and 480 B.C. and the year of his death about 420, though another and less credible tradition made him still alive in 411. Many of his adult years were spent at

---

[1] Diog. Laert. II 16. See Diels-Kranz, *Vorsokr.*[5] §60. Archelaus was said to have learned from Anaxagoras and to have taught Socrates, but it may all be an example of the tendency to link up ancient philosophers in a kind of affiliation.

[2] And still are. See for example John Mackie, 'A Refutation of Morals', in the *Australasian Journal of Psychology and Philosophy* XXIV, Sept. 1946, from which the above citation is taken.

Athens, whither he first came between 450 and 445. Here he formed a close friendship with Pericles and it may have been on his recommendation that Protagoras was invited to become Lawgiver in the new city of Thurii in 446-444 B.C. This appointment brought him into touch with Herodotus and must have involved some years' residence in S. Italy, but he then returned to Athens and made or renewed acquaintance with Socrates and Euripides. He left Athens again, perhaps about 430, for it was about that year that the decree of Diopeithes against atheistical teaching was passed and Protagoras' departure was stated to be due to an impending prosecution for atheism. About his movements after that date and whether he returned to Athens and where and at what age he died there is much uncertainty. But for our purpose the most serious gap in his biography is the lack of information about the Thurii period. Plato left to posterity some account of his own two ventures into practical statecraft (Chap. IX *ad fin.*), but we have no letters or autobiographical remains of Protagoras and do not know what kind of laws he made for Thurii. It is a plausible conjecture,[1] if no more, that he gave it a constitution modelled on Periclean democracy. Certainly he had a chance to do so, if he was so minded, for he had a free hand, and earlier lawgivers with the same freedom had had no such model. Aristotle mentions the earliest lawgivers in S. Italy,[2] too early for Protagoras to be included, but it is surprising that he makes no reference to him in connection with Thurii, which he twice mentions[3] as an example of how changes in constitution may be brought about all too easily. Aristotle gives no dates for the changes but it certainly looks as if the Protagorean constitution of Thurii was somewhat impermanent.[4]

The fame of Protagoras in his own day did not rest on his work at Thurii but on his lectures and to a lesser extent on his writings. These are now lost but later antiquity preserved a list of titles, which covered a variety of subjects. One of these was περὶ πολιτείας, the first work to bear as its title the word made

---

[1] Of A. Menzel in *Zeitschrift für Politik,* Vol. III (1910), p. 208, and *Protagoras als Gesetzgeber von Thurii* (Verhandlungen der kgl. sächs. Gesellschaft, Leipzig. Phil.-hist. Kl., LXII, pp. 191-229).

[2] *Politics* II 1274 a.   [3] *Politics* V 1307 a 27 and b 6.

[4] For reasons well shown by V. Ehrenberg in *Amer. Journ. Philol.,* LXIX, 1948, 149-170.

famous by Plato's *Republic*. Another was entitled 'About the original state (of mankind)'. It was presumably from reading these two books that Plato chiefly derived his knowledge of Protagoras' political doctrine which he used in the composition of the dialogue *Protagoras*. The Protagorean doctrine of knowledge is discussed, if not properly understood,[1] in the *Theaetetus*, and other references in Plato testify to his philosophical importance. But the *ipsissima verba* of Protagoras are few and their interpretation even in Plato's day was by no means clear. The fragment supposed to be the cause of his reputation and possible prosecution for impiety runs thus: 'About the gods I cannot know either that they exist or that they do not exist nor what they are like to look at; for many are the hindrances to such knowledge, both the lack of certainty and the shortness of human life' (Fr. 4 D[5]). This is not strictly atheism nor even consistent agnosticism and, though in his political theory he allowed but a small place for τὸ θεῖον, yet he thought it worth while and found it possible to write a book *On the Gods*. Even more obscure, yet of greater importance for our subject, is the oft-quoted 'Man is the measure of all things, of things being that they are, of things not being that they are not'. The interpretations and applications of this dark saying have been numerous. For its meaning in reference to political theory we can get a little further information, albeit only at second or third hand. Plato suggests that Protagoras would have amplified this statement, in so far as it relates to a State, as follows: 'Whatsoever things appear to each city to be right and good, those things are right and good *for it*, so long as it continues to be of that opinion'. This is later further developed thus: 'In matters relating to the πόλις each city, after determining what is good and bad, just and unjust, right and wrong, establishes in accordance therewith what things are lawful for itself and these are in truth valid for each, and you cannot say in such matters that one individual or one city is wiser than another.' Opinions, it is admitted, may differ as to what is expedient for a city, but in matters of morality the πόλις itself is the authority and the standard is to be found in the consensus of opinion, τὸ κοινῇ δόξαν.

If Plato here fairly represents Protagoras' real opinion, then we must take it that he regarded the state as the source of morality and of law, each citizen being free to hold his own opinions but

[1] So F. C. S. Schiller, *Plato or Protagoras?* 1908.

obliged in his conduct not to transgress the consensus of opinion as expressed by the laws. We are reminded of Rousseau's distinction between *la volonté générale* and *la volonté de tous*, but τὸ κοινῇ δόξαν is not the general will but 'that which has been communally decided', and it is not conceived as necessarily and unchangingly right. If the city errs, we are told (*Theaet.* 167), either in making changes or in not making them, it is the duty of wise citizens to exert a pacific influence and convince their fellow citizens that theirs is the better opinion. There is no suggestion that these wise men are to be in any sense rulers[1] and no insistence on any particular form of constitution, but it is assumed as a matter of course that the city is one governed by law and not by an irresponsible despot. Now there is nothing surprising in this setting up the state as a moral arbiter; it was part of the normal basis of the Greek city. But the significant thing is the frank recognition of the fact that if we accept the position, there must be as many different moralities as there are states. Protagoras does not therefore claim any universality for law, still less any divine origin. There is nothing here about unwritten laws. The laws of a city are the discoveries (εὑρήματα) of the good lawgivers[2] of the past, but they are none the worse for that. A man must do what is right and lawful, that means what is right for him at the time and in the place where he is. Each city requires a man first to learn its laws and then to regulate his life according to them; men cannot just behave as they like, εἰκῇ πράττειν.

Such would appear to be the meaning of Protagoras' *homo mensura* saying in relation to political theory. But it is only an interpretation of Plato's interpretation supplemented by two references to Plato's dialogue *Protagoras* (326 C D). To this dialogue we must now turn, for it gives a much fuller account than the *Theaetetus*. First, however, it must be pointed out that there is a certain apparent incompatibility between the two dialogues on one point.[3]

[1] Rather do they form a kind of 'Opposition'.

[2] And not of the gods, not a εὕρημα καὶ δῶρον θεῶν, as in a famous passage in praise of law (Demosth. (?) xxv 17). Bad lawgivers may occur too; their laws must be obeyed until wiser ones are made. Protagoras had a less static view of the state than many.

[3] On only one point, I think. Protagoras' strong social sense is conspicuous in both versions, and it is only by ignoring this that other inconsistencies can be conjured up. See D. Loenen, *Protagoras and the Greek Community*, ch. IV. But Loenen does not squarely face the one difficulty that remains.

How is it that in the *Theaetetus* the validity of τὸ δίκαιον depends on its being laid down by a πόλις, while in the *Protagoras*, as we shall see, a certain feeling for, if not actual knowledge of, the right is stated to be universal among men? Both purport to be views of Protagoras, but in the *Theaetetus* the political doctrine is not stated to be derived from Protagoras, but only to be a possible deduction. Unless therefore the two can be shown to be compatible,[1] it is safer to follow the *Protagoras*; it is the earlier dialogue and taken all round gives a much more convincing account of the man and his theories. But it is as well to remember that it is Plato's work, a dramatic reconstruction, almost a historical play, so skilfully written that it is easy to delude ourselves into thinking that we are reading a *verbatim* account. Yet we need not on that account reject the evidence; we can at least be fairly confident that the myth[2] which Protagoras tells was taken by Plato from the work of Protagoras, mentioned above, on the original condition of mankind.

The training which Protagoras professed to give was not a course of lectures leading to a professional qualification and dealing only with a particular subject, such as medicine or music. It was expressly designed for those young men who wished to distinguish themselves in their πόλις, and is described as the acquisition of political skill (πολιτικὴ τέχνη) or political goodness (πολιτικὴ ἀρετή), that is to say, being good at politics and being a good citizen.[3] If such a training can be given, it will go a long way towards solving one of the problems of practical statecraft, but as Socrates, who is depicted as the interlocutor of Protagoras, points out, experience shows that the best statesmen have not found any means of bringing up their sons so as to have the same

---

[1] The problem is too intricate to be discussed here. Loenen assumes rather than demonstrates their compatibility; but I owe to his book a reference to Max Salomon: *Zeitschrift der Savigny-Stiftung für Rechtsgeschichte* (Romanist. Abt.), XXXII, 1911, p. 135 ff., who reconciles the two by interpreting the *Theaetetus* passages so that δίκαιον is merely descriptive of law and not an obligation resting upon the state.

[2] The comments and conclusions come presumably from Protagoras' other book, the περὶ πολιτείας.

[3] It is taken for granted that a good citizen will be good at politics, since ἀγαθός and ἀρετή imply both goodness and ability. Notice how in the text (esp. 322 B - 323 B) ἀρετή and τέχνη are used, first one and then the other. 'Virtue' is itself a 'skill'.

ability (ἀρετή) as their fathers. Aristocracy had been based on the view that such ability was hereditary, or at least ran in families, and that only a poor substitute for an ἀγαθὸς ἀνήρ could be produced by training. Athenian democracy had been built up on the contrary basis, that political goodness is not a special craft, but one which all citizens, simply as being citizens, were expected to have or to acquire in addition to their professional skill. Protagoras takes up the latter position but with a significant addition. Political goodness is 'being a good citizen', but there are degrees of goodness. There are some citizens whom training and education will turn into real statesmen. We are not told which citizens are to be so trained or whether there is to be a process of selecting those with natural gifts. In practice apparently not; for the training which Protagoras gave was open to all who could afford to pay the fees. If then Protagoras intended that there should be a *corps d'élite* able to serve the State in positions of trust,[1] or to be wise and persuasive advisers on matters affecting laws and morality,[2] entry into it may have depended on wealth; but we cannot be certain, for Protagoras nowhere constructs an ideal state. On the other hand, since it did not depend on noble birth, the possibility must be open to all, unless indeed one were to suppose that the presence of money in the pocket conferred an ability not there before. We would therefore expect Protagoras to agree that in all men, unless they are quite depraved,[3] there is a disposition towards the life of a citizen and a capability of being taught. And so we do find; every man has a share of 'justice and general citizen-skill', μετέχειν δικαιοσύνης τε καὶ τῆς ἄλλης πολιτικῆς τέχνης, and the Athenians are not unreasonable in expecting every citizen to have a certain degree of ἀρετή, for without it there could be no cities (323 A). Instruction and practice, however, are necessary and the State must supplement the earlier education through the medium of its laws. There must be no citizen who is not an expert,[4] but what degree of expertness is required for all and what further

---

[1] Such as the ten στρατηγοί at Athens, an office which was frequently held by Pericles and became increasingly important.

[2] As envisaged in Plato, *Theaet.* 168 B.

[3] Hopeless cases must be put to death (*Protag.* 322 D). Crime must be punished (326 D) but always with a view to reform not retribution. This new and valuable theory of punishment is mentioned casually as being self-evident (324 B).

[4] τῆς ἀρετῆς, εἰ μέλλει πόλις εἶναι, οὐδένα δεῖ ἰδιωτεύειν.

IV. PROTAGORAS AND OTHERS

degree can be acquired by the rich, who make the best pupils, are among the things that remain obscure in Plato's report.

One thing, however, Plato makes perfectly clear: Protagoras had some answer to the question What is Man? (see above p. 48). By endowing him with a disposition towards justice and the other social virtues Protagoras has not only differentiated him from beasts in the same way as Hesiod did, but he has allied his destiny to that of the community in which he finds a home. He accepted as true what Aristotle afterwards said—Man is a πολιτικὸν ζῷον. Man has become a central figure in philosophy, usurping for the time much of the interest attaching to the cosmos and its primary matter. Protagoras was not the first[1] to make Man the centre, but he opened up a new line of thought by seeking to solve some of the problems of political theory in the light of the origins of political living. The earliest beginnings of communal life among Mankind were lost in remote antiquity and Protagoras had no historical record of fact to hand. Rousseau found himself in a like predicament when he approached a similar problem with the startling remark: 'Commençons donc par écarter tous les faits, car ils ne touchent point à la question.'[2] So too Protagoras, and after him Plato himself frequently, makes use of a myth, partly traditional, partly free invention, which will illustrate, though it cannot prove, the author's drift. All that we can expect from a μῦθος on early Man is that we may be able to throw some light on the question: 'How can men *best* live together?' by first ascertaining how they *could* first have done so. The value of the answer will depend on the light which it sheds on the major problem, not on the factual truth of the answer to the secondary question. So, even if we cannot categorically answer the question: 'Did mutual needs first bring men together (Plato *Repub.* II) or was it the acquisition of property (Rousseau *Discours* Part II *init.*)?', the discussion may prove illuminating. On the other hand Protagoras, while using the myth-form, was trying to reconstruct actual history and drawing on his knowledge of the past. He shows mankind at first living in scattered families, like the Homeric Cyclopes, and knew that the first function of the πόλις was to be a safe place. He knew that among early men the individual counted

---

[1] Before him certainly Xenophanes. See W. Nestle's edition of the *Protagoras*, Introd. p. 25.

[2] *Discours sur l'origine . . . de l'inégalité parmi les hommes*, 1754, p. 2.

for nothing and he lends no support to the theory (see next chapter) that the State depended on a contract by which individuals surrendered their liberties for the sake of their mutual protection.

Taking as a basis the myth of Prometheus he adapts and expands it freely. He notes the miserable condition of primitive man and the successive marks of civilisation—religion, language, agriculture, weaving, building and all the various means which helped to make life more tolerable. But the danger from wild animals continued and could not be overcome except by co-operation and mutual aid; and all the arts which man had hitherto acquired did not include the 'political art'. Hence they did not 'play fair' and the first experiment in living in cities broke down.[1] In order to save the human race from extermination Zeus sent Hermes to bring to men αἰδώς and δίκη, decency and right.[2] From this we infer that training in the political art can only be given when the necessary moral qualities are present. And these two qualities, we next learn, make for peace in cities and unite the citizens in a bond of friendship[3], but they do not of themselves make a cure for ἀδικία. For this education and training are essential. The myth concludes as follows: 'Hermes then asks Zeus in what manner he is to distribute δίκη and αἰδώς to men, whether he is to follow the same plan as in the distribution of τέχναι, that is to say, one person skilled in medicine to serve a number of other non-medical persons, and so with other crafts. Is he to put δίκη and αἰδώς into the world on that system or is he to bestow them on all men?' 'Upon all men,' replied Zeus, 'they must all participate in these. If only a few were to possess these, as is the case with the professional skills, there would be no cities. And lay it down as a law coming from me that anyone

---

[1] ἠδίκουν ἀλλήλους ἅτε οὐκ ἔχοντες τὴν πολιτικὴν τέχνην.

[2] On δίκη see above (Chap. II). αἰδώς is far more than 'decency'. The Greeks themselves were puzzled by its dual aspect: positive, regard for others; negative, diffidence and compunction. See Hesiod, W.D. 317-319, and cp. Ecclesiasticus IV 21. Also C. E. v. Erffa: Αἰδώς und verwandte Begriffe (1937). Perhaps 'moral sense' will do.

[3] ἵν' εἶεν πόλεων κόσμοι τε καὶ δεσμοὶ φιλίας συναγωγοί (322 c). Without a feeling of 'being members one of another' a city cannot be held together. On this passage see D. Loenen (pp. 8-11 and 108-111), who suggests solidarity as a translation of φιλία in its political sense. Similarly ὁμόνοια in Democritus and Antiphon.

who is incapable of decency and right shall be put to death as a national pest' (322 D).

Protagoras therefore had no fault to find with the Athenian practice of assuming that all citizens, whatever their particular professional skill, could acquire sufficient 'political goodness' to make their advice worth seeking in national affairs; the fault lay in the haphazard way in which it was generally acquired, in the lack, that is to say, of political education. But any free[1] man, unless he is an abnormality, has the moral qualities which make living together possible and make him fit to be educated. But though all have an equal *minimum* endowment and are equally subject to an equal law, some are more educable than others. A combination of natural gifts and good training begun in early youth[2] will produce citizens whose advice will be better worth seeking than the average. These will have εὐβουλία, 'good counsel', which Protagoras stated to be the aim of his teaching.[3]

It is difficult to sum up the contribution of Protagoras to political thought. Apart from the paucity of authentic fragments and the second-hand nature of our material we have to remember its limited scope. Plato only used what he needed for his purpose in the writings of Protagoras. We do not know how he taught the way to see both sides of a question or the need for a high, perhaps an impossibly high, standard of proof, if knowledge is to be attained, or what were his famous 'Knock 'em down'[4] arguments. But the man who tries to be fair, who withholds assent for lack of evidence, is always likely to be misunderstood and reviled as Protagoras was. Particularly we cannot say what answer he would have given to the stock question: Which is best, monarchy, oligarchy or democracy? Probably he would have refused to answer it in that form but he would have found no difficulty in providing arguments in favour of all three, and may well have contributed

---

[1] Note the limitation and cp. *supra* p. 46 n. 1. But the idea of removing such a limitation was not far off; see next chapter *init*. But it did not survive in Plato and Aristotle, for whom only a free man has moral qualities. It is worth noting too that in Protagoras' account of human history all the 'technics' of civilisation, even language and religion, belong to a pre-moral era. Contrast Lucretius; see below Chap. XIII.

[2] Frag. 3 Diels⁵.

[3] Plato, *Protag.* 318 E, that is, before his discourses in the dialogue.

[4] οἱ καταβάλλοντες (λόγοι) is the title of, or a description of, one of his lost works.

something to the source of Herodotus' 'Persian dialogue' (Chap. III). Besides, in the discourses and myth which we have just discussed there are hints of different answers and it is possible by emphasising one or another to force a reply from the philosopher. The universality of distribution at the close of the myth and other features suggest ἰσονομία, the watchword of Otanes and of democracy; the aim εὐβουλία was that of Megabyzus and oligarchy. Even the monarchy arguments of Darius have been asserted to be Protagoras' own views, as being analogous to the position of Pericles.[1] But the fact surely is that Protagoras had no advice to give about constitutions. What matters in his view is not the form of government but the *men* who make the πόλις. Political goodness has its basis in moral goodness; and this discovery was one of the foundations upon which Plato built in his *Republic*. Protagoras has left behind no written discussion that has survived. He had of course a number of guiding principles, some of which we know and some of which were in evidence in the working of the Athenian constitution in the time of Pericles. So that if he did set about constructing an ideal constitution we may be sure that he would bear in mind three things, the third being by far the most important:

1. All are equal before the law and all are responsible for their actions.
2. The able and well-trained man is of more use than the others and deserves honour and promotion accordingly.
3. That which is socially beneficial is ethically sound.

Now the individual is not the *arbiter* of what is socially beneficial; it is τὸ κοινῇ δόξαν. The individual can but speak up for his own point of view. But without the moral sense in every individual no κοινῇ δόξαν, no decision taken by the community would ever be socially beneficial; it would be socially disastrous.

The other three 'classical'[2] sophists, Prodicus, Hippias and Gorgias, are of much less importance. A careful use of language and differentiation of the terms used is essential, if thought of any kind is to be expressed, and it is here that Prodicus of Ceos made a contribution. Protagoras had already laid the foundation of

[1] See notes at the end of this chapter.
[2] The four are sometimes called the 'older' sophists.

grammar[1] but it was his younger contemporary who tried to distinguish between words of similar but not identical meaning. His best word-definition, however, is not of this type; Prodicus described the teachers of 'political goodness' as being 'on the border line between φιλοσοφία and πολιτική'.[2] Like most of the fifth-century teachers he appears as a character in Platonic dialogue,[3] but only once and then he is not taken very seriously. On the other hand he is frequently mentioned by Plato in other dialogues in such as way as to suggest that Socrates, and through him Plato, owed him a debt for his studies in the meanings of words. Plato also includes 'the excellent Prodicus' among the χρηστοὶ σοφισταί, useful teachers, on account of his fable of Heracles. This is a story preserved in something like the original words by Xenophon. In it Heracles is depicted not as a hard-drinking athletic champion nor as a Dorian cult-hero, but a man who chooses the hard path of right action in preference to a life of ease. This version of the myth was destined to have a long history in monarchical theory. But though he was a 'sound' moralist, his ethics had no divine sanction and he was one of those who derived the gods from personifications of natural phenomena (Fr. 5). Hence he was reckoned among the atheists.[4] His general pessimism was said to be due to the depressing effect of living in the island of Ceos.

Hippias of Elis travelled much and was at home everywhere, even in Sparta, but it was to Athens that he gave the name πρυτανεῖον τῆς σοφίας. His name is in the title of two Platonic dialogues, the *Hippias Major* and the *Hippias Minor*, but in neither of these does he appear to be a thinker of any account. We learn of his vanity and versatility but nothing of his mathematics. Like Prodicus, he appears in the *Protagoras* (337 c): he speaks of a *natural* kinship among men, not *conventionally* recognised, because Νόμος is a tyrant that forces men to do many things contrary to nature. Hippias' political views are further described by Xenophon in a story which tells of a discussion, which can only be imaginary, between Hippias and Socrates on justice and law. The

[1] Plato, *Phaedrus* 267 c, ὀρθοέπεια.
[2] He did not describe *all* sophists thus, but Plato found the description apt in certain cases (*Euthyd.* 304 c - 305 e); cp. *infra* p. 134.
[3] *Protagoras* 337 A.
[4] Perhaps unfairly; E. R. Dodds in his edition of the *Bacchae* of Euripides (1944) p. 99.

views ascribed to Hippias are not inconsistent with those ascribed to him in the *Hippias Major* and may be shortly summarised thus: Law and custom, though contrary to φύσις, are useful, if good. In a city in which conditions are perfect,[1] perhaps there, but only there, can τὸ νόμιμον be said to be τὸ δίκαιον. On the other hand the unwritten laws of honouring the gods, avoiding incest and rewarding benefactors are stated to be valid everywhere, though sometimes broken, and therefore *natural*. Hippias made caustic comments on one of the great evils of political life at Athens, namely διαβολή or misrepresentation (Fr. 17). It ought to be a punishable offence to filch away another man's good name. Herodotus, who knew Hippias and may have heard him on the subject, made similar remarks, and later Isocrates took up the theme.[2] Hippias also remarked (Fr. 4) on the power of beautiful and clever women in affairs of state.[3]

If *accurate* use of language is an important asset in political thinking, its *skilful* use is an indispensable aid to the politician. The arrival in Athens in 427 B.C. of the Sicilian orator Gorgias of Leontini added much to the armoury of those whose ambition it was to sway the minds of the Assembly, but little or nothing to the understanding of political problems. He did not claim to teach πολιτικὴ τέχνη as Protagoras did, but only ῥητορικὴ τέχνη. The tools of the art of rhetoric were words and its only end was to use them convincingly. It taught nothing except itself; but its possession made a man more free and more powerful to rule over others; and a man who could get things done, by persuasion and not by force, was a valuable asset to a city. But the importance of Plato's *Gorgias* lies for us not in what the rhetoricians are made to say, but in the political doctrine of Callicles (see next chapter). We have however a great deal more of Gorgias' actual words than of the other three and these include two short pieces, the *Praise of Helen* and the *Defence of Palamedes*, which are of some

---

[1] The necessary conditions (Xen. *Mem.* IV 4, 16) are not unlike those favoured by Democritus.

[2] Noted by W. Nestle in *Philologus* LXVII, p. 567, who calls it a τόπος of the sophists. But perhaps it was also an awakening of a social conscience or at any rate part of the growing awareness of the need for good relationships—φιλία, ὁμόνοια, in city-state life.

[3] Cp. Democritus, Fr. 214, who, however, was not referring to 'the power behind the throne' or to 'petticoat government' but to the power of temptation.

forensic but no political interest.[1] The nihilism of his metaphysical fragments on *Not Being* does not prove that Gorgias was one of the Immoralists (see next chapter), and even Plato does not attribute such doctrines to him. At worst he was incapable of defining goodness, but he appeared to accept the current morality of his day, and part of Palamedes' defence was that his discovery of writing had helped to civilise mankind by means of 'written laws, guardians of justice'.[2] It is significant also that in his speech at Olympia (Fr. 8 a) he urged the necessity of ὁμόνοια not only within cities, as did Democritus and Antiphon, but between the Greek states, as did Isocrates (Chap. VII).

It was not among the professional teachers only that political theory found students and exponents. Hippodamus of Miletus,[3] who was by profession a city-architect or town-planner and assisted along with Protagoras and Herodotus at the foundation of Thurii about 444 B.C. (see above p. 52), was also a forerunner of Plato in the construction of the model state. But Plato never mentions him and we owe all our scanty information to Aristotle, who in the second book of his *Politics* passed under review both the Platonic and other 'ideal' states, chiefly in order to point out their defects. He called Hippodamus the earliest of 'those not engaged in politics'[4] to attempt to find the best kind of state. He was fussy and eccentric and liked to divide everything into three. But Aristotle's criticism is perhaps not always fair and he does not comment on the significant proposal for a High Court of Appeal,[5] though he criticises other juridical reforms. The ideal city of Hippodamus, like that of Plato in the *Republic*, should not be too large and should contain three classes. But, unlike Plato's, the classes are to be equal in status and none is to have a mono-

---

[1] The passage (*Helen*, §6) about the right of the stronger (πέφυκε ... τὸ ἧσσον ὑπὸ τοῦ κρείσσονος ἄρχεσθαι) refers to the relations between men and gods, not men and men (Callicles in Plato, *Gorgias*) or men and governments (Thrasymachus). On these see next chapter. The notion occurs (*Helen*, §12) that the plea 'I did it under persuasion' is as good as 'I did it under compulsion'. Propaganda relies for its success on men's 'ignorance of the future, inability to grasp the present or to remember what happened last time' (*ibid.* §11).

[2] *Palam.* §30.

[3] He came to Athens from Miletus, where he had made his reputation.

[4] τῶν μὴ πολιτευομένων.

[5] With the result, apparently, that Vinogradoff, *Outlines of Historical Jurisprudence*, II 49, also overlooked it, though he quotes and translates Aristotle's comments on the proposals relating to return of verdicts.

poly of government. It is thus a class-society on equalitarian principles; the ten thousand citizens are to be classified according to
their professional capacity thus: skilled workers (τεχνῖται), farmers (γεωργοί), and the armed defenders of the city. The next
century did in fact see a good deal of professionalisation in the
art of war, but not exactly as Hippodamus or Plato had intended.
As for the actual work of government it is to be in the hands of
officials elected, we do not know how often, by the people. It is
stated that the function of the elected officials is to look after
three kinds of business—κοινά, ξενικά and ὀρφανικά. It is interesting thus to find the interests of strangers and orphans safeguarded not merely by the Unwritten Laws, but in the earliest of
our model constitutions. The humanity of Hippodamus is further
shown by his urging state-maintenance for those whose fathers
were killed in war and his suggestion of special honours for those
who 'made discoveries beneficial to the city'. Of uncertain date
but certainly later than Hippodamus was Phaleas of Chalcedon,
whose theories are also discussed by Aristotle in the same review
of predecessors. His point of view was more economic than political, but it would be going beyond the evidence to say that he
really understood that political equality must necessarily be ineffective without economic equality. His basic principle was simply that maldistribution of wealth was the cause of *all* disunity
and discontent. He accordingly devised a method of gradually
reducing the property of all citizens to nearly equal portions. But
he only applied the method to landed property, not to goods and
chattels—an extraordinary omission at this stage of history. But
then Aristotle's account, which is our only source, constantly refers to things which Phaleas overlooked and we cannot withhold
assent to his conclusion that Phaleas' methods would be effective
only against the minor evils of society[1], since even successful re-
adjustment of inequalities of wealth cannot of itself cure those
defects which are fundamentally moral. But Phaleas was not the
last to attempt the solution of age-long problems by means of a
single formula.

Democritus, like Protagoras, who was some twenty years senior
to him,[2] belonged to Abdera; but after early travels he stayed in

---

[1] πρὸς τὰς μικρὰς ἀδικίας. (1267 a 16).

[2] The traditional birth-date 460 is regarded by W. Kranz as much too
early. *Hermes* XLVII 1912, p. 42.

his native city aloof from the Sophists and when he visited Athens no one knew him. He was a 'physicist' and is chiefly remembered as one of the founders of the atomic theory, but like an earlier φυσικός, Archelaus (p. 51), he made contributions to the study of ethics and politics and it may well be that his work in this sphere was of more value. But Plato makes no mention of him in either capacity and, though a very large number of sayings have come down to us, there is great doubt about the authenticity of many of them.[1]

When he advised that more account should be taken of the soul than the body (187) he was thinking, as the context shows, of the importance of the reasoning faculty rather than the Socratean ἐπιμελεῖσθαι τῆς ψυχῆς. But his general ethical outlook was similar to that of Socrates in its emphasis on character and duty and on the barrenness of the pursuit of bodily pleasures (171, 217, 235, 264 et al.). Though not himself one of the professed teachers, he constantly insists, like Protagoras, on the need for adding training and education to natural ability (33, 242 et al.). His ideal for the individual is an equable frame of mind, εὐθυμία, like the ἀταραξία of Epicurus. He gives advice on how this is to be attained (3, 189) but he does not on that account advise or allow abstention from the duties of a citizen or from πολιτικὴ τέχνη (157, 253). On the contrary, he believed strongly in the πόλις and in the dependence of everything on its smooth running (252). His is therefore a secular State like that of Protagoras. He believed also in the rigorous punishment of transgressors of the law (259, 262). But laws, if obeyed, can and ought to make life easier (248); it is only because of the defects of men's characters that law appears to be something restrictive (245). Quarrelsomeness is the great bane of community life, as Hippias too saw, and as εὐθυμίη is the ideal for the individual, so ὁμόνοια is that of the πόλις (250). Its members should feel themselves to be friends, the rich and powerful lending a hand to the less fortunate (191, 255, 261). This is perhaps the earliest reference to a charitable spirit in social relationships. In the matter of constitution he expressed a preference for democracy, at least as against tyranny

---

[1] Especially those (Frr. 35-115) to which the name 'Democrates' is attached. They are not therefore here taken into account. For a discussion see Diels[5] II, pp. 153-154. Doubtful also are 169-297—from Stobaeus. See note at end of Chap. XIV.

(251), but he was no leveller, and the general tone is favourable to an aristocracy of ability whose natural prerogative is to rule (267)[1]; and he deplores a state of affairs, common in democracies with their changing officials, in which persons who show themselves honest and strict while in office may afterwards be penalised (266).[2] The oft-quoted saying about the poverty and shortness of human life (285) has no Hobbesian connotation; it is only another recipe for εὐθυμίη—not to expect too much of life. Of more political import is 'To the wise man every land is open; the ἀγαθὴ ψυχή has the whole world for his country' (247). Thus Democritus and Hippias shared a cosmopolitan outlook long before Alexander or the Stoics (see Chap. XII).

Probably contemporary[3] with Democritus was Socrates. His place in political thought will be discussed in a later chapter, since it depends on the latter rather than the earlier part of his life. But it is important to note here that the youth of Socrates, the formative period of his thinking, was spent at Athens in the intellectual atmosphere described at the beginning of this chapter. The habit of critical enquiry which he there acquired remained with him all through his life despite any changes in the direction of his interest. We have, however, no really reliable information about his early teachers. He was, perhaps, fifteen years or so younger than Protagoras, and even if he did not habitually go to hear him lecture, he can hardly have avoided coming under his influence. The Eleatic philosophers, notably Parmenides, left their mark upon him and so too did the Pythagoreans. One tradition associated him particularly with Archelaus, and Plato[4] puts into the mouth of Socrates a piece of autobiography which can hardly be totally false: he describes his own early studies in τὰ φυσικά, in the generation and decay which take place in nature everywhere, and refers not only to doctrines associated with Archelaus but also to those of Empedocles and Anaxagoras: he describes how his hopes of finding out the cause of things were raised and then disappointed; for none of these people could tell him what he really wanted to know: so he abandoned those studies which

[1] In view of what Thrasymachus says (see next chapter) about the rights of the stronger, the actual words should be noted—φύσει τὸ ἄρχειν οἰκήιον τῷ κρέσσονι.

[2] See Diels[5], p. 200, but the interpretation is not quite certain.

[3] But see p. 64 n. 2.   [4] *Phaedo*, 96-99.

depended on observation[1] and had recourse to discussion and argument[2] in the hope of finding the truth of things there. The full significance of this change of direction and the time when it took place are obscure, but the effect seems to have been that Socrates, dissatisfied with the older men, turned to the younger, more in the hope of learning from discussion with them than of teaching them anything. Here he found his mission and here Plato found him.

[1] ἀπειρήκη τὰ ὄντα σκοπῶν. 99D.

[2] εἰς τοὺς λόγους καταφυγόντα ἐν ἐκείνοις σκοπεῖν τῶν ὄντων τὴν ἀλήθειαν. 99 E.

FURTHER NOTES AND REFERENCES
CHAPTER IV

There is an abundant and varied literature dealing with the general atmosphere of mid-fifth-century Athens from George Grote's *History of Greece*, ch. LXVII, which is still well worth reading, to Werner Jaeger's *Paideia*, Vol. I, Eng. Trans. pp. 283-328. The texts and fragments are in Diels-Kranz[5] (see p. 44 n.), in connection with which the following are useful: Wilhelm Nestle: *Bemerkungen zu den Vorsokratikern und Sophisten* in *Philologus* LXVII, pp. 531-581; Kathleen Freeman: *Companion to the Pre-Socratic Philosophers*, 1946.

PROTAGORAS: Plato, *Theaetetus* 152, 167 C - 168 B, 171-172; *Protagoras*, esp. chs. I-XVII (309-329 B); A. Menzel, *Beiträge zur griechischen Staatslehre*, chs. 8 and 9 (S.B. Akad. Wien, Vol. 210, 1930); cp. p. 52, n. 1; D. Loenen, *Protagoras and the Greek Community* (Amsterdam, 1940).

Protagoras misrepresented: Aristophanes, *Clouds, passim*; Aristotle, *Rhet.* II 24, 1402a, *Metaph.* IV 4, 27, 1007b. P. favours democracy and *Gleichheitstaat*, Menzel, *op. cit.* 177, 197; favours aristocracy, A. Döring, cited by Menzel p. 187; favours monarchy, J. S. Morrison, *Class. Quart.* XXXV (1941) pp. 1-16. On Damon, a contemporary of Protagoras, see note at end of Chap. II.

PRODICUS: Choice of Heracles, Xenophon, *Mem.* II 1 21-34; Plato, *Symp.* 177 B.

HIPPIAS: Plato, *Hipp. Ma.* 284 D, E. On νόμος and νόμιμον see Xenophon, *Mem.* IV 4 12-20, but neither testimony is very strong.

GORGIAS: Plato, *Gorgias*, chs. I-XV (i.e. down to 461 but especially 450 B - 457 C); *Philebus* 58 A. His morality: Plato, *Meno* 71 D-E; Aristotle, *Pol.* I 1260a 27.

HIPPODAMUS: Arist. *Pol.* II 1267b. Town-planning, *Camb. Anc. Hist.* v, p. 463.

PHALEAS: Arist. *Pol.* II 1266-7.

DEMOCRITUS: The numbers refer to the fragments in Diels.[5]

The two quotations at the head of this chapter are of course illustrative of the exact opposite of two of Protagoras' views. Montesquieu (*de l'Esprit des Lois* I 1) and Sorel (*Le Procès de Socrate* 1889 IV §VI) make strange bedfellows.

On the multiplicity of notions attaching to φύσις and νόμος see F. Heinimann, *Nomos und Physis* (Basel, 1945), a valuable study which did not reach me till Chapters I to VI had been completed.

CHAPTER V

SOCRATES AND HIS OPPONENTS

THIS chapter, like the preceding, deals with the fifth century
and particularly with intellectual activity at Athens and its
effect on political thought. But the thinkers here treated
represent a somewhat different outlook. They differ among themselves, of course, but they take sides on questions which, though
they may arise out of the problems faced by Democritus or Protagoras, are not identical with them. This separation is not chronological and the writers now to be dealt with are not necessarily
junior to those described in Chapter IV or even to Herodotus
in Chapter III; in many cases exact dating is impossible. But just
as Herodotus in many ways typifies the early or early middle part
of the century, when the victory over the Mede was still upper-
most in men's minds, and as Protagoras and Hippias are typical
of the mid-fifth-century, so now we may without serious error
speak of a third period, dominated by the war between the Athenian empire and the Peloponnesians (431-404 B.C.). This is the
period of the φύσις doctrine and its varying applications to states
and morals, of Antiphon and Thrasymachus; but it is also the
age of Socrates and others who opposed it. It is also the time
when Aristophanes and Euripides were at the height of their
powers, using, the one the comic, the other the tragic stage, to
attack from different standpoints the social evils of the day; the
time when Thucydides was keeping a record of the events and
speeches of the war, constantly reminded on the one hand of the
weakened respect for law and morality and on the other of the
magnitude, never before realised, of the problems of inter-state
relationships in peace and in war. It is a period above all of constant antithesis, which it would be an error to think of as only
a rhetorical device, of δισσοὶ λόγοι, of a perpetual *Zwiespältigkeit*

—the moralists and the immoralists, the weak and the strong, the Just Reason and the Unjust, and the prayers for concord and cohesion, the answers of faction and disintegration.

Antiphon the Sophist, almost certainly a different person from Antiphon the orator and author of the Tetralogies, was an Athenian who lived and wrote in the latter half of the fifth century. He was the author of a book *On Truth*, probably a reply or counter-blast to Protagoras' work bearing the same title. But whereas the Protagorean 'Αλήθεια is entirely lost, considerable fragments of Antiphon's have come to light in the papyri discovered at Oxyrhynchus. These are of great political interest and certainly in some respects reveal a standpoint contrary to that of Protagoras. Antiphon is, so to speak, a φύσις-man; Protagoras was a νόμος-man; yet it was Protagoras' particular relativistic account of νόμος in relation to πόλις that made easy its rejection in favour of φύσις. As we saw above (p. 48), those who studied φύσις and τὰ φυσικά found at first no evidence of any law except the growth-process itself. What if that be truly Law, Universal Law belonging to all mankind, taking precedence over and often annulling the different man-made or city-made laws to which Protagoras and other people prescribed obedience? The first conclusion which would follow from the acceptance of such a Law would be the abolition of the much-cherished distinction between Greek and Barbarian.[1] Neither Hippias (p. 61) nor Democritus (p. 66) went so far in cosmopolitanism as this, but Antiphon did. Not only did he disapprove of the practice of honouring fellow-Greeks on the mere ground of ancestry but, since in the process of growing all men are alike, keeping alive by means of breathing and eating, so he held that Greeks and Barbarians do not differ and should be treated alike. It would follow that within the πόλις there should be no constitutional advantage attaching to high birth, though wealth could have privileges. But we have no record of Antiphon's constitutional theory, if ever he had one.

In a fragmentary context (1364 a)[2] he refers to justice as 'not to transgress the legal provisions of the city in which one is politically engaged'. This is equivalent to the theory of τὸ νόμιμον = τὸ δίκαιον and was widely accepted as a working definition.

---

[1] Equality of the sexes might also follow; but that, oddly enough, was left to Plato to deduce (*Repub.* v 455 A).

[2] *P. Oxy.* See note at end of chapter.

In its reference to separate cities it recalls Protagoras. But Antiphon draws his own inferences as follows: 'It is very useful to behave justly when there are witnesses to one's conduct, but when there is no chance of being found out, there is no need to be just.' This reasoning Antiphon bases on the doctrine that τὰ τῆς φύσεως are opposed to τὰ τῶν νόμων, for the laws are conventions made by men among themselves; punishment and disgrace only follow those transgressions that come to the knowledge of the makers of the agreement. It is very different with the laws of φύσις. These cannot be transgressed and any attempt to do so meets with nature's instant retaliation, and this retaliation is neither greater when the attempt to flout nature is seen by witnesses, nor less when it is not. And, he adds, employing the now commonly drawn distinction between Opinion and Truth, the hurt suffered is οὐ διὰ δόξαν ἀλλὰ δι᾽ ἀλήθειαν. The artificial laws which attempt to lay down what we may or may not see or hear or do have no validity. Only those laws are valid for our eyes, ears, hands and feet, which the natural capacity of these organs makes it necessary for us to observe, unless we want to blind, kill or maim ourselves.[1] Therefore although it is often advantageous and profitable to be seen obeying the conventional laws, these are fetters on nature, δεσμὰ τῆς φύσεως. There follows a much-mutilated part of the papyrus dealing apparently with the possible objection that things which we do not like may nevertheless be good for us. Antiphon then criticises laws for the inadequate protection which they give, their failure to *prevent* suffering and injury. They not only intervene too late but, when it comes to a trial, allow the aggressor-party to use all the resources of rhetoric to secure his acquittal. There is here another tantalising break in the papyrus, just when Antiphon looks like appearing among the ranks of the denouncers of ῥητορική.

Another papyrus (*P.Oxy.* 1797), probably also a fragment of the Ἀλήθεια, begins in the middle of another passage relating to *the just*, but it also fails, owing to incompleteness of text, to inform

---

[1] These are comparatively homely instances, like the neglect of the law of gravity by walking over a cliff-edge. But Euripides in his *Hippolytus* (428 B.C.) takes up the idea, perhaps from this very passage, and applies it to sexual passion considered as a law of life and the possible consequences of resistance to it. Both Phaedra and Hippolytus in different ways *resist*; the nurse is the 'sophist' who *accepts* it.

us what Antiphon's own definition would have been. We read that it is both just and expedient to tell the truth when bearing witness. On the other hand there will be cases in which he who tells the truth will not be just. For if[1] it be true that 'To do no man wrong unless you have sustained wrong' is justice, cases may well arise in which a truthful witness causes by his evidence damage to a person who has done him no wrong. He will moreover make an enemy of that man for life; thus two people suffer ἀδικήματα as a result of action declared to be δίκαιον. It looks as if Antiphon meant therefore to reject the statement that justice means doing no man injury when you have received none, but the sequel does not appear to say this.[2]

Before the publication (in 1915 and 1922 respectively) of these two papyri the work of Antiphon was known through the usual short quotations in later writers. Some came from the work on Truth, others from the περὶ Ὁμονοίας. For he too saw the need for concord in daily life (Fr. 49, Diels) but he does not seem to have elevated it to a political principle or to have equated it with justice.[3] The fragments of both works present an extraordinary medley covering a wide range of topics. Few have any direct bearing on πολιτική, but many are pieces of moral advice rising rather above the average and quite unlike the opinion of an author who would only advocate honest conduct when dishonesty would be found out. The effect of environment on character (Fr. 62), the need to be master of oneself (58), the strengthening of the character by resistance to temptation (59) make strange reading. He quotes Sophocles' Creon[4] on the evils of anarchy, but applies it not to politics but to the misbehaviour of

[1] Or 'since'. Thus it makes all the difference to our knowledge of A.'s own doctrine whether the missing letters in *Col.* 1 l.12 are to be restored ειπε >ρ or επειπε >ρ.

[2] It appears, if the text (*Col.* 11 ll.20-21) be right, to warn us not to enter into a contract under the terms 'no wrong to be inflicted or received' because of the uncertainty of carrying it out. It should be noted that here is yet another case of confusion caused by undeveloped terminology; ἀδικεῖν means not only 'to be unjust' but (1) to be guilty (of something) and (2) to wrong (a person).

[3] As did unnamed speakers in Plato, *Clitophon* 410 A. Ὁμόνοια, as we saw in the previous chapter, was a universal topic for discussion in various aspects, but there is no reason to connect the discussions in Xenophon (*Mem.* IV 4,16) and Isocrates (*Areop.* 31-35) with Antiphon's work.

[4] *Antig.* 672; see p. 28 n.

children and the need for education (61). On the other hand the fragments show him as a student of τὰ τῆς φύσεως, of weather and natural phenomena, also as a geometrician with theories about the nature of the gods and of time. Apparent references to uncivilised tribes may conceal a reference to theories about wild men of nature.[1]

Chalcedon lies on the opposite side of the Bosporus from Byzantium. Thence came Thrasymachus, who spent a good part of his life at Athens, but returned to Chalcedon to die. The years of his Athenian sojourn are quite uncertain, but they probably fell within the twenty-seven years of the Peloponnesian war and caused him to come under the influence of Gorgias. Antiphon had gathered fruits on every tree, Thrasymachus stands closer to Gorgias than to any other. His work was largely concerned with the style, diction and rhythm of Greek prose, and in his oratory he was said to be an adept at arousing the passionate emotions of an audience. The excellence of his prose style is vouched for by our one considerable fragment (No. 1) preserved by Dionysius of Halicarnassus and referred to by Plato (*Phaedr.* 267). In Plato's picture of him in the *Republic* he is bitter-tongued and loses his temper easily, and it was doubtless part of his technique to make an audience indignant by appearing angry himself. But it must be admitted that the political theory associated with the name of Thrasymachus comes entirely from his appearance in the opening scenes of Plato's *Republic* and a mere mention of him in the *Clitophon* as a person who had a theory about justice. The one reference to δικαιοσύνη in the tradition[2] about Thrasymachus says nothing about justice being the right of or in the interests of the stronger. Indeed, were it not for Plato's account of him in *Republic* I, Thrasymachus would have been marked down, on the strength of the speech partly preserved by Dionysius, as an advocate of all that was old-fashioned in morals and politics. However, it does not necessarily follow that Plato's account is entirely imaginary.[3] For in the first place the speech from which Dionysius quoted was written to order, as speeches often were,[4] for some client who wished to create a good impression by the sentiments expressed. In the second the reference in the Platonic commentator does not

---

[1] See above p. 48, n. 4.   [2] A commentator on Plato, *Phaedr.* 239. Diels[5] p. 326.

[3] So H. Gomperz, *Sophistik und Rhetorik* (1912), ch. III.

[4] As a foreigner Thrasymachus would not himself have had a chance to deliver speeches to the Athenians about their good old constitution.

profess to give the views of Thrasymachus, only to record his opinion that men found justice very useful and that the gods, if they had had any concern for men, would not have overlooked it.

The doctrine had its origin in the appeal to φύσις but the inference drawn is quite different from Antiphon's, and at one point directly opposed. From the similarity of men's growth everywhere Hippias and Antiphon had deduced a kinship κατὰ φύσιν. Thrasymachus, if we may trust an isolated reference (Fr. 2), was in favour of maintaining a distinction between Greek and Barbarian. But in looking at the realm of nature to find a law of conduct some, Thrasymachus and Callicles among them, found something else besides the process of growing and the retaliations of Nature. They observed that the larger and stronger animals devoured the weaker and that the quick-witted and clever could hoodwink the slow and stupid. This appeared to be abundant proof that it was in accordance with Nature that the strong should have mastery over the weak. Such a doctrine is capable of three applications and each of the three was made in theory and in practice. Applied to individuals it leads to the superman theory of Callicles; applied to whole states it leads to the *Machtpolitik* of the Athenians at Melos (see Chap. VI). Thirdly it can be applied so as to produce a theory of government within the state, namely that the right to govern belongs to those that have the power to do so. It is this third that is associated with the name of Thrasymachus. In Plato's account he supports the theory by stating certain facts as he sees them. He finds that in Greek city-states the laws have been framed and the constitution drawn up so as to suit the interests of the dominant power, whether that be the One, the Few or the Many, a τυραννίς, ἀριστοκρατία or δημοκρατία. Hence if a constitution is to be regarded as an embodiment of the principles of justice, it follows that the principles of justice are identical with the interests of the ruling power, and justice may be described as τὸ τοῦ κρείττονος συμφέρον. There was nothing shocking in all this; it had been the regular practice in times past. At worst one might say that Thrasymachus in modern parlance had not kept himself up to date on the theoretical side of his subject, neglecting Protagoras and making no serious attempt to understand the state and its function. Certainly neither Protagoras before him nor Plato after him held that the aim of the state should be to promote the interest of the rulers themselves. Plato further depicts Thrasy-

machus, whose name means 'doughty fighter',[1] as holding a theory
of ruler-infallibility, that the ruler, *quâ* ruler, cannot make a mistake as to what is in his own interest, that is, as to what is just.
But this, since it leads to his eventual discomfiture, can hardly
be more than a position into which Plato for his own dramatic
purpose has manoeuvred the speaker. What we miss here is a
statement of how Thrasymachus' dictum would appear as applied
to the three types of constitution. All through the argument
minority rule seems to be taken for granted and we hear of no
statement by Thrasymachus of the view, which might reasonably
follow, that justice is the interest of the majority. We do, however,
find it in the *Gorgias* (483 B), but there it is combated by Callicles
himself; for he, while agreeing that framers of laws frame them
to suit their own interest, yet maintains that the law-making
majority are not really strong but weak. About Thrasymachus
we can learn little more that is to our purpose. The argument in
Republic I moves away from the rights of government to the
rights of the individual. Thrasymachus is made to describe justice
in the conventional sense as something foolishly altruistic; the
way to success is that of injustice, not petty crime, of course, but
large-scale wickedness and self-seeking. Here again Thrasymachus
is simply arguing from facts. Moreover, he appears in this latter
part of *Republic* I as holding views similar to those of the opponents of Socrates as depicted in Plato's *Gorgias*. There Polus
the rhetorician not only defends the art of rhetoric as a means of
advancement, but puts forward 'success at any price' as a rule of
life. As Croesus in Herodotus' story (I 30) had tried to make
Solon agree that his wealth, power and prosperity as king of
Lydia entitled him to be considered most fortunate of men, so
Polus, who cites the ruthless and successful Archelaus of Macedon, and Thrasymachus fail to convince Socrates, when they try
to uphold a similar doctrine. This doctrine of the successful and
powerful man is more cogently, but in Plato's account not more
successfully, argued by Callicles with whose name the ancient
superman theory is associated.

Callicles was not a sophist or professional teacher like Polus
and Thrasymachus, but he must have been a pupil of Gorgias[2]

[1] Aristotle, *Rhetoric* II 23, 1400 b.
[2] The pupils of the school of Gorgias were very numerous. How far the
'immoralism' of a Callicles or a Meno was due to the school is impossible

and a believer in rhetoric. Nothing, however, is really known
about him and it has been suggested that he is either an imaginary
person, created by Plato to act as expounder of the doctrines, or a
real person, perhaps Charicles, one of the Thirty, given a different
name. In the *Gorgias* the dramatic starting point of Callicles' intervention is the paradox with which Socrates had silenced Polus—
'to do wrong is more disgraceful than to suffer it'.[1] To this Callicles replies by stating the fundamentals of his position, especially
the distinction between φύσις and νόμος, which, he says, Socrates
had quite neglected. Whether this distinction is really fundamental
and absolute he does not discuss, but he shows that the Socratic
paradox is contrary to φύσις, since it is natural to avoid being
hurt. Moreover, as the realm of nature shows, it is equally natural
to hurt others where there is anything to be gained. So φύσις
teaches us that it is *just* that the better[2] man should have more
than the worse, the more powerful than the less powerful. So
far Callicles' position is not more extreme than that of the 'Old
Oligarch'[3] or any other disbeliever in Athenian equalitarianism.
He notes with some contempt[4] that where the mass of citizens
have the power to make laws, they make them to suit the interests
of the masses, πρὸς . . . τὸ αὐτοῖς συμφέρον, and for the express
purpose of preventing the powerful from getting that larger share
to which Nature has entitled them. Thus Callicles is not thinking
in terms of government power but of the strong man's right to
power. But the superman is not complete unless his strength lies
not only in his own superior skill and brains, but also in his freedom from any scruples about their use. The 'immoralism' is now
complete. The justice of which the weak prate is fit only for the

to say (cp. p. 63); not all believers in rhetoric were immoralists. Meno the
Thessalian is, like Gorgias himself, not unsympathetically handled by Plato.
But Xenophon (*Anabasis* II 6, 21-29), who knew him, makes him the perfect
example of unscrupulous self-seeking, but does not mention that he was
educated by Gorgias, as Plato does. 'A man who is not a scoundrel', said
Meno, 'is not properly educated.'

[1] 482 D: τὸ ἀδικεῖν αἴσχιον τοῦ ἀδικεῖσθαι.

[2] ἀμείνων, not really different from κρείττων. Both denote the abler, the
stronger, as we might say of one of two athletes, 'the better man of the two'.

[3] Name given to the unknown author of a political pamphlet on the
Constitution of Athens *c*. 424 B.C. See below pp. 83-84.

[4] Yet this is what Lycophron (see below), who also based his political
theory on φύσις, approved. If φύσις was less changeable than νόμος, it had
many meanings and applications. See note at end of Chap. IV, p. 68.

weak, for miserable servile people 'who were better dead anyway' (483 B). Give me a man 'who has enough raw nature in him to shake off the trammels, break through and escape, trampling on our scraps of paper, our mumbo-jumbo and eyewash and all our unnatural conventions' (484 A). The only valid νόμος is that of φύσις and that is Pindar's νόμος πάντων βασιλεύς. Fancy expecting Heracles to pay for the oxen of Geryon! Nature's justice knows no such pettifogging distinctions between right and wrong.

This is the paradox of Callicles; on the basis of the absolute opposition of φύσις and νόμος it abolishes all accepted law, including the Unwritten Laws; the effect is to reverse the ordinary meaning of νόμος and to turn all the gentler virtues into vices. And this reversal of values, as Thucydides (III 82) tells us, did in fact sometimes take place. It remained for Plato to demonstrate that no state could exist on such a basis. But the Socratic paradox, that it is better to suffer wrong than do it, also involved a reversal of values. The accepted code of social behaviour did not demand such self-sacrifice, but quite expected, for example, that an accused man would use every means (πᾶν ποιεῖν) to secure an acquittal. Here again it was Plato who showed that this particular reversal of value, amounting to a change of heart, was essential for the construction of a just state. Plato, as W. Jaeger[1] has well shown, was able to understand both points of view, and perhaps himself felt keenly the Will to Power, its dangers and temptations. It is perhaps worth while here to anticipate a little further and note that Plato was constantly in search of the right kind of man to exercise personal rule and hoped to find the answer in himself. At any rate he was sure that the answer would be the exact reverse of that of Callicles. Instead of saying, 'The man who by his efforts has risen to the top is the man fit to rule,' we ought to say, 'Find the man who is fit to rule and put him at the top'. Thus it is that, with his own ideas in mind about the philosophical training necessary to make a ruler, he makes Callicles speak disparagingly of education[2] as something only suitable for young people and not worth the attention of grown men. According to Callicles people who spend all their time in the study of it lose touch with actual life. Far from being a training for ruling, it is a positive

[1] *Paideia* Vol. II p. 138.
[2] This is more nearly what he meant by φιλοσοφεῖν than an expression like 'study philosophy'. See further p. 124 n.

drawback to the strong man to concern himself, like Socrates, with the cultivation of the mind. This degrading of intellectual pursuits is one of the many resemblances between the Calliclean and the Nietzschean superman.[1] But Plato was more afraid of the effect of unregulated literary and artistic pursuits. One remark, however, which Plato puts in the mouth of Callicles expresses a contempt which Plato also felt for the professed educators of the day.[2] There are some points of contact between Callicles and Heraclitus, for both favoured free rivalry, so that the 'better man' might always come out on top. But Heraclitus, so far as can be seen, had none of Callicles' contempt for intellectual education.[3]

Other pupils of Gorgias who applied the standard of φύσις to political theory were Alcidamas the rhetorician and Lycophron the sophist. Both these and Glaucon too (see below) belong more properly to the fourth century, but it is convenient to mention them here. Alcidamas said, 'God set all men free. Nature has made none a slave.' Euripides had already (*Ion* 854-856) remarked that the difference between slave and free lay only in the word used. This marks the third and final step in the doctrine of universal equality, promoted first by Hippias and then by Antiphon. Alcidamas used to speak of laws as 'cities' kings'—a rhetorical flourish to which Aristotle objected—but he also said that philosophy was a 'bulwark against the laws', that is, presumably, against their too rigid application.[4] To Lycophron was ascribed the theory that 'law is a mutual guarantee of rights'.[5] In a state of nature there were no moral restraints and no law but jungle law. The city-state came into being not φύσει, but νόμῳ, that is, by a contract (συνθήκη). If this view of the πόλις were correct, it would, says Aristotle, be more like an alliance in war than a community and it would not be capable of exercising any morally educational power such as a Greek expected from a πόλις. Lycophron further interpreted φύσις as showing that the weak naturally become strong if they keep together, and that the power of the nobles was a figment, there being no difference between well-born and

---

[1] There are also differences. See A. Menzel, *Beiträge* (note at end of Chap. IV) p. 246 ff. Plato's and Aristotle's 'god among men' owes nothing to Callicles or to Heracles the cattle-lifter.

[2] *Gorgias* 519 E [οἱ φάσκοντες] παιδεύειν ἀνθρώπους εἰς ἀρετήν.

[3] Cp. Chap. II, pp. 29-31.

[4] Aristotle, *Rhetoric* III 3, 3 and 4 (1406). The context gives no clue.

[5] ἐγγυητὴς ἀλλήλοις τῶν δικαίων. Aristotle, *Politics* III, 1280 b.

low-born. The contract theory appears also in Plato's *Republic* Book II, where it is explained by Plato's brother Glaucon, not as being his own, but as a view of the origin of law held by other people; these, however, are not named. The following extract will illustrate the theory further. 'The theory is that to do wrong is good, to be wronged evil, and that the evil of being wronged is greater than the good of doing wrong. So when men have had their fill of wrong and being wronged, those who have been unsuccessful in avoiding the one and seizing the other decide that it would be to their advantage to make an agreement one with another on a basis of "no wrong to be inflicted or suffered", μήτ' ἀδικεῖν μήτ' ἀδικεῖσθαι.[1] And here, they go on to say, you have the origin of the making of laws and agreements and the use of the terms *just* and *lawful* to describe that which is laid down by law. . . . This justice is not welcomed as a good, but is only valued by reason of one's inability to do wrong.'

Critias, the poet-politician and many-sided genius who met his death in 403 B.C., was a relative of Plato, an associate, but afterwards an enemy of Socrates, and one of the Thirty, who misruled Athens for some months after her defeat by the Peloponnesians in 404. He was a playwright, a musician and a prose-writer but he was not a professional sophist; his rank and birth would have precluded such a thing. But the error of Philostratus in calling him Κριτίας ὁ σοφιστής was a venial one, for Critias was the embodiment of a certain type of σοφία, of many-sided and unscrupulous cleverness, which helped to bring the name σοφιστής into disrepute. The average Athenian, for whom he had nothing but contempt, disliked him also for his irreligion, his oligarchical and pro-Spartan views and even his unorthodox literary judgments (44) and practices (4). His attitude of intellectual superiority, admiration of Spartan education and Thessalian horses may be seen in fragments of two works on Constitutions, one in prose (31-38) the other (6-9) in elegiac verse. There is, however, little of constitutional theory in these fragments, which suggest that Critias was interested in habits of life, material wealth and products of manufacture. This is further illustrated by an elegiac poem (2) in which he seeks to determine the origin and discovery

[1] This formula occurs in Antiphon. See above p. 72 n. 2. It was commonly used in arranging a truce or other inter-state agreement, e.g. Xenophon, *Anabasis* VI 1, 2.

of pottery, chariots, chairs, bronze and the invention of letters and verses. It is therefore perhaps significant that the most important fragment (25) for our present purpose is also a kind of tentative contribution to the history of civilisation. It comes from a satyric drama entitled *Sisyphus*. Into the mouth of the leading character Critias puts a new theory of the state, by which it rests not on force but on fraud. The contrast between this myth and that of Protagoras is striking. The forty-two lines commence thus: 'There was a time when the life of man was disordered and like that of wild beasts controlled by brute strength. There was then no reward for the good nor any punishment for the bad. Next, men conceive the idea of imposing laws as instruments of punishment, so that justice may be sole ruler and hold violence in check. If any erred, he was punished. Then, since the laws only prevented the commission of deeds of *open* violence, men continued to commit secret crimes. At this point it is my belief that some far-seeing and resolute man saw the need for a deterrent which would have effect even when *secret* deeds were done or contemplated. So he introduced the idea of divinity, of a god always active and vigorous, hearing and seeing with his mind . . . all that men say or do.' Sisyphus is then made to recount how successful the deception was. Men readily accepted the fiction and believed that deaths by lightning and other sudden disasters were sent as punishments for wrong-doing. 'This then was the origin of belief in the gods as well as of obedience to the laws.'

Thus Critias, like his contemporary Diagoras of Melos, was a thorough-going atheist. Moreover he was the first of many others to see the political uses to which religion might be put. For keeping the lower classes in order (if that be the context of Fr. 22) νόμος was insufficient, for clever speakers could always get round the law; but they could not corrupt good character. The loss of the many works of this astonishing and unscrupulous man, hated by the pious Xenophon and by many others, the object of mixed disapproval and admiration in his own set,[1] has left a most unfortunate gap in dramatic and political literature. Cynical, super-

---

[1] Such as Alcibiades, Plato and another young cousin, Charmides. Plato's unfinished dialogue *Critias* is one of his later works and the myth of Atlantis bears no resemblance to any of Critias' known fragments and the gods, far from being a figment, are the originators of the political order (*Critias* 109 C - D). In the *Timaeus* and the *Charmides* he also appears.

cilious and contemptuous he was, yet he may have been the first to see the importance of economic history in politics, and he was certainly the first sociologist to advise pre-natal care for fathers as well as mothers (32).

While there is nothing in the Critias remains to show that he deduced any political or moral theory from the workings of nature, the general tone allows us to class him along with those who believed that since it comes naturally to men to behave badly, they may be permitted to do so. But the immoralists did not have it all their own way; Protagoras was not altogether forgotten and Socrates was winning friends as well as making enemies. Other champions of law and justice there were (Plato, *Repub.* II 366 E) but their names have not come down to us, and the only considerable piece of writing, found in a manuscript of Iamblichus the mathematician, has no name attached to it. The author, whom we call therefore *Anonymus Iamblichi*, is anxious, like Diodotus in the Mytilenean debate,[1] to show himself as a realist, a practical, unsentimental man of the world. He does not attempt to show, and this is just what Adeimantus[2] complained of, that justice is to be valued for its own sake, not for the advantages which it brings. On the contrary, his advice is to try and acquire a good reputation, which will take some time, to get training in making speeches and other forms of skill, to make oneself useful to influential people and, within limits of caution, to expend one's money to this end. But whatever power one may gain is always to be used εἰς ἀγαθὰ καὶ νόμιμα. Money has its uses, but do not let greed for it master you, or allow your eagerness to get on and prosper to degenerate into πλεονεξία. This is aimed at the doctrines of Callicles and Thrasymachus. We must not, says the author, confuse ἀρετή with the power to do well for oneself or think it weakness to obey the laws. Even the superman (ὑπερφυής), supposing him to be exempt from wounds and disease and even from the power of the law itself, can only pursue his career if he gets the laws on his side. (So Deioces the Mede rose to power by being a just judge.[3]) On the more general aspects of political

---

[1] Thucydides III 48; see Chap. VI.

[2] Plato, *Republic* II 366 E: οὐδεὶς πώποτε ἔψεξεν ἀδικίαν οὐδ᾽ ἐπῄνεσεν δικαιοσύνην ἄλλως ἢ δόξας τε καὶ τιμὰς καὶ δωρεὰς τὰς ἀπ᾽ αὐτῶν γιγνομένας.

[3] These allusions are of course not in the text. The story of Deioces is in Herodotus I 96-99; the strife at Corcyra in Thucydides III 82.

order the author has an old-fashioned flavour. Peace and good order he praises as being advantageous not only, though perhaps chiefly, to men of property, but also to those not so well off (δυσ-τυχοῦντες), because only in a law-abiding community do charity and mutual help prevail. Εὐνομία brings leisure, too, for peaceful and cultural pursuits; ἀνομία leads to external war and internal στάσις, where every man's hand is against his neighbour's and men are constantly suspicious. (So at Corcyra in 427 B.C.[1]). But his pacificism did not cause him to shut his eyes. On the contrary he was more practical and realistic than the φύσις-theorists. He warns his fellow men that in a state of ἀνομία, when men lose all sense of justice, the inevitable outcome is the seizure of sole power by the most unscrupulous. Absence of νόμος and δίκη gives the intending tyrant his chance. If it is the πόλις that makes civilised life possible, law and justice must be made supreme, for these make and keep the πόλις together.

The author thus raises a question which, as we saw at the beginning of this chapter, badly needed answering at the end of the fifth century and indeed was always felt to be supremely important by Greek political thinkers. If the city-state is to be preserved we must know what are the forces which hold together (συνοικί-ζειν, συνέχειν) men and cities. Clearly, as this author implies, some agreed conception of τὸ δίκαιον is a first requirement. Others had pointed out the need for φιλία and mutual goodwill. Clearly, too, the supply of food, of goods and services considered essential and a medium of exchange. The interchange of these and the many and various dealings of men with men form a large part of the life of a πόλις. And the continued existence of the city depends, as Aristotle[2] saw, on the fairness of the dealings and on the acceptance of reciprocal obligations. Plato, as we shall see, laid emphasis on unity as well as justice. Here again it was Aristotle who saw that excessive desire for unity and uniformity ends by destroying not preserving the πόλις.[3] Σῴζειν τὴν πόλιν, 'keep

---

[1] See footnote 3, p. 81.

[2] *Ethics* v 5, 6, 1132 b *fin.* 'The city is held together by interchange of services on a proportionate basis'; and *Politics* II, 1261 a: τὸ ἴσον τὸ ἀντι-πεπονθὸς σῴζει τὰς πόλεις. Cp. Euripides, *Phoen.* 538. The urgency of the question is even more forcibly illustrated by Euripides *Suppl.* 312-314: τὸ γάρ τοι συνέχον ἀνθρώπων πόλεις / τοῦτ᾽ἐσθ᾽, ὅταν τις τοὺς νόμους σῴζῃ καλῶς—words very much like those of *Anon. Iambl.*

[3] *Politics* II, chs. I and II.

safe the city'; but were there not some who rejected even this?
There was nothing in Nature about the State, and the φύσις-ex-
tremists, like Callicles and Critias, must, consciously or uncon-
sciously, reject the State. There was no need to wait for Plato
(*Repub.* I) to show that the unlimited right of the stronger and
cleverer can only mean tyranny or anarchy. There was, however,
with the possible exception of the Cynics (Chap. XII), no philosophy of anarchy in Greek political theory. And in practice the
power of the Athenian people, the δῆμος, exercised through the
law-courts[1] as well as the assembly, was stronger and more enduring than that of the cleverest orator. This kept the πόλις in
existence, but the individual citizens had no such restraint and no
such safeguard, though every politician of the day professed to
be able to give them just what they wanted. How far in fact all
honesty and decency disappeared from Athenian life we can
hardly tell, but the war and the plague certainly lessened and
weakened the regard for such things; and it became all too easy
to laugh at those who strove to maintain standards of conduct
as clinging blindly to outmoded ways and to a bourgeois culture
of φιλοκαλία. Were Demaratus (Herod. VII 103) still alive and
visiting Athens he would have had to say ἔπεστι γάρ σφι δεσπότης
οὐ *ΝΟΜΟΣ* ἔτι ἀλλά *ΔΗΜΟΣ*.[2] That anonymous writer who
is sometimes called the Old Oligarch, has characterised the
δῆμος-morality as 'Ignorance of moral principles (ἀμαθία) and un-
scrupulousness (πονηρία) combined with loyalty (εὔνοια) to the
popular cause'; and again, 'What you think is bad government
means power and liberty for the people'. Thus those whose grand-
fathers had fought and won the battle for *Νόμος* the liberator
now were eager to throw it off as slavery. Whenever the violence
of internal στάσις or the hardships and miseries of war opened
the way, there the bonds of 'slave-morality' were loosened and
the 'transvaluation of values'[3] might begin and men might adopt
moral sentiments wholly opposed to those of tradition. It was
now possible, and among some people habitual, to judge actions,

[1] Readers acquainted with Athenian history will not need to be reminded
of the extent to which the law-courts were used as a political weapon. See,
for example, C. Bonner, *Aspects of Athenian Democracy*, ch. 1.

[2] See p. 40.

[3] Nietzsche's phrase is similar to Plato's ἐξαλλαγή τῶν εἰωθότων νομίμων
(*Phaedrus* 265 A) where it is used to describe *what goes on in the brain of a man
going mad!*

whether of cities or of persons, by reference to non-ethical standards and to declare those to be right which serve a particular purpose or promote a particular cause such as the social good,[1] or the redemption of society, or merely, as Thrasymachus said, the interests of the ruling class. Even the Old Oligarch, who was no friend of Athenian democracy, uses 'justly' and 'unjustly' to mean conformably or not to the interests of the ruling δῆμος.[2]

It was in such an intellectual atmosphere that Socrates spent his later years, very different from the days of his youth in the Athens of Pericles and Protagoras. The man and the hour were well matched. Socrates was convinced that honesty, courage, decency, fairness and justice had a meaning of their own, and he spent much of his life discussing what the meanings really were —a life which called forth the scorn of a Callicles at one extreme and the disapproval of an Anytus at the other. Had Socrates been the kind of man to sing the praises of a stable society and the virtues that make a good citizen, instead of seeking to know the fundamental bases, both of the society and the virtues, less would have been heard of him, and he would not have been twice[3] singled out by Aristophanes as typically free-thinking and irreligious, and as sponsoring, with apparent indifference to the issue, a debate between the δίκαιος λόγος defending old-fashioned ways[4] and the new cleverness of the ἄδικος λόγος.

This strange, warm-hearted and impressionable man, who in his youth had absorbed the influences of Parmenides, Zeno, Protagoras, Anaxagoras and Archelaus, had now settled down to pursue wisdom in his own way. He had, it seems, been influenced by a reply given to his friend Chaerephon by the Delphic oracle. The Pythia, asked whether any man was wiser than Socrates, replied

---

[1] Cp. p. 60 (Protagoras).

[2] H. Fränkel, *Amer. Journal of Philology* 78 (1947) p. 309.

[3] First in 424 B.C. at the first performance of *The Clouds*, then in 422 when it was revised with additions. The play's comparative failure in 424 was not due to any public sympathy with Socrates but to its tricky subject-matter and to the fact that Aristophanes was trying to do too much, to criticise a great variety of opinions and pursuits and a very complex body of thought all in one person. The new scientific knowledge, the new morality, new forensic methods, religious scepticism, subtleties of language are all rolled into one and the result fits nobody in particular.

[4] e.g. the Just Argument protests against τὸ μὲν αἰσχρὸν ἅπαν καλὸν ἡγεῖσθαι, τὸ καλὸν δ' αἰσχρόν (*Nub.* 1020-21)—another reversal of values.

that there was none. Socrates interpreted this as a challenge not as a compliment. We do not know the date of Chaerephon's visit to Delphi, but if it did not precede, it certainly confirmed Socrates' change in outlook, his turning from the old to the young (Chap. IV, p. 66). Whatever its date, it was from then on that Socrates regarded the pursuit of truth and wisdom by means of questioning and discussion as a sacred duty. Not being aware of possessing any wisdom or knowledge, he decided that the words of the oracle must mean that he knew that he knew nothing, while others did not. To the Athenian public he was a sophist who professed no σοφία and did not teach. If he left no body of doctrine yet he had great influence and there were many who came after him and called themselves Σωκρατικοί. His influence on political thought manifests itself in three ways—in the manner of his life, in his sayings and opinions and in the manner of his death. The influence was therefore largely indirect, and to estimate and interpret it will always be a highly subjective and personal process.

Conspicuous in his own day and long after remembered were his way of living, his personal habits and appearance, his provocative and irritating way of talking, his disconcerting way of looking at you with an eye that seemed to look through you, and all the other indications that he was an uncanny person, a δαιμόνιος ἀνήρ. In private life he was virtuous and law-abiding, entirely devoid of greed and self-seeking. This to the Athenians was astonishing in a man who was clever enough to make money and poor enough to need to. In public life he performed both the military and civil duties which fell to him, but showed no great interest in holding office and, unlike most others, refrained from using it to advance himself. He had learned his father's trade of stonemason and was perhaps free of the current prejudice against manual labour. One way or another he contrived to support a wife and family, while himself spending his days in the *agora* conversing and discussing. His circle consisted of old and young, but chiefly the young, and chiefly those who had leisure to spend thus and were keen on culture and philosophy. But he did not pick and choose his companions or open a school; it would have been inconsistent with his conception of his own life as dedicated to the service of God to have restricted his audience or exacted a fee. He regarded his way of living and the care of the things of the mind rather than the body as a duty inseparable from his mission, but he did not talk much about himself; and the 'inward voice', which used to warn him, was but another indication that he was δαιμόνιος. His aim was to draw knowledge out of his companions, not to put it in. Without formulating any laws of logic, he tried to make them think clearly and to draw together different statements, analogies and examples so as to arrive at definitions. If he over-intellectualised morals, overlooking in his search for self-mastery the irrational element in us, at least he was free and kept others free of that fatal disease of politics—looking for the comforts of unreason. In general it may be said that Socrates' life demonstrated that intellectual ability was not incompatible with either honesty or patriotism, and that clever people are not and need not be exempt from doing their duty as citizens.

When we come to try and gauge his importance by his doctrine or opinions, our main difficulties begin and almost every statement made can be and has been challenged. We know the kind of things that he discussed, but we cannot say that this or that never formed a subject of discussion. We can sometimes say that he did *not* hold such and such a view, but we cannot be sure that he held the opposite view, more particularly as ancient philosophy tended to confuse the contrary or direct opposite with the merely opposing or contradictory. Not only did he leave no writings but he gave no lectures and so, though many who came after him claimed to be his followers and to derive from him, none of them had any authentic tradition or could say of their master *ipse dixit*. We should bear in mind these uncertainties.

Socrates must have made it quite obvious, as he talked, that in his view the politicians of the day simply did not know what they were about. Whatever skill or ability each might possess, Socrates held that none of them had any knowledge; preoccupied with the acquisition of power they failed to see that the first requisite in a statesman is the knowledge of the difference between good and evil. It is indeed the first thing that any man must have, but Socrates did not apparently say that all men ought to be statesmen. It is likely that he would have agreed with Protagoras that all men need the virtues of the citizen, but only an élite, men with special training, can rule. But the Aristotelian question: 'Are good man and good citizen the same?' is not yet formulated. In political institutions Socrates was not much interested, or in party rivalry; he was concerned with the individual man. He does not, however, say 'I am an individualist; show me a state which shall give fair play to the individual'. The problem for him remains one of knowledge, to the lack of which the defects of human society are due. He means not just knowledge of this or that or how to do something, but fundamental and universal knowledge. The problem is therefore how this knowledge is to be obtained. How far Socrates himself went towards a solution of this problem we shall probably never know, but it was Socrates who brought epistemology into the realm of political philosophy; so the sixth book of Plato's *Republic*, if he could have read it and have understood it, would certainly not have appeared to him to be irrelevant. But what did Socrates himself say about knowing? Apparently three things—first that he knew nothing,[1] save that he knew nothing; second, that the pursuit of knowledge, though difficult, was not impossible; and third, that the method of question and answer, honestly conducted, was the way to pursue it. Now one cannot help observing that if to the end of his days Socrates still knew nothing, the method cannot have been very effective. People therefore thought that his ignorance was a sham and a pose. All his life he had shown what we might call a 'working knowledge' of the difference between right and wrong and had with the utmost confidence and conviction based his conduct on that knowledge; it was he who seemed to know, others to be uncertain. But that is not what Socrates meant. Convictions, however strong, however right, however true, however widely shared are those of a man himself, an individual; true knowledge must be universal and to this he laid no claim.

It would be going too far astray to discuss Socrates and 'universals'. However much or little he may have done for metaphysical theory, Socrates certainly believed in Universal Right, in τὸ δίκαιον. But, as we have seen, the very existence of the goodness and justice in which he believed was at stake, challenged by the immoralists and weakened by a war-ridden mentality. He saw the dangers of intellectual fireworks; but he saw also, as Plato did not, that the perils of subversive thinking cannot be averted by suppressing the thinker, but only by helping him to

---

[1] Why is Socrates' refusal to dogmatise, to say 'I know', so often applauded, while Protagoras' similar but less sweeping saying about the gods (Fr. 4; see p. 53) is made the occasion for abuse?

think again and think better. Another truth, akin to this, was grasped by Socrates but not by Plato: that, while thinking may be dangerous, it is in the long run less dangerous than not thinking at all. He believed, like other fifth-century thinkers, in complete intellectual freedom and unfettered speculation, but where shallower thinkers stopped short, content with sensational and subversive answers, Socrates, refusing to accept answers which conflicted with the very notion of goodness, went on asking questions. He represents no break with tradition in this respect, no reaction, no diminution whatever of intellectual freedom, only unsparing ridicule of intellectual pride. It was the insolent affectation of knowledge, the claim to have science on their side that made a Thrasymachus or a Critias shocking not to Socrates only, but to many hundreds who for all the fashionable atheism could not forget the traditional and deep-seated horror of ὕβρις. Socrates realised as fully as any of his contemporaries that the demand for a basis on which law, morality and the state should rest, or for an authoritative source from which they should derive, could not be met by any reference to ancestral custom or to personifications of Δίκη or Θέμις. But he was convinced that the despairing nihilism of those who denied the existence of any such basis or authority was unreasonable. Instead of looking for universal δίκη in the observed phenomena of nature, Socrates saw that what is really universal cannot be found by observation at all, that a distinction must be drawn between δίκη, a right usage which might differ from place to place, and τὸ δίκαιον, abstract right, which is eternal, unchanging and universal.

Socrates' position in the Nature-Convention controversy falls next to be considered. On the one hand he appears to have rejected the φύσις doctrines, both the natural kinship and the right of the stronger. His notions of equality among men do not appear to have gone farther than the 'equality before the law' of Athenian democracy, and he certainly did not agree with those who found in the animal-world patterns for human behaviour. He believed in learning about men from and through men. 'Trees and country places', Plato[1] makes him say, 'won't teach me anything; give me men in town.' Nevertheless two features of Socratic belief can be connected with φύσις in its widest sense and both have a bearing on political theory. First, there is a supra-human realm of nature,

---

[1] *Phaedrus* 230 D.

whose ordinances are binding on all, and second, the realm of human nature must be distinguished from that of gods on the one hand and of animals on the other. Neither conception is new; the roots of both are deep in the past, as we saw in Chapters II and IV. But their revival and re-emphasis on the lips and in the life of one so intolerant of shams as Socrates did much to σῴζειν τὴν πόλιν, to save not only Athens from dictatorship and anarchy but European civilisation from early disintegration.

Antigone had appealed from the man-made νόμος of Creon to a higher law, which had existed for all time and was everywhere and eternally valid. She did not quarrel with the legitimacy of Creon's rule, but with its refusal to keep within its proper sphere. In forbidding the performance of burial rites due to a brother the ruler was treading on the sphere of Zeus and the Unwritten Laws.[1] Socrates too, if the conflict were simply one between his belief in a divinely-imposed mission and the authority of the state, would choose to die many deaths.[2] Whether it was his 'inward voice' or his shrewd common sense that made him keep out of political work at Athens, he knew well that his whole attitude was likely to bring him into conflict with the authority of any πόλις claiming jurisdiction over all a man's doings. If he avoided that conflict as long as possible, it was certainly not for lack of courage or because 'submission to authority saves many lives',[3] but because he believed both in the sacredness of his work and in its usefulness to his fellow countrymen. But the conflict was there all the time and the accusers of Socrates were not wrong in seeing in him a menace to the authority of the πόλις. For Meletus and Anytus, who brought him to trial, were not among the immoralists. They too believed that they were saving the polis, but they could not see that a city would still be a city, and perhaps a better one, if its power were less absolute.

The other aspect of φύσις which is reflected in Socrates' work

---

[1] When Pericles (Thuc. II 37) spoke of ἄγραφοι νόμοι, he passed lightly over them, as if they only meant the accepted conventions of Athenian society; and perhaps for him they meant only that. On Antigone's or Sophocles' view, see C. M. Bowra, *Sophoclean Tragedy* (1944) pp. 96-101.

[2] *Apol.* 29 D, but the issue was more complicated than that; see below, p. 92 ff.

[3] Sophocles, *Antig.* 676. Socrates had probably seen the *Antigone* performed about 442 B.C. One could wish that he had recorded his impressions.

is that which was referred to in Chapter IV (p. 50)—the *nature of man*. Every animal has his own nature; men differ from each other in many ways, but there is something which they have in common, something which makes them men, not dogs or elephants. Man must exist not merely κατὰ φύσιν, as others said, but κατὰ τὴν ἑαυτοῦ φύσιν, according to his own nature. Now, as we have seen, Socrates believed that it was in accordance with man's nature to act rightly, as soon as he knew what was right. If then we have laws, human laws, made so as to embody τὸ δίκαιον, then νόμος will no longer appear as an unnatural restraint on human conduct but as something in itself according to nature. Thus the third of the four analyses (p. 50) of the φύσις-νόμος position now comes to the fore; though rejected by the Cynic followers of Socrates, it was accepted, but much modified by new theories of divinity, by Plato. The whole realm of nature is large enough to include the old φύσις and the old νόμος, which are seen to be different, but not to be mutually exclusive, or the absolute opposite the one of the other. But the fundamental question is *how* to make laws so as to embody τὸ δίκαιον. Plato, though out of sympathy with Socrates at many points (above, p. 88), followed the same quest here and spent much of his life seeking a solution of the problem. Socrates' answer cannot be positively stated; probably he never gave one. Xenophon, it is true, makes him assert firmly in the argument with Hippias[1] that the just and the legal, customary or constitutional, τὸ δίκαιον and τὸ νόμιμον, are the same. So, of course, they ought to be *if* the laws and customs of a city are all made according to justice. But Xenophon was hardly capable of seeing this point, simple though it is now after twenty-four centuries of familiarity. In any case Xenophon was only designing a conversation to illustrate the facts which he had just been stating about the law-abiding habits of Socrates. There can indeed be no doubt about these; though far from satisfied with Protagoras' view of justice as city-made, he was never known to break with the city-law. But he does seem to have drawn a distinction between abiding by the law and implicit obedience to those in authority. He refused to carry out a command of the government of the Thirty because it would have involved the arrest and execution of a man without trial. He did not question, any more than Antigone, the legitimacy of the government, but

---

[1] Xenophon, *Mem.* IV 4, 18; cp. *supra* pp. 61-62.

their command was, says Xenophon, παρὰ τοὺς νόμους, unconstitutional and, says Plato, ἄδικον καὶ ἀνόσιον, unjust and immoral.
But for the fall of the Thirty, whose brief régime was marked by
the characteristics of the immoralist way of thinking and was led
by Critias, he would doubtless have paid for his courage with his
life and the story of his martyrdom would have been different. On
another occasion he refused to put an illegal proposal to a meeting over which he had been obliged by the fall of the lot to pre-
side. This too showed great courage, for he knew that, although
at the moment he had formal authority on his side, the courts of
law could easily be used against him. Socrates, indeed, whatever
Xenophon may say, can hardly have missed seeing that the same
act might be 'according to the laws' and therefore νόμιμον, and
yet not in accordance with the principles of justice. Plato makes
Socrates in his defence refuse to obey hypothetical orders of
Athens requiring him to give up his way of life, and there is no
reason to suppose that such orders would have been παρὰ τοὺς
νόμους. The verdict and the condemnation he believed to be unjust, but the indictment was not illegal and the trial was carried
out according to law.

The story of the trial and execution of Socrates in his seven-
tieth year is too well-known to need repetition here. If a wide
sense of the terms be granted, it will be conceded that Socrates
was both a saint and a martyr. Though he preached no doctrine
and performed no miracles,[1] he had that mysterious power of
calling forth both unwearied devotion and bitter hatred. Some
hovered long between the conflicting emotions. Some of his
greatest admirers understood him least. Attracted in the first instance irrationally, emotionally or even erotically, they sometimes
failed intellectually or morally. Blame for the infamies of Critias
and Alcibiades was laid on him; and the virtuous Crito misunderstood him no less than they. Georges Bernanos[2] has defined
a saint as one who 'renders unto Caesar that which is Caesar's,
but would rather be hacked to pieces than render unto him anything else' and, he adds, 'it is just that which is *not* his that Caesar
nowadays most wishes to get'. Socrates rendered to the Athenian
people his loyalty and devoted service, but refused to surrender

[1] Unless we believe that he was a successful fortune-teller! Xeno phon
Mem. I 1,4.
[2] In his *Lettre aux Anglais*, 1942.

that which did not belong to them. Doubts begin to arise only when we consider not the saint but the martyr, when we raise the question 'What did Socrates die for?' It is never easy to know in what cause a man lays down his life, since two men may fight and die in the same struggle for different reasons. Yet Socrates' place in political thought can hardly be determined without attempting an answer.[1] He was indicted for impiety, as others had been before him. He was the first to lose his life on such a charge; his refusal to admit any sort of guilt led to the imposition of the extreme penalty. But we can hardly be satisfied to say that he died a martyr either for religion or for irreligion. Again, he was accused of corrupting the young; but no one would say that he died on the altar of Educational Reform. It is possible that the motives behind the prosecution were mainly political, being kept obscured because of the amnesty. But this is doubtful; even Plato[2] admitted that the restored democracy behaved with moderation. Though many people wanted rid of him for personal reasons, he can hardly have been politically dangerous as a rallying point for another oligarchical *Putsch*. Besides, even if his accusers' motives were primarily political, that does not tell us the real significance of his death. He very nearly, as we have seen, met his death at the hands of the oligarchy of the Thirty. He did not die in the cause of either democracy or oligarchy nor was he strictly a political martyr.

The significance of his death is perhaps rather that he died in the cause of freedom of conscience. All his life he had urged upon his fellow men that each had an individual duty to perform, the duty of ἐπιμέλεια τῆς ψυχῆς, and that each was responsible for its performance not to the πόλις but to himself. His own attempts to live a life in accordance with this principle had brought him into conflict with the πόλις and are a testimony to his belief in the ethical freedom of the individual. He never surrendered this freedom even when, being in prison and awaiting death, he received his friend Crito and heard his offer to arrange an escape from the prison and from Attica. He rejected this offer for the same reason that he disobeyed the Thirty; it was not right. This is not inconsistent with the view that the verdict was unjust;

---

[1] Unless we prefer to believe that he was playing for a death-penalty because he preferred death to old age. Xenophon, *Apol.* 1.

[2] *Epist.* VII 325 B.

Socrates would never agree that wrong done by one party justifies wrong-doing by another. In refusing to yield to Crito's entreaties and insisting that he must abide by the official verdict Socrates was true to the same principle which on the earlier occasion had made him disobey authority. The verdict, even if unjust, did not require him to act unjustly and Socrates, though he never found, or refrained from offering, any universally valid account of τὸ δίκαιον, had a very fair notion of what it meant for him; and once he knew what was right, he could have no hesitation about doing it. But in Greek as in English 'right' can mean not only something that you do, but also something that you claim for yourself. Crito therefore could take the view that Socrates, having been unjustly condemned, had a right to leave the prison. Socrates held that it would be contrary to τὸ δίκαιον and therefore could not possibly be among τὰ δίκαια, 'rights'. No reconcilement is possible between these two views and it is hard to believe that Socrates ever really converted Crito to his way of thinking. But in the dialogue entitled *Crito* Plato not only depicts Socrates as scoring a dialectical victory over his well-meaning friend[1], but he puts into his mouth arguments which presuppose some sort of theory of the State. Outside the Platonic dialogues there is nothing in the Socratic tradition that can be called a theory of the State. Yet Plato here ascribes not one but two theories to him. First, that every citizen by his continued residence in a city has entered into an implied contract with that city to do all that may be required of him. The second draws an analogy between πόλις and parent and endows the state with the *auctoritas* and *potestas* of a Roman father. Now either of these theories, or both if they are compatible with each other, provides cogent arguments against trying to escape, but that does not prove that Socrates used them; they could also be used to provide arguments in favour of doing many things which Socrates might consider wrong. It is improbable that Socrates ever believed in or acted upon either of these theories or that he theorised about the State at all. He certainly did not die in defence of any theory as to what a πόλις should be. His concern was with man.

A retrospect over the life of Socrates brings us back to the heyday of Protagoras and reminds us that he too was concerned

---

[1] Crito, the chief interlocutor, is reputed (Diog. L. II 121) himself to have written a dialogue, Πρωταγόρας ἢ πολιτικός.

with men rather than institutions, that he too was aware of the
moral and intellectual qualities necessary for successful living
together. But there are fundamental differences between the two
chief figures in fifth-century political thought which should here
be noted. The great difference is that Socrates did not regard
education and philosophy as a training in how to do things, but
as a process of acquiring a knowledge of the nature of things.
Protagoras, with the easier educational aim before him and living
in a world where things generally did not seem to be going amiss,
had on the whole an optimistic outlook. Socrates not only saw a
very different piece of history in the making, but had set himself
a higher and harder task. His ἐπιμέλεια τῆς ψυχῆς demanded a
high standard of intellectual honesty, and the Delphic 'Know thy-
self' was a constant reminder of man's intellectual limitations.
But if our limitations are serious, still our responsibilities remain
great, and each man must face his own and find an answer to the
question πῶς βιωτέον; 'how shall a man live?' Another change is
one of method. Protagoras expounded and Herodotus imitated
the method of debate, of seeing both sides of every question.
Socrates was eager to know which was the *right* side and hoped
to track down the truth by means of question and answer. Both
methods have their uses and both had a large future, but the
Protagorean method was more easily applied and more immediately influential. We have already (p. 84) referred to its parody
in Aristophanes' *Clouds* and, apart from the influence which it
must have had on everyday life, literature is permeated with it.
Drama in particular afforded opportunities, and many scenes in
Sophocles and still more in Euripides are debates between opposing sides. There is a fragment of Euripides (189 N.) which says,
'anyone who is a clever speaker could make up a set of twin arguments about anything'. And this is exactly what an anonymous
writer about 400 B.C. set out to do, to compose twin arguments,
δισσοὶ λόγοι, dealing briefly with pairs of opposites, the true and
the false, the just and the unjust, or with the two sides of such
oft-discussed questions as 'Is it possible to teach ἀρετή and σοφία?'
or the democratic use of sortition in appointing officials. The
unknown writer is neither original nor profound and the most
interesting of his pairs of λόγοι is the second, τὸ καλόν and τὸ
αἰσχρόν, much of which is clearly derived from Herodotus on
νόμος. There is indeed more political interest in the debates in

some of the plays of Euripides, especially the *Phoenissae* and the *Supplices*.[1]

The rival propositions in the *Phoenissae* are Absolutism and Equality, τυραννίς and ἰσότης. The arguments in favour of the former have no moral basis except that it is cowardly to throw away such advantage when it has been won. If crimes must be committed, then let them be, provided that they are necessary for the maintenance of the tyrant's power; otherwise he should conform to morality, εὐσεβεῖν. Jocasta's defence of the other λόγος is even more 'full of good quotations'.[2] She says that this desire to outstrip one's fellows is an unrighteous thing. Equality is the principle upon which human relationships must be based and warrant for this can be found in the doctrine of φύσις; for in the realm of nature night and day, summer and winter have equal shares of time. This application of the φύσις principle, turning the tables on the superman theory, is clever and unexpected and, though shallow in itself, shows the equal shallowness of the other. The standards provided by φύσις are no more fixed and sure than those of νόμος. Equality is thus approved both by nature and by convention.[3] In another play, the *Children of Heracles*, the unlimited self-seeking of the 'Callicles' man is contrasted with justice and is condemned as unpatriotic and anti-social.

In the *Suppliants* Aithra, mother of Theseus, is made to give her son advice on how to rule and especially on the dangers of neglecting religion and the laws: 'What keeps the cities of men from falling asunder is each man's good observance of its laws.'[4] In the same play there is another set of δισσοὶ λόγοι occasioned by the arrival at Athens of a messenger who began with the tactless words τίς γῆς τύραννος; and was sharply rebuked by Theseus with engaging anachronism: 'Look for no tyrant here.

---

[1] Apart from these two the *Medea*, *Hecuba*, *Helen* will all provide examples of political or semi-political debate. From the very numerous fragments one might select, 205, 251, 256, 284 (cp. above p. 22, athleticism), 288, 329, 1035 as being of political interest.

[2] γνωμῶν μεστὸν πολλῶν τε καὶ καλῶν. So says the author of the *Argument* prefixed to the play.

[3] τὸ γὰρ ἴσον νόμιμον ἀνθρώποις ἔφυ (538). The paradox is deliberate and telling and occurs also in *Bacchae* 890-896, where religion, too, is 'both customary and natural'. Cp. *Ion* 643 and see Heinimann, *Nomos und Physis*, 166-167.

[4] 310-311. Cp. p. 82 above and esp. *Anon. Iambl.* 3.6.

The city is not governed by one man but is free. The people is sovran, rulers succeeding annually in turn. No extra privilege is given to the rich man; the poor is his equal.' When the messenger is bold enough to defend the monarchic principle, Theseus, for all the world like a fifth-century Athenian, takes up the challenge with gusto. To the traditional arguments against tyranny (see Chap. III, p. 36) are added some of the advantages of democratic Athens, such as equality before the law and the right of all to participate in forming a national policy. In the end the antagonists agree to differ, since the play must go on and all this arguing has nothing to do with the story.[1] But it is a good example of the way in which political thought invaded Euripidean drama.

[1] As a kind of concession to realism Theseus blames the other man for starting an argument (427-8). Did Euripides ever notice that he used the same gambit, word for word, in the Jason-Medea debate? (*Medea* 546).

FURTHER NOTES AND REFERENCES

CHAPTER V

ANTIPHON: The two Oxyrhynchus papyri are numbered 1364 (Vol. XI) and 1797 (Vol. XV). They are Frag. 44 A and B in Diels[5]. Their relation to the previously-known fragments is a matter of great difficulty. See E. Bignone, *Studi sul pensiero greco*, most of which are concerned with Antiphon problems, and a review by O. Regenbogen in *Gnomon* XVI, 1940, p. 97, and on their style, etc., also J. H. Finley in *Harvard Studies in Classical Philology*, Vol. 50 (1939) p. 63 ff. The numbers refer to the fragments in Diels[5].

THRASYMACHUS: Plato, *Repub.* I, esp. 338 c - 344 c, and *Clitophon*. The fragments of the speech on πάτριος πολιτεία in Diels[5] fr. 1.

CALLICLES: Plato, *Gorgias*, esp. 482 E - 488 B, and cp. W. Jaeger *Paideia* II ch. 6.

LYCOPHRON, though hardly pre-Socratic, is included in Diels[5]. Alcidamas is not. Glaucon's speech: Plato, *Repub.* 358 c - 359 b.

CRITIAS: The reff. are to Diels[5]. Of Anon. Iamblichi the text is given in Diels[5] pp. 400-404. 'Just and Unjust' debate, *Clouds* 886-1023.

OLD OLIGARCH: Ps.-Xen., *Aθ. Πολ.* is printed in Vol. 5 of the O.C.T. Xenophon, also ed. by E. Kalinka (Teubner) 1914.

SOCRATES: Where to look for the authentic Socrates in ancient literature is a question with so many possible answers that the reader will not expect to find it discussed here. The *main* sources here used are: Plato, *Apology; Epist.* VII 324 E - 325 C; *Crito* 43 A - 49 C. Xenophon, *Apology; Memorab.* I 1, 10-19 and IV 4, 1-4. Aristotle: the various reff. are conveniently collected and discussed by Th. Deman in *Le témoignage d'Aristote sur Socrate* (Paris, 1942) where Nos. 11, 16, 24-34, 39 are most important for political thought.

Διϲϲοὶ λόγοι in Diels[5]. EURIPIDES, *Phoenissae* 503-585; *Heraclidae* 1-5; *Supplices* 301-319, 399-466.

CHAPTER VI

THUCYDIDES

History is a preceptor of prudence, not of principles.—BURKE

As was observed at the beginning of Chapter V, the war between Athens and Sparta formed a constant background to much of the political thought of the latter end of the fifth century. This war is known to us chiefly through the *History* written by Thucydides and while it would be superfluous here to describe the war or Thucydides' account of it, it is essential to consider certain aspects of the work and its importance in the history of political thought.

Apart from certain digressions, inserted for various reasons, the narrative parts of Thucydides' *History* are concerned chiefly with naval and military operations; there is little, except in the eighth book, about the internal history of Athens, from which he was an exile for twenty years (424-404 B.C.), or about constitutional questions; he was not writing political history in that sense and his few personal expressions of approval or disapproval are generally more connected with the conduct of the war than with political principles. Yet political action, if not political principles, is just what interested Thucydides most—the behaviour of men and states and of men in states. It was because he understood men in that context that he could write an intelligible history of their behaviour, and that history thus written, being the first of its kind, has a place in political as well as in historical writing. Herodotus knew a great deal about human nature in other contexts; a tyrant's wrath or amorous fancy often appeared to be and indeed often was the mainspring of political action, but the generation which separated Herodotus from Thucydides had seen great advances

in the study of man as well as great social and political changes
(Chaps. IV and V). Thucydides approached the study of contemporary history, even as Euripides approached social and religious
problems, equipped with the new education, with wider knowledge and a more critical spirit. With this he combined practical
experience as a naval commander in war, and with his immense
intellectual powers applied himself to the writing of the history
of the war. In his account of the Revolution of 411 B.C. he was
applying historical study to politics, but he was elsewhere far
more concerned to apply his political knowledge to history.

The work is thus primarily a historical one, not a contribution
to the study of πολιτική. Yet there are good reasons[1] why it should
receive in a history of political thought special and separate consideration not given to the work of Aristophanes or the Greek
Orators, full of politics though they may be. The first and chief
reason lies in the fact that Thucydides included in his history
speeches and discussions. Others had done this but Thucydides
is anxious that his readers should realise the historical value of
the speeches and not mistake them for the semi-dramatic pro-
ductions of his predecessors. He has in this way preserved for us
some of the political thought of the prominent men of his time,
of Pericles, Alcibiades, Cleon and others and of unnamed persons
speaking on their city's behalf. Naturally not all that was said is
important in the history of thought, but the matter of the speeches,
combined with Thucydides' manner of reporting them, resulted
in frequent enunciations of general principles or generalised discussions. The speeches and debates in Thucydides are neither the
artificial δισσοὶ λόγοι of the Sophists' lecture-rooms nor yet purely
local and immediate discussions about what to do next. They
avoid the vacuity of the one and the narrowness of the other in
a way which shows how deeply not Thucydides only but all contemporary thought was permeated with the education in φιλο-

---

[1] And perhaps some bad ones. For example the book has been called
'a handbook of political theory in disguise'. Some hold that Thucydides'
main purpose was to produce a handbook for future *politicians*. This is to
read too much into the historian's claim (I 22) that his work is both 'an
accurate record of events now past and a useful guide as to how they might
be expected to fall out in the future'. It is, however, quite possible that
Thucydides' determination to write history was helped by the misfortune
of exile, which deprived him of an active political career. See further in the
note at the end of this chapter.

σοφία. It is, of course, certain that Thucydides infused something of himself into the speeches. He did not profess to give a *verbatim* report, but only to 'keep as nearly as possible to the general purport of what was actually said'. How far in each case this process affected his report we shall probably never know. Doubtless it went deeper when he was reporting a plurality of speakers, and when his knowledge of the original was not detailed, and when the original itself was inadequate. At any rate such a way of working would permit a historian to improve upon arguments actually used, and if the speaker had failed to say some of the things which really needed saying or needed doing[1] at a particular juncture, the historian might add them. The result would be a truer analysis of the situation and a fuller account of reasons for and against a course of action, though a less accurate account of the speeches made. But how far Thucydides allowed himself this licence is impossible to say.[2] Certainly he himself had a deep understanding of πολιτική, especially in its relation to war, and so, though he endeavours generally to keep himself in the background and to avoid passing moral judgments, he too, by his analysis of political behaviour and his understanding of the nature and effect of political power demands a place in the history of political thought. Lastly, the subject of his history obliged him to deal frequently with problems of inter-state relationships—a subject generally somewhat neglected by Greek political philosophers and by us too regarded usually as a part of legal rather than political studies.

Of the politicians of the day whose ideas are worth studying none can be compared with Pericles, though indeed his great days were behind him when the war came and he died when it had been two years in progress. No other possessed that power of knowing beforehand the kind of situation likely to confront a state and of discerning the measures necessary to meet it. It was

---

[1] τὰ δέοντα: the term includes both, as has been shown by J. H. Finley (*Thucydides*, pp. 96-100), to whose reff. add Gorgias *Epitaphius*, τὸ δέον ἐν τῷ δέοντι καὶ λέγειν καὶ σιγᾶν καὶ ποιεῖν.

[2] For the present purpose this summary statement of a difficult problem must suffice. The interested reader may begin by consulting J. H. Finley, *Thucydides* (Harvard U.P., 1942) and A. W. Gomme, *Essays in Greek History and Literature*, ch. IX (Blackwell, 1937) and J. B. Bury, *The Ancient Greek Historians* (1909), Lecture III, to mention only a few works in English. See further note at the end of this chapter.

this faculty (πρόνοια) that Thucydides most admired in him, regarding it as the most valuable πολιτικὴ ἀρετή (cp. p. 55). Among great men of the past Themistocles had it; it came easily to him, a kind of natural flair. But it *was* capable of being taught; the study of human behaviour in the past gives a good indication of the way in which human beings act and react. Now Pericles exercised his power over the Athenian people by virtue of his character and ability. He was no sole ruler, but such was the strength of his personality that what was nominally a democracy was under him in a fair way to becoming[1] rule by a leading citizen. In so far as a Periclean political theory can be constructed from Thucydides, it would seem that his ideal state was very much like the Athens which he describes and idealises in the Funeral Speech. — Uninterrupted possession of its territory generation after generation is essential for the working of the πόλις. The constitution must be one of the Many not of the Few. But, while legal equality among the citizens is essential and no man is to be preferred before another on the score of wealth, the democratic principle of 'every man in his turn' must be modified by a proper recognition of merit.[2] A city should have an easy social atmosphere, not rigidly hide-bound; yet there must be proper submission to law, to authority and to the accepted code of behaviour. (There is no reference to duty to the gods.) In order to provide such a social life and easy circumstances, the state must be rich and powerful, an imperial and commercial city with a strong navy. But this is by no means to say that individual citizens are to be rich and prosperous.[3] It is the quality of the citizens that counts and their training is all important. He rejects the hard, narrow Spartan school; citizens must be educated not simply trained. Even in warfare it is character that counts, for courage in action depends more on that than on training. On the other hand there must be no softness (μαλακία); the attention paid to literature and the arts should not be excessive and above all never exclusive of national interests. A citizen of a πόλις is failing in his duty if he does not make his city his first concern and aim not merely at obeying her orders but understanding them. This is not the place

---

[1] ἐγίγνετο, II 65, 9. The imperfect tense is generally missed by translators.
[2] II 37. See A. W. Gomme in *Class. Quart.* XLII 1948, p. 10.
[3] II 60. But this is just what the propertied classes would like to believe, e.g. Nicias in VI 9, 2.

to criticise Pericles' Utopia or to discuss how far it is tinged with Thucydides' own retrospective longing. But it should be noted that some of the topics anticipate the themes of Platonic dialogues. Character and education as the basis of state-building did not begin with Plato's *Republic*. When Thucydides sums up the career of Pericles he speaks chiefly of his long-sighted policy in the war, but it requires no reading between the lines to see that he himself, while he believed in democracy, believed also in leadership. After Pericles Athens failed to produce leaders, because politicians were too much wrapped up in their personal ambitions and rivalries and opportunities to enrich themselves. Plato's idea that political power must be divorced from money-power lay ready to hand.

Among the power-seeking and unscrupulous politicians of the years 428-423 B.C. Cleon was the most prominent, and Thucydides' dislike of him is as conspicuous as Aristophanes', though less often expressed. There is one Cleon speech in Thucydides and a reply to it. The question was how to punish the people of Mytilene in Lesbos, who had changed sides, or rebelled, as the Athenians put it, during the war. Hence both speeches deal with ἀρχή, the rule exercised by an imperial power over her satellite states, and both speakers draw a distinction between inter-state relations among equals and the relationship of Athens to her subject-allies (ὑπήκοοι). According to Cleon humanitarian feeling and common decency are quite out of place when dealing with subject states, though useful enough with other great powers from whom one may expect similar consideration. The principles and methods of government called δημοκρατία are also quite inapplicable. If you have an empire you must rule it like a tyrant and regard objectors as rebels. (In this respect there is no difference between the imperialism of Cleon and that of Pericles, who also (II 63) compared Athenian ἀρχή to a τυραννίς, though a little more apologetically.[1]) Cleon expresses the fear of appearing to be subject to persuasion, of changing one's mind. From its own people too a government should demand implicit obedience and not allow citizens 'to think themselves wiser than the laws'. Here there is a clear and presumably deliberate contrast to Pericles' idea of citizenship. For a critical and independent spirit is discouraged; docility and stupidity are to be preferred to disobedient

[1] The analogy became generally accepted: e.g. the Athenian Euphemus at Camarina in Sicily in 415 B.C. Thuc. VI 85 *init.*

cleverness; a city which keeps its laws and does not tamper with them, even if they are inferior, is in a better state than one where the laws are good but impotent to control.

In presenting the case for a less harsh treatment the otherwise unknown Diodotus also denies any feeling of sentiment in favour of the rebellious Mytileneans; he is concerned only to discover what is expedient for Athens. What he has to say on general political principles is somewhat reminiscent of both Protagoras and Pericles, with its insistence on εὐβουλία and on the duties of a good citizen. To Cleon's doctrine of unquestioning obedience to unchanging laws he replies with a quite Periclean statement of the principle on which practical political thinking must always be based, however much the so-called practical men may deride it —*discussion is action's teacher*.[1] In a democracy especially every citizen must do his share of political thinking, and a corollary would be that every government must make its government intelligible.[2] A second feature which Diodotus would demand, though he has to deplore its absence at Athens, is real freedom of speech, and freedom from any fear of the consequences, even should they be mere unpopularity and misunderstanding, of speaking for an unpopular cause or advocating a policy not acceptable to the authorities. It should be an elementary principle that decisions are taken as a result of discussion, from which haste, passion and the browbeating of opponents are absent; no man should be penalised for saying what he really means. It is noteworthy that the speaker not only has to point out that such conditions do not in fact exist in Athens less than four years after Pericles had given his glowing account of it, but has also to safeguard himself from being laughed at as old-fashioned and sentimental by disclaiming all humanitarian feeling.[3]

To be supremely rich and supremely clever seemed to many an Athenian the greatest blessing that the gods could bestow: and if ever the gods did bestow these gifts on a man, he was not only admired and envied, but also feared as a potential tyrant. How to

[1] λόγοι πραγμάτων διδάσκαλοι (III 42). The Periclean statement is quoted on page 2.

[2] Diodotus does not himself say this, but it is not unlike the principle of Pericles and of Plato's προοίμια νόμων. See Chap. X.

[3] On any view of the composition of Thucydides' speeches, it is surely legitimate to see the historian's own mind behind Diodotus' appeal for Reason and Freedom.

use a man of outstanding ability without allowing him to become your absolute master was a constant problem in a small state and Aristotle in his *Politics* devoted much attention to it. A conspicuous example was Alcibiades, that lion's cub reared in the bosom of Athene. His enemies had little difficulty in turning his popularity into envy of his wealth and they so played upon the fear of tyranny that they brought about his downfall. His one public utterance at Athens recorded by Thucydides defends the rich man's right to use his wealth extravagantly and even ostentatiously, since this redounds to the credit of his country; but the occasion was a debate, in which he was speaking against the more cautious Nicias, on the proposal to send an expedition to Sicily, so that the principles of imperial policy or ἀρχή are the chief topic. Here (VI 18) he speaks in the same vein as Pericles (II 63): a state which rules over others must continue to do so; to this end it must be ready to spend its resources instead of merely husbanding them (ταμιεύεσθαι). If a powerful state suddenly reverses its policy of telling lesser powers what they must do, the result will always be disastrous. Having thus appeared as a champion of the imperial policy of the Athenian democracy, Alcibiades, when he fled from prosecution and escaped to Sparta, had some difficulty in posing as a friend of Lacedaemon. It was for Spartan ears that he made his famous remark that democracy was 'an admitted folly'. Here too he gave utterance to a view of patriotism which has acquired added significance in Europe since 1934. He claimed the right to fight against his country, because he was fighting to recover that which had been unjustly taken from him, and because Athens' real enemies were those who by abuse of their power were driving her friends into the opposite camp. Political freedom is a condition of political allegiance; political oppression absolves its victim from patriotic duties.[1]

Long before the Athenians sent their great expeditionary force to Sicily, the inhabitants of the island had had many causes for alarm and endless discussions took place. Not all these were worth recording but Thucydides singles out the speech of the Syracusan Hermocrates at the Gela conference in 424 B.C. as sum-

---

[1] It is doubtful whether this sentiment does really underlie the twisted and equivocal language of τὸ δὲ φιλόπολι οὐκ ἐν ᾧ ἀδικοῦμαι ἔχω, ἀλλ' ἐν ᾧ ἀσφαλῶς ἐπολιτεύθην (VI 92), but Alcibiades may have had Athens' interests at heart. See Thuc. VIII 81 and 86.

ming up the arguments in favour of a policy of Sicilian collective
security. The speaker expresses no righteous indignation at the
Athenian expansionist policy; his wrath is reserved for those who
will not resist it. It is *according to man's nature* (IV 61) both to
dominate the obedient and to forestall the aggressor. The advantages of peace over war need no advocate; but a cause which is
just, as others' experience shows, is not necessarily successful.
(He does not add, nor yet deny, that a cause which is successful
is not necessarily just.) Some nine years later, when the Athenian
fleet is already on its way to Sicily, Hermocrates addresses his
fellow-Syracusans. He has little to add on general principles, but
his opponent Athenagoras is more concerned with political ideo-
logy than with the danger from abroad. In constitutional theory
he strikes the same note as Pericles and Protagoras—a democracy
with no privileges for wealth but proper recognition of merit
and ability. He is alive to the danger that the increase of armed
power to meet an external foe may at any time lead to the oppression of the citizens instead of their defence. Certainly when the
invasion came and the Syracusans suffered their first defeat, Hermocrates was able to carry through a narrow concentration of
military power into fewer hands.

The relations between one city and another were not a subject
to which Greek political philosophy gave much attention; but its
practical importance was hardly less than the choice of constitution or the method of selecting officials, and it presented problems which cities and citizens had to face. International relations
were governed either by specific treaties, to which two or more
cities might be parties, or else by a somewhat vague conception
of established usage, τὸ καθεστὸς τοῖς Ἕλλησι νόμιμον. Just as
opinion was divided (see Chap. V) between those who still asserted the supremacy of ΝΟΜΟΣ and those who would sweep
it away as something contrary to ΦΥΣΙΣ, so in relation to whole
cities; some were for disregarding all established usage, the sanctity of treaties and unwritten laws of decency and fairness, while
others clung to them. When the individualism of a Callicles is
applied to individual cities, it means that the city which is cleverer
and wealthier will outstrip the rest; and by the age-old principle
of city-state autonomy each city was an individual aiming at its
own advantage. But this same principle of autonomy was also
quite incompatible with the domination of one city by another,

to which the policy of self-aggrandisement inevitably led. This impasse was complete even before the outbreak of hostilities between Athens and Sparta, and the speeches made at both places bring it out very clearly. These are not without some reference to the old-fashioned notion of δίκη or right usage, but the claim of one city to lay down what is right for another is resented by Pericles as a first step towards loss of freedom. On the other hand the view was expressed by some Corinthians that great cities have a responsibility in international affairs: they should be prepared to check excessive domination by other great cities. Where the relationship is already one of ruler-state and subject, formally even if forcibly entered into, as the superior strength of the one is the cause of the relationship, so in practice it is the only principle governing it. Where there was no formal subject-ruler relationship but a free city threatened by a great power, as Plataea by Sparta or Melos by Athens, there was nothing, then as now, that the weaker could do except either to ask for aid from a third party or appeal to the better feelings of the oppressor. In short, in the international field at any rate the immoralists appeared to have won the day. The war had opened with an attack not preceded by a declaration, a fact which Thucydides is careful to record, though he makes no comment.[1]

Yet even those who no longer believe in the sanctity of treaties continue to make them; they serve to mark the conclusion of a war and to secure at least a period of peace. On the making of treaties there is a short but striking speech in Thucydides. It is made by a Lacedaemonian mission sent to Athens after six years of warfare. Nothing came of the mission, but it is clear from the narrative of events in the chapter following the speech that Thucydides thought that peace might well have been made then. After remarking on the folly of supposing that a nation can enter a major war with reservations, hoping to limit the extent of its participation, the speakers stress the necessity of mutual consent in the making of peace-treaties; the object should be to put an end to hostility as well as to war. To do this with any hope of permanence means abandoning the notion that 'that party which has had the greater success in defensive and offensive operations should bind the other by a forced oath to unequal terms'. Even when the victor is in a position to impose terms, he ought to have

---

[1] It is however noted as a breach, VII 18.

regard to fairness (τὸ ἐπιεικές)[1] and 'with an unlooked-for victory over him in generosity, make a mutual and reasonable peace'.

Such sentiments are naturally more often expressed by the weaker party. The stronger follows the opposite rule: impose your will wherever you are strong enough to do so. It was on this principle that the Athenians acted at Melos, declaring quite truly that it was not their own invention. Melos was one of the few islands not members of the Athenian confederacy in 416. Being Dorians by race the inhabitants mostly favoured Sparta and expected the great naval power to be satisfied with their neutrality. When an Athenian force of overwhelming size came demanding their submission, a discussion took place which Thucydides has reported in the form of a dialogue. The Athenian side of this is the classic expression of the principle just mentioned— οὗ ἂν κρατῇ, ἄρχειν—but pure *Machtpolitik*, being the exact counterpart of tyranny, is no more important in political theory than the idea of τυραννίς. It is just because the Athenians make no claim to have justice on their side that their exposition is of less significance than that of their victims. The Melian side of the dialogue is in part an attempt to make out a case for fair-play in inter-state dealings and in part an attempt to expose the weakness of the opposite theory. Notions of merit earned by past services, though the Athenians were glad to use them at Sparta, of divine approval or of moral obligation are all ruled out: they had not availed the Plataeans in their appeal to their Spartan conquerors in 427. Thus restricted, the Melians produce three major arguments: the first is based on the common interest of the weaker and the stronger; the second attacks the idea that an expanding imperial policy can ever bring security; and the third, which is akin to the second, states that an empire which is based on force cannot endure. The Athenians would listen to none of these arguments and the Melians would not give in; the history of the next ten years was to show their force.—That which binds the weaker and the stronger is the mutability of fortune; danger is ever recurring and if it threatens the weaker to-day, it may reach the stronger to-morrow. It should be a principle 'not to destroy that which is to the good of all'—μὴ λύειν τὸ κοινὸν ἀγαθόν. Then in

---

[1] According to Cleon, who opposed these proposals, as he had opposed any concession to the Mytileneans, there was no place for ἐπιείκεια in the rule of an empire, any more than in 'international' dealings.

reply to an Athenian assertion that they expected by subduing Melos to gain for themselves not only an extension of empire (πλεόνων ἄρξαι) but also security for the future (τὸ ἀσφαλές), the Melians are quick to point out that there soon comes a point in an expansionist policy where these two advantages cannot be had simultaneously. Every fresh country subdued means not only conflict with the next, but increased alarm and enmity among those not yet affected. To try to limit the process, as the Athenians hoped, was a delusion, just as great a delusion, we may add, as a limited participation in a war (p. 106) or a voluntary reduction of imperial power (p. 104). Lastly, the determination of the ruling city to maintain its authority by force without any regard to ἐπιείκεια must be in perpetual conflict with the desire of the subject to be rid of it. Of course some will bow before the storm, and the Athenians urge that such a course brings no disgrace, since it saves a city from destruction; it is folly to wait for a miracle to happen, such as help from Sparta. In short, so long as immediate preservation (σωτηρία) remains the first object, the debating honours, so to speak, rest with the Athenians. To them therefore it seemed completely unreasonable (πολλὴ ἀλογία) that at the end of the discussion the Melians should throw aside conclusions logically reached and choose according to a 'foolish sense of decency and honour'. Possibly the Melians did really trust in Lacedaemonian aid, but surely the Athenians must have known that more than safety was at stake, that they were matching themselves against something which could not be conquered by force of arms at all. Some among them must have recalled the stand which their allies at Plataea had made against the Spartans earlier in the war. When they told their victims, 'You deem the future more real than what is before your eyes and wishfully look upon the unseen as already with you', they were intending to condemn the senseless folly of the Melians, but they were actually foretelling the spirit which kept alive the resistance movements between 1940 and 1945. Thucydides himself with his historical sense, his political understanding and his philosophic training saw the whole matter in relation to its past and its sequel and understood the ever-recurring nature of the problem; but he does not step in to censure either the folly of the weak or the brutality of the strong nor to applaud the courage of the one or the success of the other.

Thus, throughout these various speeches and reports Thucydides has generally kept himself and his views well in the background. Sometimes he has recorded his opinion, as well as others' opinions, about certain politicians, but through most of the work he refrains from giving judgment. But as his philosophic training had helped him to see clearly issues involved, so his work under other sophists, teachers of medicine, also bore fruit; and that not only in his account of the symptoms of the plague at Athens, but also in his detached diagnosis of diseases of the body-politic. Disease appeared to him to be as inseparable from the human character as from the human body; and so long as human nature remains as it is, it will have to contend with rifts within the state, with στάσις. Plato, as we shall see, concludes that we must therefore set about changing human character; but Thucydides, while diagnosing the disease, offers no cure. In a well-known passage in his third book he analyses the causes and effects of the acute political dissensions which rent Corcyra early in the war, for these were typical of conditions often found elsewhere. The perpetual instability caused by recurrent outbreaks of στάσις was the most urgent and difficult practical problem in Greek politics. Where the ascendancy of one party means the virtual exclusion of the other from political life, disasters always occur; human nature (ἡ ἀνθρωπεία φύσις) being what it is, this is inevitable. Now in a city-state among the Greeks party-ascendancy did emphatically mean such exclusion and often actual banishment. Thucydides points out how all these dangers are accentuated in time of war, when the chance of external aid was often seized, to the utter detriment of the coherence and stability of the πόλις. Even more serious were the decline in honesty, moderation and all decent feeling, the general reversal of values (cp. Chap. V) and that negation of all political thought[1] whereby the stupid act without thinking and the clever think without acting.[2]

In the eighth and last book of his history Thucydides records no speeches in full but contents himself, for whatever reason, with brief summaries indirectly reported. On the other hand when he is telling of the mid-war revolution at Athens in 411, he does make some personal comments. Though he admires the skill shown by Antiphon the Orator, he expresses no approval of either the methods or the policy of the Four Hundred. One reason for the short life of the new régime may be found in a kind of law of

---

[1] II 40, v. supra, p. 2 n.   [2] III 83.

political change—that oligarchy replacing democracy is particularly unstable because of personal rivalries.[1] 'For all [the new rulers] instantly refuse to consider each other as equals and each asserts his claim to be first. But under a democratic constitution, when a choice of leaders is made, he who is passed over accepts the result the more contentedly because he knows that he has been beaten by better men' (VIII 89). Thucydides is not suggesting that the transition from democracy to oligarchy is either likely or unlikely; he is but observing its effects. Plato on the other hand disregards and presumably thinks unlikely this type of change; but his outlook is here quite different from that of the historian. We cannot help asking, however, what form of government Thucydides really believed Athens needed. The catchwords and clichés of oligarchy and democracy keep on recurring in speeches but these στασιωτικοὶ λόγοι cannot all give Thucydides' own views. But towards the end of his unfinished history he expresses the opinion that the proposal to replace the oligarchy of the Four Hundred by a modified democracy was the best piece of constitutional reform which the Athenians had undertaken within his lifetime. The main modifications were two in number, but to an uncompromising democrat both were serious, since they would put an end to the power of δῆμος. One was the restriction of the franchise to five thousand citizens on a property qualification; the other was the abolition of pay for holding office. But though these are the most definite and concrete things that Thucydides has to say, they are perhaps the least important.

Previous thinkers had neglected history as a factor in political thought. They had utilised the evidence of contemporary society at home and abroad, collecting and comparing customs and institutions, and the wider they cast their view, the more surprising their results (see Chap. III). Thucydides, instead of looking east and west on the contemporary scene, began to look forward and backwards in the realm of time. He does not of course peer into the future like a seer, but he often stresses the value of πρόγνωσις and πρόνοια for the practising statesman and it was, as we learn from an oft-quoted passage, with an eye to the future that he wrote. He believed that his history would be useful to all those

---

[1] κατ' ἰδίας φιλοτιμίας. Of course these have always to be reckoned with. Thucydides uses very similar language to mark the conditions after the death of Pericles (II 65).

coming after him who might need a guide to past events. His own generation had no such guide. There were works of history, such as those of Herodotus and Hellanikos, there were plentiful reminiscences of former glories in speeches and encomia, there were epic verses, especially those of Homer, there were the fanciful reconstructions of the early life of mankind by a Protagoras or a Critias; but these were not accurate records of past events. Some were myth pure and simple, others highly coloured by τὸ μυθῶδες. Their various writers had various aims, to give pleasure to an audience or to illustrate a thesis, or had some other purpose. None was aiming at the factual record which Thucydides needed for the past and hoped to provide for the present; though of course many historical facts were thus recorded. He found himself obliged to supplement and correct existing histories[1] and to write for himself an account of early Aegean civilisation, especially in its bearing on the history of warfare. His own subject was a war of unprecedented magnitude. Small wars may be fought because people are hungry and seek sustenance[2] at the expense of their neighbours, but large wars can only be fought where there are a surplus of wealth,[3] material and technical resources, such as were not known in early Greece, and a settled and organised life. In the special circumstances of the Aegean Sea there must be added a fourth factor—a large fleet and men to man it. Thucydides' prolegomena to his own history provide an aid by means of comparison and contrast to the understanding of the events and the speeches which he has to record in his own time. The present can only be understood in the light of the past; but the day soon comes when contemporary events are past history, and Thucydides was anxious that future generations should not be hampered, as he had been, by inaccurate and false information, least of all in regard to the 'Great War'.

How then can these complicated relationships be summed up so as to set Thucydides over against his predecessors not in historical but in political writing—Protagoras, Hippias, Antiphon and the rest? The man himself, his broken career, his historical work, his opinions and his reporting of others' opinions, these

[1] e.g. in Bk. I, chs. 20, 97, 89-117, 126, 128-138.
[2] Or additional sustenance, a higher standard of living. Plato *Repub.* II 373.
[3] περιουσία χρημάτων, I, 2 and 7.

must be considered in relation to the subject of πολιτική. Thucydides had absorbed the lectures of contemporary sophists, as Karl Marx absorbed the British Museum reading-room, and the effects of his studies went very much deeper than the acquisition of an antithetical style. As previous chapters will have shown, there was a great deal of variety among the fifth-century sophists. Thucydides acquired a general knowledge of legal and political theory as then understood and of the ideas of various exponents; this enabled him to interpret convincingly in his history opposing points of view. But not all that he heard was equally valuable for the historian's purpose. He had little or no use for theories of ruler-infallibility or about the origins of religion or law. On the other hand he profited greatly by the study of speech and rhetoric and of medicine, and his outlook was predominantly secular and Anaxagorean. He is not concerned, not being himself a sophist, with the methods by which political success may be acquired or with any superman theory; but the success of a πόλις in its dealings with other states is for him one of the most important parts of history. This presupposes the maintenance of the πόλις, but on this problem—how in such an age as this can the πόλις be maintained?—Thucydides casts only a kind of negative light by analysing the increase of disunity and the decline of morality. Indeed, what Thucydides appears to have got out of his sophistic education is an interest not in right and wrong, just and unjust, but in questions of truth or falsehood. For example τὸ ξυμφέρον, expediency, is not a piece of doctrine about the nature of justice, as Thrasymachus said (according to Plato), but merely an expression of a fact or a motive in human activity. Power, too, is not described as a good thing or a bad thing, but as something to be reckoned with. As for the νόμος-φύσις controversy Thucydides recognises both of them as factors in history. For this purpose he rejects equally the φύσις-doctrine which makes all men kin, and all those mixed and contradictory theories which may be deduced from a superficial observation of the realm of nature. He takes the rational point of view, which was shared by many,[1] that men behave according to the φύσις *of men*. He does not ask whether that is νόμιμον or δίκαιον, he does not say that, because

---

[1] References to ἀνθρώπειος τρόπος, human character, and ἡ ἀνθρωπίνη φύσις are frequent in the speeches of Thucydides and of fourth-century orators, in medical writers and in Plato.

men do behave in such and such a way, that therefore is δίκη, the way to behave. Men differ so widely that you cannot deduce what ought to be done from what is done by them (p. 48). On the other hand they are sufficiently similar to each other to make it probable (εἰκός) that men acting together, men in a πόλις, will act in ways in which men have been observed to act. So long then as human nature remains as it is, we must expect trouble in a city. But Thucydides, though he does not set out to alter human nature, is far from believing that nothing can be done to improve human society. There is no ineluctable ἀνάγκη driving men to their doom. Certainly military or political necessity dogs the steps of a nation at war, and Thucydides would have often agreed with Rudolf Binding: 'Sie sagen sie führen Krieg aber der Krieg führt sie.' But that is something different from fatalism, and to remain in-active, whether out of despair or out of a blind hope in provi-dence, was very far from Thucydides' mind. He would not have written his κτῆμα ἐς ἀεί for so blank a future.

But whatever his debt to his teachers and to fifth-century philo-sophy, Thucydides' fame rests on what he himself achieved; and that achievement was his *History*. His first aim was historical not philosophical truth. He was not concerned with the antithesis of the philosophers, ἀλήθεια and δόξα, Truth and Opinion, but with true opinions as opposed to false. Finding false opinion to prevail about the sons of Pisistratus and the Lacedaemonian kingship, he deems it his duty to turn aside to correct these errors. Regard for factual truth was not a characteristic virtue of the Greeks, and few, as Thucydides says, were willing to make the effort to find it out. To him it was all-important. He wanted future generations to have a true account of the war so that they should not make errors of fact. Errors of policy, if he believed them to have been committed, he recorded; but he did not conceive his work as a warning to future Athenians. Of course, like a true Greek, he wrote with his city in mind; all that he did was hers, even in exile. But he was not using history in order to propound political theory; he was using πολιτική in order to write history.

FURTHER NOTES AND REFERENCES
CHAPTER VI

The Funeral Speech of *Pericles*, Thuc. II 35-46, should be read in conjunction with his 'war' speech, II 60-64. Thucydides on Pericles, II 65.

The Mytilenean debate in 427 B.C.: *Cleon*, III 37-40, especially 37; *Diodotus*, 42-48.

Alcibiades' Athenian speech in 415: VI 16-18, cp. esp. VI 18 with II 63 (Pericles: impossibility of retrenchment); at Sparta, VI 89-92.

Conference at Gela in 424, IV 58-64; Syracuse in 415, VI 33-39.

The 'international' situation; speeches at Sparta, I 68-86 (Responsibility of Great Powers, I 69); at Athens (Pericles), I 141.

Mutual consent as a basis for post-war treaties, IV 18-19.

The Melian dialogue, V 85-112.

Disease of the body-politic, III 82-84; cp. Plato, *Republic* VIII; Aristotle, *Politics* V.

The eighth book, 68-71, 89, 97. (In ch. 24 he notes that the people of Chios, in spite of long peace and prosperity, kept their heads.)

Thucydides on his own work, I 20-22.

Any account of the place of Thucydides in political thought must depend on answers to questions about the composition of the work, especially of the speeches, and on the interpretation of passages in which Thucydides speaks about his own work. For the historian can not be separated from the πολιτικός. The Greeks, not having a modern University education behind them, did not divide up knowledge and thought into 'subjects' and 'departments'. The reader will therefore find much that is relevant in the many books written about Thucydides and his *History*. Particularly concerned with the subject of the above chapter, but not at all agreeing with it, are: Otto Regenbogen, 'Thukydides als politische Denker' in *Das Humanistische Gymnasium* XLIV 1933 (unprocurable but for its author's kindness) and a chapter in Jaeger's *Paideia* Vol. I, 'Thucydides: Political Philosopher'. As already mentioned, the *History* of Thucydides is of particular interest for its study of inter-state relations, especially between large states and small. I therefore also mention here A. E. Zimmern, 'Thucydides the Imperialist' in *Solon and Croesus and other essays*, Oxford, 1928; G. Méautis on the Melian dialogue in *Revue des Etudes Grecques* XLVIII 1935; V. Martin, *La Vie Internationale dans la Grèce des Cités* (1940); and Jacqueline de Romilly, *Thucydide et l'Impérialisme Athénien* (1947).

CHAPTER VII

PLATO AND ISOCRATES

The long war which formed the subject of Thucydides' unfinished history ended with the defeat of Athens in 404 B.C. After a short period of misrule by the 'Thirty', a régime set up by the Spartan victors, the democratic constitution was restored in 403 B.C. (the archonship of Eucleides). Thucydides died about that time; Socrates drank the hemlock in 399. Of writers whose work has survived in any measure and who had made their names in the fifth century, only Aristophanes and Andocides the orator were still active. But many of the writers of the new century had grown to manhood at Athens during the Peloponnesian War and had been accustomed to hear discussed the questions which formed the subject of our fifth chapter. It would therefore be a mistake to over-emphasise the change in outlook at Athens after the loss of her empire. On the other hand it was inevitable that this post-war period should be marked by social and economic as well as political changes and that these should leave their mark on political thought. The reverse of this process, political thought shaping political change, is much less prominent now than in earlier centuries. The Athenian empire was built by men who had participated in the educational movements of the early and middle fifth century; farther back the connection was even closer, and Solon could combine the rôles of thinker, educator, poet and statesman. In the fourth century such a combination would have been impossible in action, and it was in the fourth century that Plato lived—the one man whose mental powers would have been equal to the task and who longed for the chance to perform it.[1] We may well doubt whether we would choose to live in a Plato-planned Athens, even in preference to

[1] He himself thought that he was born too late in history (*Epist.* v 322 A).

that unstable and self-centred city which Demosthenes strove to rouse against the menace of Macedon, but we cannot deny his comprehensive intellectual mastery.

The end of the Peloponnesian war was not followed by a period of peace but by continued struggles between the Greek states. The Spartan hegemony was challenged and had to maintain itself by force. The Thebans and Corinthians soon fell out with their fellow-victors. The Athenians had suffered immense losses both of men and material. The devastation had been great and did not cease; fields were sown with a very uncertain prospect of reaping the harvest; and as the population increased again, the need to import food became greater. The peace of 386 B.C. led to some improvement, and later in the century attempts were made to study agriculture more scientifically. But landed wealth, which had already suffered the competition of the more mobile kinds in the middle-class revolution of Cleisthenes, was in many areas decreasing in value as compared with the fortunes that could be made by the manufacture of arms and utensils, by slave-labour, by underwriting and insurance at high premiums and most popular of all, since it required no capital, military service under some successful employer in lands far richer in booty. But those who were neither clever enough nor strong enough to acquire wealth naturally far outnumbered those who were; and the inevitable rise in prices benefited those who had abundance of goods, manufactured, plundered or inherited, and added to the misery of those who had not. At Athens there were attempts to redress the balance by the obvious and afterwards traditional method of increased taxation on the one hand and increased distribution of state-aid on the other. But nothing could disguise the widening gap between rich and poor, or, as Greek sometimes put it, between 'those who could' and 'those who couldn't' (οἱ δυνατοί, οἱ ἀδύνατοι). The comedies of Aristophanes, which a generation back had reflected the current controversies about ethics and politics, now confront us with this social problem and, significantly enough, with a woman's imagined solution for it. 'All men ought to be partners, sharing all things with each other; all should live on the same income instead of having one man rich, another poor; one man tills land in abundance, another has not enough for his own grave; one has many servants, another has no one to attend him. I want one way of living, common to all and the same for all. . . . (Then) poverty will never be the mainspring of any action; for all will have all they need, food, drink, clothing and amusement.'[1] Thus spoke Praxagora, one of Aristophanes' 'women in parliament'. The demand for a more equitable distribution of wealth is behind the comedy *Plutus*,[2] in which Wealth and Poverty are personages in the action. Their rival claims and exchanges of argument reveal the serious social problem that underlies the comic situation. For now, as never before since the time of Draco, political problems are seen also as social problems and the existence of poverty recognised as a menace to society as well as a cause of misery. The economic aspect thus comes to the fore also; so often the material resources and technical means were wanting, even when ends were clear. The pamphlet *Ways and Means*[3] attributed to Xenophon is a testimony to the growing interest in economic problems, as the *Oeconomicus* to an interest in agriculture. The pamphlet aims at greater self-sufficiency at Athens and attempts to show how it can be attained; how poverty can be abolished without either increased taxation or imperialist expansion, how the standard of living may be raised and a surplus income attained, out of which all manner of public and religious works may be financed.

Further survey of the conditions in the Greek world after the Peloponnesian war would be impossible here, and the reader must be referred to books dealing with Greek history. But perhaps enough has been said to show what kind of thing must have been constantly in the mind of any political thinker. Such things are more explicitly stated in Isocrates, who wrote partly with a view to converting a wide public to his way of thinking about the Hellenic world, than in Plato, who had no such intention. For example, writing about 380 B.C. Isocrates says: 'Already there are many evils which in the course of nature afflict mankind; but we have gone out of our way to discover others beyond those which necessity imposes; we have inflicted on ourselves wars and civil war. Some meet their end in lawless anarchy in their own cities, others with their wives and children move from place to place in foreign lands; many in order to get daily bread are driven

[1] From *Ecclesiazusae*, 590-605, *c*. 391 B.C.
[2] Πλοῦτος, *Wealth*, 388 B.C.
[3] Πόροι or *De Vectigalibus*, the Latin name being a translation of the poor sub-title περὶ προσόδων.

to become hired soldiers and die fighting for their foes against their friends.'[1] Thus Isocrates looks more widely than Plato at conditions in the Aegean world, and is perhaps more alive to the economic effects and social calamities of the wars. But Plato is more acutely aware of the narrower, yet in his view more funda- mental, problems which confronted the city-state. If he does not keep on referring directly[2] to contemporary events or conditions, he has two good, but entirely different, reasons; one is that the problems of political theory are for him at bottom always the same and always moral; the other is that the Socratic dialogue, the form which he used for most of his writings, required a dram- atic setting within the lifetime of Socrates. None the less, Plato's analysis of political evils (e.g. *Repub.* VIII) is based just as much on his observations of post-war Athens as on his recollections of Athenian democracy during the war-period.[3] Again, Isocrates was most deeply affected by the evils of internecine warfare among the Greeks and by the amount of good which a strong but benevolent ruler like Evagoras of Cyprus might do. Plato, despairing of all politicians ever since the execution of Socrates, saw the urgent need for disinterested public service, and tried to devise an educ- ation which would inculcate it. The cleavage between the rich and the poor so alarmed him that he feared nothing so much as the splitting of society into 'two nations'. His almost morbid insistence on the unity of the state has its roots here.[4] Equally alarming was the concentration of much wealth in few hands, causing him to abhor capitalism in all the forms of it known to him. The need for increased technical efficiency in times of short- age led to increased specialisation, notably in military science. This is reflected in both Plato and Xenophon. The power of efficient military autocracy to produce order out of chaos was

---

[1] IV (*Panegyricus*) 167-8.   [2] He does so occasionally—and anachronistically.
[3] See G. C. Field, *Plato and his Contemporaries*, ch. VIII.
[4] And not in any imaginary longing for ancient tribal conditions, as K. R. Popper would have it in *The Open Society and Its Enemies*, Vol. I, esp. chs. 5 and 10. Many of Popper's shafts are well directed against Plato's hostility to a free society, but many others are wide of the mark, and there is no need to invent a cumbrous and even erroneous terminology which can only add to what he calls (p. 27) the 'pretentious muddle of the philoso- phers'. Isocrates (VII 54) was also worried by the contrast between rich and poor, but he thought that old-fashioned charity would be able to mend it. Plato, whatever one may think of his solution, knew better than that.

demonstrated by the career of Dionysius I of Syracuse and stimulated a revival of the 'strong man' fallacy and the belief in the
leadership of one man. The weakness of the smaller states as compared with the greater led to the formation of groups and leagues.

Herein lie two pointers to two notions about government which
were prominent in the fourth and third centuries before Christ:
federations or leagues of states, and the belief in a sole-ruler.
What may be called the Federal idea owed nothing to the theorists and received little attention from them. This is in keeping
with the already-noted tendency to neglect problems of inter-
state relationships except in war and concentrate attention on the
city-state. But it was most unfortunate; we have no record of a
Greek political philosopher discussing such questions as 'How
can a group of states be welded together for mutual aid and
protection without sacrificing too much of their separate auto-
nomies?' Yet men of intelligence and understanding were asking
these questions and trying out possible answers. One answer was
interchange of citizenship; each citizen becomes a member also
of the other cities in the group, but each city manages its own
affairs. This was called ἰσοπολιτεία, equality of citizenship. Another form of federation was sympolity, συμπολιτεία. In it each
man, in addition to being a member of his own city, is a member
of a larger body, and this larger body is organised as a federal
union. In various parts of the Greek world various forms of
federation were tried by groups of cities in need of support. Unfortunately these efforts at co-operation among the lesser powers
were met with hostility and suppression by the greater; and it is
hardly likely that the support and interest of political theorists
would have rescued them. The time-honoured principles of city-
autonomy, recognised in theory even by the Persian king,[1] could
easily be invoked against such experiments, when it suited, for
example, the Spartan domination to do so. But there could be no
such formal objection to a state ruled by one man, a wise and
successful leader of his people. The age of the tyrants was past,
the general disorder seemed to call for a firm hand, and the time
seemed ripe for a man of courage and ability. This idea, unlike
the other, permeated much of the political writing of the century.
It was far more easily assimilated into the general trend of poli-

---

[1] In the terms of the Great King's Peace or the Peace of Antalcidas,
387-6 B.C.

tical thought than the federal ideas and got perhaps more than its share of attention. On the other hand it is significant that in practice there was not the slightest tendency among the large and well-established states to look for a single ruler to govern them. In outlying parts Archelaus, while Athens and Sparta were still at war, had done more than all his predecessors to put Macedon on a war-footing; Dionysius I of Syracuse was keeping the Carthaginians out of Eastern Sicily. But these examples appear to have affected theory more than practice. The *Hiero* of Xenophon and the Evagoras essays of Isocrates are attractive expositions of the 'benevolent despot' theory, to which the man-in-the-street readily succumbs; but in effect he only believes that autocracy is good *for other people*. At Athens, if another Alcibiades had appeared, he would probably have met with the same fate. The old fear of tyranny, the same mixture of distrust, jealousy and half-guilty admiration would have been stronger than the political theories. Of course, now that Alcibiades was safely dead, there was a tendency to praise him, to make his memory into a kind of cult; like Socrates, he became a centre of controversy and the subject of many essays and speeches. He had been a close friend of Socrates, and the defence of one was part of the defence of the other. Thus if the 'democratic' dread of the man of outstanding ability was less strong now, it was partly because there was a dearth of such men.

However important it may be to remember the economic and historical background of the writers of the fourth century, the major influence at work is to be found rather in the previous thinkers, in the thought which we have traced in earlier chapters, particularly from Protagoras to Socrates. The influence of Thucydides is as yet scarcely discernible; no one had learned from him the connection between history and politics.[1] But the influence of Socrates is widespread and paramount. It extends to every school of thought, Cynic and Cyrenaic no less than the Academy, the Porch or the Peripatos. Many 'Socratic discourses' and some anti-Socratic writings appeared in the early fourth century. We possess only those of Plato and Xenophon, with a little of Aeschines Socraticus and a few fragments of Antisthenes. None of these followed every step of the master. Probably none, not even

[1] The rhetorical influence of Thucydides is another matter. See W. Jaeger, *Paideia* III, p. 102.

Plato, entered fully into understanding that enigmatic and δαιμόνιος personality; and if Plato owed him most, he also added
most, having most to add. At the same time we must not forget
the earlier influences. The old question 'What is the best πολιτεία,
best form of constitution?' is still to the fore. But there is a
difference. As well as asking 'What is the ideally best city?' men
asked 'What is the best possible city?' A hundred years before
this time there was hardly any difference between these two questions. Freedom had been won, all things seemed possible, perfection might well be attained. But in the state of the Greek world
in the fourth century B.C. the gap between the perfect and the
attainable was all too wide. Nor could anyone be any longer
satisfied with the simple choice of the One, the Few or the Many,
as in Herodotus' Persian debate; and Plato, as we shall see, returns more than once to classification of constitutions. Moreover,
a century of political experience and the work of fifth-century
educationists and their study of Man had shown that in any form
of government the personal quality, ἀρετή, of the men in it counts
for a great deal. It was a matter of great practical importance to
know how, and indeed whether, this 'political goodness' could
be acquired and by whom. It was inevitable that Plato, Isocrates
and Xenophon for all their differences should each address
himself to the problem of educating citizens and statesmen.

Plato was born about 427 B.C. Thus his formative years were
spent in the Athens of Euripides and Aristophanes and the Peloponnesian war, not in the post-war period. But to judge from his
writings, that war, which so profoundly affected Thucydides, had
not in itself much to teach Plato. As a boy he must have known
of the fate of Melos, of the Athenian expedition to Sicily and its
disastrous end, but the strongest influences on his youth were his
friendship with Socrates, and his family circle. The latter inclined
him towards an active life in politics, the example of the former
towards abstention from them. This tension continued all his life.
His talents were altogether remarkable. We remember him here as
a political philosopher, but he was or could have been also a poet,
a dramatist, a mathematician, a story-teller, a mystic, a metaphysi-
cian, a statesman, a theologian. What indeed in the intellectual
or artistic sphere could he not have been, except a historian?
The events of human history, their accurate and truthful recording, which meant everything to Thucydides, meant nothing to

his one intellectual equal. For Plato historical truth hardly deserved the name. But if facts were of little account, time was of less; only eternity really mattered.[1] Others before Plato had attempted to view human life not as a record but *sub specie aeternitatis*, but Aeschylus and Sophocles were poets. To the poet's and to the dramatist's vision Plato added the insight of the philosopher and the mystic. His belief in an ultimate reality, which is unseen and eternal and 'laid up in heaven', his belief that emotional as well as intellectual effort is needed in the approach to truth, these, beginning early and intensified later, were part of his very being and deeply affected his political thought.

Towards the end of his life Plato wrote a number of letters, some of which, in addition to serving an immediate purpose, were intended to justify and give a true version of incidents in his own career. Here for once Plato was at any rate professing to set down actual facts, and the autobiographical portions of the letters are not only useful as information about his life, but have a bearing on his political thought. A passage at the beginning of the seventh letter bears on his early life and on the effect which the death of Socrates had on his attitude to politics. So, though often quoted, it shall here be reproduced in full:

'In my youth I had the same idea as many others; I thought that, as soon as I grew up and could lead my own life, I would take part in the affairs of my country. And it so happened that events took a lucky turn for me. The existing constitution at the time [404 B.C.] fell into disfavour with many people and a change took place, whereby the government passed into the hands of fifty-one persons, eleven in Athens itself, ten in Piraeus (each of these two groups was concerned with trade and other local matters in the two towns), and Thirty were appointed governors of the whole state with absolute powers. Among the Thirty were several of my own relations and friends and they at once invited me to join them. "Just the very thing for me", they told me, and I was too young to question it. I thought that their aim was to turn the city from its life of injustice to the way of justice and so to govern it. I therefore paid particular attention to see how they would act. In a very short time I found that the previous régime was a golden age beside this one. One of their crimes was to send Socrates, an elderly friend of mine, whom I would not hesitate

[1] See for example *Repub.* x 604 c and *Laws* vii 803 b.

to call the most righteous man of his time, in company with some others to make a forcible arrest of another citizen with a view to his execution [Leon of Salamis, p. 90]. Their object was to implicate Socrates in their activities whether he liked it or not. But he refused; he was prepared to suffer anything sooner than be a party to their unlawful actions. The sight of these and other no less heinous crimes aroused my indignation and I withdrew from any participation in those unhappy events. Not long after the whole government of the Thirty collapsed. Then my desire for a life of political activity drew me back again, though only very slowly. In the new government, uncertain of itself, there was plenty to find fault with; it is not surprising that the change involved some cases of vengeance on foes. But on the whole the restored democrats behaved with great fairness. Some influential persons, however, as ill luck would have it, brought my friend Socrates into court on a charge that was most unfair and particularly inappropriate to the man. They actually indicted him for being irreligious, and the court found him guilty and put him to death. Yet this was the very same Socrates who on the previous occasion had refused to participate in the unlawful arrest of one of their own friends at a time when their cause looked hopeless.

'I reviewed these facts; I thought about the men who take part in public affairs, and about law and morality, and the more I thought and the older I grew, the more difficult it appeared to be to manage the affairs of State *aright* (ὀρθῶς). In the first place it was impossible to do anything single-handed, to act without firm friends and loyal supporters; and there were few of these left in a city where life was no longer lived in accordance with the old traditional morals and habits, while new friends could only be made with difficulty. In the second place the disregard of every precept of law and morality was increasing so vastly that I, who at first was full of eagerness for a political career, now looking on all this and seeing everything in a state of confusion finally lost my bearings altogether; and, while I could not refrain from seeking to know how things might be improved in these respects and in the whole business of πολιτεία, yet so far as doing anything was concerned, I had to continue to bide my time. In the end I came to the conclusion that all modern states without exception are badly constituted and badly governed, because the condition of their laws and customs is well-nigh incurable without the aid of abundant resources and exceptional good fortune. So I was forced to the conclusion that the solution lay in right education as the only basis for right action by cities or by individuals; and further, that the nations of mankind would never be rid of their troubles until either men who were rightly and truly educated should come to hold the ruling offices in the state or else by some miracle those who hold power in cities become truly educated.'[1]

Such were the comments of the elderly Plato looking back at a critical period in his early life. The two tendencies, one towards and the other away from politics in action, are still vividly remembered, but the figure of Socrates the master is somewhat faded. It is easy for an old man to attribute to his younger self ideas and knowledge gained only in later years, but unless Plato is doing this here, he early saw that the would-be practical reformer must lead a band of fellow-workers and not live in isolation, that disorder and confusion in morals mean disorder and confusion in politics, so that right education becomes the prime need. In the state of mind described in that letter he left Athens for a time on a visit to Eucleides of Megara, himself a philosopher and a writer of dialogues. Plato may have begun to write dramatic sketches about Socrates during that visit, but we do not know how long he stayed. At any rate the first period of his literary activity may be put between the death of Socrates in 399 and the travels of 387 which immediately preceded the foundation of the Academy. This journey took him to Sicily and to South Italy, and its outcome was important for Plato's future life and thought. At Syracuse he met (and disliked) the great Dionysius I, who had made such a name for himself, and his brother-in-law Dion, with whom he formed a close friendship. At Tarentum he met Archytas, who was not only ruler of his city but a man well-versed in Pythagorean philosophy. This combination of political power and philosophical education must have interested Plato greatly, for, whatever the political teaching of Pythagoras himself may have been (see Chap. II), Plato held the Pythagoreans of his own day in high esteem and shared many of their beliefs and enthusiasms.

---

[1] Plato says ὀρθὴ φιλοσοφία, ὄντως φιλοσοφεῖν. 'Education' is inadequate but 'philosophy' is not right either; it makes the statement far more paradoxical than it sounds in Greek. Isocrates and many others accepted the principle, but differed widely as to what education in philosophy comprised. Cp. p. 77 n. 2 and see further below.

So much the more unfortunate then that he did not write an account of the Archytas régime at Tarentum, of the combination of ruler and mathematician. It is reasonable to infer that he was favourably impressed; for as soon as he returned to Athens he set up a school, which soon acquired a reputation for turning out able, practical statesmen, the famous Academy of Plato. Indeed this new institution had some resemblance to the old brotherhood of Pythagoras: it had a religious basis and its activities were part of a cult of the Muses; mathematics were of fundamental import-ance. For a thousand years it continued to exist, but under later directors it became less political. In the years that followed its foundation, however, many students from many parts came to the Academy, hoping to get from Plato what an earlier generation had asked of Protagoras and his contemporaries—an education which would help them to realise their political ambitions. Many indeed were very successful in their careers afterwards and bear witness to the practical value of the Academy training.

Unfortunately, however, we know very little about that train-ing. It must have been directed towards the attainment of high intellectual and moral standards. For the former end, and perhaps for the latter too, the subject of mathematics was considered es-sential. Mathematics was the only branch of knowledge sufficiently advanced in Plato's day to provide a first-class intellectual disci-pline; there was nothing at all in the linguistic sphere and very little in the legal or scientific. Besides, number was incorporeal and eternal, and therefore of supreme importance to Plato as an object of knowledge. Logic and dialectic too there must have been, but of practical lessons in running a city there was almost certainly little or nothing. Plato had a horror of those who thought it sufficient to pick up a few tricks of the trade, acquiring superficial knowledge like a coat of sunburn in order to avoid the long and arduous but exciting pursuit of philosophical knowledge. Nor could a true philosophical education be acquired from books. 'On these matters', he writes,[1] 'there is no book of mine and never will be; it cannot be put into words like other subjects. Know-ledge of it can only be attained by long association and joint con-centration' (by master and pupil). He goes on to compare the process to a brand catching fire from another and thereafter feed-ing its own flame.

[1] *Epistle* VII 341 C.

It does not tell us much about the training at the Academy to know that it relied more on inspiration than on information and discouraged the use of text-books; and in the only direct reference in the seventh letter (329 B) to his work there, Plato only says that he liked it very much. But this hint is perhaps just enough to mark what will become clearer later on, that Plato's methods were very different from those of fifth-century teachers of 'political goodness' and from those of his contemporary Isocrates, who also claimed to teach φιλοσοφία. What is most puzzling, however, is to know how these and other such remarks[1] about books are to be related to the dialogues of Plato, from which inevitably we derive most of our knowledge of his political thought. Presumably Plato is warning his readers that his works are not to be regarded as treatises on a particular subject, but simply as dialogues, dramatic sketches showing how the search for truth may be conducted by the question-and-answer method which Socrates had used. In this form, it may be, Plato felt able to give play to his desire to write and create works of art, while still maintaining his mistrust of the written word. However, in later life the desire to instruct, to put his own thoughts on paper increased, and the dialogue-form becomes less of a reality. If no one would call the *Gorgias* a text-book, neither would anyone mistake the *Laws* for a real dialogue; it is much more like a treatise on government than Plato would have allowed himself to write in his younger days.

We are in no position to say with any exactitude what is the relationship between the text of the Platonic writings and the spoken words of Socrates. But since in an earlier chapter an attempt was made to assess the contribution which Socrates through his life and his convictions brought to the study of the πόλις, now therefore it would be well to state, again tentatively and with reserve, what Socratic positions Plato adopted when he began to

---

[1] He returns to the subject later in the same letter (344 B - D) where he singles out laws as being particularly unsuitable as a subject for written work. Yet he himself at 73 was probably already writing his *Laws*! Objections to the written word are made in the dialogues; and in the Second Letter (314 C) he goes so far as to call his writings 'sayings of a rejuvenated Socrates'. Whatever that may mean, it cannot be applied to the *Laws*. The mistrust of the written word is not confined to Plato. It was an affectation shared by other Socratics (O. Gigon, *Sokrates*, Bern, 1947, p. 18) and goes back not to Socrates merely but to Pythagoras (*supra* p. 27).

write dialogues, and thus to indicate some of the ways in which the influence of Socrates on political thought persisted. In the first place Plato shared the belief that there is Universal Knowledge and Universal Right and that lack of knowledge is the main reason for the lack of goodness, both in the conduct of our lives and the management of our cities. Everywhere he found politicians ignorant, yet the first requisite of a statesman is knowledge, especially knowledge of good and evil. And this for Plato means not simply right opinion, but knowledge of Universal Right, of τὸ δίκαιον. As time went on, he became more than ever convinced that Socrates was right in 'bringing epistemology into political philosophy' (p. 87), and he worked out a theory of kinds or degrees of knowing, in which the supreme knowledge was that of the Good. Again, Plato, and after him Aristotle, regarded the πόλις as something natural, as Socrates did; it was κατὰ τὴν φύσιν, in accordance with the nature of man, not of animals. Thirdly, he shared Socrates' view that it is better to suffer than to commit injustice, since it does less real harm to the man; it does no harm to his mind or soul, and that is the part of him which he ought always to look after. What degree of submission to authority and what kind of authority the acceptance of this view involves is a fundamental problem of ethics, on which, as we saw in Chap. V, Plato parted from Socrates, even as Socrates had parted from Protagoras. Does moral autonomy belong to the πόλις, or to the individual, or only to God? Plato, accepting the third view, is faced with the task of bringing transcendental morality down to human life, of bridging the gap between God and man. The older Plato grew, the more this question pressed itself upon him (see Chap. X).

The first of the dialogues[1] to deal with questions of right and wrong in relation to the πόλις is the *Crito*, to which reference has already been made. As was there (p. 93) pointed out, two theories of the state are used to support the case for absolute obedience to

---

[1] It is assumed that *Crito* and *Apology* belong to the decade following Socrates' death and that *Gorgias* is not much later, at any rate before 387; that *Republic* and *Politicus* were composed between 386 and 367; that *Laws*, like the *Letters*, were written in his last years, when both his Sicilian ventures (see below) were over. It is assumed too that, while in *Crito*, *Apology*, *Gorgias* there is a good deal of the real Socrates overlaid by Plato, in the dialogues after 386 we have mainly Plato.

its decrees and to the verdicts of its courts. The comparison of the
πόλις to a father or mother, to whom all citizens owe love and
allegiance, is not peculiarly Platonic. In the great days of the
city-state the relationship was not unlike that of benevolent parent
and loyal son, and the πόλις, while encouraging and recognising
family obligations, had taken over or canalised much of the power
of the family. There is indeed some successful archaising[1] in the
arguments which Plato makes the personified constitution of
Athens use: many of Socrates' contemporaries were rejecting
them and asserting the right of the son or the citizen to hit back.[2]
'Have you forgotten', say the Athenian laws, 'that your country
is of more account than your mother or father or all your ancestors put together, more august and sacrosanct and held in higher
honour both among gods and among men of understanding? You
ought to pay it respect and deference, and make more efforts to
placate the anger of a fatherland than of a father. If you cannot
win it over to your view, you must do as it commands and bear
without murmur the burdens it imposes, be they stripes or im-
prisonment, wounds or death in war ... it is impious to offer
violence to father or mother, still more to one's country' (*Crito* 51).
Of the other theory, that of a contract between city and citizen,
what little is said in the dialogue relates almost entirely to the
case in question. The long-continued residence of a citizen in a
city is taken as evidence that he has undertaken to obey its laws;
and it is argued that the acceptance of this contract was free,
since he could have gone elsewhere to live, if he did not like the
city in which he was born. How like Plato to forget that the vast
majority of people have no freedom of choice as to where they
shall live! But no attempt is made on this contract-basis to work
out a theory of the relationship between the state and its members
and it would be unfair to take much notice of it. What is of more
significance for Plato's future is the hint at the end of the dialogue
that there is a life after death, and that laws in this world have
'brethren' in the world hereafter and are not less divine than they.
If Socrates has been unjustly treated it is by men and not by οἱ νόμοι.
Many years later Plato returned to this conception, and his last

---

[1] That is, if we assume, as was done in Chap. V, that Plato is not deriving
them from what Socrates actually said.

[2] τυπτόμενον ἀντιτύπτειν, *Crito* 51. Similarly of son and father in Aristophanes, *Clouds* 1321-1344.

great political work, the *Laws*, seeks to devise a constitution both legal and theocratic.

Of Plato's *Gorgias* something has already been said (pp. 76-78), as illustrating both the superman theory of Callicles and the rhetorical training for politics given by Gorgias and Polus, and the connection between them. Rhetoric, in itself neither moral nor immoral, furnishes its possessor with power over others, and thus readily becomes a tyrant's weapon, a source of a superman's strength. But the Socratic-Platonic side of the arguments in this dialogue has a positive value in political thought. The art of πολιτική is conceived as relating to the mind (464 B), a counterpart to those arts which relate to the body—medicine and physical culture. In this analogy the statesman is compared to a trainer or physician, whose aim is to produce health, while the rhetorician is like a cook, who is trying to tickle the palate. If the aim of the statesman is to secure the well-being of the state, rhetoric provides no clue to what that condition is. Thus, more broadly speaking, the purpose of the *Gorgias*, as one of Plato's later followers[1] said, is to discuss 'the ethical foundations from which we may proceed to political well-being'. The famous Gorgias is not depicted as an immoralist, and the eager Polus even goes so far (482 D) as to agree with the Socratic dictum 'it is more disgraceful to commit than to suffer wrong'. But for Callicles πολιτική has no ethical foundations whatever; he has nothing in common with Socrates except (and it is an important exception) intellectual honesty (487 B - 488 B). If the keynote to the Platonic Socrates' view of life is *self-control*, that of his opponent here is *self-expression*; and since political well-being depends on the life and character of the man (*supra* p. 35), the question 'What kind of man to be and what aim to pursue'[2] is of prime importance. 'For you see,' says Socrates in the dialogue (500 C) 'that the subject of our discussion is one which anyone with any intelligence must take seriously. After what manner ought we to live?' This is a question which must have been constantly in the mind of the historical Socrates and to which his whole life was his answer. But for Plato there still remained the problem how to relate Socrates' answer, which must have been right, to the lives of other men. For, since civilised life meant life in a city, this question ὄντινα χρὴ τρόπον

---

[1] Olympiodorus, an Alexandrian neo-Platonist of the fifth century A.D.
[2] Ποῖόν τινα χρὴ εἶναι τὸν ἄνδρα καὶ τί ἐπιτηδεύειν.

ζῆν; can only be asked in relation to the πόλις. At this point one is tempted to ask which of the two is to be considered first? Ought we to say that such and such is the right way for men to live and that the city must be organised accordingly? Or are we to start with the city-life, determine its nature and purpose and require men to conform to it? But, as was pointed out at the beginning of this book (Introd. p. 6), a question formulated in that way implies an antithesis which in the Greek city-state was unreal. We recall this fact here because it is important to remember that Plato, for all his revolutionary ideas about the whole basis of politics, was thoroughly orthodox and old-fashioned in linking city and citizen indissolubly.[1]

Broadly speaking there are two ways of life. They can be variously labelled, but a label can do no more than indicate a single feature or a typical example: on the one hand there is Socrates, on the other his accusers; on the one hand the politician, on the other the philosopher. One of the two might be described as the Way of the World, of the successful man, the ruthless Archelaus of Macedon, powerful and efficient, or of the older politicians—Pericles, Themistocles and even Solon himself. In the *Gorgias*, which took its start from a discussion on rhetoric, the emphasis is on the politician or ῥήτωρ on the one hand and the philosopher on the other. What matters therefore is the relationship of these two kinds of life to the life of the community. Isocrates, as we shall see presently, denied that there was any opposition between the two. But for Plato it was fundamental, and the reason for it was that the politicians lacked knowledge. A training indeed they might have; since the middle of the fifth century there had been many who professed to teach political 'goodness', being 'good at politics'. But if we accept the doctrine that goodness is knowledge and if the professed teacher or σοφιστής has no knowledge, the pupil learns nothing but a routine, a set of tricks and so becomes a mere persuader, πειστικὸς μόνον, skilled in the use of words, but incapable of telling you anything worth knowing. The

[1] There is, however, another issue here and it transcends the Greek πόλις. Is the State to be so organised that all men may *have a chance* to live the right life or so that all men *shall* live the right life and be forced to do so? This is not discussed in the *Gorgias* but, as we shall see (*infra*, Chap. IX) Plato held the view that once you have found for certain what is the right way, it is your duty to *compel* men to live according to it. The patient must do as the doctor bids him.

same complaint is made by Plato about poets, both here in the *Gorgias* and elsewhere, that they use their skill in words to amuse and not to instruct. But the true statesman ought both himself to instruct and employ artists with a true message to deliver. It is not the business of either poet or statesman to provide pleasure or amusement, but to educate. This is just where in Plato's view Athenian statesmen in the past had failed; Cimon, Miltiades, Themistocles and Pericles are all condemned because they did not educate the people, but only tried to please and flatter them. This is manifestly unfair, but Plato was not concerned about historical truth. Nor was he self-consistent[1] in his errors; in the *Phaedrus* (270 A) he allows Pericles to have had some philosophy. In the *Protagoras* Pericles and Themistocles are cited as examples of political 'goodness', when the question is raised why they did not transmit or teach it to their sons. In the *Meno* (99 B) a similar question is asked, and the answer is given that they could not transmit it because they had no knowledge but only right opinion. But here they are not credited with either ability or right opinon. However, it matters little to Plato's argument that this picture of Pericles as an obsequious servant of the Demos is grossly inaccurate. It still remains his view that if the statesman is to be an educator, he must have knowledge. What the object of that knowledge should be is discussed fully in the *Euthydemus* and the *Republic*; only a hint is given in the *Gorgias*. The central question now is what kind of man should he be into whose hands political power may be put? He must be really capable of educating, διδασκαλικός, not merely πειστικός, persuasive, possessed of skill at his work and also righteous, δίκαιος, ἀγαθός, and he must not aim at securing advantage for himself. He must regard the people as a doctor regards his patients, sparing no pains to make and keep them healthy, but being concerned more with their minds than their bodies. Like a physician he will demand strict conformity to his regimen; a doctor cannot be expected to cure a patient who goes on eating and drinking to excess.[2] Over-indulgence in bodily pleasures is harmful also to the soul, and the statesman-

[1] Any more than Isocrates, who himself calls our attention to the fact XII (*Panath.*) 172.

[2] A favourite analogy in Plato. See especially *Epist.* VII 330 D - 331 D. He would not have used it so constantly, had it not suited so well the authoritarian trend in his political philosophy.

educator must be ruthless in reducing or forbidding these and eager to inculcate self-control and other virtues. He who, failing to control himself, commits faults needs punishment, actually needs it as the patient needs medicine, because it is good for him, and he will not be well in soul, $\epsilon\mathring{v}\delta\alpha\acute{\iota}\mu\omega\nu$, until he has had it. Righteousness and good-conduct are essential to happiness and the aim in life both of city and citizen is to secure these. Political well-being depends on maintaining the virtues and punishing the vices; you can only make men happy by making them good. The true statesman has no doubt whatever that it is a greater disgrace to do wrong than to suffer it. Naturally men want to avoid suffering wrong; but he who is justly punished is not wronged but 'righted',[1] and even he who is unjustly punished (like Socrates, whose death is 'foretold' in this dialogue) is not any the worse for it. For though his body may show stripes and bruises, his soul never will, not even when he passes to a life beyond the grave.[2] The citizens must be taught that the soul is of more value than the body, that they must not merely obey those in power, but copy their whole way of life. Authority sets the standard, whether the ruling power be the One, the Few or the Many. He who copies well will be most successful. If he is a good king's man or a good party-man he may expect to be rewarded with material advancement as well as by the preservation of his life. But for all his success in life, such a man is still a copyist. Though he may fancy himself a statesman, he is not $\pi o\lambda\iota\tau\iota\kappa\acute{o}s$ in the true sense, since he is not an educator. If Plato had to interview a candidate for a political career, he would question him thus: 'Which of the citizens have you made a better man? Is there any-one, slave or free, citizen or foreigner, who was formerly a bad man, utterly unrighteous and uncontrolled, and who is now, thanks to you, honest and respected? . . . Have you done any-thing in your private life which shows your fitness for a political career? . . . You may have your own ideas on being a statesman among us, but let me tell you that his one duty is to make us, the citizens, as good as he can' (515 A - C). The so-called improvements of the so-called statesmen, the shipyards, the docks, the

---

[1] Like the Scots term 'justified'. Plato, like Protagoras, (p. 56 n. 3) moves away from the traditional view of punishment as purely retributive.

[2] The 'myth' of the *Gorgias* 523-527. The soul after its separation from the body will still show the sins which it has committed.

walls, the tribute, these are all dismissed as so much rubbish.

To the problem of the right kind of person to be a ruler Plato returns again and again, and the founding of a school for statesmen may already have been in his mind when he wrote the *Gorgias*. But the Academy was not the first such school. Isocrates, who was a few years older than Plato, but outlived him, began his school about 392 B.C. and opened it with a kind of manifesto or prospectus entitled *Against the Sophists* in which he attacked the other educationists of his time for their triviality, their extravagant pretensions and high fees. In his youth he had heard both Socrates and Gorgias and in his plan for the training of statesmen he owed something to both. Plato mentions him by name at the end of the *Phaedrus* (279), making Socrates express the view that the young Isocrates would 'go far', as he had the love of wisdom in him. Certainly all his long life Isocrates remained devoted to φιλοσοφία as he conceived it, to general education as the first requisite of a statesman. Though he differed widely from Plato as to what philosophy was, he shared his dislike and distrust of the experts, the sophists of their day, and his indignation at the travesty of education which they provided. The difference lay in the fact that Isocrates did not accept Plato's firm division of ways of life into two and only two kinds (*v. supra*). If it was not possible to reconcile them, at least we could take what is good in each. To say of rhetoric that it teaches the aspiring statesman a potent technique but not how to use it, is a criticism which must be met not by rejecting rhetoric altogether but by combining it with a training in its right use. In Isocrates' view the art of speaking, of writing, of prose composition has in itself an educational value. It is unfair to regard it as a technique for propaganda or for distorting opinion or tickling the fancy (XII 271). Admittedly it does not directly teach morality (XIII 21), but the mere learning of the art is conducive to good behaviour (XII 27). Moreover Isocrates was trying to give a training not merely in the use of words, but in getting things right, finding the best course of action, the best statement of fact and the most appropriate exposition, in short, the right λόγος. This required a high degree of intellectual ability, and for Isocrates the Socratic ἐπι-μέλεια τῆς ψυχῆς was simply the training of the mind and had no transcendental significance, as it had for Plato. Isocrates wanted to see in his pupils a courageous and hard-working spirit, so that the statesman might be a man of character, with the courage of his convictions, and not a mere mouthpiece (XIII 17). He would need knowledge, but the kind of knowledge to which Plato would have denied the name; knowledge of how to get up a subject, of the right kind of things to say and the right time for saying them. In thus making speech and language his guide Isocrates was following Gorgias (λόγος ἡγεμὼν πάντων[1]), but he was not, any more than he, an immoralist. On the contrary, he was as far removed as Plato from the doctrine of self-seeking, and his perfectly righteous man is he who has power to enrich himself but refrains (1 38).

Such in bare outline are the contrast and the resemblance between the educational ideals of Plato's *Gorgias* and of Isocrates. It cannot, however, be said that Isocrates' attempt to bridge the gap between the two was successful. As often happens to would-be mediators, he came under fire from both sides. To the end of his long life he was still battling against the attacks of the sophists, while Plato disagreed entirely with his view of φιλοσοφία, regarding it as no better than the σοφιστική which he was trying to replace. In the previous century, as we saw (p. 61), Prodicus had spoken of a certain kind of sophist as being on the borderline between the philosopher and the politician; Isocrates was the fourth-century counterpart. He believed it to be his task to make politicians better educated, and if he expected Plato's sympathy in this attempt to relate φιλοσοφία to πολιτικὴ πρᾶξις, he had on the face of it good reason to do so. But Plato rigorously condemns such a compromise as a cowardly attempt 'to pluck the fruits of learning without facing its dangers and trials'. Such men, in attempting simultaneously to be philosophers and politicians, fail to be either. We cannot be quite certain that Plato is here[2] referring to Isocrates, but it looks very like it. If so, his judgment was not at fault, for Isocrates met with little success in either field. His school, however, was successful as a training ground of speakers, writers and military commanders; and if his own written work had little influence on contemporary politics,[3] it had great importance in literary history.

Its importance in political thought is harder to estimate. There

---

[1] The phrase is Isocratean, XV 257 =III 9, but the sentiment is thoroughly Gorgianic, *Helen* 8-12.

[2] *Euthydemus* 305-306.

[3] It is greatly disputed what effect Isocrates did have. On the educational

are two things about Isocrates' work which prevent it from holding a high place: first, it is largely second-hand and derivative;
second, it is very much attached to the time, place and situation
which the author at the moment has in mind. He has ideas about
politics rather than political ideas. For example his Pan-Hellenism,
the idea for which he is most often remembered, in all essentials
goes back to Aeschylus and Herodotus and closely to Gorgias,[1]
who wished to extend to inter-state relations the ὁμόνοια of Antiphon and others (p. 63). There is something of his own in his
conception of 'Hellenic' as a cultural rather than a racial term
(IV 50), but his Pan-Hellenism is essentially a plan to secure certain
objects and meet an immediate situation and is not based on a
political principle of general application. It is totally different from
and bears no relation to the Federalist ideas which were noted
earlier in this chapter. These too were limited in their application
to certain situations and received no theoretical treatment that
we know of, but at least they were capable of being so treated.
Isocrates' eloquent appeal for unity among warring Greek states
and for a common front against Persian interference will always
make excellent reading, but the place of the *Panegyricus* in political
thought will never be high. So it is wherever we look among his
many writings. We do not find political principles because he
himself did not set out in search of them, but only of the right
way to deal with a situation; and that for him meant primarily the
right thing to say about it. He had no powers of abstraction, of
seeing how the immediate situation stands in relation to others,
ancient or modern, real or imaginary. But he did not believe this
to be a defect. He owed much to Protagoras and Gorgias, but he
so little understood their greatness and his own weakness that he
poured contempt on their theoretical abstractions (X 1-5) and
claimed to be the really practical man. When he discusses the
merits of a form of constitution, it is always with a particular

theories of Isocrates see Jaeger, *Paideia*, III and H.-I. Marrou, *Histoire de
l'Education dans l'Antiquité* (1948).

[1] Aristophanes, too, is imbued with a sense of Hellenic unity, in the
Acharnians and the *Peace* and later (411 B.C.) in the *Lysistrata* (1112-1135);
cp. also a fragmentary *Olympiac* speech of Lysias (33) and a Funeral oration
doubtfully attributed to him (2), which is full of Isocratean echoes. In fact,
as V. Martin, *Museum Helveticum* I (1944) 15, has shown, there was probably
more Pan-Hellenic feeling, especially in the years 390-387, than Xenophon's
Hellenica would lead us to believe.

place and a particular audience or reader in mind; and since his chief object is always to say the right thing at the right time, it is not surprising that he speaks now with one voice, now with another and is not at all put out by his own inconsistency.[1] He does not ask 'What is the Ideal State?' and even the question 'What is the best possible State?' is one which he prefers to put with reference to a particular set of people and circumstances. In Cyprus the reign of good king Evagoras had shown how well monarchy suited the people, and so for the Cypriots monarchy was a good thing. The Athenians on the other hand had prospered under a moderate democracy and the Spartans under their dual kingship.

Notwithstanding these weaknesses it is worth while to give a brief account of what Isocrates has to say both about one-man government and about πολιτεία or government by a constitution.[2] In his opinion monarchy is not suitable for the majority of Greeks, but the Macedonians cannot live the life to which they are accustomed without it (v 107-108). But it is very different from the Persian monarchy (IV 150) with its degradation of humanity, where all are equal but all are slaves and there is no free association or political life. There is no such objection to the Spartan monarchy, but the best type is that held by Evagoras of Cyprus and after him by his son Nicocles, a pupil of Isocrates. It is morally superior, and in writing a eulogy of Evagoras and exhortations to his son the author is simply describing the ideally perfect ruler, possessed of all the virtues, for which later generations of the Greek world would be hopefully looking in Hellenistic kings. Clearly in one-man rule the character of the ruler is all-important and his education becomes an urgent political problem, while he himself, as Plato saw, must be the educator of his people, both by precept and example. His rule should be based on respect and admiration, not on fear; his high office demands high standards of conduct and ability (II 9-26). Literature should be designed to improve and instruct; but, unlike Plato, Isocrates has here no fault to find with the old Greek poets, traditionally used for in-

---

[1] p. 131 n. 1.

[2] Isocrates sometimes uses πολιτεία in this sense as opposed to government by one man. Aristotle (*infra*, p. 224) restricts it still further. Both writers use it to denote the rights of a citizen (III 15, IV 105). It was Isocrates who coined and repeated the phrase πολιτεία ψυχὴ πόλεως (VII 14, XII, 138), on which see W. Jaeger, *Paideia*, III, p. 112 and W. Nestle in *Philologus* LXX, 1911, p. 34.

struction (II 40-49) or with tragedy, if only men would learn from it. The qualities necessary for a monarch are not the severity associated with the τύραννος, but wisdom, moderation and justice and in particular, gentleness (πραότης), a virtue on which Isocrates laid stress. To educate such a ruler is of course difficult but Isocrates believed that he had found a way. There are various restraints on the lives of ordinary people which keep them from going astray, but the sole ruler must rule himself (II 2-5). The question whether, given the chance, a man should choose to be a single ruler was a stock one and one of no importance, though Xenophon devoted his *Hiero* to it. But Isocrates has things to say on the advantages of sole rule, and these, if not profound, are a good example of the arguments which were current in its favour at a time when it was much discussed (*supra*, p. 120). But it should be noted again that there is no intention of imposing it where it is not wanted.

Monarchy avoids one of the worst features of constitutional governments, whether oligarchic or democratic, their insistence on equal rights and privileges for all citizens irrespective of merit.[1] This kind of equality favours the poorer sort. 'But monarchies give the largest share to the best, the next to the second-best and so on. And even if this has not everywhere taken place, still it is the intention of the constitution that it shall' (III 14-15). Here Isocrates does call monarchy a πολιτεία, and he also ascribes to it something very like the Platonic and Aristotelian proportionate equality[2] and in so doing is ascribing to monarchy advantages which on a different occasion (VII 21 ff., see below) he ascribes to 'ancestral democracy'. Other good features of a monarchical régime call for no comment except scepticism—that decisions are quickly reached, that officials are permanent and know their work and are not distracted by their private interests, that there is greater efficiency in war (III 16-26).

If Isocrates had a conception of an Ideal State, it was not, as Plato's, laid up in heaven nor, as for modern Utopians, in the

[1] The inclusion of oligarchy in this condemnation (usually reserved for extreme democracy, see p. 221) is surprising, but Isocrates is thinking of oligarchies in practice, where only 'The Few' were allowed to be citizens, to share in πολιτεία (IV 104-105).

[2] Plato, *Repub.* VIII 558 C, *Laws* 757 C; Aristotle, *Polit.* III 1280 a. *v. infra*, p. 221 n. 1.

future; it was comfortably wrapped in a roseate past. He believed that the right constitution for Athens existed in the good old days of Solon and Cleisthenes under the good moral influence of the Court of the Areopagus; and his essay called *Areopagiticus* is largely a reconstruction of an idealised 'ancestral constitution'[1] with criticism of fourth-century democracy. If we discard the quasi-historical dress and put Isocrates' Best State into a short summary, the following points emerge:

1. The aim of the State is prosperity (εὐπραγία) and this depends primarily not on military strength or large population but on good government (VII 13).

2. The people should appoint officers of government and demand an account of them (VII 26 f.).

3. Equality is not absolute and the choice by lot is therefore disapproved. The principle of 'proportionate equality', each according to his deserts, is accepted (VII 21-23).

4. There should be no scramble for office; it is right that office should be an expense and not a profit to the holder. Hence the posts of power and responsibility can only be held by persons of means. The democratic principle is thus replaced by the timocratic (XII 131 ff., VII 24-27).

5. A high standard of public service is to be expected (IV 79), and especially it should be the duty of the rich to help the poor so that none shall be in want (VII 83).

6. It follows that the security of property must be maintained in the interest of both rich and poor, but its usufruct must be made available for the needs of all (VII 35).

7. The good government on which εὐπραγία depends will be secured not by excessive legislation (VII 39-42) but by the high moral character and practical ability of those in charge (XII 132-133, XV 79-83).

8. Similarly the good behaviour of citizens generally cannot be maintained by innumerable detailed rules, the existence of which is a symptom of social malaise (VII 40).

9. It follows that the education of the young is a prime duty of the State, but since only the well-to-do will hold office, only they need have a higher education (VII 43).

---

[1] διοίκησις πατρία VII 58. According to Jaeger, *Paideia* III, p. 114, Isocrates avoids the commoner πάτριος πολιτεία as being too much of a political catchword going back to Theramenes.

10. The State should take its religious duties seriously and sensibly (VII 29).

It is no part of our present duty to ask whether this was a feasible political programme or how far it was typical of fourth-century Athenian conservatism. What does concern us is to note that Isocrates considers this to be a pattern of a *democratic* state and himself to be a friend of the people, not μισόδημος, still less ὀλιγαρχικός. Yet some of its features (4, 5, 7 and 8) appear in Plato's aristocracy or his timocracy (see Chap. VIII) and may indeed be borrowed thence.[1] The oligarchy of the Thirty was for him the worst possible government, not indeed a form of government but of force, a δυναστεία.[2] Compared with that even contemporary democracy was tolerable (VII 70). 'But let no one suppose', he adds, 'that my approval applies to those who are in power to-day; the exact contrary is the case' (76). He finds contemporary society to be suffering from the same kind of immoralism that had marked the years of the Peloponnesian War and had incurred the disapproval of Aristophanes and of conservative writers like the Anonymus Iamblichi (Chap. V). The upsetting of all standards and the reversal of moral values were still stock charges brought against popular politicians. Isocrates joins in this attack, accusing them of distorting such terms as Freedom and Happiness, as if they meant unlimited scope for self-gratification.[3] But he is at pains to point out that the ancestral democracy was free of this. So all through his writings Isocrates by his strictures on contemporary moral and political conditions calls to mind on the one hand the attacks of Demosthenes, on the other those of Plato. Once again he appears as half-politician, half-philosopher.

So little has survived of the work of other philosophers in the early part of the fourth century that it is difficult to form a clear picture of their place in political thought. We have some pieces of the Socratic dialogues of Aeschines of Sphettus, but they are

---

[1] The *Areopagiticus* (VII) was written long after Plato's *Republic*.

[2] Cp. Thucydides III 62, and see p. 34 above. Plato (*Laws* 680 B) says δυναστεία was used of a primitive, uncivilised way of life.

[3] It would be an interesting study, both ethical and linguistic, to follow these various 'transvaluations'. Hesiod, *W.D.* 271-272, Thucydides III 82, Plato, *Repub.* VIII 560 D, Isocrates VII 20, XII 131, XV 283 and the παραχαράττειν τὸ νόμισμα of Diogenes (Chap. XII).

not of political interest and he founded no school. Aristippus of Cyrene came to Athens and became an associate of Socrates. His works have all perished and there is hardly anything that we know to be his actual words. But he appears as an interlocutor in Xenophon, who on one occasion depicts him and Socrates discussing ἀρχή and the proper training for those who are to rule and those who are to be ruled. It is assumed that they will be different persons. Socrates lays it down that self-control in all bodily pleasures and fortitude in bodily toil are very necessary in those who are to rule. Aristippus agrees that those who hold office and govern have to work very hard and are obliged to sacrifice many of their pleasures; for his part therefore he would have nothing to do with governing. 'A man has enough to do to look after himself without undertaking also to provide for the other citizens.' The work of holding office is just as much slavery as the life of the underdog; the sensible man will avoid both. 'I think there is a middle path, that runs, not through ἀρχή or through δουλεία, but through Freedom and this is the path that leads to happiness.' It is demonstrated that this application of Cyrenaic hedonism is in practice impossible; such a man will either be without citizen's rights, a foreigner in a city, or else he will be one of the 'ruled' who will have to perform the citizen's duties. Aristippus has no answer to this but to return to the subject of the hardships of office and the painful process of learning the art of ruling. To this Socrates is made to reply that those things which are worth having can only be had by πόνος, by striving for them, as the wise men of old, Hesiod, Epicharmus and Prodicus have shown. There follows *in extenso* the myth of Prodicus on Heracles' choice (p. 61) and we hear no more of the alleged political philosophy of Aristippus. Xenophon's sketch seems to be designed to show that Aristippus did not represent the Socratic traditions of self-control and bearing hardships, while Antisthenes did.

Of this third Socratic, precursor, if not founder,[1] of the Cynic sect, we have also a scene in Xenophon, but it is much less informative. We have a number of sayings and a long list of titles of lost works. Cicero said that he was 'magis acutus quam eruditus'

---

[1] Ancient opinion regarded him as founder. This is rejected by D. R. Dudley, *A History of Cynicism* (1937) and many others, but supported by R. Höistad, *Cynic Hero and Cynic King* (1948) and other historians of philosophy. See further in the notes to this chapter and to Chap. XII.

and modern opinion about his merits is divided. At all events our knowledge of non-Platonic political thought in the fourth century would be greatly enriched if we had any of the political writings attributed to him. Aristotle in discussing the supreme and perfect man[1] refers to Antisthenes' anecdote that when the hares demanded equality among animals, the lions replied 'Where are your claws and teeth?' A different kind of superiority of a leader is exemplified by the shepherd-ruler analogy, which is expressly attributed to Antisthenes by Xenophon (*Symp.* IV 6), though the comparison ultimately goes back to Homer.[2] It is a slender basis on which to build any political theory of Antisthenes. The most that can be said is that his ethic was not centred on the city and its νόμοι, to which he was generally opposed, but on the individual: 'The wise man will not live according to the law laid down by the city but by the law of virtue.' This is one answer to the problem of the 'conscientious objector', but it is not one which Socrates, whose life had raised the problem, would himself have given. Such extreme individualism would soon become incompatible with any form of government, which seems to have been the view of Diogenes the Cynic (Chap. XII). But Antisthenes' quite Platonic dislike of politicians and of contemporary society did not cause him to reject human society altogether. Xenophon (*Symp.* IV 64) makes Socrates praise him as a very useful person for promoting good will among men and in cities. Characteristic of him was the doctrine of πόνος, which went farther than that of Prodicus and made hard work a positive good: 'Whatever the Wise Man does, he works at with all his ἀρετή' (fr. 31). He wrote about Heracles, second only to Prometheus as benefactor (εὐεργέτης) and civiliser of mankind, a notion familiar to Isocrates, who recommended it to Philip of Macedon as an example (Isocr. V 76 and 114). The barbarian counterpart was Cyrus the Great founder of the Persian empire, the typically hard-working king, on whom Antisthenes wrote more than one book, doubtless quite as

---

[1] Aristotle, *Pol.* III 1284 a.

[2] ποιμένα λαῶν. The analogy is used in Plato, *Repub.* I 342-343, not very successfully, rejected as between mortal men in Plato, *Politicus* 267-275. It forms the basis of a discussion in Xenophon, *Mem.* III, chs. 2-7, and lies behind much of the monarchical ideas of his *Cyropaedia* (see Chap. IX). It is therefore possible that Xenophon was indebted for these passages to Antisthenes, who also wrote in praise of Cyrus. (K. Joel, II 1053-1061; see notes at end of the chapter.)

unhistorical as Xenophon's (Chap. IX, p. 172). That Antisthenes looks forward not merely to Cynicism, but to Hellenistic kingship and the philosophy of the Stoics hardly needs to be pointed out.

FURTHER NOTES AND REFERENCES
CHAPTER VII

GENERAL. *Cambridge Ancient History*, Vol. VI, ch. III (M. Cary) and ch. XVI (E. Barker). W. Jaeger, *Paideia* II (Eng. Trans.), pp. 126-160. G. C. Field, *Plato and his Contemporaries* (1930) Part II. The 'cult' of Alcibiades really began in his lifetime. Cp. Xenophon's description of his return (*Hellen.* I 4, 11-20) and see I. Bruns, *Das literarische Porträt* (1896), pp. 509 ff.

PLATO: *Epistle* VII 324-327 B. *Crito* 50-end. *Gorgias passim* but especially 488-522.

ISOCRATES: His writings are voluminous and repetitive. The references are to the numbering of speeches and sections in the Teubner text (Blass, 2nd edit., 1886). No. XIII *Against the Sophists* is incomplete. On monarchy—chiefly the Cyprian speeches II, III and IX and V *Philip*, with J. Sykutris on the *Evagoras* in *Hermes* LXII (1927) and F. Taeger, 'Isokrates und die Anfänge des hellenistischen Herrscherkultes' in *Hermes* LXXII (1937). On 'polity'—chiefly VII *Areopagiticus* and XII *Panathenaicus*. (The latter, like XV *Antidosis*, belongs to his old age, but he is constantly looking back, and defending his early career.) X *Helen* and I *Ad Demonicum*. Also G. Mathieu, *Les Idées politiques d'Isocrate*, 1925, chs. XI, XII, XIV, and W. Jaeger, *Paideia* III pp. 46-70. (Jaeger dates *Against the Sophists* after Plato's *Gorgias*, to which he thinks it is a reply.)

ARISTIPPUS: Xenophon *Mem.* II 1, 1-18. Diogenes Laertius has mostly anecdotes. A saying is attributed to him in Stobaeus (Ecl. IV, ch. VIII 18 = Hense IV, p. 30) that there is the same difference between kingship and tyranny as between law and no-law (ἀνομία), freedom and slavery.

ANTISTHENES: The fragments (Mullach, *Fr. Philos. Gr.* II) are a disappointing relic of a large output which was early lost. The reconstruction of A.'s thought, its relation to that of Socrates, Plato, Diogenes and others is extremely hazardous, and even the little that is here said (Xenophon *Symp. passim*, Diog. L. VI ch. I) must be taken with reserve. Those who complain of short measure may read R. Höistad's misleadingly entitled *Cynic Hero and Cynic King* (Uppsala, 1948), pp. 104-115, where they will find a *maximum* reconstruction of A.'s political thought. The nature of the arguments used against Aristippus in Xenophon *Mem.* II ch. 1, especially the Heracles πόνος conception, suggests that we may have something of Antisthenes there. K. Joel, *Der echte und der Xenophontische Sokrates*, saw Antisthenes also in *Mem.* III chs. 2-7 and throughout much of the *Cyropaedia*.

CHAPTER VIII

PLATO'S *REPUBLIC*

Πολιτεία γὰρ τροφὴ ἀνθρώπων ἐστίν.[1]

WHEN children have to take an unpleasant medicine, they can be more easily induced to swallow it if the rim of the cup is smeared with honey. On this principle Lucretius (I 936-950) says he used verse to convey his philosophic doctrines. The analogy might be even more aptly applied to Plato's *Republic*, whose exordium is pure honey, giving no indication of the abstruse and difficult, if not actually ill-tasting, draughts in the middle of the cup. A scene of comfort and elegance, men of good taste and good manners engaged in conversation neither too profound nor too trivial—about youth and age, about wealth inherited and acquired, its uses and abuses: and then very gradually we are led on and away. The kindly old host retires and his hospitable house vanishes. But for an occasional dramatic touch the *mise-en-scène* is forgotten. There is no break; the aged Cephalus, before he leaves the company of Socrates and the rest, remarks that one great advantage of having money is that you do not need to be dishonest; you can afford to be good. Questions such as 'What is being good?' and 'Why should men be good?' naturally follow and before long we are drinking the first draughts of the cup which Plato offers, resuming consideration of the problem of the *Gorgias*, that 'most serious of all questions to a man of intelligence—after what manner ought he to live?'[2] The answer of the 'average decent man', which would make righteousness consist in common honesty combined with a readiness to help friends and thwart enemies, is examined and found wanting. The

[1] Plato, *Menexenus* 238 C.   [2] *Repub.* I 352 D, *Gorgias* 500 C.

answer of Thrasymachus, denying that man has any duties, is less easily disposed of, and the challenge to Socrates to show that the just life is better than the unjust is the starting point of the whole discussion; it is not finally answered till the ninth book and the myth of rewards and punishments hereafter in the tenth and last book. On the face of it the just life is hard and is only advantageous, said some of the older moralists,[1] because men had agreed to abstain from wronging each other in the interests of all.[2]

Though the main purpose of this preliminary sketch is to show the inadequacy of some current definitions of justice, both moralist and immoralist, a close reading shows Plato at several points foreshadowing some of the features[3] of the πολιτεία which he later constructs—that rule should be exercised for the benefit not of the ruler but the ruled, that money power and political power should be divorced, that holding office in the State should be unattractive and unprofitable, that strife and disunity in the State are identical with strife and disunity in the human mind. No one, however, could guess what was to come; but readers will be well aware how much was comprised in the Greek notion of πολιτεία, the title which we misleadingly translate *Republic*. Certainly the stress laid on the education of rulers will come as no surprise to readers of Isocrates or of Plato's *Gorgias*, though its content strikes a new and unexpected note; but the concern with nursery and elementary education is striking, its stress on environment, on the learning of the good by imitation and the exclusion of all that is unseemly. These have received the attention, critical and uncritical, of educationists; here we must observe that it is at all times directed towards the needs of the πόλις. Education is valued not for its own sake but because it can and should render a man a fit member of his State. For although the discussion took its start from individual morality and consideration of the just life of the just man, we soon become aware that for Plato justice is *par excellence* the virtue of the community. Justice or Righteousness (δικαιοσύνη) and Injustice (ἀδικία) are the virtue and vice of the State, as of the individual. This shifting of the central interest

[1] See Chap. V.

[2] But especially the interests of the weak. This differentiates it from Thrasymachus' interest of the stronger. Plato ignores the difference. See K. R. Popper, *The Open Society* I 102 ff.

[3] They are of course not necessarily peculiar to Plato; cp. what was said on p. 102.

from the citizen to the city marks a difference in point of view between Socrates and Plato, but not any departure from Socratic principles.[1] Plato was faced with the fact that there was no place for a Socrates in the public life of a Greek state, yet a Socrates, he felt, was just what politics most needed. To construct a state in which the true philosopher should be a guiding influence, and not despised as useless or feared as dangerous, was a task which Plato set himself. Perhaps he did not succeed; the man Socrates would have met his death sooner in the Platonic city than in the Athenian; but Plato was not really thinking of the historical Socrates but of the perfectly just man, who could not fail to be at home in the perfectly just State.

What, then, of the πόλις itself? Whence does it derive and on what does it depend? For Plato, as we saw (p. 127), it had a transcendental basis. The theory of Forms or Ideas can be applied to the State as to other and simpler products of human activity. Just as all tables, for example, have in common a certain *form* (εἶδος, ἰδέα) which makes them to be tables and not some other thing, so there must be a *form* of the πόλις. Existing cities like existing tables are copies, more or less imperfect, of the Ideal City. The Ideal City has a real and not merely a nominal existence, but its existence is incorporeal, 'in heaven perhaps', and any knowledge of it is extremely difficult to acquire. Hence a considerable part of Plato's book is devoted to theory of knowledge and the training of the mind for its pursuit. Plato does not give a direct answer to the question, What is the Idea of the πόλις? How indeed could he, since the written word (p. 125) is incapable of expressing and conveying an answer? The true answer can only be emotionally felt and mystically perceived; for a passionate devotion (ἔρως) is an essential part of a philosopher's equipment and indispensable in one who would see visions of Eternity. All this seems strangely remote from the would-be political reformer, but it was the same Plato who wrote the *Phaedrus* and the *Symposium* who also set out to understand the πόλις; and we can readily see why so much of the language of the *Republic* looks quite inappropriate to political problems. In the 'Form' city there are no political problems, everything is unchanging and eternal. Only those who devote many years to the understanding of the unseen world and earnest contemplation of its wonders will have

---

[1] There were differences of principle too. See pp. 87-88.

the knowledge on which to base real work for the πόλις. You cannot reform what you do not understand.

This duality is one of the things that make the interpretation of the *Republic* especially difficult. One cannot always be sure how much is intended to be descriptive of the essential nature of the city, its Form or Idea, and how much belongs to the mundane existence in which people eat and fight. The latter undoubtedly predominates; words cannot adequately deal with the former. But since the aim of the political reformer is to approach the Ideal as nearly as possible, there is no question of any fundamental difference. Nevertheless Plato does write on two different planes. Sometimes he has clearly Athens in mind,[1] the city where he himself had made no headway, the recalcitrant patient who will not be cured. Yet the highly abstract and metaphysical parts of the work are its very kernel, however remote they may seem from practical politics; and not only are they the basis of the philosophic wisdom of the ruler, but they serve as a vast demonstration of Plato's cardinal doctrine that proper political activity does not depend on the possession of a particular skill, called πολιτικὴ τέχνη, but on transcendental knowledge of the Supreme Good.

To these two preoccupations, the Ideal State and political reform, must be added a third, which is common to both; the parallel between the life and habits (βίος, τρόποι) of a man and those of his city. There is nothing new about this βίος-πολιτεία analogy and nothing abstruse; it was an accepted fact (see p. 35) that the character of a state is reflected in the character of its citizens and *vice versa*. But in the *Republic* it is something more than an analogy. The life which a man leads depends on his mind or soul (ψυχή) more than on his body; so too the State is regarded not as an aggregate of administrative activities but as a mind or soul, exercising over the whole community the same power as the individual man's soul over his body. Socrates had urged that care of the soul (ἐπιμέλεια τῆς ψυχῆς) was a far more important business than those to which most men devoted their energies. Plato now says that this is the duty of the πόλις too, for the State is itself soul as well as body and in its structure is identical with the human soul.

This view will have important consequences; but the discussion

---

[1] e.g. *Repub.* VI 495 A - 496 D and IV 425 C - 427 A (with which compare *Epistle* VII 330 C - 331 B) and II 372 D - 374.

of the State does not start from it. It starts with an examination of the minimum material basis and most elementary form of the πόλις. This is neither an analysis of any existing city nor a historical account of the origin of the πόλις, but an attempt to state what are the minimum requirements necessary for its existence. There is no need to raise the old question whether it exists φύσει or νόμῳ; since it answers to human needs, it must be in accordance with the nature of man. The material needs, food, clothes, houses, and the simple mechanical contrivances required to produce these, can all best be provided, not by the extravagant individualism of a Hippias who could make everything for himself,[1] but by each man specialising in his own craft and contributing his skill to the common good in return for his share in the product of others' skill. Whatever cannot be produced locally must be imported and a surplus of local products will be exported. This commerce is also a specialised occupation. So too, above all, is work of defence; soldiers must be professionals. Whether an army will be needed for aggression as well as defence depends on the standard of living aimed at. If to the simple minimum needs we wish to add all the luxuries of a modern civilised state, these can only be had by encroaching on one's neighbours. Plato knew well that the magnificence of fifth-century Athens had only been created at the expense of her subjects, and he regarded the attempt after the war to maintain the same standard of luxury as not merely economically unsound, but morally and physically unhealthy, calling for the presence of lawyers and physicians in greater numbers than a healthy city ought to have.

So far, then, we have not been learning about a Platonic theory of the state or of government, but merely looking at what a city-state is in its simplest form and in its luxurious form. But there are two anticipations of the Platonic State: first, each man is considered not as a person but as a functionary, the embodiment of a certain skill or craft which he exercises for the benefit of the community. This attitude persists throughout. Second, though there is no talk yet of formal government, the protection (φυλακή) of the State is stated to be in the hands of a professional body of men, endowed not only with skill and courage but with intellectual ability and a love of wisdom. 'But how shall these guardians

---

[1] There is no reference to Hippias in the text. But Plato often refers to the views of others without naming them.

be reared and educated?' asks Socrates (376 C) and then the construction of the Platonic city begins, and begins characteristically with the education of the young of a select group. No special provision is made for the education of the citizens in general; we do not even know whether Plato intended them to learn anything beyond their profession,[1] that they might become weavers or carpenters, merchants or bankers, and so serve the economic needs of the community. Those whose function is to protect the community must possess that rare combination of courage, even fierceness, with gentleness, be ruthless towards external foes, watchful and gentle with their own folk. Their education as future protectors of the people must begin in early childhood and we must therefore presume, though nothing is yet said, that the infants are selected because of the courage and intelligence of their parents, in the hope that these qualities will prove to be hereditary. Their education will be both mental and physical, that is, will cover both μουσική and γυμναστική; but the two are not entirely separate, since each has its value for the other. More particularly 'gymnastic' should have a beneficial effect on the mind or soul, the improvement of which is the chief purpose of all education. In this respect the existing materials used in education are found to be largely unsuitable right from the nursery years on; the common myths are full of unseemly stories about the gods, the dramatic literature is designed to arouse excessive and unhealthy emotions and much of the music is open to similar objections. It is most important that future protectors should have a proper understanding of theology, of which the current accounts were quite false; the divine nature is good, unchangingly good and cannot be the cause of evil either in this life or another. The whole process of education is conceived as putting before the young all that is beautiful, noble, good and true and excluding or suppressing all that is ugly, unworthy, evil and false.

Assuming then that we have successfully selected and properly educated up to the age of twenty a body of men, and, as we see later, women, who by their loyalty, courage and intelligence are well fitted to look after the others, we must go a step further and

---

[1] But unless they also receive a general education, they cannot hope to be eligible for promotion. See G. F. Hourani in *Class. Quart.* XLIII, 1949, pp. 58-60. On the other hand Plato pays so little attention to promotion that he may not have seriously intended it. K. R. Popper, *op. cit.*, and *contra* J. A. Faris in *Class. Quart.* XLIV, 1950, pp. 38 ff.

'choose from among the protectors those who after scrutiny appear to us to be doing eagerly and at all times whatever they deem to be in the interest of the city, the sort of men who would never consent to do anything contrary to that interest' (412 D). These will generally be the older men, but a watch should be kept from youth upwards not only to see which are the most intelligent and courageous, but to find out by testing which have the most unshakable belief in the commonwealth which is in their charge. There will thus be three classes in the State: Rulers or Guardians, who are the supreme protectors, the Auxiliary protectors (ἐπί-κουροι) organised as a military and police force and carrying out the rulers' orders in a variety of ways, and thirdly, as before, the general citizen-body, who carry on their trade, profession or craft but do not participate in the government. Now a firm belief in the goodness of one's own πόλις is necessary in all sections of the citizens. No kind of State, ancient or modern, can endure and be stable unless its members believe in it and grow up in that belief. Every nation has its story and the patriotism of its people is partly a reflexion of the belief in that story. The story itself may change, little or much, in the course of time and there will be variations in historical exactitude. But there must be a history and it must be accepted as true. Plato's imaginary city could not have a history in fact, so it must have one in fiction (ψεῦδος, 414). There is perhaps some grain of fact in the popular myths that make Solon the author of all the liberties of the Athenian citizen and Magna Carta the guarantee of an Englishman's rights; but there is so little that each might almost be classed as a γενναῖον ψεῦδος. For the myth must be a really fine one (γενναῖος), not something paltry or trivial that will command neither belief nor respect. Unfortunately we find that the myth offered to us is to our minds paltry and trivial. Plato must have felt its inadequacy; for he depicts a very reluctant Socrates telling a tale which he admits educated people of his day would not believe, though it is just the kind of myth that ancient poets told. It is a combination of the myth of earth-born men, sprung ready-made and fully equipped from the soil, and of another myth, associating types or races of men with certain metals. This is intended to demonstrate that, although all members of the State have a common origin and are therefore all kin, some have 'gold' in them, some 'silver' and the rest only 'iron or bronze'. In this way the division into three classes becomes part of the historical tradition by which the city lives, and successive generations of its citizens are expected to accept the framework of the constitution as the expression of something inherent in their own natures. But though the workings of heredity may normally be expected to produce children of the same quality as their parents, it cannot always happen so. Arrangements must therefore be made, though Plato is vague about what they should be,[1] for the promotion to the Auxiliaries (or even to the Guardians) of highly exceptional children from the families of the third class; and for the relegation to a lower grade of children unsuitable for the higher into which they were born. The essential is that the work of the State should be done by those best qualified to do it and particularly that the tasks of ruling and protecting should not fall into the hands of the money-loving general body of citizens. The myth might be reinforced by a reference to a command of the gods and a prophecy foretelling the ruin of the country, if ever it should be ruled by the people of iron or bronze. That would be as if the sheep were to usurp the functions of the shepherd and his dog.[2] A dog can be trained not to worry the sheep and the Auxiliaries will receive an education which will strengthen their boldness to face enemies and their carefulness for their own people, make them swift to carry out the commands of the Rulers and to suppress disobedience everywhere.

From this point on (end of Book III) we hear virtually nothing about the mass of the citizens[3] and very little about the Auxiliaries, who are not always carefully distinguished from the senior protectors or Guardians. These are Plato's main preoccupation; the welfare of the flock depends more on the shepherd than on his dog.

[1] See above p. 148, note.

[2] Plato's 'philosophic dog' is briefly treated by the author in *Classical Review* LXII, 1948, p. 61, where the suggestion is made that Plato is turning the tables on those who taught (cp. *supra*, p. 48, n. 4) that man's behaviour can be based on that of animals. But Plato himself makes much use of analogy from animals.

[3] Slaves are not actually mentioned; they have no place in any State. But Plato did not intend his citizens to be without them, as casual allusions show, e.g. the advice to enslave barbarians rather than Greeks (469 B). Thus Plato, if he knew of Antiphon's arguments (Chap. V, *init.*) ignores them. He had no feeling whatever for the brotherhood of man, only for that of the Hellenic race (470).

It is therefore necessary here to add a further word of comment on Plato's three-class society; for those who praise as well as those who disapprove are apt to misunderstand what was intended. The use of the word 'classes', though perhaps inevitable, is unfortunate in view of its modern associations. Plato's classification is based on function in society and on fitness for those functions. His third class embraces employers as well as workers; his Auxiliaries would include parts of a Civil Service as well as Army and Police. The Guardians proper are the supreme authority of government but educationalists and judges (433 C) are included. None of these corresponds to a social class anywhere. But it will be observed that in any form of polity, short of anarchy or despotism, there are in fact three groups—the government, those employed by the government, and the rest of the population. Since these are the necessary components of any State, the difference between one and another will depend largely on the composition of each group and the powers which it can exercise in relation to the others. There is here infinite possibility of variety, notably in regard to:

1. the method of choosing Rulers or a government;
2. the qualifications for being a Ruler;
3. the length of tenure of any power-wielding office;
4. the degree of power and responsibility that is allowed to the agents of the Rulers;
5. the number and variety of the activities which the Rulers through their agents control and direct; and the number left to the free action of all citizens.

This list could be well extended but it will serve to illustrate some of the features of Plato's three groups. (1) Reliance on heredity, though somewhat modified (see below), as a guide to choice of Rulers and Auxiliaries is clearly a reflexion of Plato's own background of hereditary aristocracy; and taken together the two groups do resemble a social class. But (2) the qualifications of a Ruler do not depend on birth but on character; they are intellectual and moral, not technical. No one can be a Ruler until after a long and elaborate philosophical training. (3) The Rulers appear to hold office from the age of fifty for life or until they are too old. But can an unsatisfactory Ruler be dismissed by his colleagues? It would be a potent cause of στάσις if it were so, but Plato appears to have been satisfied that no unsatisfactory person would have survived the thirty years of training and apprenticeship. He condemns as unsound the democratic idea of holding office by turns for a limited period. (4) We learn so little about the duties of Plato's Auxiliaries that we cannot say much about the powers or responsibilities, yet for the general working of any State this is a matter of great moment. Plato passes very lightly over the relations between the second and the third groups, but he does realise that he is leaving out much detail and that for example (425 D, E) it will be necessary at some stage to make regulations governing taxation and certain commercial transactions. So it may perhaps be said that the Auxiliaries have little authority of their own, but have to carry out orders of the Rulers and to act under written (?) regulations. But the inference is doubtful. (5) Plato's government would control education very closely and minutely, paying particular attention to the moral training of the two ruling groups, encouraging music and the arts, but exercising a strict censorship and insisting on the maintenance of unchanging norms. Beyond a vague injunction to see that there shall be no undue disparity in wealth, we hear of no control over trade, economic policy or the means of production, whether of food or machinery. All these are left to the free initiative of the third group; they alone are interested, whether as owners or workers. But there is a general understanding that each will serve the community according to his capacity.

Plato, then, regards it as essential that in a State constructed on natural principles[1] its members should be classified according to their ability to perform the work required of them. The citizens need, not that illusory 'political goodness' which the fifth-century teachers had pursued, but in the first instance moral qualities. The goodness of a Ruler is Wisdom, of the Auxiliaries Courage, of the Rest Obedience. But clearly there can be no rigid separation of these virtues; the Rulers must have courage and the Auxiliaries, though not requiring supreme wisdom, must have a love of knowledge and acquire right beliefs; they must also be obedient. Moreover the virtue of σωφροσύνη is wider in its meaning than obedience to authority and includes loyalty, steadiness and self-

---

[1] κατὰ φύσιν 482 E *et saepe*. He uses the expression with obvious approval, so that G. R. Morrow, 'Plato and the Law of Nature' in *Essays in Political Theory presented to George H. Sabine* (1948) argues that for Plato the realm of φύσις was the world of Ideas.

control; it is indispensable in all three.[1] But the third and largest group will not need and could never acquire any real wisdom or knowledge but only that of their several crafts.[2] What then of Justice? Like steady loyalty it belongs everywhere and is described as a principle governing the relations between the groups; it is *just* that each group should confine itself to its own duties and not interfere with others, the contrary is *unjust*. The notion that justice is a quality of a social order could hardly have been more strongly put, but it bears little resemblance to the quality of the just man from which the discussion began. Plato therefore sets out to see (434 D) whether it is really applicable to the individual man; if so, all will be well; if not, we must go back to the πόλις. In any case the quality of justice will be the same whether in the individual or in a society. Now if the structure of the State is analogous to that of the human soul, the latter will consist of three parts corresponding to the groups in the State. Plato therefore[3] divides the human mind into three—a deliberative and controlling part, an executive part, and a productive and acquisitive part. This applies to all human beings, as the triple division applies to all States, but the character, whether of State or individual, will depend on which of the three predominates.[4] A man dominated by his desire for material prosperity is like a State dominated by its men of bronze and iron; a man who is full of courage but lacking in knowledge and self-control will be like a semi-civilised community of warriors. As in the perfect State wisdom, knowledge and reason hold sway, so in the perfect man. The virtues summed up in the word σωφροσύνη are as needful for the individual as for the city. In man pugnacity and acquisitiveness must accept a subordinate role, as do the Auxiliaries and the ordinary

---

[1] Demosthenes expressed what Plato meant by σωφροσύνη when, in praising the loyalty and patriotism of men of the good old days, he said σώφρονες ἦσαν καὶ σφόδρα ἐν τῷ τῆς πολιτείας ἤθει μένοντες (*Olynth.* III 25). They were true to the character of their country's πολιτεία.

[2] τὴν τῶν τεκτόνων ἐπιστήμην (428 B).

[3] In saying that Plato's psychology is based on the structure of his πόλις rather than *vice versa* I follow F. M. Cornford in *Class. Quart.* VI, 1912, pp. 246-265. But see next note.

[4] For a detailed treatment of this topic see, in addition to Cornford's article, the fourth essay in H. W. B. Joseph's *Ancient and Modern Philosophy* (Oxford, 1936) who says, 'It is Plato's political philosophy that order and disorder alike in States are the outward and visible sign of order and disorder in the souls of men'.

citizens. Finally, as justice was found to be a principle governing the relations between the parts of the State, so now it appears as a principle governing the relations between the parts of the soul. A just man is he who performs his own function; in an unjust man the parts of the soul are at war with each other. Justice is a right order, a healthy condition within the soul of man or State. It cannot but be better than injustice.

Such in bare outline is the constitution of Plato's ideal State. It is intended to be in the strictest sense ἀριστοκρατία, rule of the best, that is the wisest; and when Plato comes to compare this constitution with others in the eighth book, this is the name which he gives to his own. But before discussing defective constitutions he has more to say about these 'best and wisest' and about the political principles upon which they are to act. Their first aim should be to secure unity and coherence.[1] The danger of disintegration was a very real one. Men were still looking for that which binds cities together. Earlier writers had stressed the need for a common sentiment, for ὁμόνοια. Plato adds an even stronger word ὁμοδοξία, a common set of beliefs, and he agrees with Damon[2] that a fixed standard of musical taste is essential for the stability of the State. By dividing society into three classes it might seem as if Plato was making this condition unattainable; but he is constantly emphasizing the common interest of all three groups. Not only the masses but the guardians must hold fast to their belief in their own city and the myth on which it is based. Community of belief or opinion is especially important for the ruling and auxiliary groups; for beyond this general acceptance the majority are not expected to have any beliefs or opinions or to do any thinking for themselves. Even the Auxiliaries take their opinions from the Rulers; this ensures not only that they are right but that the two ruling groups shall be in complete agreement among themselves and with each other. This is most essential for keeping the city, σῴζειν τὴν πόλιν. More will be needed for this purpose than education, important though that is. The

---

[1] Ultimately of course the aim is justice, but it is justice as the expression of perfect order; and disunity is its negation. See further below.

[2] See note at the end of Chap. II. Damon is one of the very few of his predecessors to whom Plato acknowledges his debt; and the debt in *Republic* is probably much larger than actual citations indicate. So H. Ryffel, *Museum Helveticum* IV, 1947, p. 25.

so-called constitutional safeguards, prosecutions for infringements and the like, he had seen too much of these and their ineffective workings at Athens to put any trust in them. He must find a way to abolish any *motive* for disbelief in, or interference with the constitution and to remove any cause for dissension among the protectors of society. Greed for money might, he hoped, be confined to the producing and acquisitive group and there kept in check and harmlessly exercised; from the two other classes it might be eradicated by training and tradition. But even that will not be enough; the mere possession of anything, a house or a piece of land, a wife and family, raises up in the soul of man a rival interest, a personal loyalty which, as experience shows, is liable to win first place in a man's devotion. It follows, since the protectors of the community must have no other loyalty, that they must go without private property and family life. They do not indeed take vows of poverty or chastity, for they will be well looked after and must, under strict official control, beget a new generation; but they are to own nothing, to have no private house or children; no one of them may say 'This is my husband' or 'These are my wife and children'. They cannot even entertain their friends or go abroad; they will have no money to spend on the most innocent of enjoyments, but will be like a company of soldiers always on duty with no prospect of leave. The only people who could live in such conditions are those whose only happiness lies in the performance of duty; not indeed that their happiness is the aim of the State. The well-being of the whole is all that matters; but it must be a true well-being; we are constructing a city, not a fun-fair (421 B).

The prohibition of private property, if it is intended also to apply to auxiliaries, will bind these two ruling groups together, and Plato does not fear that it will create dissension between them and the rest. Among those who may own property wide disparity of wealth must be avoided. Plato had in his own lifetime seen the evil effects of this disparity (Chap. VII, *init.*). A city at war is always glad when its enemy suffers from a cleavage between rich and poor (422 E). Great size is no more desirable than great wealth; for both are obstacles to unity.[1] In a large city-state the education of the Guardians could not be properly carried out, and

[1] Plato does not conceive the State itself as a property-owner on a large scale.

they would be unable to exercise that close supervision and control which is vital to the scheme. Least of all could they manage the breeding system, that is the arrangement of temporary unions between eugenically selected couples and the segregation at birth of children from their mother. For the authorities[1] will be unable to carry out this scheme without much secrecy and deception.

The unity of the State would be further promoted by equality of the sexes. The proposals under this head are put forward with more diffidence than the breeding-scheme, as if they were more likely to shock public opinion or excite greater ridicule. The subject of the position of women had been discussed for many years. The *Alcestis*, the *Medea* and other plays of Euripides had awakened the minds of some of the Athenians to women's social disabilities; and their political rights too were being canvassed, not with much success, but widely enough to make a subject for Aristophanic comedy.[2] Plato, however, is not thinking of the rights of women. How could he, when he thought so little of the rights of man? He is merely pursuing the logic of his own principles. Each member of the community must perform the task for which he or she is best fitted. There is nothing in the difference between the sexes to warrant the exclusion of women from any of the professions or from higher education,[3] nothing to warrant the restriction of weaving and cooking to the female sex. In short, 'there is no function in the working of a city which belongs to women *quâ* women or to men *quâ* men' (455 D). Women will therefore be eligible to become warriors, auxiliaries and guardians. How indeed could they be allowed to become mothers of guardians, unless they possessed the qualities of mind and body required? And these qualities are not so common that we can afford to leave their possessors to menial tasks. There is thus no humanitarian feeling[4] behind Plato's desire for the emancipation of women, as

---

[1] οἱ ἄρχοντες. Perhaps he had in mind a sort of sub-committee for this degrading and dishonest procedure. The social aim is an adequate supply of 'good' births; they are not likely to have too many of these. At the same time, since the city is not to be too large, over-population among the citizens in general would have to be prevented. We are not told how this could be done; the stud-farm methods are applied only to the ruling classes.

[2] The *Ecclesiazusae* referred to on p. 117 above.

[3] Cp. Euripides, *Medea* 1085.

[4] On the contrary, witness the callousness of the 'breeding-rights' of the brave soldier in war time (468 c).

there was in all that Euripides wrote about them. Those of either sex who have ability must use it to serve their fellows whether they wish it or not. Therefore in the two highest classes women and men will receive the same education from birth.

These two features, the abolition of married life and the equality of women, are closely dependent on each other. The substitution of communal life for separate households will release many women of high courage and intellect to play their part as Guardians. The principle of specialisation is followed in giving communal nurseries and communal kitchens into the hands of those men and women best fitted for those tasks.[1] It illuminates Plato's uncompromising rigidity in adherence to his own principles to observe how on the one hand he sees that living in cities answers a human need, yet refuses to his best citizens a place for the far deeper need of a child for its own mother or a woman for her child. He recognised the power of these affections and saw in them only a rival loyalty, a danger to the State. His aim was to direct them all towards the πόλις itself; the solidarity of the family, which was still strong at Athens, as the surviving law-court speeches show, must give way to the solidarity of the City. 'No greater evil,' says Plato, 'can afflict a State than whatsoever divides it and makes it Many instead of One, and no greater good than whatsoever binds it together and makes it one' (462 A).[2]

Plato's ideal constitution now exists, as we might say, on paper. So far as words can do it, the Idea of the πόλις has been described. No actual city on earth can be identical with it, but that will be best which most resembles it; more than that it is unreasonable to ask (473 A). No known city is like it, but there is nothing inherently impossible in the scheme, however difficult it would be to induce a Greek city of the time to adopt it, and to create a *tabula rasa* on which to build it. If only political power were in the hands of those who *know*, not those who merely think they

---

[1] The actual work of ministering to the daily needs of the community will fall on members of the majority class; these may marry and live as they please. On the non-mention of slaves, see above, p. 150 n 3.

[2] Aristotle at the beginning of the second book of his *Politics* sharply criticises this part of Plato's *Republic*, and remarks how this excessive striving after unity defeats its own ends by destroying that diversity which is an essential mark of the πόλις. But for Plato the more unity, the better; and it is in retrospect to the ideal city of the *Republic* that he writes in *Laws* v 739 D οἵτινες νόμοι μίαν ὅτι μάλιστα πόλιν ἀπεργάζονται.

know or, as more often, do not understand what is meant by knowing, the thing would be possible. To join together supreme power and supreme wisdom was the dream of all his life[1] and the essence of all his thinking on practical political reform. There is a natural affinity between them.[2] But the wisdom which Plato had in mind was something very different from the cleverness of the orators or the culture of Isocrates, from whose conception of φιλοσοφία, as we saw in Chapter VII, he dissociated himself entirely. Plato's philosopher will pursue a wisdom quite unlike that offered by even the best educators of the day. He will devote his whole attention to ultimate truth, to the world of Ideas or Forms, not to beautiful *things* but to Beauty itself. For this he will need to be a man of the highest intellectual power, deeply emotional and devoted to the search for truth. Such a philosopher is the born ruler. This is not the popular opinion or the opinion of those who have their own brand of culture to sell; and it is admitted that those who devote their lives to higher things often make a sorry exhibition of themselves in mundane affairs. But the fault is in society not in the philosopher. In a corrupt, ignorant and pleasure-loving community the true philosopher will always be a misfit, as Socrates was at Athens. Worse than that, potential philosophers will be corrupted in their youth and, as often as not, their brains and ability will find an outlet in crime (491 E). These are discouraging observations, but they are not held to invalidate the claim that the philosopher-ruler is a practical possibility. 'There will never be a perfect city or constitution, or a perfect man either,[3] until by some good fortune those rare and excellent philosophers who are now dubbed useless are compelled, whether they like it or not, to take control of the city' (499 B). For they are not really useless and perhaps one day even the general public will realise that the philosopher's daily contemplation of Eternal Perfection will make him, when he turns to mundane things, the best 'creator of justice, loyalty and all civic virtue'. Only a painter who uses a divine model can paint a picture of perfect bliss.

We will not attempt to summarise here the advanced education of the philosopher-ruler, the allegory of the cave and the shadows,

---

[1] Cp. *Epist.* VII 326 B (quoted on p. 124).

[2] πέφυκε συνιέναι εἰς ταὐτὸν φρόνησίς τε καὶ δύναμις μεγάλη (*Epist.* II 310 E). The context of this letter is obscure, but the sentiment is thoroughly Platonic.

[3] No perfect man without a πόλις.

the theory of knowing and degrees of knowledge, the years of studying mathematics and dialectic, the weeding out of the unfit, the experience of military and other practical work and all the thirty years' work, between the ages of twenty and fifty, that are needed to produce a full Guardian. But it should be noted that in planning the making of a philosopher-ruler Plato is thinking of himself and his own career. He cannot have been more than a year or two over or under fifty when the *Republic* was completed; he had spent many years studying mathematics and metaphysics and at his own Academy had had experience of selecting and training the best pupils on these or similar lines. He felt himself ripe for political power and he knew of no one with whom he would be willing to share it—certainly not Isocrates or Antis-thenes, reputed philosophers. Thus he could not collect a team of philosopher-rulers, an aristocracy of wisdom. It would, how-ever, be no departure from the principles of the Ideal State if one were to rule alone (540 D); and he had in mind (see below) a way of classifying constitutions different from the old One, Few and Many principle. For himself, he had to wait till he was over sixty before he had his chance and even then, as we shall see in the next chapter, it was no chance at all. He was not in his own city and hardly any of the necessary conditions were to be had—the clean sweep (501 A, 541 A) and the absolute loyalty of the executive arm.

The Ideal State, that is the Pure Form laid up in Heaven, can suffer no change or corruption. It is eternal and always the same. If there exists anywhere on earth some very close copy, then it will be far more stable and less liable to change than any other earthly State; it would be the best possible answer to the Greek city-state's demand for permanence and stability and freedom from στάσις. But it could not last for ever. Things do not last for ever except in the world of ideas, the unseen reality; in this world nothing ever stays the same, πάντα ῥεῖ, as Heraclitus said. There are degrees of impermanence; the rocks last longer than the waves that dash against them. So too the Best State will last longer than the bad. All existing States were found to be bad, and Plato, while constructing his Ideal State, had the contemporary situation always in mind. If he did not actually write the eighth book before the rest, he had its material constantly before him. Why, for example, does he insist so strongly on the need for coherence of the two ruling groups? Because he observed that among all the city-states only Sparta, where the ruling caste kept to themselves and acted solidly together, had reached anything like a permanent constitution. But he knew, too, that Sparta had not really solved the problem, but lived under threat of revolt; he saw faults as well as merit in Spartan education and still more in Spartan character. But his main conclusion was that the chief danger to a city's stability lay in disagreement among its rulers. By definition, so to speak, the rulers of Plato's state do not disagree, but the means employed to secure agreement may not in practice be entirely successful. The hereditary basis is admittedly insecure; the eugenic breeding has to be carried out by those who are themselves products of it. They cannot know all that they are doing or be sure of their results. If there is a mathematical certainty[1] in eugenics, that too belongs to the unseen world and cannot be known by men and women, who have to make their calculations according to their observation and experience.[2] The result will be that one set of Guardians may be just a little inferior to their predecessors, just a little less careful about keeping unchanged all education in music and the arts. The next generation will be slightly less well educated, not so fit to exercise the ruling and protecting function. The purity of the 'metals' will have been lost and division or στάσις will creep in.

Gradually, when once there has been a deviation from the best possible, things will become progressively worse and each form of corrupt constitution will be worse than that which preceded it.[3] For, though there is only one Best State, there are many bad ones; not all equally bad, but corresponding to different types of badness and of bad men. Justice is One but Injustice is Many. One might have expected Plato to say that a bad constitution is one marked by the absence of σωφροσύνη (cp. *supra*, p. 152), and no doubt he would have agreed. But it would hardly serve as a

---

[1] Something of this kind seems to be implied in the cryptic passage about the perfect and the geometric numbers (546 B - D).

[2] λογισμὸς μετ᾽ αἰσθήσεως (546 B).

[3] Is this intended to be a universal law of history? Does Plato say that at any given moment in any given State, whatever its constitution or previous history, everything is going from bad to worse and will go on doing so through predictable stages till each is ruled by a ruthless maniac? *Credat Iudaeus Apella.* On the other hand, as Solon had long since urged (Chap. II), once you let Good Order slip, despotism lurks around the corner.

basis for classifying them[1] and it is to this age-old occupation of Greek political philosophy that Plato's *Republic* now turns. 'You know, I presume, that the number of possible characters of men is the same as the number of possible constitutions that is, ways of life.'[2] There must therefore be a large number of possible πολιτεῖαι and Plato, disregarding intermediate and foreign types, classifies the bad constitutions into four main forms; their degree of badness depends on how far they depart from the one good form in point of character, habits and manner of living. These four, in Plato's descending order of merit, are Timocracy, Oligarchy, Democracy and Tyranny. Each of these is associated with a certain type of man.[3] Tyranny is included, although old-fashioned people still regarded it as a mere negation of πολιτεία. Plato was well aware of this and indeed would not have denied it; but he needed tyranny just because it was the complete and perfect negation of the Just State and the τυραννικὸς ἀνήρ the complete antithesis of the Just Man. To illustrate the four types Plato does not describe actual states, though he does mention Sparta and Crete as examples of Timocracy.[4] Athens of course is in his mind constantly, and many of the features both of plutocratic Oligarchy and Democracy are drawn from his experience of his own city. If he were actually describing Athens, the picture would be most unfair.

Giving the name aristocracy in the strict sense of 'rule of the best' to his own constitution, in which the most wise rule, he considers next how it may degenerate into something like the Spartan way, something intermediate between aristocracy and an

[1] But a preliminary dual classification into those resting on force and those on consent is made in *Politicus* 276 E.

[2] 'Ways of life.' These words are added to the quotation (544 D). Plato simply says πολιτεία, of which our 'constitution' is only half a translation, for πολιτεία is βίος and springs, as Plato here says, ἐκ τῶν ἠθῶν τῶν ἐν ταῖς πόλεσιν. As St. Thomas Aquinas says, *diversas vitas faciunt, et per consequens diversas respublicas*. Cp. also the quotation at the head of this chapter; for the converse is equally true.

[3] Cp. what was said in Chap. III, p. 35, on types of men. But it was the boast of Athenian democrats of the fourth century that their constitution did not depend on the personal character of anybody, but on impersonal and impartial law. See for example Aeschines *Ctesiph.* 6. Plato here takes no notice of this claim.

[4] Aristotle has an entirely different sense for τιμοκρατία in *Eth. N.* VIII 1160 b 19 and 1161 a 28. See below p. 225.

oligarchy of the rich. This he calls Timocracy because in it great importance is attached to Honour (τιμή). Errors in breeding will be followed by others, such as failure to keep a proper balance of wealth. Some members of the third class will become much richer than the rest and this will make it harder for the rulers to keep them in obedience to the established constitution. Force is used and the rulers, being armed, are victorious[1] and enter into private possession of the houses and lands. The general citizen body, instead of being free men voluntarily supporting their benevolent protectors, become agricultural serfs. The rulers become a military caste, practising only war and self-defence. Though they are now landowners, they do not farm, but continue to live a communal barrack-room life. But they no longer form a community of lovers of Wisdom and Courage. The military clique neglects the true Muse and all intellectual culture; there is no love of knowledge in them and γυμναστική counts for more than μουσική. Moreover, they have become greedy of money, not spending it generously, but hoarding it in secret, for it is still a forbidden and lawless pleasure. Plato need hardly have told us that this is a Laconian kind of society, so closely does it resemble contemporary Sparta and the Spartan military type, who gets his own way by violent methods, is fond of hunting and athletics but lacking in intellectual culture.

The next kind of constitution is Oligarchy, which might also be called Plutocracy,[2] since it is defined (550 c) as one 'based on a property qualification, one in which the rich rule and the poor have no share in government'. The secret hoarding of gold among the rulers in a timocracy continues and wealth comes to be prized more highly than honour or military skill. That love of money which Plato sought to suppress and confine now becomes open and universal. Wealth is the recognised standard by which fitness to rule is estimated and this is as disastrous as to choose for navigator the seaman who has most money in his pocket. Furthermore, such a constitution violates the principle of specialisation;

---

[1] Plato glosses over this and speaks of 'coming to an agreement' (547 B), but the result is no compromise. Oligarchy and democracy are openly stated to need force and terrorism (δι' ὅπλων ... διὰ φόβον) for their establishment (551 B, 557 A).

[2] Plato does not use πλουτοκρατία, though he might well have. It is used by Xenophon, *Memorabilia* IV 6, 12.

there is nothing left of the professional army, and land-owners engage both in agriculture and commerce and, if need be, in warfare. Others do not trouble to engage in anything at all; they live on their wealth, drones in society, neither rulers nor subjects, merely consumers. The dreaded division into rich and poor follows and all the evils of capitalism are seen. This time there is a double danger of revolution, revolt from below as well as dissension among the ruling class. In the race for riches there is bitter rivalry and those who are eliminated join the ranks of beggars and paupers. The successful wax fat and fall an easy prey to the lean and hungry masses and the democratic revolution has taken place.

One by one the safeguards of Plato's aristocracy have been abandoned and two forms of wrong constitution have been shown. The education of the human soul has ceased, its baser elements overtop the good. A dominant class with no pretensions to knowledge has been substituted for a team of experts. The State is split into two. Yet worse is to come; first democracy or, as its extreme form came later to be called, ochlocracy[1] or mob-rule. Eagerness to make money keeps the oligarchic man on some semblance of a path of virtue; he 'keeps steady' and does not 'take to drink', like the tyrant type (573 c). But the mob, when it has killed or driven out the capitalists and the drones, has its soul dominated by sheer love of liberty and has no thought but to throw off all restraint, exterior and interior. As for government, they regard specialisation as undemocratic, think it right that every man should have his turn, and allocate important offices by lot. Much of the criticism of the rule of the Many goes back for a hundred years (Megabyzus in the 'Persian' dialogue, Chap. III) but Plato adds more detailed criticism, based partly on his own prejudices, partly on his knowledge of Athens and partly also on his reading of such authors as the Old Oligarch and his uncle Critias (Chap. V). For Plato it was inconceivable that the masses should ever have sufficient goodness and intelligence to rule. The principles to which democracy clung—equal rights for all, freedom of speech and action, were for him positively evil; so too the freedom from official control of private life, that proud boast of Periclean Athens. Variety, so much prized, was for Plato a sign of instability, of an unbridled soul. It is meant as a serious reproach when he says

[1] ὀχλοκρατία first occurs in Polybius. See below Chap. XIII.

(557 C) that in a democratic State you will find all manner of people. A democratic constitution is not one but many, for there are many ways of life to choose from. This too is meant as a reproach. It does not seem to have occurred to Plato that it was in virtue of this very 'defect' at Athens that Socrates was able to live there his own particular way of living. Nor does he choose to remember that the theoretical basis of Greek democracy was Law, respect for the νόμοι and the whole constitution as the guarantee of personal freedom.[1] As he grew older, he came to realise more and more the importance of Law, but only as part of the equipment of ruling, not as a guarantee of liberty. Thus, if in the *Politicus* (see next chapter) he recognises that there may be a better type of democracy than the worst and in the *Laws* (Chap. X) includes a certain democratic element and legal checks, these are not evidence of change of heart or change of principle.

Just as oligarchy is liable to perish through its excessive devotion to riches, so democracy eventually succumbs to its own craze for liberty. In a manner reminiscent of the Old Oligarch (p. 83) Plato describes how liberty degenerates into lawlessness and the passion for equality extends, so that distinctions between master and servant, parents and children, rulers and ruled are blotted out. 'The combined effect of all this is a weakening of the moral fibre of the citizens, indignation and resentment at any suggestion of compulsory service, ending in complete disregard even of the laws, written or unwritten; they will have no master over them in anything. . . . Excessive action in one direction is apt to provoke a violent and contrary reaction; this can be seen in weather, as well as in plants and animals, and is especially true of πολιτεῖαι. Extreme liberty seems to lead inevitably to extreme subjection. . . . Little wonder that always out of democracy springs despotism and the greater the extreme of liberty the more thorough-going and harsh the tyranny.'[2] Plato does not here develop this theme. Why not? Because he knew, and his readers would know, that Greek tyrants had often come into power by being, first, champions of the people against their rulers, then demanding armed protection for themselves and using this to make themselves

[1] Prosecutions for attempting to alter the Constitution (γραφαὶ παρανόμων) were frequent at Athens, largely, if we can trust the orator Aeschines (*Ctesiph.* 6), because any such change was felt to be a threat to an Athenian's παρρησία.

[2] 563 D - 564 A abbreviated and paraphrased rather than translated.

masters of the city. He must therefore bring these facts into the picture when he comes to show the fourth kind—tyranny or despotism or dictatorship. But Plato seems not to be aware that the two origins are quite different, though both may occur. The process by which a despot comes into power through championing the masses against the entrenched privilege of property (566 A) is not the same as that just described. Plato treats them as stages of one process, as if τυραννὶς ἐκ δημοκρατίας were necessarily the same as τύραννος ἐκ δήμου.

The resulting tyrant, however, will be much the same in one case and in the other. However mild and beneficial his rule may be at first, he cannot escape the deterioration that goes with absolute power. Our minds go back a second time to Herodotus (III 80), to Otanes and all the traditional Greek hatred of oriental despotism. But again Plato penetrates more deeply. His picture of the 'tyrannic' is more a psychological than a political study.[1] Love of money keeps some people honest, even love of pleasure does not lead the democratic man into the worst excesses of which our more bestial nature is capable. But there is nothing to check the path of the tyrant. Unnatural lusts, homicidal mania, all the darkest depths of the soul, the existence of which in all of us is revealed in dreams (571-2), come to the surface and find expression in action. Whether he be in fact a τύραννος of a city, one so afflicted with megalomania that he expects to rule over gods as well as men (573 C), or simply a τυραννικὸς ἀνήρ or 'criminal type', he is carried along by forces over which he has now no control. He is no mighty prince or strong man, but the most abject and powerless of slaves; for has he not *lost his reason*? So the other extreme is reached. Not wisdom but insanity sits in the saddle; folly not knowledge is united with power. Whatever one may think of Plato's ideal state, his picture of its opposite is convincing enough; there are those who have lived through the rule of a paranoiac and can testify to Plato's insight as well as to Aristotle's when he said, 'The man in the street does not discern evil in government as it creeps in; it needs a statesman'.[2]

Plato's *Republic* is the despair alike of those who hate him and

---

[1] Like, and yet how unlike, the *Characters* of Theophrastus some fifty years later. Theophrastus has no democratic or tyrannic in his thirty types but he has an oligarchic (No. 26), Chap. XII, p. 248.

[2] Or rather a πολιτικὸς ἀνήρ. Aristotle *Politics* v 1308 a, *fin.*

those who admire him. His enemies cannot forgive his influence
and prestige and so cannot ignore him; and he will not toe the
line which his friends draw for him, but strays across to the enemy
camp. He attacks in the name of stability the pillars of bourgeois
society—private property and family life. You can find in the
Republic warrant for preaching social revolution, the overthrow
of capitalism and of money-power; but you can also find warrant
for the existence of two different systems of education, one for
the Few and one for the Many, and for a hereditary ruling class.
Political principles of Rousseau, Burke and Marx jostle each other
in its pages. It can be cited in support of two directly opposite
theories of government—a Cabinet with members professionally
trained in the work of their ministries, or a Cabinet of amateurs
from a University debating society. Plato's estimate of the human
race is at once incredibly low and incredibly high: the flower of
a country's men and women to have their lives and loves directed
down to the last detail by a 'committee of experts', the majority
to live the unthinking life of sheep. Between the wisdom of the
few and the docility of the rest the human race has never been so
exalted or so abased. His reputation has suffered as much from
adulation as from attack. Blinded by his glory and bewitched by
his poetry many see only what they wish to see and pass over
the evil; others, infuriated by his inhumanity and his lordly affectation of knowledge, lose patience with the task of trying to
understand him. But perhaps the strongest objection to the political theory of the *Republic* lies in the notion of an absolute government by a set of persons whose claim to superior wisdom and
infallible knowledge must never be questioned.

FURTHER NOTES AND REFERENCES
CHAPTER VIII

The *Republic* of Plato, being one of the world's most influential
books, has been endlessly studied and commented upon. Below will
be found (*a*) a list of select passages in accordance with the plan of this
book and (*b*) a very small selection of modern works useful for the
understanding of the *political* aspects of this variegated work. But the

reader ought not to confine himself to the author's choice under either of these heads, though he has attempted to be fair and catholic. Inevitably, however, much has been omitted which Plato regarded as part of πολιτική but which we do not include in Political Thought; most notably his discussions (in Books II, III and X) on literature and the arts. But these have in recent times been brought back into the political sphere: Plato might have written the following extract from *Pravda* (21st August 1946): 'The task of Soviet literature is to help the State properly to bring up its youth, answer its needs, educate the new generation to be brave, to believe in its cause, to be fearless before obstacles and ready to overcome all barriers. . . . (Its strength is that in it) there are not and cannot be any interests other than those of the people and the State.' Cp. *infra* Chap. X, p. 201.

(a)

The *mise-en-scène* and the preliminary discussion of moral problems occupy Book I and part of Book II (368).

The minimum State and the luxury State, 369-374.

Qualities needed for the 'protecting' class: their early education, 375-412.

The three classes and the myth of the metals, 412-415.

(The 'noble lie' has been more often criticised for being a fictitious tale than for not being noble. In any case as a means of securing conformity it is perhaps preferable to whipping, torture and burning at the stake, and the lack of factual truth was not heinous in Greek eyes.)

Goodness in the State and the individual, 427-444.

Abolition of private property among rulers, 416-426, and of marriage and family, 457-465.

Equality of women, 450-455.

The true philosopher, 470-487. Popular view of him as useless, 487, *Theaet.* 172-175, *Gorgias* 486 (Callicles).

The philosopher-ruler, 499-502, *Epist.* VII 326 B.

Constitutions: Timocracy, 545-549 C; Oligarchy (Plutocracy) 550 C - 553 D; Democracy (Ochlocracy) 555 B - 558 C; Tyranny, 562 A - 569 C.

How the corresponding type of man in each case comes into being is told in between (tyrannic type, 570 ff., bk. IX). If Plato had chosen the career of dramatist, we might have had three first-rate plays, domestic comedies as it were, based on these passages: mother and son think father an unambitious failure and join forces against him; or again, the son rebuilds the family fortunes; the son of the self-made man, will he follow his father's ways or will he rebel against the seemingly virtuous moneymaking?

M

(b)

F. M. Cornford, *Plato's Commonwealth*. Dill Memorial Lecture for 1933. Printed in *Greece and Rome* IV 1935, p. 92, and reprinted in *The Unwritten Philosophy*, 1949.

R. L. Nettleship, *Lectures on Plato's Republic*. It is interesting to compare this fine work of mid-Victorian scholarship (1887) with the older work of Grote (*Plato and the Companions of Sokrates*, vol. 3) and with later works such as: Ernst Cassirer, *The Myth of the State*, ch. VI (1946), R. H. S. Crossman, *Plato To-day* (1937), H. W. B. Joseph, *Ancient and Modern Philosophy*, Essays I-IV (1935).

A. Verdross-Drossberg, *Grundlinien der antiken Rechts- und Staatsphilosophie*. Vienna, 1946, 2nd ed. 1948.

K. R. Popper, *The Open Society and Its Enemies*, Vol. I, 1945.

Ernest Barker, *Greek Political Theory: Plato and his Predecessors*, 1918.

There are several translations into English. F. M. Cornford's (1941) is the most readable and is also a valuable guide to the whole.

CHAPTER IX

XENOPHON AND PLATO

THE Royal Science of Ruling, the Education of a Prince—
expressions such as these at first sounded strange in connection with the Greeks, a people so proverbially attached
to freedom and so horrified at the notion of a master. But the
two previous chapters will have accustomed the reader to monarchical ideas in the Hellenic world of the fourth century B.C.
and to education conceived as a preparation for the work of a
statesman. Both Isocrates and Plato were in their different ways
seeking at their two schools to provide a training which should
fit a man to rule either singly or in conjunction with others.
Among those whose social position and education were sufficient
to warrant expectation of exercising authority there was a good
deal of support for the idea of personal rule. It was the name and
associations of tyranny rather than its absolutism that was disliked, though strict and old-fashioned people could take Plato to
task for his readiness to associate with tyrants.

The four books of the *Memorabilia* of Xenophon contain a mass
of material professedly Socratic, but in all probability put together
from various sources, including Antisthenes and Aristippus (Chap.
VII, *fin.*), as well as Socrates, and others of whom we have now
no trace; to these Xenophon added something of his own. It is
not of great importance in political thought, springing mostly
from Xenophon's admiration for Sparta and for great and good
men wherever he found them, or thought he found them, from
Lycurgus of old to Agesilaus of his own day. Such democratic
devices as popular elections and sortition are condemned; the
emphasis is on the 'best' people and much of it might have been
written in the days of Theognis (Chap. II). The Socratic insistence

on the importance of knowledge is interpreted as if it meant no more than learning a certain method, a professional training, whether in leading an army or leading a people. 'Kings and Rulers are not those that hold the sceptres or those that have been selected by a particular body of people or have had the luck of the lot or got their way by using force or deceit, but those that know how to rule.'[1] There are imaginary conversations on a variety of topics, some being of political interest. In one of these Xenophon puts into the mouth of Pericles the following definition of law. 'All that the sovran power in the city shall after deliberation lay down as obligatory—that is called νόμος.' Challenged to say whether this definition includes tyranny, Pericles replies that it does. This recalls a fragment of Heraclitus,[2] but the definition is modified by the assertion that in each case the sovran power must use persuasion not force to impose its will. It follows that the majority, the sovran people, cannot impose its will on a property-owning minority save with their consent. Thus the whole anecdote is staged in order to score a point at the expense of Pericles and Athenian democracy, and to defend the rights of property. This is characteristic of Xenophon[3], as is also the identification of justice with all that is legal and traditional, all that is according to the νόμοι. This is put forward in another anecdote[4] by Socrates. The old objection that laws and traditions differ from city to city is brushed aside and all that comes out of the conversation is the supposed universality of certain Unwritten Laws, such as the avoidance of incest and the obligation to reward good with good. A community which is marked by good-will and well-being will find favour with the gods.[5] Of more value than these anecdotes is a note on the familiar topic of the classification of constitutions as follows:

[1] *Mem.* III 9, 10. Cp. below, Chap. XIV, *init.*

[2] Fr. 33; see p. 30.

[3] The sacredness of property is legal and therefore just, as in the Socrates-Hippias anecdote. This is the point too of a story about Cyrus, who, when a boy, made two other boys change coats, because each fitted the other better; he was punished for his mistake in justice (*Cyrop.* I 3, 17).

[4] For the point of this anecdote see p. 90. It is assumed that Xenophon gives us some information about what Socrates *did* but not about what he actually *said* or *thought*. But many hold quite the opposite view.

[5] Xenophon's piety was strong. A city permeated by ὁμόνοια was a long-standing dream, and εὐεργετεῖν, though Democritus Fr. 248 said that the *law*

Kingship. Constitutional (κατὰ νόμους) rule of one man over subjects consenting to his rule.

Tyranny. Sole rule over unwilling subjects, based on no νόμοι, but only on the tyrant's will.

Aristocracy. State offices held only by those (few) who carry out the duties imposed by law and tradition.[1]

Plutocracy. State offices filled by those possessing a certain property qualification.[2]

Democracy. State offices open to all.

It is impossible to know where Xenophon obtained this interesting fragment.[3] He adds nothing to it himself but a few trivialities. The distinctions between constitutional and unconstitutional and between government with and without the consent of the governed, here applied to one-man rule, were used also by Plato in reference to other forms (below, p. 174).

Xenophon had neither philosophical training nor practical experience to bring to bear on problems of politics. But he had other experience, notably that of handling a body of troops in difficulties and hardships. He had played a part, according to himself the chief part, in bringing back the Ten Thousand Greeks from the heart of Persia to the Black Sea and thence home again. He had used his powers of persuasion to advantage and knew well how much depends on a commander's eloquence. It is therefore hardly surprising to find that he tended to regard the problem of government as one of securing and maintaining discipline[4], and the good citizen as identical with the good soldier, or rather the good officer. The way to secure obedience is by prestige and persuasion not fear or force. Men are not naturally disposed to be constant in loyalty and obedience; they are not like sheep, who have never been known to rebel against their shepherd or even to go on strike (*Cyrop*. 1 1, 2). They must therefore be led, not driven. The weaker and inferior must obey the stronger and

should aim at doing good, is now becoming the typical activity of the good *king*. On these twin ideas in antiquity see Eiliv Skard *Euergetes-Concordia* (Oslo, 1932), and see Chap. XIV generally.

[1] ἐκ τῶν τὰ νόμιμα ἐπιτελούντων. Cp. *Lac.Pol*. X 7, ἐκτελεῖν τὰ νόμιμα, of Spartiatae maintaining what Lycurgus had laid down.

[2] Aristotle called this 'timocracy'. See p. 223.

[3] Xenophon, *Mem*. IV 6, 12. See note at the end of the chapter.

[4] As also the task of running a farm in the *Oeconomicus*. See P. Chantraine in the introduction to his edition, Paris (Budé series), 1949.

superior. But the 'superior' must be genuinely so, loyal and patriotic and capable of inspiring loyalty in others. Though only the
few can be real gentlemen, all should make καλοκἀγαθία their
aim and ideal. This is what Lycurgus had done for Sparta long
ago, 'the only city where being a gentleman was part of a national
policy' (*Lac.Pol.* x 4). Xenophon never strayed far from this
ideal of 'an officer and a gentleman', and his political thought,
such as it is, is coloured by this conception. Hence his Ideal
Monarch will be one possessing these virtues and he will sur-
round himself with men of like character with himself, disciplined
and self-controlled, always setting a good example to those be-
neath them. Such a one must Cyrus the Great have been, who
established the Persian empire. So, with the merest shadow of
historical fact, Xenophon in eight books of his *Cyropaedia* describes the education and career of the perfect monarch under
the name of Cyrus the Persian. He disapproved of the degeneracy
and luxury of contemporary Persia, just as he had found fault
with Sparta for not keeping strictly to 'Lycurgus' (*Lac. Pol.* xiv).
But he found, or rather he pretended to find, the ideal monarch
in Persia's early history. That he should have found it, even in
his imagination, in an oriental king might seem to put the *Cyropaedia* outside the scope of Greek political thought; but it is only
in part Persian; a great deal of it is Greek, especially Spartan.
The two are not compatible, and the work is full of contradictions,
great and small. At one time Cyrus is the embodiment of all the
Spartan virtues, his moral prestige sufficing for his safety, at another he is the oriental despot with an entourage of eunuchs and
a large armed bodyguard. But the book found many readers; they
were not put out by the inconsistencies, for most of them came
in search of stories and romance, not of political theory; and those
others who found in it abundant material for Hellenistic kingship
welcomed the mixture of Greek and Persian ideas. The elder
Cyrus was reputed to have had a great capacity for hard work
and taking pains, so that Antisthenes too had chosen him for a
model. Xenophon thought that a king should not only work
hard at being a king, but also at acquiring accomplishments, especially those of a military or sporting kind, so that he might be
able to do things better than others. A king's ἀρετή must be
supreme; it is not enough to put on the right clothes and merely
look the part. At the same time appearance is very important;

a king should spare no pains to look like a king. His majesty
(σεμνότης) should raise him high above his subjects. Oriental
pomp, high heels and painted face, and other methods of exercising fascination (καταγοητεύειν) are mentioned. The king's rule
is not a thing to be trifled with.[1] If he is eager to acquire wealth,
it is only that he may have the more to give away; for his bene-
factions will be the source of his influence and popularity. The
king's favour should be the highest reward, the king's disfavour
the greatest penalty. In piety, honesty, self-discipline and consideration for others (αἰδώς) he should be a model to all, adding
his own example to the educative power of the written laws. The
good ruler is a 'watching law' (βλέπων νόμος) and his trusted
friends will be 'the eyes and ears of the king'.

Some twelve or fifteen years after completing the *Republic* Plato
wrote the *Statesman* (Πολιτικός, *Politicus*).[2] We do not know what
kind of reception the *Republic* had among readers at Athens. Those
friends who frequented the Muses' shrine of the Academy must
have discussed and perhaps criticised the book; and Plato himself
would have admitted that there were many aspects of πολιτεία
scarcely touched upon. No clear and detailed indication had been
given about the actual powers of the supreme guardians; their
authority was to be unchallenged and there was no talk of a written
constitution. Yet they certainly had no authority to change the
general structure, the threefold division and the μουσική or cultural
tradition; so their powers were not absolute. In his classification of
bad forms of constitution he had stressed the character and habits
of certain types of city and citizens, but had said little of their
constitutional bases. Whether these comments were made or not,
Plato took account of these matters in the *Statesman* and the *Laws*;
but neither work is on the face of it an answer to criticism of the
Republic. Had that famous work been lost, we could not have inferred from the Πολιτικός that Plato had already written a Πολιτεία.

Those who may be expecting to find a handbook on the duties
of a ruler or the qualifications for a statesman will have cause to
remember Plato's warning about the written word. The subject

---

[1] μὴ εὐκαταφρόνητος, VIII 3, 1. The actual phrase recurs in 'Diotogenes'. (See
Chap. XIV, p. 295.)

[2] It is assumed that the *Politicus* was written before Plato's final visit to
Sicily in 362 B.C. His experiences during his brief visit in 367 B.C. may have
helped to form some of the ideas expressed in the *Politicus*. On Plato and
Sicily see further below.

of the *Politicus* is regarded primarily as an exercise in the definition of terms. Knowledge is divided into practical and theoretical, that is 'knowing how' and 'knowing' (γνωστική). The art of ruling, the knowledge needed by king, statesman or even master of a household is classified as 'gnostic', because it depends on *knowing*. This is subdivided into judging (κριτική) and commanding or controlling (ἐπιτακτική). But the control of man over man differs from that of man over animals and the oft-used comparison between ruler and shepherd is only valid when the ruler is a god. Men are not nowadays directly controlled by gods, but there was a time, according to an ancient myth, when such conditions did exist. In that age of Kronos the gods ruled over men and looked after them, so that they did not need to do anything for themselves; they had no need of any of the institutions of civilisation, no family, no πολιτεία. In those days the sun and stars moved in the opposite direction to their present-day motions. But when Zeus replaced Kronos, the motions were reversed and the gods ceased to look after human beings. These therefore had to look after themselves but, as they were ill-fitted and ill-equipped to do so, the gods allowed them the discoveries of Prometheus and Hephaestus. Such is the condition of mankind until the circle revolves again in the other direction and gods again look after men as a shepherd looks after his sheep. But in the meantime the parallel between herdsmen and the βασιλικοὶ καὶ πολιτικοί is not applicable.[1] 'Man looking after man' is something different and it is this ἀνθρωπίνη ἐπιμελητική that is the business of king and statesman.

Government then is the exercise of this function; it may be based entirely on force, in which case it is τυραννική, or it may be based on consent; and this is βασιλική. This way of distinguishing between tyranny and kingship was perhaps common in the fourth century, for Xenophon, as we have just seen, had read of it somewhere. It did not exactly correspond to the difference as usually expressed, since subjects might be unwilling to accept a king and willing to accept a popular upstart. But the doctrine of

---

[1] This seems a poor return in political theory for a long digression (267-275) but its interest is theological. H. Ziese (see end of chapter) analyses the relation of the myth to the theory which follows and shows how the dualism of god and world, god ruling world and world ruling itself, is matched by the antithesis between true statesman and false, true state and imitation.

consent was useful in political theory and could be applied to other forms of government than monarchy. Plato here (291 E) uses it also to distinguish between aristocracy and oligarchy, and he recognises the distinction between democracy by consent and by violence, though he has no other word than δημοκρατία for both. But the principle of consent is not further developed. For Plato, as we shall see, it was never more than a secondary consideration, useful in distinguishing between second-rate and third-rate. Here it is not further used, but is quietly dropped in favour of another, but equally secondary, criterion—that which distinguishes between rule according to written laws and strictly personal rule. Even with these distinctions Plato is no more satisfied than he was when he wrote the *Republic* that any of these forms of government is positively good. He has varied his description of the bad forms; he no longer, as in *Republic* VIII, illustrates their differences by showing how one badness leads to another; and later in this dialogue shows a changed view as to the order of merit. The difference between bad and less bad is a difference in form of constitution; but the difference between good and bad is still, as always for Plato, the difference between knowledge and ignorance. The only really good State will be that which is ruled by the man or men possessed of the 'kingly knowledge'. Existing politicians, priests and prophets, all who guide cities and peoples are a motley crew[1] with only their ignorance in common. If a man can be found who has this royal knowledge, he deserves to be called kingly[2] (βασιλικός), whether he is actually a ruler or not, exactly as in the *Republic* a τυραννικὸς ἀνήρ need not be a tyrant.

It is important to note that for Plato, as for modern Communists, when the government is in the hands of those who really know the truth, then the consent of the governed is of no importance. 'Though they put some to death and banish others in order to purge the city for its own good, or reduce its size by detaching colonies, as bees do, or increase its size by admitting foreign immigrants to citizenship, so long as they by their knowledge and justice maintain it and improve it by every means in their power, then we are bound to say that thus described this is the only right (ὀρθή) constitution. If we mention others, we must

[1] Plato abhorred variety (ποικιλία). To do anything 'just for a change' was for him the worst possible reason. Cp. p. 163.

[2] The prototype here of the wise man of the Stoics. *Infra* p. 258.

speak of them not as real or genuine, but only as imitations of this one' (293 D). Nor does legality matter; there is no need of a 'constitution', only for such 'laws' as the rulers may from time to time make or alter. The familiar Platonic comparison between the ruling art and the healing art is made; neither depends on the observance of laws. The knife and the poultice are applied to the patient whether he likes it or not, and the surgeon works by his skill,[1] not according to written instructions. As it is the duty of a physician or trainer of athletes to make his man better, so, as we saw in the *Gorgias*, it is the duty of a ruler to make the citizens better, that is, to make them just. In either case we must judge according to results and not ask whether some pre-arranged set of regulations has been observed. Best it is, not that the laws should have sovran power, but the wise and kingly man. Law is incapable of meeting every situation; the field of human activity is too vast and too shifting. This theory of government, so far as it goes, is thoroughly in keeping with the philosopher-king of the *Republic*; Plato still insists that the prime need of the true states-man is knowledge. The royal art is not described in detail, nor are we told how this knowledge may be acquired, if at all (308 E); but anyone who possessed it would indeed be, 'as it were, god among men' (303 B), so vast a gulf separates him from ordinary folk. This phrase became a sort of shorthand description of the perfect king.[2]

It is certain then that no really wise and expert king or ruler would consent to fetter himself (295 B) with laws and rules which he could not break. No expert in the art of medicine or of navi-gation goes always by some book of instructions; if he did, it would be disastrous, not merely for patients or passengers, but for the whole science of medicine or of navigation (299 E). The same in Plato's view applies to the art of statecraft. Yet some people (he means the Athenians) do not think it at all ridiculous to impose many rules of their own devising, and pride themselves

---

[1] κατὰ τέχνην. Translated into Latin *secundum artem* and into English 'according to art' this phrase still puzzles readers of handbooks on medicine and nursing.

[2] In Aristotle *Politics* III 1284 a θεὸς ἐν ἀνθρώποις used to be taken as a reference to Alexander. This is now rejected; as a proverbial expression it goes back to Theognis (339); Isocrates (IX 72) quotes it as a familiar exag-geration of the poets (*Iliad* XXIV 258). The expression is far less strong in Greek than in English.

on the fact that it is open 'to any man who wishes to bring an accusation for non-observance of the rules' (299 A), thus allowing any one at all, not an expert but a mere charlatan, to set himself above the laws and seduce and corrupt the young similarly.[1] Yet if we look at the world in which we live, we find that we cannot afford to laugh at the limitations and weaknesses of the rule of law. Since no one exists who is great enough and wise enough to rule without it, law becomes indispensable in practice. Judged by the one and only right form of government, those which are actually found on earth are not really deserving of the name of πολιτεία at all, they are but imitations.[2] Any such constitution, be it of the one, the few or the many, will never be anything but a second best, a δεύτερος πλοῦς (297 E, 300 C).

'As things are, then, there is no living person in our cities who is as naturally a monarch as a queen-bee[3] in a hive, supreme in body and mind, as you can see at a glance (εὐθύς); and so it seems we are obliged to come together and make written terms and then keep running along the track of the truest πολιτεία' (301 D, E). This is the only road to survival; there is a certain toughness about a πόλις (302), but it must eventually succumb, if it is exposed to ill-treatment by those who think they know and do not. Our best chance of permanence is the 'best second-best', a condition in which 'none of the inhabitants dare do anything contrary to the laws and he who does is punished by death or other severe penalty' (297 E). There was nothing of this in the *Republic*, but it is very similar, *mutatis mutandis*, to the strict observance of existing law at the end of the *Crito* (p. 128) and it clearly looks forward to the *Laws*. There too, as we shall see, the distinction is kept between the best State and the second best. The *Republic* dealt with the former, the *Laws* with the latter. The *Politicus* is a stepping stone from one to the other.

It seems strange that Plato, after ridiculing the Athenian practice of γραφὴ παρανόμων, should turn round and recommend such

---

[1] The allusion to the Athenian habit of prosecution for illegal proposals (γραφὴ παρανόμων, p. 164 n. 1) is clear, and the allusion to Socrates hardly less so. Plato is thinking how his old teacher (who is not a figure in this dialogue) had fared in a city which prided itself on its adherence to law, but whose lawmaking was done not by those who knew, but by anybody and everybody.

[2] Cp. *Laws* IV 712 E.

[3] The Greek, of course, has 'king', for so the ancients regarded the queen bee. Cp. Virgil *Georgics* IV 106.

a strict and unbreakable rule of law. But the inconsistency is only apparent. In order to be even a second best, the constitution of a law-state must be framed by those who know; it must really be an imitation, an attempt to copy faithfully and without any variation a set of laws already laid down by wise men of the past and sanctioned by ancient usage. The politicians and rulers must remember that they are *not* endowed with supreme knowledge and must not act as if they were. To alter or set aside the ancient laws is tantamount to claiming possession of the 'royal science', which by definition, so to speak, they cannot have. They must be obeyers of the law, not makers of it. It seemed to Plato impossible that the same people should both make laws and obey them. 'All actual constitutions', he says (300 E-301), 'if they are to copy effectively that one true polity ruled by one man having knowledge, must never, once their νόμοι have been established, do anything contrary to that which has been written down or to the customs of their fathers.' This is not simply conservatism, it is fossilisation; to such absurd lengths was Plato driven by fear of the perpetual flux of his age. This rigid adherence to ancient ways can occur in any form of government, even what we call the 'most advanced'.[1] A monarch who always ruled in strict accordance with law and custom would not indeed be skilled in the royal science, but as a second best we call him king, having no other word. If he rules according to his own devices, behaving as if he really knew, he is a τύραννος. Whenever the Few, that is the rich, rule according to law, we call it aristocracy; if otherwise, oligarchy. To equate the few with the rich was in general accordance with the facts and it is of actual conditions that Plato is here speaking, not of ideal conditions with an imaginary, unpropertied aristocracy as in the *Republic*, where the distinction between one and several is of no account. Democracy too can be similarly divided, but no separate names exist; so adjectives such as 'lawful' and 'law-less' must suffice. These are then arranged in order of merit. Monarchy attached to good laws is best; uncontrolled monarchy or tyranny is worst. The rule of the many, being the weakest and most ineffective, is capable of doing least harm and least good; it will therefore be the worst of the lawful forms

---

[1] The metaphor would of course be meaningless to Plato. In English it has an accepted sense. It is only as a deliberate paradox that we can say 'advanced Tory' or 'last-ditch Radical'.

and the best of the unlawful. The rule of the few will occupy the two remaining places; so that while its legal (νόμιμος) form is higher than democracy, its illegal (παράνομος) form is lower. In the *Republic* no form of rule by the few was regarded as inferior to democracy and there was no mention of legal monarchy. The whole scheme might be tabulated thus:

RIGHT	Rule by a 'god among men' not requiring law			
WRONG (numbers showing descending order of merit)	*Lawful*		*Without law*	
	1. Rule of One: Kingship		4. Many (Poor) Democracy	
	2. Few (Rich): Aristocracy		5. Few (Rich): Oligarchy	
	3. Many (Poor): Democracy		6. One: Tyranny	

But for all their respect for Law none of the three lawful forms really deserves the name πολιτεία. Each is lacking in unity and solidarity. The rulers in each case govern according to a set of rules drawn up to suit that particular form and having therefore only a partial validity; thus the rulers cannot help being στασιαστικοί, not truly πολιτικοί.

These imitations are now (303 D) put aside again; they have been sufficiently differentiated from the true and perfect Statesman, and to him we now return. It ought to have been pointed out that, if laws cannot be framed so as to cover every eventuality, neither can a sole ruler, however wise, personally superintend everything. But nobody in the dialogue says this; the perfect wisdom of βασιλικὴ τέχνη must not be sullied by any derogatory criticism. Plato knew perfectly well that it was a pure abstraction, indeed that is just why he would allow no imperfection in it; he was thinking of it as a Form or Idea. However, as if in answer to an unspoken criticism he concedes that the perfect ruler will need expert assistance in many fields of activity—military leadership, judicial work, rhetoric (for he will need official spokesmen), all that is comprised under μουσική and all the technical skills. Each or any of these may be dignified with the name ἐπιστήμη or τέχνη, but they do not hold these titles, as it were, in their own right, and their possessors act not on their own initiative but only as directed by the supreme science of πολιτική. The dialogue at its conclusion (306-311) picks up again an earlier-made (287) comparison between the work of a perfect ruler and the work of a weaver. Both are constructive artists; and the statesman is conceived as employing diverse materials, that is, men of different capacity and temperament, to make the warp and weft of a harmonious whole. The absolute power which the weaver has over his material will cause a critical reader to point out that this analogy is even less valid than the shepherd analogy already rejected. But it is not so much the power of the ruler that is illustrated by the weaver picture as his skill in blending contrary elements and even contrary virtues.[1]

It is clear from a reading of the *Politicus* that the years that had elapsed since the writing of the *Republic* had taught Plato much about the practical side of politics, that is, about handling men. It would be too much to say that he had learned toleration. That was not a quality which Plato or the Greeks generally esteemed very highly. Perhaps their nearest word for it was ῥᾳθυμία, which really means 'not taking things too much to heart', a habit which was not at all to Plato's liking. He certainly had not learned to tolerate what he believed to be error: that would be unthinkable. But he had perhaps become more tolerant of *people*. His Academy had been a success and had brought him into touch with people from all parts. If few of them turned out to be philosophers of high quality, many proved to be men of merit and ability. He came to see that the people who most effectively do good in the world are not always the first-rate intellectuals but the second-best. It is true that second-best men will only make second-best cities, but they will be cities in which human beings can live as citizens. Of course even the second-best men are far outnumbered by the rest, and Plato never abandons his paternal attitude towards the general run of people; they must always be told what to do.

To his experience at the Academy must be added his work in Sicily and his relations with Dion of Syracuse, who studied at the Academy during his exile,[2] that is, between Plato's two attempts to assist at Syracuse, and at a time when possibly Plato was actually writing the *Politicus*.[3]

[1] It is outside our scope to discuss this apparent breakaway from the doctrine that Virtue is One or its anticipation of the Aristotelian Virtue as a Mean.

[2] On Dion's studies at the Academy see W. H. Porter in his forthcoming edition of Plutarch's *Life of Dion*, supplementary note v.

[3] See above, p. 173 n. 2. It is however possible that the *Politicus* was not written or not completed until after the 362-361 B.C. visit.

In 367 B.C. there came an invitation from Syracuse which
seemed to offer him a chance to show himself in action in political affairs. True, it was not the chance which he formerly hoped
for; he was to be given no political power, only an opportunity
to use his powers of persuasion and education on the young ruler
of Syracuse. This man, Dionysius II, had just succeeded his father
as sole ruler of Syracuse and all eastern Sicily. The elder Dionysius
had kept the Carthaginians at bay; it was said that he did not
drive them out of the island entirely, because his own military
power depended for its justification on the existence of the Punic
menace. He had acquired a reputation throughout the Greek
world as a ruthless but efficient tyrant. Twenty years before this
(see p. 124) Plato had met Dion, uncle of the new tyrant, a man
of strict and puritanical ideas, who ever since had stood out
against the licentious ways of the tyrant's court. The new ruler
had expressed a desire to study philosophy under Plato and there
seemed to be just a chance that he might become 'converted';
perhaps even some sort of union of political power with philosophic knowledge might be brought about. Plato must have
known that there were great difficulties in the way. He knew from
his previous travels that the so-called upper classes in Sicily and
South Italy were particularly licentious and gluttonous, the sort
of people who always dominate and set the tone for tyrants'
courts, the τυραννικοί of *Republic* IX. At Syracuse the character
of the πολιτεία was 'tyrannous'; the removal or conversion of the
tyrant himself would not alter that character. But it seemed to
Plato cowardly to refuse; he felt that he owed it to his friend Dion
and that it would be false to philosophy not to go. After
much thought he decided that 'if ever anyone was to set about
really accomplishing all that had been thought out περὶ νόμων
τε καὶ πολιτείας, now was the time to try' (*Ep.* VII 328 C). So
despite his sixty years he accepted the invitation and came to
Syracuse.

The story of this first association with Dionysius II, which
ended in 366 B.C., and of the second attempt in 361 B.C., equally
unsuccessful, can be put together from letters which Plato wrote
after both visits were over.[1] It cannot be retold fully here: the
intrigues against Plato, the waywardness of Dionysius and his
jealousy of Dion, who was banished soon after Plato's first com-

---

[1] The other main source is Plutarch's *Life of Dion*.

ing, the lack of response to Plato's teaching and his powerlessness to act—all these do not properly belong to our subject. But it is instructive to see Plato confronted with a political situation and attempting even in thought to apply his ideas to it; he never really had any chance of putting them into practice. There were two Sicilian questions, both such as are apt to occur when a military autocrat dies. Dionysius I had established not only a tyranny at Syracuse, but an empire over the other Greek cities in Sicily. These were both contrary to Plato's first principles; the government of Syracuse could not continue to be a tyranny and the Greek cities must be re-established in their independence. Verbal assent to the latter proposal was obtained; indeed Dionysius claimed that he had always had such an intention. But to interfere with the internal government of Syracuse with a reigning tyrant secure in office was a different matter, and no one can deny Plato's courage in entering upon such a dangerous task.

It is not difficult, after reading his political writings from the *Crito* to the *Politicus*, to guess in general terms what Plato's advice was likely to be. There could never have been any question of establishing in Syracuse the Ideal State of the *Republic*, that is, of course, an earthly copy of it. None of the conditions needed for its establishment was to be had[1] and he was given no thirty years in which to train Guardians. Nor was there ever any expectation that Dionysius II would prove to be a god among men and so become the perfect ruler of the *Politicus*. Plato never imagined any mortal man in that exalted rôle except himself; and he was offered no such post at Syracuse. He had no doubt some hope of establishing an ascendancy over the young tyrant; but Dionysius himself turned out to have little real power. Plato's letters, when they speak of constitutions, envisage not the ideal but the second-best, the practically possible, the rule of Law. As we saw earlier in this chapter, there were three *lawful* constitutions to choose from. At Syracuse single rule had existed for some forty years and there was a ruler in office; the choice of monarchy seemed obvious and the simple answer was that tyranny must be changed to kingship. To induce Dionysius to accept a written constitution, to the νόμοι of which he himself and all his court would be as subject as any other Syracusan, that was the aim of Plato and Dion. It was to be a process of conversion, beginning

---

[1] See above, pp. 157, 159, and *Republic* 541 A.

with Dionysius himself, who was to be taught to master himself
and to have friends—two things impossible for a tyrant, requisite
in a king; the conversion was then to proceed until everywhere
a decent way of life should replace the τυραννικὸς βίος. Very
naturally the tyrant's entourage resented this and interpreted it
all as a plot to abolish the tyranny, as of course it was. On the
constitutional side Plato got as far as drawing up memoranda
showing the general purport of his proposed laws—a useful idea
in civic education which he used in his next large work, the *Laws*.
But he got no farther. From the time when Dionysius fell out
with Dion and banished him there was no more political co-
operation (πολιτικῶν κοινωνία) between Plato and Dionysius.
That was in 366 B.C. In 362 after much hesitation he accepted
another invitation, hoping to prepare a way for Dion's return to
Syracuse. But, as Aristoxenus aptly remarked, his Sicilian venture
was 'just about as successful as that of Nicias'.[1]

As the years went on Plato kept firmly to his belief in a Law-
state for the practical purposes of this world. 'Do not put Sicily
or any city in subjection to human masters but to laws' (*Epist.*
VII 334 C). But as to which of the three legal forms of constitution was the best for Syracuse he was not quite so certain. It had
proved impossible to make a law-abiding monarch out of Dionysius. Plato was sure, though others were not, that Dion had no
wish to rule Syracuse himself; in any case, though he took to
arms and defeated Dionysius, he was himself assassinated in 354
B.C. The changes of the past seven years caused Plato's opinion
to veer towards Law-Aristocracy rather than Law-Monarchy.
The latter would have been better; but the civil war between the
friends of Dion and those of Dionysius must be brought to an
end by agreement, not by force; and there was more chance of
agreeing over the rule of the Few than over the choice of a sole
ruler. But there could be no compromise with the 'tyrannous'
men; so long as they dominated the scene, there could only be
bad and lawless constitutions, any one of the three with constant
changes; there would be no πολιτεία that could be called δίκαιος
καὶ ἰσόνομος (*Ep.* VII 326 D). Plato therefore suggests that from
other parts of the Greek world a team of lawgivers of good
reputation and ancestry should be invited to come and make a
settlement; they are to enact laws which do not favour one

---

[1] Lucian, *De Parasito* 34 (862) = Aristoxenus Fr. 62 Wehrli.

faction or the other but hold the balance between them and are equally binding on both.

A few months later, while still urging the need for a settlement, he writes slightly modifying these suggestions (*Epist.* VIII). The family to which Dionysius and the murdered Dion both belonged was a kind of royal house. They had some claim to the loyalty and gratitude of the people of Sicily. The elder Dionysius had saved the Sicilian Greeks before, and now not only the Carthaginian menace, but Italian barbarians away to the north would be a danger, if those who spoke Greek did not agree among themselves. Monarchy was needed, and if they had two kings in Sparta, why not three at Syracuse? (Dionysius, his half-brother and Dion's son).[1] As before, experts are to be called in to assist in drawing up the laws. The outlines of a constitution are given: the duties of the kings are to be largely, though not entirely, religious; much power will be in the hands of thirty-five 'guardians of the law' (νομοφύλακες). There are also to be a citizen-body and a council, for which the Athenian terms δῆμος and βουλή are used. Thus democratic and oligarchic and monarchic principles have a place in this, Plato's last word on the Syracusan problem. The compromise bears a significant resemblance to the vast structure in Plato's *Laws*.

[1] On the identity of these persons see R. S. Bluck, Appendixes I and II to his edition (1947) of the seventh and eighth letters.

FURTHER NOTES AND REFERENCES
CHAPTER IX

XENOPHON

Memorabilia: I 2, 40-46 (Alcibiades and Pericles); III 5, 13-24; IV 4, 9-25 (Socrates and Hippias); IV 6, 12 (Constitutions); see below.
Lacedaemonian Polity, chs. VIII-X.
Cyropaedia: I 1 and 2, and 6, 7-24; VII 5, 58-86; VIII 1 and 2, and 3, 1-14.

PLATO

Politicus: 268 C - 276; 291 C - 303 D; 303 D - 305 E. These are the parts most immediately relevant, but it must be emphasized that they belong to a dialogue only incidentally concerned with government. For a detailed analysis, especially of the relation to the *Republic*, see Hans Ziese, *Der Staatsmann* (1938) (Philologus Supptbd. XXXI 3).

Epistles. The third and the eighth letters. Of the long seventh chiefly 326 B - 330 E; 350 B - 352.

G. R. Morrow, *Studies in the Platonic Epistles* (Illinois, 1935), pp. 114-173.

G. C. Field, *Plato and his Contemporaries* (1930, repr. 1948), ch. II.

NOTE ON THE 'FRAGMENT' IN XENOPHON, *Mem.* IV 6, 12

The paragraph is isolated; it is preceded by nothing that leads up to it and what follows has no direct bearing on it. Xenophon may have got it from some other political dialogue of the time, such as that of a certain Florentine papyrus. This contains in Greek of the fourth century B.C. a few lines of a discussion about oligarchy and democracy, an examination and rejection of a theory that ability to speak is of more consequence in a democracy than in an oligarchy. *Papiri della Società Italiana* XI, 1935, *Aegyptus* XXVIII, 1948 (M. Gigante) and XXIX, 1949 (M. Gigante and R. Merkelbach).

CHAPTER X

PLATO'S *LAWS*

θεὸς ἡμῖν πάντων χρημάτων μέτρον.
Laws 716

ἀνθρώποις γὰρ διαλεγόμεθα ἀλλ' οὐ θεοῖς.
Laws 732

WHEN men grow old they are apt to become more confirmed in their opinions and more verbose in their exposition of them. But some, while becoming less tolerant
of opposition to their beliefs, become also mellower, more tolerant
of human beings and more ready to make allowances. Plato, it
seems, was one of these. The *Laws*, a work of his old age never
finally revised, is diffuse and garrulous; it lays down the law with
paternal authority, it sticks firmly to main principles and allows
no tampering with them and no mercy to those who would undermine them. But it also makes concessions to our human weaknesses, our liking for pleasure and amusement and our fondness
for what is our own; it recognises that men are neither devils nor
angels or rather, *more Graeco*, that they are men not gods, that
they are, if properly educated, rational beings, who are more likely
to behave according to certain standards if they understand why
they are expected to do so. But they cannot be allowed to choose
the standards for themselves, for these are fixed and eternal and
come from the gods. Protagoras had said 'Man is the measure of
all things'. Plato says, 'No. It is God.'

The philosopher's new task is thus to describe a city which
shall on the one hand be orderly, friendly and 'liveable in' by
human beings and on the other conformable to God. He does not
forget, indeed he often repeats (711-712, 875) his conviction (pp.

186

176-177) that the best way to accomplish this would be to put everything under the personal control of the wisest, the most devoted to righteousness, the perfect and divine ruler, if such could be found. But 'no human character is capable of exercising complete control over human affairs without becoming deeply infected with ὕβρις and ἀδικία' (713 C) and 'no man has natural gifts sufficient to enable him to discern what is best for men in their πολιτεία or, having discerned it, to be able and willing to do it' (875 A). The absence of family life and private property from the lives of rulers and the suppression of every interest save that of the city—these too are still desirable but 'we are talking to men now, not gods' (732 E). This being so, as was shown in the *Politicus*, we must accept the rule of law with all its limitations and with the knowledge that it is only second-best. The control exercised by human beings must be subject to a code of laws, and no person, since we have no divine ruler, may set himself above the laws. Plato does not forget (822) the objection raised in the *Politicus* that written legislation cannot cover everything, but the fact is that a legislator must do far more than draw up a code. He must educate the citizens in the morals of the code, teaching them to understand and follow the underlying principles and strengthening their belief in the divine origin of law. Matters too minute for legislation will be the subject of advice (788). The citizens in turn must not merely be receptive and obedient, but actively participate in their own education (724); they must remember that the soul is more than the body, must cultivate the intelligence and generally 'pay heed to whatsoever in them savours of immortality' (713 E).

The troubled years of Plato's life (366-354 B.C.) had left their mark on Plato's thought (see Chap. IX *fin.*) and the composition of the *Laws* was probably begun towards the end of that period and continued nearly until his death in 347. With many repetitions and digressions it proceeds on its way for twelve[1] books of pseudo-dialogue. The problem is still[2] How best shall man live? It is of course taken for granted that he can only live in a city-state, that the good life is the righteous life and the only happy life. This lesson is to be driven home by the power of persuasion; for per-

---

[1] Or thirteen, if we include the *Epinomis*, an appendix to the *Laws*, edited, or worked up from Plato's words, by Philip of Opus. To that extent, at any rate, the *Epinomis* is genuine Plato, unless indeed one rejects the *Laws*.

[2] 714 B; cp. *supra* p. 143 n. 2.

suasion is better than force, even if it involves deception (662-663). The value of the art of rhetoric as a means of moral and political education is now freely admitted. As in the *Republic*, the character of the citizen is the first concern of the state and the treatment of the subject of education is wider and more general than in the earlier work. With it goes strict censorship of art and literature. The Dorian type of city-life, as exemplified in Crete and Sparta, is in general approved; the weaknesses which were pointed out in *Repub.* VIII are here overlooked and it is accepted that each constitution had its divine sanction—Zeus for the Crete of Minos, Apollo for the Sparta of Lycurgus. It is not for its constitutional defects that Sparta is here criticised, but for its excessive devotion to military training. Military training is important (829 and 942), but not as an end in itself, for the courage which it professes to inculcate is not the only virtue needed in a πόλις. These defects are not held to invalidate the claim to a divine origin, and for Plato, unless you can get a divine ruler, you must have a divine law. Of course he does not accept the Spartan or Cretan laws as they stood in his day. The chief merit of the Spartan constitution had always been its relative permanence, which had been maintained in spite of frequent helot-revolts.

In the hope[1] therefore of drawing practical lessons from the past Plato in the third book surveys the whole history of πολιτεία right back to its beginnings and brings the story of civilisation from the Deluge down to historical Sparta. This is a process which the political thinker need not disdain, though it cannot take the place of actual thinking; but it must be based upon fact not fancy, not upon τὸ μυθῶδες but upon τῶν γενομένων τὸ σαφές.[2] Unfortunately, however, the lesson of historical accuracy which Thucydides taught was never learned either by Plato or the orators, and the third book of the *Laws* is both obscured and vitiated by the fact that Plato reconstructs history and constructs theory almost simultaneously. The emphatic way (684 A) in which Plato insists that he has got hold of real historical facts is in itself a warning, though he admits that in reconstructing the earliest history he is either relating only what may probably (κατὰ τὸ εἰκός) have happened or relating an ancient tale (παλαιὸς λόγος). He bases his account to some extent on Homer, which is just what one would expect

---

[1] And a very confident hope; see 692 C.
[2] *Thucydides* I 22; cp. Chap. VI.

(Introd. and Chap. I). Four stages of development, spread over an immense period of time, are noted. The first is that of isolated families, as of the Cyclops in the *Odyssey*; but Plato describes their mode of life as one of piety, virtue and simplicity, uncorrupted by gold or by the use of the other metals. Its defect is lack of knowledge.[1] The second stage sees the advent of agriculture, but it is only in the third, when the various families are merged in larger groups, that the establishment of laws really begins. The ruling authority set up by the earliest lawgivers was always either aristocracy or kingship, that is, either the heads of families acting together or a single chief ruling the others. Finally, cities of the 'modern' and more complex type are formed. The lesson for πολιτεία which this is held to contain is that an agrarian, land-owning aristocracy has the merit of antiquity and therefore of stability. A second lesson is drawn from the history of events after the Trojan War, much of which is Plato's own invention. Having found that the monarchy declined in Argos and in Messene but flourished in Sparta, he adds, 'Is monarchy ever dissolved, or has any government ever been dissolved by any persons other than its own members?' (683 E). In other words Plato is finding or creating confirmation for his view (Chap. VIII) that in good governments the danger of rebellion by the masses is negligible compared with the danger of failure from within. Perhaps he was not far wrong; the masses in antiquity were ill-organised and their grievances were apt to be exploited in the interests of some ambitious politician or even a foreign invader; moreover they were divided into slave and free.[2]

These two lessons both point to a Dorian model; but the excessive concentration in this type of community on military excellence is always accompanied by the neglect of the intellectual and emotional virtues. This is regarded as a serious defect; ignorance must give way to knowledge. But what does Plato here mean by ignorance? He means ignorance of right and wrong, a sense which the Greek ἀμαθία can easily bear; he means folly, the sense-

---

[1] Thus the primitive way of life, though good, is not perfect. This whole reconstruction looks like an attempt to combine two contradictory theories of a decline from a golden age and a progress in civilisation, as Hesiod too tried to do. See notes and reff. in my edition of the *Works and Days* (Macmillan, 1932), pp. 15-17, and cp. the attitude of Lucretius, *infra*, Chap. XIII.

[2] On this topic see F. W. Walbank: 'Causes of the Greek Decline' in *Journ. Hell. Stud.* LXIV, 1944.

less 'refusal to accept as right and good *that which has been decided upon*[1] and the deliberate choice of what is counted as bad and wrong' (689 A). And if we ask who has made this decision about right and wrong, Plato would answer that it was the gods and that their decisions are embodied in the laws. Only if people have a religious conviction about obedience to the laws can the ever-to-be-sought unity and conformity within the state be found. He even goes so far as to let slip a remark, which seems to annul the claim that intellect counts for much, when he says that the title of σοφός and the offices of the government are to be reserved for those who conform, even though they are 'not very bright'.[2] Thus Plato, here surprisingly like Cleon[3], was really afraid of brains not politically controlled.

A third lesson deduced from this pseudo-historical survey is that the constitution will be more lasting if political power is not unduly concentrated. This was demonstrated by the success of the Spartan constitution with its dual kingship, balanced by the authority of the elders and of the ephors. Spartan monarchy was not really autocracy but a mixed, well-balanced constitution.[4] Autocracy exists in Persia; and Greece had been saved, he rightly says, not only from Persian domination but from Persian education.[5] The Greek cities had had the chance to be 'free, intelligently conscious and self-friendly' (693 B). Only Sparta in Plato's view had come near to doing this; she had attempted to steer a middle course. The Athenians had failed to maintain the principle whereby the whole people 'entered into a voluntary subjection to the laws' (700 A) and had fallen into the same error as the Persian monarchs—unbridled licence and lack of self-control. Nowhere was this more evident than in music and the arts, about which at Athens one man's opinion was as good as another's. For Plato artistic anarchy still[6] meant political anarchy.

[1] δόξαν. Protagoras left the decision with the community, τὸ κοινῇ δόξαν. See p. 53.

[2] The colloquialism is appropriate; the Greek saying was 'can neither read nor swim' (689 D).

[3] Cp. p. 102 and read *Laws* 689 A-E alongside *Thucydides* III 37.

[4] σύμμεικτος καὶ μέτρον ἔχουσα, 692 A.

[5] 'Here is the real truth about Cyrus: he was a good and patriotic leader in the field, but of true παιδεία he had not the remotest conception and he gave no attention whatever to οἰκονομία' (694 C). Is this an attempt to show the folly of Xenophon's *Cyropaedia*? Or is it aimed at Antisthenes?

[6] *Repub.* 424 B-C; *Laws* 701, 812-813.

With these three lessons from the past before us Plato turns our attention to a possible future and the interlocutors (for the *Laws* too is a dialogue) begin the task of 'verbally laying the foundations' (702 E). We are invited to suppose that a lawgiver has been commissioned to found a colony somewhere in Crete and that practical advice is needed. We may be permitted to believe that young men who were studying πολιτική at the Academy in 355 B.C. received instruction more like that of the *Laws* than of the *Republic*. Plato had learned much; he now recognises how much the success of a city-state, or any experiment in government, will depend on external factors, on race and climate, on the compatibility of mixed populations, on the suitability of a constitution for a people and a place. In sketching his new colony, therefore, Plato has more to say about economic conditions than in the *Republic*. He postulates an area of land large enough to maintain the population, but not to raise an exportable surplus. This is a precaution not only against too much wealth, but against the foreign influences which overseas trade inevitably brings. For the same reason the best site would not be on the sea-coast but off the beaten track. (The sea was a highway.) Besides, there must be no temptation to build a fleet, this for fear not of 'international incidents' but of evil social consequences such as Plato had seen at Athens in his early manhood during the Peloponnesian War.

The founder of a city will meet many difficulties at the outset and will often feel himself powerless; decisions will be forced upon him by external causes that he cannot control. But resolute action settles many problems and at the beginning courage and a strong hand are called for, the hand of a dictator, of a man who can get things done quickly and efficiently. To begin with, therefore, the city must be governed by a τύραννος, not of course the τυραννικὸς ἀνήρ (p. 165) but 'a young man with a good memory, intelligent, brave and high-principled' (709 E). He must rule himself, have control over his own mind. These are the conditions which Plato had hoped to find at Syracuse—himself as lawgiver, Dionysius as a converted tyrant. Dionysius was young and intelligent but he would not be converted to σωφροσύνη and would not, as is here required, give up his power in favour of a law-bound constitution (cp. Chap. IX, p. 182). But one of Plato's reasons for advising a lawgiver to have a tyrant to assist him in starting the city and in getting rid of undesirable elements (735) is that he is more easily removed when the need for him is over (710 D), far more easily, for example, than a highly privileged and firmly entrenched oligarchy. Moreover, the good influence which the lawgiver will exercise will be more quickly reflected in one man and passed on through his resolute leadership to the people at large. But the essential is the 'conversion' of ruler or rulers, a 'deep and divinely inspired longing (ἔρως) for all orderly and righteous conduct' (711 D). Whether it be for the actual work of personal rule, as in the *Republic*, or for setting up the rule of law, this combination of political power with understanding and self-control is essential. This is very much what he had often said in his younger days; no existing State is really deserving of the name πολιτεία.

The new city must therefore not be under personal rule absolutely, but under the rule of law, and for the construction of a Law-state there are three fundamental principles: (1) The only true laws are those which are promulgated for the common good; (2) The laws come from the gods, so that the state is grounded in religion; (3) The citizens must not only be acquainted with the laws, they must understand the reasons for them. None of these is entirely new; the first goes back to Solon (p. 24) and the second is equally old-fashioned; the third was implicit in Athenian democracy. But Plato has something to add to all three.

As he had advised the followers of Dion (p. 183) to come to terms with their political opponents, and with the aid of expert νομοθέται, set up a constitution which should not favour one set of people and penalise another, so now Plato protests against the use of such terms as 'city' and 'citizen' as if they were truly applicable to places where one party drives out another and there is no ὁμόνοια. 'We cannot call these constitutions nor give the name ὀρθοὶ νόμοι to any laws save those which have been laid down for the common good of the entire city. . . . In your new city we shall put no man in office because he is rich or because he is possessed of strength or size or good birth or anything like that' (715). A man may win a victory over his fellow-citizens only by being more obedient than the rest to the established laws; and it is to such a victor only that we shall give the highest office, making him a servant of the gods[1] and of the laws.—How much the

---

[1] θεῶν in 715 C 4 should *not* be changed to θεσμῶν.

principle of the common good was really worth will appear shortly; the entire city was very far from being everybody (*infra.* p. 199).

The belief that the gods have given men laws and will protect those who keep them was for long the mainstay of the old city-state. But the *Laws* of Plato envisages a more theocratic kind of state, a more dogmatic religion and a new and additional kind of gods. The theology of the *Laws* is intended to be universal and everywhere accepted. This makes the close association of religion with the city at once more important and more difficult than, say, at Athens in the hey-day of Athena: more important because the new divine laws are made to govern human conduct in far greater detail: more difficult because citizens are apt to feel that a civic religion is their own, while a cosmic religion belonging to everyone is something remote. In the old city-state the conformity which was expected of a citizen in matters of religion was mainly conformity in outward observances. It was his duty to perform certain rites and discharge certain obligations in relation to family and city; but not to hold one particular set of beliefs about the existence and nature of the gods.[1] It is just this that Plato now demands. Orthodoxy in religious belief is a necessity in a theocratic state and the good life is dependent on right belief about the gods (888 B). It is not of course the only requirement; the performance of religious duties is no less strictly enjoined than before, and these are not only prayer and sacrifice and the like, but also duties to society, neglect of which cannot be tolerated, since it would affect the whole community. The religious regulations are therefore held to conform to the first of the three principles and to promote, not hinder, ὁμόνοια. They must also conform to the third principle (see below) and show reasons why they are good laws. If atheism is to be suppressed we must first confound its arguments and only when persuasion fails, resort to force. Plato therefore inserts an attack on all his old philosophical enemies,[2] the physicist materialists, the tellers of unseemly myths, the advocates of the so-called natural right of the stronger and, most dangerous of all, those who assert that the gods either take

---

[1] From time to time, however, as the prosecutions for impiety show, the Athenians at any rate took alarm at the expression of unusual opinions about the gods.

[2] See also p. 206 n. 1.

no notice of men's deeds or can be bribed and cajoled into disregarding them. He protests too against the view that the science
of politics has no basis in φύσις, but only in artificially-contrived
conventions. This is followed by a series of metaphysical arguments about the soul, about motion, about number and reality,
which leads up to a new theology and a new kind of god, visible
yet supernatural—the heavenly bodies.[1] These do not supersede
the traditional gods but appear to be added to them. The conception of Apollo, Dionysus, Zeus, Themis and others has been
purified and the imitation of god is urged as a way of life (716 C).
For Plato's natural inclination was not to destroy institutions hal-
lowed by age, but to reform them; and his own belief in the value
of Apollo, Delphi and the Muses is conspicuous. But he does not
seem ever to have faced the task of deciding how far existing cults
and the whole notion of a city-state were consistent with an astral
and universal theology.[2]

The insistence on the divine nature of all the laws of the state
has for Plato great political consequences. Sacrilege and treason[3]
become equally crimes against the state and against the gods.
Unorthodoxy in religion is both a crime and a danger; it angers
the true gods, and private or secret cults undermine a state which
is itself run as a religion. For much of the activity of the law-state,
and especially everything connected with judicial procedure, is
closely wrapped up with religious ritual, as indeed it was at
Athens. A lawgiver or founder of a city is warned (738) not to
interfere with existing religious observances, many of which serve
a useful social purpose. But the charge of impiety which brought
Socrates to his trial and death would in Plato's new city bring
even the best-behaved unbeliever or heretic into a 'place for mak-

---

[1] On these see M. P. Nilsson in *Harvard Theological Review* XXXIII, Jan.
1940. Other works dealing with Plato's theology are: A. J. Festugière,
Contemplation et vie contemplative selon Platon (1936); Friedrich Solmsen, *Plato's
Theology* (Cornell Studies, 1942); and an article by E. R. Dodds, 'Plato and
the Irrational', *Journ. Hell. Stud.* LXV, 1945. It is treated with particular reference to the *Laws* in O. Reverdin, *La Religion de la Cité platonicienne* (1945) and
to the *Epinomis* by E. des Places in *L'Antiquité Classique* VII, 1938, 186-200.

[2] O. Reverdin, *op. cit.* p. 246, thinks that there may have been two grades
of belief, one for the wise, who really understand, and one for lesser folk.
The existence of both astral divinities and the unseen and anthropomorphic
is mentioned as self-evident in 931 A.

[3] Proximum sacrilegio crimen est quod maiestatis dicitur.—Ulpian.

ing people good and obedient', a σωφρονιστήριον. Here he suffers solitary confinement, sees no one save members of the Nocturnal Council, who visit him regularly for the purpose of 'instructing him and restoring his mind'.[1] For his mind must have gone wrong, if he holds such impious beliefs. If five years of steady mind-conditioning do not succeed in making him σώφρων again, it is best that he should die.[2]

The third principle requires that citizens shall be intelligent, politically conscious and fully aware of their own constitution. At first sight this adds nothing much. It had long been expected of a citizen that he should understand the laws of his country; it was part of his education to learn them. And the education which the laws gave was better in Plato's view[3] than that which was based on Homer or other poets. As examples of lawgivers who really attempted to educate he instances Lycurgus, Solon and Charondas. Of this third lawgiver we know little except that he and Zaleucus had a principle 'not to publish a new law without first speaking in praise of it'.[4] Plato too, while at Syracuse, had begun to draw up preambles to the work of legislation (*supra* p. 183). The view was widely held[5] that a law should not simply follow a formula such as 'Let a man do this, or else be punished thus', since that is no better than the order of a dictator (τυραννικὸν σύνταγμα), which is in its nature unconstitutional. To give

---

[1] ἐπὶ νουθετήσει τε καὶ τῇ τῆς ψυχῆς σωτηρίᾳ (909) which must not of course be rendered 'for the saving of his soul'. There is no reference here to a life after death. Like the persecutions which go on in modern secular states, the aim and the excuse is *security*.

[2] Or perhaps be imprisoned for life. The point is not made clear.

[3] e.g. *Laws* IV 719, *Repub.* X 599, where the ancient lawgiver Charondas is mentioned.

[4] Cicero, *de Legibus* II 14, and the doubtful testimony of Stobaeus about these two and other 'Pythagoreans' collected in Mullach, *Fr. Philosoph. Gr.* (Didot), pp. 532-543. See A. Delatte, *Essai sur la politique Pythagoricienne*, pp. 177 ff; and *infra* note at end of Chap. XIV.

[5] So much seems to be already implied in *Laws* 720-721 and is proved by F. Pfister (see note at end of chapter). Even if we cannot accept as genuinely ancient the προοίμια given in Stobaeus, the fact remains that there is really nothing new in the idea of uniting πειθώ and βία, in spite of Plato's claim (722 B) to originality. Nor need we take much notice of his claim to have been the first to apply the word προοίμιον to a πολιτικὸς νόμος as well as to a κιθαρῳδικός (722 D). He makes no such claim in *Epist.* III 316 A (about 356 B.C.) where he uses the expression τὰ περὶ τῶν νόμων προοίμια of his work in Syracuse, not as something out of the ordinary.

no reasons, but 'simply to state what is to be done and what not, threatening punishment, and then go on to the next law without adding a single word in order to exhort or convince' (720)—that is not the proper way to treat men free and intelligent, who are expected to be able to do a good deal for themselves in the matter of education (724). The novelty in Plato's *Laws* on this point consists not in prefacing law with explanation, but first, in paying greater attention to the basis of legislation, to the doctrine lying behind it, and second, in regarding the inclusion of doctrinal matter as normal[1] and authoritative. 'When the laws and the whole constitution have been drawn up in the way prescribed, the best word that can be said in praise of the outstandingly virtuous citizen is *not* that he has best served and obeyed the laws. A more perfect citizen would be he who passes his whole life in obedience to *all* the written words of the lawgiver, both the legislative and the 'approving and disapproving'.[2] . . . The true lawgiver must not only make laws, but in addition to the laws and interwoven with them insert a statement about what he holds to be right and wrong; and the finest citizen will be bound by these just as much as by the provisions of the law that carry penalties with them' (822 E).

It will be noted that these lessons need not be prefixed to the laws but may be incorporated in them. The emphasis on the preliminary nature of the preambles is not on their position in relation to the actual text,[3] but on the need for thinking well beforehand and preparing the doctrinal position upon which the law will be based. So, whether one prefaces a law with a preamble or incorporates instruction (νουθέτησις, 822 D) in it, the essential is that the preliminary work (προοιμιάζεσθαι) must be done before embarking on the task of sketching a constitution (νόμους πολιτείας ὑπογράφειν). Once it is finished and written down, it will stand for ever (such of course is Plato's view) and *be constantly referred to* (891 A). How can legislation for a theocratic state proceed except as based on theological doctrine? How can any of the problems of political science be discussed without a doctrine of the nature of man? Thus the whole of the *Laws*, but especially the first third

---

[1] φύσει, 722 E; cp. p. 50.

[2] This is contrary to 715 C, but it is by no means the only inconsistency in the *Laws*.

[3] From which of course they can be distinguished (723 B.) In 723 E τὸν τυχόντα λόγον means 'the text, as it will eventually be', not 'chance discourse' or the like, which makes no sense.

of it,[1] is to a large extent a 'making the preliminaries'. We have to do this ourselves with the help of the gods and not rely on the moral or theological standards of the poets, as our forefathers did. In constructing new standards we are writing new poems (811). In addition to illustrations of the work of 'preliminaries' the *Laws* also provides us with some typical, completed preambles, both general and particular (for both are needed, 723 B). Sample προοίμια attached to sample laws occur all through. One passage (715 E - 717 A) inculcates the lesson that God, not Man, is the standard; another offers (719) to a lawgiver a προοίμιον showing why poets are deficient as legislators. Clearly, too, legislation about burial of the dead must be based on a doctrine of the soul (959); legislation about marriage must be accompanied by a lesson in sociology (721).

A much longer 'preamble', expressly (726) continuing the lesson of πάντων μέτρον θεός, ostensibly winds up the preliminaries. It may be described as the first sermon in European literature. As we saw in Chapter IV, many of the problems of political science are inseparable from questions such as What is Man? and What is his place in the Universe? In a theocracy, such as we are here dealing with, the immediate answer is that Man is next below the Gods and is in everything subject to them; he is, moreover, soul first, body next and possessions last of all. This lesson of inferiority to a higher being is one which men find very hard to learn, especially in their youth when they 'think they know everything' (727 A). For ignorance is never so hard to eradicate as when it thinks it is knowledge (886 B *Epinom.* 974 A). In his younger days Plato had indirectly made extravagant claims for his own infallibility and it is tempting, if not very convincing, to believe that he looks back with disapproval on his own youthful ignorance and intolerance as one who has been reformed and converted.[2] There is certainly a sermon-like quality about this 'preamble'. But as a religious lesson the sermon fails; the question, so vital in a theocratic state, What is the relation between divine law and human? is not answered[3] and we are not told how the

[1] See note at the end of the chapter.

[2] There may well have been a *conversion* in Plato's life, though it cannot easily be placed nor can its quality be determined. See E. R. Dodds in *Journ. Hell. Stud.* LXV, 1945, p. 24.

[3] It is not answered by 'Law shall strengthen the link between the city and the gods' (921 C).

human lawgiver is going to learn from his divine superiors.[1] The process by which the *just* and the *lawful* are to be equated is, so to speak, secularised thus: 'To sum up, the lawgiver after consideration shall lay down what things are evil and bad and what things are noble and good'. He who deliberately refuses to abstain from the one and practise the other with all his energy really punishes himself by inflicting damage on his own soul. And so the discourse proceeds to moralise without carrying the basis of the state or of morality back to its divine source. The laws and the legislator should aim at producing the true citizen, him who is ἐν ἤθεσι νόμων. He alone is just; he alone is happy.[2]

Having thus finished his general exhortation, Plato prepares to begin the process of legislation. He first clears the ground by postulating favourable conditions for a good start, a population of a convenient size—5040 citizens,[3] eugenically selected and ruthlessly purged of all moral incurables. He next reminds us that he is not attempting to construct an ideal state but the best that could be managed in practice; there is still for him only one best state, but there are one or two others which may be worth trying. From this point on,[4] therefore, much of what Plato has to say is by way of sample and illustration, not fixed doctrine. He makes use of the lessons which have been drawn in the third and fourth books: the constitution should be 'mixed' to ensure permanence and stability and the whole fabric should aim at being harmonious, religious and self-conscious. He is showing how such a society can be realised and by what laws, but is far from suggesting that in the matter of legislation the last word has been spoken (859). He does not forget the lesson of his own *Gorgias*, that moral education is the first essential for living together, but he finds it necessary to supplement and strengthen it by a comprehensive criminal code. The claims of one set of people to rule over others personally and permanently (690) are modified or rejected (715).

[1] He does, however, return to this question, *infra* p. 206.

[2] cp. *Laws* 733 E - 734 E and 662 D with the *Republic*. There was no change of view about the nature of happiness. 'The very rich are not good (politically, that is) and if not good, not happy' (*Laws* 743 c).

[3] $1 \times 2 \times 3 \times 4 \times 5 \times 6 \times 7 = 5040$. As A. E. Taylor has shown, the choice of 7! is not merely an illustration of mathematical perfection; it is administratively convenient.

[4] See note at the end of the chapter. The method is one which he had recommended legislators to follow (718 B).

In the second-best State the laws will be above all persons.

In the *Republic* only the rulers and their auxiliaries had any part in political life or even knew what they were about; but in the Law-state, in accordance with the third principle, we are to have intelligent, free and politically-conscious citizens. Riper experience and greater knowledge of men and affairs had taught Plato the necessity for widening the basis of the political life of a city and for finding a place for the best and most stable elements in democratic constitutions—notably the practice of electing officials by means of the votes of the whole body of citizens. It follows that all citizens, and not an élite only, must be sufficiently educated to take part in the life of the city. These are significant changes and justify the statement that Plato's second-best State is more democratic than the *Republic*. But we must not delude ourselves. The basis of citizenship in the *Laws* excludes slaves and foreigners, as in any other Greek State. This was a normal 'democratic' practice. But the exclusion of all manual, professional and agricultural workers from citizenship of the Law-state makes the use of the word democracy look ridiculous. Certainly even at Athens the term 'all the citizens' did not mean all the free adult male residents; but the number of non-Athenians was relatively small. In the city of the *Laws* the number of non-citizens will be very large, since all the economic and commercial activity, as well as manual labour, will be carried out by slaves or non-citizens. Large numbers will therefore be needed, even with all Plato's restrictions on trade; and, as Aristotle[1] saw, to maintain 5040 non-productive persons would require far more agricultural land than Plato thought. Thus the Platonic Law-state, though formally conforming to current 'democratic' practice, wears a very different guise when looked at as a whole. It is a body of some five thousand men ruling over others of uncertain number, who have either as foreigners no political rights, or as slaves no legal existence.

These five thousand citizens are not, like the rulers in the *Republic*, compelled to renounce property-owning and family life. Property looms large in the *Laws* and was destined to loom larger than ever in political thought. The first step to be taken is to divide all the land into 5040 inalienable lots, as indeed would be a normal practice in starting a colony. The citizens are thus all land-owners, like the Spartans, but they must all remember that

[1] *Politics* II 1265 a.

'each man that owns a piece of property must count it the common property of the whole πόλις. It belongs to his native land and he must tend it with even greater care than a mother her children' (740). Having made this reluctant concession to private ownership, Plato hedges it around with numerous restrictions. Ownership of property other than land is very strictly regulated. Gold and silver possessions are prohibited; the use of coinage is permitted for business purposes as being 'pretty well unavoidable'. But to own foreign currency or currency accepted by Greek states generally (κοινὸν Ἑλληνικὸν νόμισμα) could only be permitted for the purpose of travel abroad and for that, needless to say, official approval must be sought. Speculation, whether in land, houses or currency, as well as money-lending at interest are all to be firmly repressed. There must be no such thing anywhere as a rich man; for the rich man is a bad citizen. — It might be supposed from all this that Plato intended that there should be complete equality in all forms of wealth. But that is not so. The aim, as in the *Republic*, is the avoidance of extremes of wealth. Even so, it comes as a surprise to find Plato dividing the citizens into four grades on a property basis and so giving the constitution a timocratic[1] element, the two richer classes having certain privileges at elections. Marriage and family life are also hedged about with very many restrictions and interferences that would seem hardly credible if Plato did not pause to remark (781 A) that 'there are many things now unrestricted which would be the better of some legal control'.

These five thousand 'landed gentry' will receive an education appropriate to their station. They will not be trained in any profession, though they will learn the use of arms and must know something about the cultivation of the land. The rulers and auxiliaries of the *Republic* were full-time specialists. Now, however, all citizens are to receive the same education. It begins in infancy and lasts till manhood. The schools are to be built and equipped by the State, the curriculum prescribed and resident teachers appointed and paid.[2] In none of these matters is the parent of the child to have a free hand, nor indeed ought he to want to; the child's *ethos* is to be that of the laws, and the environment and

---

[1] In the Aristotelian sense, i.e. based on a property-qualification.

[2] The teachers cannot be citizens since they are paid professionals. They will be foreigners! (804 D).

handling of the infant child play an important part in the formation of the future citizen. The right life (ὀρθὸς βίος) depends not
on externals, not even on the presence or absence of pleasure or
pain, but on a mental balance, a kind of poise which keeps a man
cheerful.[1] The educator will use various ways to produce this
frame of mind in children so that they may become good citizens;
a discontented child will be a disaffected adult. What has to be
said under this head will include ancient customs and traditions,
laws not yet written. 'So there is no need for surprise if our body
of laws is greatly swollen by the addition of a host of seemingly
minor provisions relating to customary habits and practices'
(793 D). For example, existing governments 'do not seem to realise
that the kind of games that children play is a most important
factor in legislation, because they affect the *lasting* qualities of the
laws' (797 A). That 'all children should play the same games on
the same occasions and in the same way and be fond of the same
toys'—that is the first step towards that stability which Plato
craved. His dream is of a people 'who have the divine good fortune to live generation after generation under the same laws so
that none shall remember or even have heard of any other' (798 B).
What is true of children's games is even more true of music,
dancing, ritual, festivals and all those varied physical and artistic
activities which meant so much in Greek life. So these must all
be brought within the framework of the laws and purged of any
emotionalism and irreligion. There must be no poem written,
no song, dance or play performed that does not conform to the
city's standards; and these are standards not of artistic taste but
of right and wrong, the standards that are νόμιμα καὶ δίκαια. All
the young citizens will receive the same education for another
reason; as adults they will all be performing the same function.
Some will be elected to important offices; all will perform public
duties. No life of idleness on a country estate awaits them, but a
career of public service, an endless succession of meetings, sacrifices and elections. Self-education is a continuous duty, the study
of the Laws and of the general principles of Law. Military training and the study of mathematics will occupy some time, but
there will be much to do and often work will have to be done by
night as well as by day (961 B). No matter how good the laws may

---

[1] εὔθυμος (792 B) the opposite of which is δύσκολος. On εὐθυμία as a social
asset cp. Democritus (*supra* p. 65).

be, the working of the constitution will largely depend on the quality of those holding office (751). Thus, while all citizens are by education qualified for public service, elections to some of the highest offices are in various ways restricted.[1]

Since the first duty of all officials in a Law-state will be to keep the laws, the chief officials will be those appointed to supervise the whole and see that the laws are kept—the Guardians of the Laws or νομοφύλακες. The word is not new; there were νομοφύλακες in the Athenian constitution, though the scope of their work was narrow by comparison,[2] and Plato had suggested such officers to the followers of Dion (p. 184). They are to be thirty-seven in number and are to be elected to office by a series of eliminating processes. At the time of his election a guardian must be over 50 and under 60; he may continue to hold office till he is 70. One of the duties of the law-guardians will be to keep records of the income and property of the citizens; for here evasion of the law is particularly easy. They will have judicial powers and will regard as particularly heinous the crime of 'disregarding the law in order to make a profit' (754). Thus αἰσχροκέρδεια becomes not merely socially reprehensible (Theophrastus, *Char.* xxx), but an indictable offence.[3] The most important individual νομοφύλαξ is the one in charge of education (765). He is selected not by general election, but on a vote taken among the holders of the various other offices. The voting is secret and the tenure is for five years. Many other officials, military, civil and religious, are mentioned and a general Council or *Boulè* of 360 members. Plato pleads strongly (Bk. IX) for a proper criminal code, one which will take into account the various *kinds* of wrong done and the *motives* behind their commission, and for legislation to prevent or punish breach of contract, commercial dishonesty, perjury and so forth, all based on the belief that men take to crime against their will. But for all his interest in Law, and that was clearly very great, Plato does not hide his preference for the personal rule of a god-like man of supreme wisdom and knowledge. If by some divine dispensation he were to turn up, he would need no elaborate code

---

[1] By artificial and complicated devices which are hardly worth reproducing here.

[2] See M. Cary in *Journ. Hell. Stud.* XLVIII, 1928, p. 232.

[3] As in England, France and Belgium about 1917. Love of money-making (φιλοχρηματία) is often the cause of attempts to thwart justice (938).

of laws by which to rule nor would he himself be bound by any written law. 'Neither law nor ordinance is superior to knowledge. It is utterly wrong that Intelligence should be made to obey blindly; it should rule over all, if it is really in its own nature true and free. But as we have none such, save very occasionally, we must fall back on laws and ordinances' (875). Thus does Plato in his old age fall to regretting the past and the career which never came his way. But we find here also anticipation of the future, of Aristotle's similar comment (*Pol.* III 1284), and of the Divine Reason of the Stoics (*infra* Chap. XII). However, in the world as we know it and with human nature as it is, we must have a fixed code binding upon all.

Plato was well aware how easy it is for any legal or political machinery to break down (945). The various officials from time to time appointed have all received the education proper to a citizen, but this is quite unlike the long and exacting discipline of the *Republic*, and less reliance can be placed on the men it produces. All officials will therefore be subject to a scrutiny (εὔθυνα) in respect of their work. The scrutineers will be an elected body of twelve, all between the ages of 50 and 75. An official who believes himself to be wrongly blamed may appeal against their decision and the scrutineers themselves will be scrutinised. Everything is to be elaborately safeguarded and the εὔθυνοι will be priests of Apollo and hedged about with all manner of impressive ritual in the hope of instilling respect for religion and the law. Yet Plato is still not satisfied that he has created a system which will work of itself and will go on working. A great army of loyal and public-spirited citizens is constantly engaged in carrying out their many duties. They have all received the same moral and artistic education, the same in each succeeding generation, and the whole is protected by a code of laws, by checks and safeguards so that everything is supervised.[1] But the system still lacks both vitality and permanence. Now the writer of the *Republic* could hardly conceive a city which had no life or soul. The rule of a divinely derived Law has been substituted for the rule of divinely inspired men; so the soul of the State must be dependent on the eternal, cosmic and universal Law of God. But where in the Law-state does the soul manifest itself? Where are the brains

---

[1] To the mottoes at the head of this chapter we might well add a third: ἀφρούρητον δὴ μηδὲν εἰς δύναμιν ἔστω (VI 760 A).

behind all this elaborate political machinery? If the laws are of divine authority and obedience to them is equal to obedience to the gods, then there must in practice be some persons who know the law of the gods and the whole theocratic system. The religious interpreters (ἐξηγηταί), appointed according to law, are not expected to do more than advise on questions of ritual and procedure; they know no theology, only τὰ θεῖα νόμιμα. The written word he had long ago found to be incapable of expressing the highest truth. So there must after all be some men of superior wisdom having special responsibility, some union of Knowledge and Power.

So, with his task nearing completion and his life nearing its end, Plato looks back at his own masterpiece, the *Republic*, and to the constitution of the Law-state adds yet another official body, a committee of *those who know*, the famous Nocturnal Council. Its members will not indeed be above the Law, for only God is above the Law, nor are they themselves to be equated with the divine ruler of the *Politicus*, for only the law itself is divine. But they will provide a link between the divine law and the human, a link which can only be furnished by the divine part of man, the human mind. The need for a committee armed with religious knowledge and judicial powers was stated in the tenth book, when the task of suppressing heresy and converting heretics was committed to them (p. 194). The Nocturnal Council is now brought into the very centre of the picture and invested with authority and responsibility greater even than those of the thirty-seven law-guardians (νομοφύλακες), though some of these will also serve on it. This committee's task is, characteristically, also described as one of protection (φυλακή). For the laws must not only be observed but preserved; they must be outwardly respected and inwardly accepted. By εὐνομία ἐν ταῖς ψυχαῖς, minds rightly conditioned, and σωτηρία τῶν νόμων, the vitality and permanence which the more mechanical arrangements appeared to lack will be secured. The Nocturnal Council will consist partly of older men selected from the law-guardians and partly of younger men, who will be active in finding out all that is going on; for the committee is to be the eyes and ears of the State as well as its brains and soul. It will meet at night[1] as its name (νυκτερινὸς σύλλογος) implies. Energy,

---

[1] That is, before dawn, for such was the way among Greeks and Romans of 'burning the midnight oil'. The day time was already overcrowded with public business (961 B).

ability, loyalty but above all knowledge and wisdom are required of its members. They must know the aim and purpose of the State and how it is to be attained. Other states may make military strength, or freedom, or riches their goal, but such aims only end in self-destruction. The purpose of our State is and has been all along[1] Goodness, ἀρετή—courage, justice, self-discipline, intelligence. But the new protectors must not merely understand the virtues taken singly; they must be able to see the unity in their diversity, the One in the Many. Though nothing is here said about the theory of ideas, there can be no doubt that Plato has it in mind, as he once again harks back to his earlier writings. For the knowledge required of the protector of the Law-state, so far as we learn of it, is not radically different from that of the supreme Guardians of the *Republic*. The most significant difference is, as we should expect, the increased importance of theological knowledge, since 'God is the measure of all things'. The *Republic* had not, it is true, overlooked (II 364) the three main tenets,—the power and goodness of the gods, their concern for what men do and their incorruptibility. But the training of the rulers was not there theological nor the structure of society theocentric. The new guardians of the Nocturnal Council will exercise political influence through theological knowledge. They must be able not only to assert but to prove the cardinal doctrines about the gods and the soul, both the human soul and those divine souls that give life and motion to the heavenly bodies (cp. 899 B).

Such men must first be found and then trained. But there is no provision for this in the Law-state, where identical education for all citizens has been the rule. We seem once again to be looking backward and to be facing the old question of παιδεία and πολιτεία as we saw it in the *Republic*, where everything depended on the success of a long moral and intellectual training of a select few. It looks as if the success of the Law-state is going to be similarly dependent. Plato will have to begin afresh and plan a ruler-education as well as a citizen-education. He fully realises that that is what he ought now to do (968), but he shrinks from such a task. Even if the right type of man can be found, Plato is not sure that he knows all that they ought to learn. He can only say in a

---

[1] Not only from the beginning of the *Laws* (I 630, III 688) but all through Plato's work on πολιτική.

general way that mathematics and astronomy will be needed, since their study leads not, as used to be thought,[1] to atheism, but, through a knowledge of celestial bodies and their motions, to a knowledge of things divine. But he declines to go further, making excuses that do not ring very true (968): it is likely that he was too old and too tired. All the same the question was on his mind and he was not the man to shirk a duty. So, though he did not revise the *Laws* or attempt in any way to superimpose a second educational system, he left 'among his papers'[2] some further remarks. For the *Epinomis* is quite clearly intended to fill the gap left at XII 968. It opens thus (973): 'We have now, I think, gone over all the ground as far as making laws is concerned; but we have not yet either put or answered the important question: What shall a mortal man learn to make him a wise man?' It ends by stating that the kind of learning described can only be acquired by long training and will endow men with that supreme wisdom which is essential for holding high office or membership of the Nocturnal Council. The body of the work, in length comparable to a book of the *Laws*, is an account of that learning, which, however little its importance in political thought, was immensely influential in other ways. It is thoroughly Platonic, that is aged-Platonic, the Plato not of the Syracusan days or even of the beginning of the *Laws* but of the very end. It is a Plato no longer certain of himself or of his superior political wisdom, scarcely any longer believing in politics, but holding fast to the truth of arithmetic, geometry, astronomy and theology.

The end of the *Laws* shows furthermore that Plato was divided in his own mind on a matter even more fundamental than education for rulership or citizenship. He was in doubt whether his proper task was to build a city in this world or in the next, here again harking back to the *Republic*, where the crowning effort belonged to the world of Ideas. Even in the *Laws* the non-material has been given precedence over the material, the soul over the body, but the city of the *Laws* is very much of this world. It is only at the very end that his old longing for the other world re-

---

[1] He is thinking of Anaxagoras chiefly, dead eighty years before, though there may have been contemporary 'disciples of a somewhat degenerate Anaxagoreanism not sufficiently distinguished to leave any of their names behind'. J. Tate on *Laws* 889 C D in *Class. Quart.* XXX, 1936, pp. 48-54.

[2] See p. 187 n. 1.

asserts itself and the feeling (for it is hardly more than that) comes to him that the starry heavens will provide a quicker path to that world than the Theory of Knowledge. For unity amid diversity, for permanence in a world of flux he had sought all his life. He had tried to construct a State which should conform to these principles and had early given up all thought of seeing it actually in existence. Now, at the end of his life, he has to abandon the project even in theory. Oneness and Eternity do not belong to a world of becoming and passing-away but only to the Other World. Plato's last thoughts about the State were not about the Greek πόλις at all, but foreshadowed the *Civitas Dei* of St. Augustine.

FURTHER NOTES AND REFERENCES
CHAPTER X

The *Laws* has been translated into English with introduction, occasional footnotes and an index by A. E. Taylor (Dent, 1934) and by R. G. Bury (Loeb).

There is another Socratic dialogue on the subject of Law—the *Minos*, which may or may not be by Plato. It will be referred to in Chap. XII (p. 247).

The two quotations at the head of the chapter single out two of the main characteristics of the city of the *Laws* as compared with that of the *Republic*. In the *Laws* theocracy is aimed at and Plato is talking to ordinary people, not to impossibly perfect Rulers, gods upon earth. The *Republic* gives us a 'secular' city in heaven, the *Laws* a 'religious' city on earth.

The general principles of the Law-state are to be found mainly but not entirely in the first third of the work—down to about Book V 740. At this point Plato begins to give samples of legislation, with comments and discussions. Aristotle was no doubt thinking of this break in Book V when he said (*Pol.* II 1265) that 'the greater part of Plato's *Laws* is about laws not πολιτεία', but he must have seen that the division is not clear cut, for in the most 'legislative' Books, VIII, IX and XI, there is much discussion and teaching, while Book X is nearly all προοίμιον. He does not comment on the change at XII 960. A writer of a modern text-book (which Plato did not want to be) would have divided his subject more rigorously, e.g. (1) 'Prolegomena to the study of Politics' and (2) 'Social and political applications'.

The following are the page numbers (Stephanus) of the *beginnings* of the books of the *Laws*: I, 624; II, 652; III, 676; IV, 704; V, 726;

VI, 751; VII, 788; VIII, 828; IX, 853; X, 884; XI, 913; XII, 941; *Epinomis*, 973.

CHIEF PASSAGES IN THE LAWS

626-631   objections to the military state.

643-644 ⎫
653-662 ⎬ fixing of educational standards cp. Book VII.

676-686   reconstruction of history (see also G. Rohr *Platons Stellung zur Geschichte*, Berlin, 1932).

688-689   wisdom and virtue as political conformity.

691-694   more lessons from history.

697-701   example of Athens; extremes to be avoided.

709-711   how to set up a state or colony, the preliminary firm hand.

711-714 ⎫
875   ⎬ the need for a Law-state.

The three principles of the Law-state:

(1) 663, 714-715, ὁμόνοια, cp. *Epist.* VII 337.

(2) 716-718, 828-831, 853-857 (sacrilege = treason) and for the religious basis generally Book X *passim* with the literature mentioned on p. 194 n. 1.

(3) 693, 701 (πόλις ἐλευθέρα τε καὶ ἔμφρων) and 718-723, 822-823, its education by means of προοίμια, with Fr. Pfister, *Die Prooimia der Platonischen Gesetze* in *Mélanges Boisacq* (1938) II 173-179.[1]

726-734   'the first sermon', cp. 716-717.

735-738   the elimination of undesirables.

738-739   the best and the second-best states.

742-744   the restrictions on coinage and wealth.

Book VII *passim* (with more detailed references above) the education of the five thousand.

960-969   second thoughts on education, the nocturnal council.

---

[1] N.B. p. 175 *Laws* IV 722 C 1 † μάχην. Pfister ἀπειλήν.

CHAPTER XI

ARISTOTLE

ARISTOTLE differs so much from Plato that it is sometimes said that all thinking men must, knowingly or unknowingly, be followers of one or the other. All such generalisations are at best partial and unsure; and to those who consider the political philosophy of the two masters there appears at first glance to be little truth in the remark; they had so much in common. To begin with, there is the whole background of political thought and moral and educational theory from Homer to Socrates. This inheritance belonged to both; but Aristotle received it a generation later, with yet another layer of thought and experience added. Both looked with alarm on the instability of Greek political life and on the moral anarchy which they believed to be its cause; and both accordingly believed that the antidote lay in education for a better way of living. Both believed that the good life could only be lived in a πόλις of moderate size, could not be attained by all men, but only by those who had sufficient means and sufficient schooling to do so. Both therefore wished to limit citizenship so as to make this possible, and both thought it right that all manual labour should be done by slaves or by non-citizens. It would, however, be a mistake to conclude that Aristotle has but little to add to Plato or to the Greek view of life, and wrong to suppose that Aristotle's express criticisms of Plato are all that marks the difference between them. These are indeed frequent, sometimes significant, sometimes trivial and carping, but they are not all that separates them.

Aristotle was not an Athenian. His father was physician to the king of Macedon but the family was not Macedonian. Stagira, where he was born, was Ionic Greek, and his early upbringing would be based on Homer, like that of any other Greek boy (and of Alexander the Great). The Macedonians, with whom he thus came in contact, were not βάρβαροι and not wholly uncultivated (or Euripides would not have gone to live among them); but they never adopted the city-state way of life. Philip was an hereditary monarch and the kingdom of Macedon had continued to grow in spite of dynastic feuds and assassinations, border warfare and periods of weakness. This background Plato did not share, though he knew something of it (*Gorgias* 470 D). Aristotle turned his back on it, when as a young man he went to Athens in 367 B.C. to study at Plato's Academy, where he remained as student or teacher for twenty years, that is, until Plato's death. Speusippus, a mathematician as well as a biologist, was appointed to succeed Plato. Aristotle left Athens and went to Atarneus in Mysia, where he joined a group of former pupils of the Academy. At the head of these was the ruler, Hermeias, whose niece he married. At various places[1] on the coasts and islands of Asia Minor he pursued the practical study of marine biology, which interested him far more than the mathematical studies at the Academy. Plato shared none of these experiences, not even marriage. This life was interrupted after five years by Aristotle's appointment as tutor to Philip's son, the future Alexander the Great, a post which he held for about three years (343-340 B.C.). Thus he became more closely than ever associated with Macedonian kingship, and the world has never ceased to wonder why in his later writings Aristotle makes no reference to the career of his former pupil.[2] About 335, being now fifty years of age, he is at Athens again, where in spite of some anti-Macedonian feeling he was able to set up his own school, the Lyceum, the future home of the Peripatetic philosophers and the biological sciences.

To these differences in background add the difference between a middle-class professional man, a husband and a father, scientific observer and practical administrator and Plato the Athenian aristocrat, mystic, ascetic, puritan. We shall not then be surprised to find the political thought of Aristotle marked by such non-Platonic features as the value of family life, the pursuit of health

---

[1] H. D. P. Lee in *Class. Quart.* XLII (1948), p. 61.

[2] See for example M. Tierney in *Studies*, June 1942, p. 221, and V. Ehrenberg, *Alexander and the Greeks* (1938), ch. III.

and happiness, to use Jefferson's phrase, the importance and value of property, respect for public opinion and for the tastes and preferences of the man in the street, above all, his sense of the possible, his conviction that one half at least of politics is making the best of what you have. What you might do, if you could throw it all away and start afresh, is not indeed a useless question; on the contrary, it is well worthy of philosophy, for the study of perfection is never to be despised. But the construction of ideal states is not the whole of political science; to improve and preserve the actual is equally a part. Whether the aim of our study be practical or theoretical, the basis will be the same—the understanding of everything connected with the πόλις and of man in his relation to it, man as a ζῷον πολιτικόν, a creature made for society. The political art is all embracing. It is nothing less, Aristotle tells us at the beginning of the *Ethics*, than the knowledge of the supreme good. He arrives at this conclusion by a characteristically teleological argument which may be summarised thus: 'All that we do or think or say has for its *end* some *good*, medicine has health, shipbuilding ships and so on. The *supreme* good must be one which we pursue for its own sake, not because it helps us to some other end. A knowledge of it will therefore be a great influence (μεγάλη ῥοπή) in our lives, so much so that, as it is the part of the art of medicine to have knowledge of health, so to have knowledge of the supreme good is the part of the art of living itself.' To this Aristotle gives the name πολιτική. For the good life can only be lived in a πόλις and to secure the good life for the whole body of citizens is better worth striving for than the good of an individual. Most people are agreed that the aim of the πόλις should be happiness, but there is great difference of opinion about what makes happiness. Aristotle could not conceive of a man being happy unless he were doing something, acting or thinking, and unless his deeds, words and thoughts had *merit*; whence his famous definition of happiness—ἐνέργεια κατ' ἀρετήν. Recognising that this condition needs financial support, he adds the proviso that a man to be happy must be 'sufficiently equipped with external goods'. The virtues and vices which help or hinder the attainment of the good life are discussed in Aristotle's ethical works, and towards the end of the Nicomachean Ethics he returns to link up this subject with that of the πόλις. Moral qualities, he tells us, will not be acquired by attending lectures on ethics given to adult audiences, but only by early teaching and training in good habits. So the first duty of a state for Aristotle, as for Plato, is to educate its citizens in accordance with its own ἦθος and laws; its second duty to correct and punish those who break the laws. But, he says (*Eth. N.* x 9, 18), the making of laws has never been satisfactorily handled either by the professors or the practitioners, the σοφισταί or the πολιτευόμενοι. Yet this is surely the next step in the study of the science of human affairs. (He does not here make any mention of Plato's *Laws*.) Accordingly he goes on (x 9, 23): 'First then let us endeavour to survey whatever good, though only partial, treatment has been written by our predecessors, then from a study of collected constitutions note what are those things which preserve and what are those which destroy cities and their several constitutions; and what are the reasons why some are well governed, others not. When we have done that, we shall also be better able to see what is the best constitution and how its powers are distributed and on what ethical and legal basis it rests.'

This concluding paragraph of the *Ethics* foreshadows and gives a partial account[1] of the contents of the work which we know as the *Politics* of Aristotle; and this work with relevant parts of the *Ethics* and the *Rhetoric* is our chief source of knowledge of Aristotle's approach to questions of political science. This approach was two-fold, and 'approach' is the right word. For Aristotle looks upon the topics of his discourse as problems (ἀπορίαι). He gives the impression of standing before his subject and considering it as impartially as his prejudices will allow. Analysis and classification, division and sub-division were the normal processes of his mind; and the division of political science into two kinds (the 'absolute best' and the 'best possible') is followed by a sub-division of the second into two. For to the study and verbal construction of ideal states are opposed (1) the search for the best practicable, having regard both to the people for whom the constitution is being made and to the conditions, material and historical, confronting the legislator and (2), since no work on politics could take into account all possible variations, the search for that which on the average may be expected to work best. To answer such questions with one of the stock answers, democracy or oligarchy, is futile. It is necessary to go into much greater detail, since there

[1] See note at the end of the chapter.

are many different constitutions each capable of bearing the name democracy or the name oligarchy. The πολιτεία depends on a variety of things—public appointments, how they are filled; power,[1] where it finally rests; the end or purpose of the association (κοινωνία) of persons which makes the πόλις. Moreover two πολιτεῖαι may be similar yet have different νόμοι. This is a distinction which early writers did not readily draw; so much of the law and custom of the city-state was regarded as part of the constitution. Aristotle advises that the laws be considered as operational rules within the framework (of sovranty, distribution of offices and general aim), which is the constitution.

The political philosopher must also face such questions as, What is the *nature* of the political association, the κοινωνία which we call a city? What constitutes membership of it? On what ethical basis does it rest or ought it to rest? Such questions belong equally to the enquiry into the Absolutely Best State and to the search for the 'best in the circumstances' or the 'best on the average'. In reply to the first question Aristotle lodges an objection against those who, like Plato in his *Statesman*, make no difference in kind between the relationship of master and slave and that between governors and governed in a city, but assume that the science (ἐπιστήμη) of government is one, whether in a household or in a State.[2] Aristotle, while agreeing with Plato that the rule of master over slave is natural and proper where it belongs, disagrees with this analogy with the government of a city, even if we assume a monarchical form of government. Aristotle's own answer to the question is, as one would expect, on the one hand biological, on the other teleological, though he does not say much about the relationship between the two answers. The progress of civilisation is part of, not opposed to, the growth-process of φύσις; there has been, we might say, an evolution: family—household—village—city. This process is not of course identical with the growth-process in men and animals, for politics is a practical not an observational (θεωρητικός) science, and human interference can 'make things otherwise'. All the same, we may reasonably look for a norm, a φύσις of city as of man or animal

---

[1] τὸ κύριον (1289 a 17) sometimes rendered *sovranty*, but it really means not the source of power, or the right to it, but the fact of its exercise.

[2] *Politicus* 258 e. Aristotle does not here refer by name to Plato or to the dialogue, but his comments (1252 a) follow the passage closely.

(cp. *supra*, p. 49). It should not be abnormally large or small, or out of proportion in any respect. Moreover life in a πόλις is also part of the 'normal nature' of man, distinguishing him from beasts, none of which, however gregarious or industrious they may be, can reasonably be called ζῷον πολιτικόν. Add that the πόλις is the *final* stage in the process, the *end*, for the attainment of which the other stages exist, and we conclude that though the family and the village may precede the polis in time, the logical priority[1] and pride of place belong to the City or State. The nature of such a κοινωνία must further be moral; man is distinguished from beast by his power of seeing the difference not only between things beneficial and things harmful; but also between just and unjust, right and wrong. Any association of human beings, whether it be large or small, household or city, must be of this kind. With most of this Plato would have had no quarrel; the opening of the *Politics* is not so much an attack on Plato's *Politicus* as a defence of the traditional institution of the city-state, both against the older immoralists (see Chap. V) and still more against those thinkers of the fourth century who regarded city-life as an unnecessary encumbrance, or as an unwarranted interference with 'nature' (Chap. XII, pp. 244-246).

The chief basis of the State will then be Justice or Righteousness, as Hesiod said long before. But for Aristotle, as for Plato, Justice is inconceivable except in a πόλις, because it governs our dealings with other people; it is πολιτικόν and πρὸς ἕτερον. The material needs of the city, though it was not these that created the πόλις, will have to be met partly by slave-labour; but slaves are not 'other people', they are possessions, and their treatment, though it should be kindly, is not a matter of political justice (τὸ πολιτικὸν δίκαιον), for this, he says, 'can only exist among those who, aiming at self-sufficient independency, share a way of life, men free and equal, either proportionately or arithmetically' (*Eth.* v, 6, 4). In all this there is nothing new; Aristotle is still defending the traditional institutions of the Greek City. What makes his discussions of the political virtues interesting is the way in which he analyses and classifies, observing the behaviour of individuals and groups and marking the reasons why they

---

[1] Aristotle, says W. L. Newman (*The Politics of Aristotle*, Vol. I, p. 31, 1887) 'makes no subsequent use of this principle'. It is here insisted on for polemical reasons. In *Eth.* VIII 14 he said ἀναγκαιότερον οἰκία πόλεως.

behave in their several ways. He often, both in the *Ethics* and the *Politics*, writes rather as a sociologist than a political philosopher in the modern sense. But he is unshaken in his belief in a Universal Justice, though he does not, like Plato, give it a transcendental existence; it is immanent in man, part of his φύσις. But man, though not a beast, is not a god either, and when it comes to establishing justice in the πόλις, the risk of allowing a mere human individual to be the sole arbiter is too great, and law must rule —οὐκ ἐῶμεν ἄρχειν ἄνθρωπον, ἀλλὰ τὸν νόμον (*Eth.* v 6, 5). Thus Aristotle comes to the same conclusion as Plato in the *Politicus* but with much less reluctance.[1] Like Plato too he has reservations about it in favour of the highly exceptional man. But in practice justice can only become effective through just laws, whether we are thinking of justice as rewards and punishments, or as the distribution of office and power, or as the fixing of standards, whether of conduct or merely of weights and measures.

But Justice, though all-pervading, is not the only moral basis of the political association; there must be Friendship and Good-will, φιλία and ὁμόνοια. This too had been said by others long before, but Aristotle's reason for stressing it was not merely political stability but moral goodness. It is possible to conceive of a relationship based on justice and carried through justly, yet not adding anything to the goodness of the life of its members. That, however, would not be a πόλις, for the aim of the city is not merely life, but good life, life worth living. Freedom from want and a fair and acceptable distribution to each according to his deserts will not in Aristotle's view suffice to secure a good life. There must be a feeling of friendship and affection for one another and for the community as a whole. Life without that is not *good*. Incidentally, this is the way to promote unity in the State. Plato's desire for unity overreached itself and his methods tended to destroy the diversity between individuals which is essential to the good life (II 1261 A).

It had long been a commonplace[2] that what makes a city is men, not ships or houses; but there is clearly much more in the question, What is a πόλις? than that. Certainly a city is its citizens.

[1] F. D. Wormuth, 'Aristotle on Law' in *Essays . . . presented to George H. Sabine*, 1948, seems to me quite at fault in reducing Aristotle's regard for law to a vanishing point.
[2] e.g. Alcaeus, Fr. 35 D, Soph. *O.T.* 56-57, Thuc. VII 77 *fin.*

But who are they? What makes a citizen? This question of membership of the political association is equally important for the theorist imagining an Ideal State and for the framer of an actual constitution. Birth, place of birth, descent, residence, age—such considerations provide the material for working rules but do not give a definition. Plato had said (*Laws* VI 766 D) that 'a city without regularly established law-courts would not be a city at all'. And Aristotle here, as often, tacitly following the *Laws*, finds a tentative definition of citizen in 'one who has a part in judicial decisions and in holding office'. He does not regard this as a dual definition but as one, since to serve in court as judge or juror is in itself to hold office, even if it be, as in democratic constitutions, only for a limited period. That is indeed its weakness as a definition; it is merely descriptive. There are many different ways of constructing law-courts and offices. To be a citizen where citizens are Few is very different from being a citizen among the Many. A πόλις is πολιτεία as well as πολῖται. Moreover any such definition leaves untouched the question of continuity of membership when the kind of political association is altered. This was and is a question of practical importance. What authority has a newly set up government to deprive former citizens of their membership, what authority either to reduce or to add to the number of citizens? This is, as Aristotle saw, part of a larger question—the continuity of contractual obligation from one government to its successor. We can either take the view that the πόλις itself has entered into a contract, which therefore is binding on the new government; or we can say that the contract was made by the ruler, or by the government, or even that it was made by the democracy (or oligarchy) and is therefore not binding on the oligarchy (or democracy). Such questions therefore as, When is an action an action of the πόλις and when is it not? and, When are we to say that a city has become other and not the same? remain unsolved ἀπορίαι, though Aristotle inclines to the view that a change of constitution, being, as we might say, a change of ethos, is in fact a change of identity, just as a tragic chorus is something different from a comic chorus, though consisting of the same persons.

Returning to consideration of the members of the political association, Aristotle raises a question whose immediacy is stronger and clearer in the twentieth century than ever before. When we ask: Are the goodness of the good member and the goodness of the good man the same goodness? we are discussing a fundamental problem in the relation of ethics to politics, as Aristotle was well aware. He had expressed his doubts in his *Ethics* (v 2, 11): 'Perhaps to be a good man is not always the same thing as to be a good citizen.' What, first of all, is the goodness of the citizen? As citizen his goodness must be that which promotes the good of the city. But that good will vary according to the character of the constitution, whereas the goodness of the good man cannot thus be made relative. Moreover a citizen must be good at something, if he is to play his part in the service of his city. Citizens cannot all perform the same service, so they cannot all have the same goodness; but the goodness of the good man must in Aristotle's view be *one*. This is not intended to depreciate the goodness of the citizen; it is essential that if a city is to be good, its members must be good citizens. Similar, though not immediately relevant to the question of membership, is the relationship between the goodness of the good ruler and that of good man or citizen. A good ruler must be a good man. But that will not suffice to make him a good ruler; he must be good at ruling. Will he also need to be a good citizen? As a ruler his goodness will not be exactly the same as the goodness of a citizen. Ruling requires greater wisdom than being ruled. Both require justice and moderation but not in quite the same sense. Aristotle is not happy about such a cleavage; the notes which he has left us are neither orderly nor full. He seems, however, to conclude that the goodness of the good ruler, the good man and the good citizen would all coincide if certain conditions were satisfied: (1) the πόλις is itself good and ruled by the very good; (2) no ruler is an absolute master but rules over citizens, of whom he is one; (3) the ruler has learned to obey as well as to command; (4) all the citizens are good citizens. He does not quite commit himself to saying that all the citizens must also be good men. It would follow from this that political education should be education for citizenship and not for ruling. Aristotle would have liked Rousseau's remark about the education of royal princes: 'Il ne paraît pas que cette éducation leur profite; on ferait mieux de commencer par leur enseigner d'obéir.'[1] Plato's view on education for ruling had, as we have seen, fluctuated. Aristotle, as usual, comes nearest to the

---

[1] *Contrat Social* ii 6.

Plato of the *Laws* and agrees that the mark of a good citizen is ability both to rule and to be ruled, both to command and to obey.[1] The practical value of this view of education is illustrated by an anecdote of the Thessalian Jason of Pherae. This fourth-century prince apparently complained that because he was good at ruling and at nothing else, he would be liable to starve if he lost his present job.[2]

This discussion of the virtues of a ruler, with its implied commentary on Plato, has thrown some light on the main question of membership of the κοινωνία. If fitness both to rule and to be ruled, both to command and to obey is to be the mark of the citizen, we have some measure with which to decide who shall be members. Now, these, taken together, cannot describe the relationship of master and slave, but only of free persons, who can both hold office and obey authority; free, intelligent and self-friendly, as Plato put it. But persons may be free, yet so occupied with earning a living that they have neither the time nor the ability, that is the ἀρετή, goodness, to hold office. They are by definition (p. 216) excluded from citizenship. Aristotle does not therefore discard the definition which makes citizenship depend on office. It would have been simple to reverse it, for holding office is normally confined to citizens. But that would have deprived him of any definition of πολίτης. He believes that 'citizen' is capable of definition and that it is preposterous (1275 b 30) to say that any persons can be made citizens just by calling them such.[3] If there is such a thing as the goodness of a citizen, then only those are citizens who have acquired that goodness. The gainfully and degradingly occupied, the βάναυσοι, have no chance to acquire it, and the harder they work, the less fit they become to be good citizens and exercise the functions of ruling as well as being ruled. Their work is useful and valuable, their presence is necessary for the working of the city, they may have much ability and make much money,[4] but all, rich or poor, clever or stupid,

---

[1] ἄρχειν καὶ ἄρχεσθαι (Plato, *Laws* 643 E, 942 C, etc.).

[2] *Politics* III 1277 a 24.

[3] Did he disapprove of the practice (which he records, *Ath. Pol.* LIII, 5) of 'unmaking' citizens (ἀτιμία) for failure to perform certain obligations? Cp. Andocides, *de Myst.* 73 ff.

[4] The point is that they might thus, so far as property-qualification is concerned, become eligible for citizenship.

who are continually and professionally employed and paid, are βάναυσοι and therefore cannot be πολῖται. Rather than sacrifice this conviction Aristotle accepts a state of affairs in which possibly a large part of the adult male population is without the rights of a citizen. He is well aware (1278 a 7-40) that this narrowing of citizenship is not generally approved, but, perversely as it must seem, he throws away one of the chief advantages of the city-state—that its small size makes it possible for all its inhabitants to share fully in its life—and clings to his high standard of individual excellence for citizenship.

The classification of constitutions into three, according as the sovran power lay with the One, the Few or the Many had long been modified by postulating a good and a bad in each class. The good might be those in which the government had the consent of the governed, the bad those based on force; or else the good might be said to be those based on law (supra, Chap. IX). Aristotle uses a third criterion—whether government is exercised for the benefit of the governed or of the governing persons. On this basis he distinguishes Tyranny from Kingship, Oligarchy from Aristocracy, and Democracy from a good 'Polity'. Plato had been obliged to use δημοκρατία for both the bad and the good. Aristotle, looking for a different word to describe the good democracy, either simply uses πολιτεία by itself or, since in his view a property qualification is always necessary for citizenship, τιμοκρατία. 'There are three kinds of constitution and an equal number of deviations or corruptions. These three are Kingship, Aristocracy and a third depending on property-assessments (τιμοκρατία), which is appropriately described as timocratic, though most people habitually call it simply 'polity' (Eth. VIII 10, 1). Plato arranged the six in order of merit (see Chap. IX) and Aristotle also does so—twice, with different results.[1] He evidently attached little importance to such schemata, and his analytical methods found many weaknesses in the old three- or six-fold classification. For example, the difference between the Few and the Many is in effect the difference between Rich and Poor, and this difference Aristotle regards as more fundamental than the difference in number. He would even use the term oligarchy to describe the rule of the majority, if the

---

[1] In the Ethics (VIII 10) he follows Plato (Politicus); in the Politics he does not. In the Rhetoric (1 8, 1365) he uses a four-fold classification for the purpose of advising political speakers.

rich outnumbered the poor, but he leaves us without definitions of these words.

Royal rule may be of several different kinds—the Spartan kingship, the non-Greek or oriental kingship, the non-hereditary, sometimes temporary, rule of an elected dictator (αἰσυμνήτης), whose election distinguishes him from a tyrant, and the heroic kingship of the Homeric poems. In all these four the absolute power of the monarch is in some measure limited. A fifth type would be monarchy quite unfettered by elections, laws or constitutions—the purely personal rule which Plato so longed to exercise. This is a possibility worth discussing, although in practice it will be found that all government must depend on law. So Aristotle, when he has discussed the relationship of νόμος and βασιλεία and demonstrated by the now familiar arguments the superiority and impartiality of the rule of law, returns again to the absolute ruler, and considers the possibility that for certain people absolute rule (παμβασιλεία) may in fact be best. But the man who could exercise such rule for the sake of the general welfare and not for his personal advantage is rare indeed, nothing less than a 'god among men' as Plato had often said.[1] Over such men there is no law; they are themselves law, just as the truly well-bred man needs no rules of polite society; he is law to himself.[2]

In the city-state, however, the forms of constitution which really counted were those of the few and the many, oligarchy and democracy. Apart from numbers and from the rich-and-poor division these two differ also in their conception of Justice, in their ideas of right and wrong, fair and unfair. In the distribution of rights, benefits and privileges, always a matter of prime importance to a Greek, the democrats hold that all, being all equally free, have an equal claim, oligarchs that wealth confers a preferential right. A third principle, that of aristocracy in the literal sense, would confer privilege only on merit and this Aristotle

---

[1] *Politicus* 303 B, *Laws* IX 875 C, Aristotle, *Pol.* III 1284 a.

[2] νόμος ὢν ἑαυτῷ, *Eth.* IV, 8, 10. On the vexed question whether Aristotle thought of monarchy as a practical possibility see V. Ehrenberg, *Alexander and the Greeks* (1938), pp. 71-85. It seems clear that Aristotle is all the while rejecting mere number as a basis for classification. He has decided that oligarchy is properly rule by the rich rather than rule by the few; so kingship proper is a matter of outstanding ἀρετή, not of one man rule; hence it is in principle identical with aristocracy. Plato would have agreed. Cp. *Pol.* III 1284 a *init.* with Plato, *Repub.* 540 D, and see Chap. VIII, p. 159.

follows. But what constitutes merit in this connection? Aristotle's answer is to say that rights and privileges should be distributed in proportion to the contribution made to the common weal, that is, to the good life, which is the end or aim of the State. Those who contribute most receive most. But we are not dealing with a commercial company or with a mutual defence pact, but with an association having a moral aim. The contributions, therefore, cannot be assessed in terms of wealth or armaments. The shareholders must be paid in the one case, and the defence provided in the other, no matter whether the persons concerned are just or unjust. They must of course commit no wrong in respect of their contract; but the moral aim of the State is something more than keeping a bargain, and 'if we are really concerned with good government, we must take note of goodness and badness in the city' (1280 b 6). Those citizens, therefore, who by their moral excellence and superior ability contribute most towards making their country a good place to live in, they and they only are entitled to office and honour above their fellows. That is not the arithmetical equality[1] so loved of the extreme democrats, but it *is* equality (τὸ ἴσον), proportionate equality—to each according to his deserts. This kind of equality is *just* and essential to the good life. Justice must also be made manifest in correcting crime and redressing wrongs; there could be no good life where there was no chance of legal redress, just as it would be no life without friendship.

Since the establishment of these and other assurances of a good life depends on the constitution, which is in a sense a city's life,[2] it becomes doubly important to decide where sovran power lies or ought to lie; for there too will lie the power to make or mar the lives of the people. There are many objections to entrusting sovran power to any class, as classes are generally understood, and it is no answer, though it is perfectly true, to say that Law is sovran; for written law may favour one class as easily as another and so deprive the city of that ὁμόνοια which is indispensable for the good life. On the whole Aristotle finds the balance

---

[1] This is mentioned by Plato too (*Repub.* VIII 558 c) as one of the marks of extreme democracy along with variety, pleasure and anarchy. It is ἰσότης ... ὁμοίως ἴσοις τε καὶ ἀνίσοις as opposed to the ἴσον ... οὐ πᾶσιν ἀλλὰ τοῖς ἴσοις. Aristotle, *Pol.* III 1280 a and similarly in Plato, *Laws* VI 757.

[2] ἡ γὰρ πολιτεία βίος τίς ἐστι πόλεως (IV 1295 a).

to rest in favour of the larger body, τὸ πλῆθος. 'For the many,' he writes (1281 b), 'though *individually* none of them may be a good man, yet may possibly when assembled be *collectively* superior to the others.' With this view of collective wisdom Plato strongly disagreed; he would not have understood Aristotle's regard for public opinion, least of all when Aristotle finds it particularly valuable in matters of artistic taste and literary judgment.[1] But collective wisdom is no substitute for expert ability, which can only be had individually. It is to individuals 'skilled in goodness' that we must look when we seek those services to the whole community which alone may be made the occasion for the assignment of rewards and privileges. Rank and fortune need not be excluded, for these may be serviceable, and within limits it ought to be possible to measure the various services rendered. But, as Greek democracies knew well, a serious political problem is apt to arise when one or two citizens far outstrip their fellows in wealth, ability and everything else. In most Greek states, where the government was a 'perversion', exercised not for the good of all classes but only for its own, it was usual to get rid of the outstanding man as a source of danger—a practice which called forth the indignation of Heraclitus but had the support of Solon (Fr. 10). Aristotle clearly does not like such a waste of ability, but history had shown it to be apparently useful to all three perversions, tyranny, democracy and oligarchy; banishment by ostracism might be said to be *just*, but only in the narrowly limited sense that it is according to a particular constitution. Even a city with a good, not a perverted, constitution may find this treatment of an outstanding man desirable in the interests of the whole community; but it is better to arrange the constitution so that it can be avoided. There is, however, the extreme case where the practice of elimination would be out of the question: where the constitution is the very best of its kind and the outstanding man owes his brilliance not to wealth or strength but to real goodness, moral and intellectual. Such a man is clearly marked out for the rare and highly exceptional status of a king ruling in his own person, the παμβασιλεύς mentioned above. But it is vain to hope that education and training will produce such a man of themselves. The pursuit of a 'Royal Knowledge' (see Chap. IX) is illusory.

---

[1] With 1281 b contrast Plato, *Laws* 670 b and 700 e.

It becomes increasingly clear that the three- and six-fold classi-
fications of constitutions are of little practical value. They depend
too much on the numerical principle and they are not based on
accurate observation of present and past constitutions and their
workings. Democracy, for example, is the name which we apply
to those political associations which are based on political liberty
and majority rule; and this, broadly speaking, serves to distinguish it from oligarchy. But there are many varieties of constitution to which the name could legitimately be applied. A state
consists of many parts, of many groups of citizens, divided and
classified in a variety of ways. If we classify them by trades and
occupations, we shall find that in a 'modern' civilised state they
will be more numerous than Plato's farmers, weavers, leather-
workers and builders (*Repub.* II)—a statement of minimum requirements which Aristotle calls 'neat but inadequate'. They may
also be grouped according to wealth or birth; and it is not contrary to democracy to use these as criteria of citizenship, provided
that the assessment ($\tau\iota\mu\eta\mu\alpha$) is not fixed too high, or the birth
qualification made too narrow. A different constitution will result
according to the emphasis laid on this or that factor and on the
fixity of law. Again, it is characteristic of democracy to avoid
long tenure of any office by one man and to provide pay for
attending to public duties. The character of any one democracy
will partly depend on how far it carries out and can afford to
carry out these precepts; it may not have the necessary man-
power for the one or wealth for the other. The greater the number of duties paid for, the less becomes the power of wealth and
the greater the power of the poor. And if this power becomes so
great that the will of an assembly of citizens can override the
provisions of the law, then we have demagogy and mob-rule,
the worst form of democracy, which Aristotle describes thus:
'Another form of democracy exists when all share in holding
office, . . . and the people is sovran, not the law, that is, when
the decisions of the Assembly have a greater validity than $\nu\acute{o}\mu os$.
This is due to demagogues. For in cities governed democratically,
but also legally, there are no demagogues; the best among the
citizens take the lead. It is where the laws are not sovran that
demagogues come into play. . . . This kind of democracy is closely
akin to tyranny, having the same $\mathring{\eta}\theta os$ and both being intolerant
of the better kind of citizens' (IV 1292 a).

Again, the social and economic background will differ, and this will mean constitutional differences. In a society predominantly agrarian the mass of the citizens will not be able to exercise direct control, as in a city-democracy, still less among a pastoral people; yet some important features of democratic government may be found there, such as the right of electing officials and calling them to account and the right to sit as judges or jurors. But an agrarian community may equally well be governed by the Few and the agricultural oligarchy is, like the corresponding democracy, much more to Aristotle's liking than the factions in the town. The satisfactory running of any State depends on the right choice of officials, but also on the kind of offices they hold and the work they do. The town and the country, revenues, markets and harbours, the courts of law and the execution of their decisions, defence and military training, temples and religion—much of a city's happiness and success will depend on these many and important matters being in good and able hands. This in practice will mark the difference between good States and bad far more clearly than the formal differences between oligarchy and democracy. Indeed Aristotle's own favourite 'Polity' or 'really constitutional constitution' can be described either as a democracy that is nearly an oligarchy or as an oligarchy that is nearly a democracy. The balance between the two forms is often extremely nice and the line to limit democracy can only be drawn at the point at which the power of the people exceeds, but only just exceeds, the combined power of the rich and notable (1319 b 14). Beyond that point it becomes an oligarchy. Thus the name may mean very little. A constitution may be labelled oligarchic or democratic yet in practice work out in the opposite direction. A democracy may be administered so as to favour the rich; an oligarchy which has a low property-qualification and grants full privileges to all who reach it will soon, if the standard of wealth rises among citizens generally, become indistinguishable from a democracy. The name aristocracy need not be confined to the few, if the many are ἄριστοι and the democracy is permeated with the idea of goodness.

The choice then lies not between three forms of constitution but among many, one shading off into another. One may be democratic in its administration of justice, oligarchic in its preference for elections rather than the lot; another will pay judges (δικασταί) for their

work, if they are poor, and fine them for non-attendance, if they
are rich, and so on. There may be reasons in a particular case for
choosing a more oligarchic constitution, a more democratic in
another. But by and large the most evenly-balanced will be the
best, that which lies midway between the extreme forms of oligarchy and democracy. For as these two approach each other, they
shed their extreme features. The mean between them will on the
average be best; for the mean between two extremes is always
good.[1] This middle way will be 'polity', Aristotle's constitutional
constitution, a timocracy with a τίμημα fixed neither too high nor
too low. It will be democratic, for the will of the majority pre-
vails; but it will also be aristocratic,[2] for the essence of aristocracy is 'distribution of offices according to goodness' (1294 a 10)
and this is the principle which Aristotle wishes to combine with
the majority principle (κύριον εἶναι τὸ πλῆθος). Good distribution
is a part of Eunomia and is the mark of all good societies. Obedience to bad laws is not εὐνομία.[3] Such a combination of aristocracy and the will of the majority will be well adapted to promote
the good life. 'For if we were right in saying in the Ethics that
the happy life is unhampered [by want] and according to virtue,
virtue being a middle term, then the middle life must be the best,
the mean attainable by all classes in the state' (1295 a 36). This
'middle life' is that associated with the middle class, that is, those
of moderate wealth, neither rich nor poor. The rich are apt to be
insolent and unruly, the poor to be bitter and to turn to crime.
Those who are moderately well off neither covet the wealth of
their rich neighbours nor incite the envy of the poor. The relationship between rich and poor too easily becomes like that of
master and servant, and that has been shown to be inappropriate.
There can be no friendship in such conditions and friendship is
an important element in the political association. Only a middle
class knows how to command and how also to obey as free men.
'The greatest likelihood', therefore, 'of good government is to
be found in those cities in which there is a large middle class,

[1] Aristotle is here drawing upon his own ethical doctrine of Virtue as a
Mean, e.g. Courage as a mean between Cowardice and Rashness. He had
difficulty in fitting justice into this scheme; cp. Eth. II 6 with Eth. V 5, 17.
[2] Aristotle uses ἀριστοκρατία loosely; it is any constitution based on ἀρετή.
He makes little use of the term as a norm from which oligarchy is a deviation.
[3] See note at the end of Chap. II.

larger if possible than the other two put together, or if not, then taken singly. The addition of a large middle class has a great steadying influence and checks the opposing extremes' (1295 b).

This account of the middle polity, which, since it includes the best elements and gives scope to goodness, is also a true aristocracy, is a good example of the way in which Greek political thinking merged the social and the political into one. It is not stated or even implied that the creation of a balanced political constitution will of itself produce a middle-class society; the converse is much more likely, the influence of a strong middle class will tend to make the constitution moderate. But Aristotle hardly seems to view them separately or to regard one as prior to the other; they are simply inseparable. All the same, he uses, to support his contention, the traditional moderation and steadying influence of the middle classes. This tradition was certainly strong, but it was largely literary. The Delphic Oracle had urged 'Nothing too much'; but the real motto of Greek politicians had always been 'Do nothing by halves'. Aristotle cites the sixth-century Phocylides, 'Things generally turn out best for the middle-class, may that be my station in the city', which merely expresses the poet's view of his own advantage. The middle-class outlook in politics had, however, found expression in drama—in Aeschylus and particularly in that argumentative[1] play, the *Supplices* of Euripides, where words are spoken curiously prophetic of Aristotle—'There are three sections of citizens: the rich refuse their help and always want to increase their wealth: the "have-nots" are unable to support themselves and are a menace; too prone to envy, they aim hostile shafts at the "haves", carried away by the oratory of demagogues. Of the three classes the one in the middle is the saving of cities; it keeps whatever order the city lays down.'

This law-abiding tradition of the middle class gives Aristotle the assurance that his constitution will have something of that ever-to-be-desired stability. He has no fear that a middle class now numerically strong, will seek merely its own advantage, like the other two, or that it will be violently at variance within itself. On the contrary, he claims for his moderate polity that 'It alone will be unsplit, for where the middle class preponderates, there faction-fights and rifts in constitutions[2] are less likely' (1296 a 8).

---

[1] See above Chap. V, *ad fin.* These allusions to Aeschylus (*Eumen.* 526 f.) and Euripides (*Supp.* 238-245) are not in Aristotle.   [2] Reading πολιτειῶν.

He thinks that a strong middle class is more likely to emerge in large states than in small, and in democracies more than in oligarchies. But it is admitted that in practice the strong middle class rarely occurs. In the past cities have generally been either oligarchies or democracies, the winning faction excluding the other. Only once, says Aristotle, has one of the leading cities of Greece had a middle polity, and that was when one man was jointly prevailed upon (συνεπείσθη) to grant such a constitution.[1]

Thus does Aristotle turn the ideas of moderation, of the middle way and the Mean into principles of practical politics; for all this is part of his attempt to find an answer to the question, What on the average is the best State? He thinks that the answer has now been found and that good States and bad may be measured by their closeness to this model. But the *best on the average*, as was stated earlier (p. 212), may not be the *best practicable* in any particular case. Differences of territory, population and general conditions all play their part, and the best plan is to try and arrange matters so that that section which desires the continuance of the constitution is superior, quantitatively or qualitatively, to that which does not; and at the same time to remember that 'the better the constitution is mixed, the longer it will last'. A description is given of the process of mixing, inducements and counter-inducements, fines and exemptions. The methods of strengthening the well-to-do are reminiscent of those in Plato's *Laws* (VI 756), but much is taken from actual practice and is not intended to be advice. Whatever kind of constitution a lawgiver may choose to meet a particular situation, he must see to it that it is equal to performing the functions required of it. These may be divided into three main divisions and the success of any constitution will be judged by its performance in all three.[2] These are (1) deliberation on matters of general policy; (2) all that concerns the offices of state, what they should be, what powers they should have and

---

[1] Aristotle names neither the man nor the city, but he can hardly have meant anyone less conspicuous than Solon at Athens, who was in a position, as διαλλακτής, to grant a constitution and who was jointly chosen (εἵλοντο κοινῇ, Aristotle, *Ath. Pol.* v). He used his powers to mix society and bring rich and poor to see their common interests. See Aristotle, *Ath. Pol.* v-ix and cp. *supra* Chap. II.

[2] Distinguish this functional analysis from the earlier passage (1290 b, above, pp. 223-224) which was an account of the activities of the πόλις.

what should be the manner of election to them; and (3) the judicial functions. It will readily be seen that those do not correspond to the modern threefold division of power into legislative, executive and judicial. Even the third is different, since the usual Greek 'judiciary' was not professional, but a body of laymen taking their turn. We must here think ourselves back, as has been well said,[1] 'into a Greek framework essentially different from the modern and abandon any idea of a differentiation of powers on the model of Montesquieu's theory, or of British (or American) practice'.

The search for stability has its counterpart in the study of the causes of instability, and this in turn should point the way to safeguards against incessant and unnecessary change. It is not therefore surprising that Aristotle devotes a book of the *Politics* to these subjects. But it is surprising to find how loose is the connection with the subject of the best practicable constitution. Aristotle seems almost indifferent to the quality of the régime whose permanence is to be secured. His own middle-class Polity receives honourable mention, but not any favoured treatment, and even tyrants may here learn how their position may be maintained by methods worthy of Macchiavelli. One might have expected also that advice would have been given on how a good and moderate constitution may be attained, by what processes of change an oligarchy or a democracy may be made to approximate to 'polity'; instead, we find an underlying assumption that all changes in constitution are to be avoided. Certainly, as we have seen, political and social change went together and constitutional change meant social revolution, so that those who had 'more to lose than their chains' naturally feared change. But one feels that if Aristotle seriously believed in his middle-class Polity, he would have studied more closely the political changes necessary to bring it into existence by peaceful means. The idea of Reform does not enter into these discussions. Changes in the life of a city are represented as being due to a great many different causes, great and small, but scarcely ever as part of an agreed policy. But in spite of these apparent defects and of incongruities with other parts of Aristotle's work the fifth book of the *Politics* contains some of his most striking observations. Nor should we forget the age-

---

[1] By Sir Ernest Barker, *Trans.*, p. 193.

long (Chap. III, *init.*) connexion between the idea of a constitution and the idea of security; men feared that any alteration in
the one, and in particular a series of apparently trivial alterations
(1307 b 31), might cause a diminution of the other. And, since
the πολιτεία was a city's way of life as well as its constitution, it
was a not unnatural error to suppose that political stability always
implies a static order of society.

Political change[1] had long been studied. Some part of the discussions of the fifth-century Athenian lecture-room are reflected
in Herodotus. Thucydides had recorded some of its more violent
manifestations at Corcyra. Plato had studied it as part of a pro-
gressive deterioration of human character. Aristotle refers only
to the third of these and criticises Plato, fairly enough, on the
ground that his account is often far removed from actual fact—
an objection which applies equally to Aristotle's own remarks in
the *Ethics* (VIII 10). He himself has something of Thucydides'
accurate observation and of Plato's imaginative insight and he
adds a wealth of historical illustration.

In general, political changes take place owing to dissatisfaction
with things as they are. This dissatisfaction may be widely shared
or it may be confined to a small group; but in either case it is apt
to express itself in violence, the occasion for which is often provided by some accident or disaster. The revolt may be suppressed,
or it may be successful and lead to the overthrow of the existing
régime and its replacement by one of the opposite kind. Sometimes the result is less a revolution than a modification of the
existing order. When the discontent is not general, it is often due
to the ambitious self-seeking of some men or the affronted self-
importance of others. And however trifling the cause, the danger
and the seriousness of the issues are the same. But in general the
causes of revolution must be looked for in the minds of the
citizens, be they few or many. Since justice and friendship are
the moral bases of the πόλις, injustice and ill-will are the most
potent causes of discontent and instability. The absence of proportionate equality, of a fair deal, leads to a lack of ὁμόνοια and
splits the city into factions. There can be no fellow-feeling when
one section of the community is convinced that its rights are
being denied to it and that justice is not being done. Agreement

[1] H. Ryffel's book *ΜΕΤΑΒΟΛΗ ΠΟΛΙΤΕΙΩΝ* (Bern, 1949) is referred to
in the Preface.

about what is just is essential. This is true both of the Few and the Many, but some causes of revolution apply more particularly to democracies, others to oligarchies, as can be shown by examples from history. Democracy is perhaps less liable to violent changes than oligarchy; but one of its most potent dangers is the extremism of many of its leading men. For these, by their demagogy and 'soak the rich' policy, drive the men of distinction (οἱ γνώριμοι, the 'notables'), whether resident or in exile, to plot their overthrow and set up an oligarchy. In the old days, too, a demagogue often made himself a tyrant, and sometimes a 'revolution' is merely one tyrant replacing another. In oligarchies oppression of the people is clearly the most obvious cause of discontent and therefore of revolution. But oligarchs are also prone to quarrel with each other, and this may lead to a change simply from one set of rulers to another. The better-governed states, such as an aristocracy, where the few are really the best, and a constitutional democracy with a strong middle-class, are of course more stable, but in the former there is always some danger of revolt and even in the latter those who are not well off are apt to get it into their heads that they are being unfairly treated (1307 a 24). And indeed it may happen even in a good constitution of this kind that there has been a failure to observe the proper balance of democratic and oligarchic elements.

The same principles apply also to one-man government where that exists, but in all forms of monarchy there is greater likelihood of quite minor and partial discontent leading to political revolution. Personal spite, court intrigue, love-affairs, insults and quarrels are apt to be dangerous and are hard to guard against. Hereditary monarchies may collapse for want of able men to succeed, but something can be done to check this by limiting the power of the monarchy, as at Sparta, so that the ability of one man is of less moment. A tyrant, of course, tries to escape the almost inevitable downfall by many means. Deceit and concealment are more effective than terrorism; he should always pretend to be less wicked than he is. Even the worst government must make some show of goodness, if it is to survive at all. But, leaving aside kings and tyrants, shams and deceits and various devices for hoodwinking the populace are not the best ways to guard against revolution. Real goodness in government is indispensable. Aristotle objects to what we may call a Fascist motto, 'Given

power and a willing populace, what need have we of virtue?'
(1309 b 9). A good government will have the dual aim of protecting the poor from oppression and the rich from confiscations.
This will involve the separation of office-holding from profit
making (cp. Chap. VIII, *init.*), the encouragement of the middle
class, the avoidance of family feuds among the nobles and of
strong party-leaders among the people, or any other abnormal
excrescence on the body politic. In this way we may perhaps
ensure that the majority of the citizens *desire* no change in the
constitution, for that is the best guarantee of stability. But if the
majority are to be so minded, they must be so educated, that is
brought up from childhood to believe in the constitution of their
city and to *like the life* which it provides. 'For', says Aristotle,
'even the most beneficial laws, mutually agreed upon by all members of the πόλις, will be of no use at all, unless all are reared
and drilled in the πολιτεία' (1310 a 14). It is therefore the greatest
mistake to imagine that a stable political life can be secured on a
basis of every man living his own life as he likes; for each member
of a city must live the life of the city. Nor is this to be regarded
as a surrender of liberty but as a means of security; οὐ γὰρ δεῖ
οἴεσθαι δουλείαν εἶναι τὸ ζῆν πρὸς τὴν πολιτείαν ἀλλὰ σωτηρίαν
(1310 a 35).

When Aristotle turns to consider the other half of political
science, the planning of a State with the ideally best constitution
and advantages, regardless of place, men or materials, he allows
himself freedom only to imagine arrangements that are within
the bounds of possibility (1325 b 39). Even so, he is less at home
in this more speculative approach, and on occasion almost loses
patience with it (1331 b 20). If he ever finished it, its conclusion
has not come down to us; and what has survived is partly derived
from earlier work of his own[1] and of Plato. He does not say that
any of it is based on the *Laws*, though much similarity is obvious,
but he does admit (1323 a 23) that he makes use of his own
previously published work on the good life. For, since the city
exists to further the good life, discussion of the ideal city must
begin by determining what is the best life, what kind of life is a
happy one. Then it will be possible to describe the conditions
in which it may be lived. The external conditions will be found

---

[1] W. Jaeger, *Aristotle*, Eng. Trans., pp. 275-278, believes that the *Pro-
trepticus* is the work referred to.

to be less important than the internal; the good life must derive
from within. To the Platonic doctrine, 'You will never be happy
till you are good', Aristotle assents. No one could be called happy,
if he were devoid of Courage, Self-control, Justice, Intelligence;
nor yet if he were destitute and penniless, though this is not the
heart of the matter. But, while all are agreed about the necessity
of goodness, there may be difference of opinion about the good
way of life. Aristotle, as we have seen, believed that happiness
could not be inactive; a man must be either doing or thinking.
But some will lean to one more than to the other, to thought
rather than action, to philosophy rather than politics; and many,
like Philo centuries later, were torn between the two. The answer
therefore is clear; the city must provide for both kinds. But the
city itself has a way of life, which is its whole constitution or
make-up. It too must have the four chief virtues, so that it too
may have a good life. It must have all four and not courage only,
as some think. The military way of life is not the good life, for
war can only be a means to an end, not an activity to be valued
for its own sake. Certainly the city needs to maintain its independence, but it is no more part of the virtue of a State to rule over
other States than it is part of the virtue of man to dominate man.
Some indeed do hold that this is the virtue of a man, particularly
of a great man, and still more think that the virtue of a State is
to have dominion over other States. But Aristotle will not separate
the two, the domineering man and the domineering State; both
are wrong. Nor will he separate the self-contained man and the
self-contained State. For both are right, and the interests of the
two are identical.

Thus armed, as it were, with weapons of his own forging,
Aristotle begins to describe the perfect constitution, which will
ensure the good way of life. It is here that he follows most notice-
ably Plato's *Laws*. The city must be of moderate size; mere bulk
is no criterion of greatness and over-population leads to trouble;
besides, it should be possible for all the citizens to get to know
each other. Neither should territory be too large; it makes defence
difficult; but it should be large enough for the supply of food.
The site must be healthy, well-supplied with pure water and easy
to defend. Plato was strongly of the opinion that it should not be
too near the sea; but for Aristotle there are two sides to the
question: the danger of foreign influence must be weighed against

the value of foreign trade, and the establishment of a naval as well as a military defence force need not be made such a drawback as Plato thought. We should choose carefully the race as well as the numbers of our citizens. Here Aristotle brings to bear his knowledge of the medical and anthropological theories of the Hippocratic schools. He combines these with his own doctrine of the mean, and advises the choice of the Hellenic race, as being mid-way between the freedom-loving but unintelligent races of the cold north and the clever but abject orientals. He does not say whether he regards Macedonians as Hellenes or not, nor does he differentiate between the Greeks, but he adds, 'The Hellenic race is both energetic and intelligent; so that it continues to be free and to have good polities and to be capable of universal empire, if united under one government' (1327 b 31). This has set later generations wondering whether he had Alexander's empire in mind, or the Pan-Hellenism of Isocrates, and whether he ever seriously considered the possibility of a larger form of national state than the πόλις.

Coming to the social and political structure of the Ideal State we find that Aristotle has still no hope of finding, nor even any intention of looking for, a constitution which will enable all the inhabitants to live the good life. Even in imagination he cannot conceive of this, or else he regards it as fantastically impossible and therefore outside the scope of his enquiry. And when one thinks how immense was the amount of manual labour required to maintain life and how little mechanical assistance there was, one cannot but admit that it was impossible for a whole popu- lation to live the life of a full citizen. So in the ideal as in the actual city Aristotle requires numbers of slaves and non-citizens for carrying out essential, but so-called menial tasks. His attempts to justify slavery as natural are too well-known, as well as too muddled and ineffectual, to bear repeating here; but at least Aris- totle was aware that the institution had been attacked and stood in need of defence. Again, slavery apart, if Aristotle could have abated some of his demand for leisure for his citizen, if he had been content to have him a little less lordly and more ready to turn his hand to some of the essential tasks of his own country, he might, we feel, have produced a worthier ideal citizen. But this is exactly what Aristotle denied. The menial occupations of handicrafts and business would not merely distract but disable the mind of the good citizen, and so interfere with the high standard of mental and moral excellence which Aristotle required of him. The only kinds of work which would not damage his mind and soul would be the deliberative, the judicial, the military and the religious. All these belong to τὰ πολιτικά and can only be performed by a πολίτης. The influence of this doctrine may still be seen in English social history and in the prestige attaching to offices in Church and State, in the Law and the Services. In Aristotle's Ideal State the younger citizens will serve as soldiers, in middle and older life they will take on the other duties. They will thus form a ruling class, a closely kept caste, which Aristotle defends by referring to something similar in Egypt and in Crete. The members will not at all times be actively engaged in ruling, for they will also in turn be ruled. But they alone are citizens and they alone eligible to rule.

The question whether the good citizen and the good man are identical is not here reopened in that form. In the Ideal State their identity may perhaps be assumed[1]; we have but to produce the virtuous man and he will be both good citizen and happy man. And that city will be virtuous where all the citizens are good. The problem thus inevitably again becomes one of education, and Aristotle has to face the question about which Plato could never make up his mind—whether there is to be a different education for ruling and for citizenship. Aristotle in Book III came to the conclusion that the goodness of the good ruler was not exactly the same as that of the good citizen, but that under certain favourable conditions they might be very similar. These conditions may be presumed to exist in the Ideal State now under construction, and it should follow that the education for the one would be fitted also for the other. This was apparently Aristotle's own view (p. 217) but he does not wish to ignore entirely Plato's point of view, namely, that if the goodness of the good ruler differs from the goodness of the good subject, the education for goodness cannot after all be quite the same. But then in the Ideal State of Aristotle they will be the same people. 'We conclude that

---

[1] In Book III (1276 b 16 ff.) Aristotle said that they could not be identical, even in ἀρίστη πολιτεία, because the goodness of the good man was one, while citizens needed many different 'goodnesses'. But the whole of the above account inevitably over-simplifies the relations between the arguments in Book III, treated earlier in this chapter, and those in Book VII.

in a sense the same persons both rule and are ruled, in another sense different persons. So too their education must be in one sense the same, in another different. For the first essential for a good ruler is to have been ruled.' With these qualifications, then, we may perhaps say that in our Ideal State 'citizen-ruler and good man have both the same goodness and that the same man must become ruled first and ruler afterwards' (1333 a 12).

In the unfinished sketch of education with which our *Politics* concludes Aristotle's aim is to produce the citizen-ruler, one who is capable both of ἄρχειν and of ἄρχεσθαι—an aim very similar to that of Plato in the central books of the *Laws*. So Aristotle does not hesitate to advise State-regulation of marriage and family-life, of the rearing of infants and the discipline of children. In the next stage of education he stresses the value of music and literature, not because they are useful and necessary like other subjects, but because the very fact of their being neither useful nor necessary like other subjects makes them particularly suitable for those who will not be engaged in any professional activity. 'To be looking on all occasions for utility in everything' (or 'to be asking always What is the good of ... ?') 'is unfitting in those who are free and whose minds have been brought to the highest pitch' (οἱ μεγαλόψυχοι). Of course the study of music and literature can and ought to be good for the character in a way that learning to cook cannot be; and it will therefore play a big part in moulding the future citizen-ruler. Moreover as relaxations of the mind literature and music have after all a certain utility. But this raises awkward questions; at least Aristotle felt them to be so. For example the best musical performances come from the skilled professionals, who are not citizens but βάναυσοι. How then are we to secure for our good citizen the benefits of a musical education without subjecting him to the taint of professionalism, the vulgarity of public performances and competitions? It would not be sufficient to teach him only to look and listen, as the Spartans do. He could not thus acquire a critical judgment of his own. Aristotle decides that during childhood he should learn to play and to sing, but that no attempt should be made to reach the level of virtuosity in execution. The adult citizen, if he plays and sings at all, will do so only in private and in a mood of conviviality (1339 b).

The importance of education in the making of a πόλις is not

new; it has been with us since Protagoras. Aristotle was emphasising the value of good habits, not saying anything new about
πολιτεία, when he wrote 'Lawgivers make citizens good by accus-
toming them to be good; and making them good is the aim of
every lawgiver; therein lies the difference between a good and
a bad constitution' (*Eth.* II 1, 5). Broadly speaking, the aim of
Aristotle's education is to produce an all-round good man, an
able man as well as a virtuous, dignified and courteous, magnani-
mous and liberal, as well as courageous, just and self-disciplined.
He believed that it was possible to produce this type by training
and practice and that it was politically important to do so. Plato's
idea of a good citizen was not the same, and he had in the *Laws*
a much less confident belief in the efficacy of education. He then,
as we saw in Chapter X, devised a series of checks, controls and
censorships, culminating in the ever-vigilant nocturnal council of
the most-knowing, in order to see that good citizens remained
good, that is ἐν ἤθεσι νόμων, as they had been brought up. Aristotle, unless the remainder of Book VIII contained something
of the kind, did not think it necessary thus to restrict and control
the members of the city. He saw in his good citizen primarily a
reflection of himself, or of himself as he would wish to be seen,
dignified, intelligent and moderate, full of good-sense, knowledge
and manly virtues. Plato, if he could have pictured himself in the
city of the *Laws* at all, which is doubtful, would certainly be
sitting on the Nocturnal Council. But Plato was devising a city
for other people, for ordinary people, not for himself. Aristotle
was planning one where he and his friends could have lived
happily; he pictured the Ideal State as one which would both produce such men and provide them with the right kind of life.
Plato knew of no men like himself; and if he had, he would not
have been happy among them. The only happiness which he
found (*Epist.* VII 329 B) was in the direction of his own Academy;
for there he exercised the authority which no city had ever given
him, among men who resembled him only in their devotion to
philosophy and politics and who were often deeply attached to
him personally. He certainly desired that his pupils and the good
citizens of the *Laws* should be intelligent and virtuous, like those
of Aristotle; but there is a difference in quality, which can perhaps be expressed as the difference between the well-born or
well-bred and the well-educated, or, rather more vaguely, as the

difference between the *ancien régime* and the Victorian era, or between the landed gentry and *la bonne bourgeoisie*. The liberal public-spirited citizen of the nineteenth century, interested equally in science and literature, educated under a system based more on the ἀρετή of property than of birth, would have won the admiration of the author of the *Politics* and the *Ethics*. But in a world where wealth as well as birth has lost much of its aura of worship and community of effort means more than dignity and moderation the high-souled man of Aristotle seems strangely unreal and remote.

FURTHER NOTES AND REFERENCES

CHAPTER XI

The traditional order of the books of Aristotle's *Politics* has now generally been restored, that is, IV, V, VI or IV, VI, V no longer appear as the final three. But there are two entirely different divisions of each book into chapters and sections. These are therefore here dropped and Bekker's pages alone used for references to the *Politics*, generally without the addition of the title. The *Ethics* means *Ethica ad Nicomachum* and is referred to by book, 'long' chapter and section. In the conclusion of the *Ethics*, cited on p. 212, the reference to 'collected constitutions' must be to the 158 constitutions which Aristotle and his pupils are known to have described. Of these only one has survived—almost entire—the *Constitution of Athens*. These historical surveys were presumably used, as this programme said they would be, in the writing of Books IV, V and VI of the *Politics*. Book II has references to actual as well as to imaginary constitutions. Books VII and VIII, the latter incomplete, are anticipated in the last sentence of the programme in *Ethics* X. But the first book of the *Politics* seems not to have been in the author's mind when he was finishing the *Ethics*; it is far from being a link between the two works. Nor can Book III, important though it is, be said to be envisaged. It has been suggested that Aristotle planned *two* works on *Politics* and that we have parts of the material of both. It is impossible to say with certainty in what order the books were written or to what period in Aristotle's life they severally belong [e.g. W. D. Ross, *Aristotle*³, ch. VIII and p. 19 n., W. Jaeger, *Aristotle* E.T.², ch. x, E. Barker in *Class. Rev.* XLV (1931) and, better, in the Introduction (II §4) to his translation of the *Politics* (1946)], and in this connection the word 'book', as J. L. Stocks wisely remarked (*Class. Quart.* XXI 1927, p. 177), is 'a device of the ancient bookseller, not the unit of composition'. It is a gratuitous assumption that those parts of Aristotle which most resemble Plato in subject-matter are necessarily earlier than the rest. It is just as likely that towards the end of Plato's life, that is in his most mystico-religious period (Chap. X, *ad fin.*), Aristotle was least sympathetic with him and that in his own mellower years, while criticising freely, he paid more attention to his old master's views, when these were expressed in a matter-of-fact kind of way, as in most of the *Laws*.

The scope of πολιτική	*Ethics* I, esp. chs. 2, 7, and 8
The two aims and the two methods	*Ethics* X 18-23, *Politics* IV *init.*
The nature of the πόλις-association	*Pol.* I 1252 a - 1253 a.
The bases of the association:	*Pol.* III *passim.*
Law and Justice	I 1253 a; *Eth.* V 6-7.
Laws as rules	IV 1289 a 15.
Friendship, etc.	*Eth.* IX 6, *Pol.* II 1261 a, III 1278 b, 1280.
Citizenship and ability, continuity	*Pol.* III 1275 a - 1278 b.
Classification; old style	*Pol.* III 1279, *Eth.* VIII 10.
Aristotle's more detailed analyses:	
Monarchy	III 1284-1288 (tyranny IV 1295 a).
Democracy and Oligarchy	III 1281-1284, *Eth.* V 3-4.
Subdivisions and degrees of these	IV 1290-1293 a, VI 1317 a-1321 a.
Polity and Aristocracy	IV 1293 b - 1294 b.
The choice; the middle way and the middle class	IV 1295 a - 1296 a.
Different conditions, different safe-safeguards	IV 1296 b - 1297 b.
The three functions of government	IV 1298 b, 1299 a, 1300 b.
Political and constitutional changes.	
Causes and cures	*Pol.* V *passim.*
The Ideal State:	
The good life in the ideal city	VII 1323 a - 1325 b, 1332 a, 1333 b - 1334 a.
External conditions	VII 1326 a - 1328 a, 1330 b - 1331, cp. the Hippocratic *Airs, Waters and Places,* 23-26.
Social and political structure	VII 1328 a - 1330 a.
The ideal citizen	1331 b - 1334 a.
Plans for educating him	1334 b - 1342 b.

CHAPTER XII

AFTER ALEXANDER

A LEXANDER THE GREAT died in 323 B.C. and Aristotle in the following year. The task of tracing the course of Greek political thought becomes from that point onwards much more difficult and its material more elusive. There are no outstanding political philosophers, and no great political writings have come down to us; so that a river, whose course it was previously possible to trace, now suddenly comes to an immense area of sandy desert in which it dissipates or sends underground its own waters. It is little wonder that to many it has seemed as if the subject were exhausted and political thinking at an end: Alexander's conquests had changed the world; the Greek city-state seemed out of date, insignificant in size and power compared with Macedonian armies, powerless and even useless in its traditional function as an arbiter of morals and social habits. Philosophers who thought otherwise must have had their minds in the skies and politicians were burying their heads in the sand. The end of Greek freedom had already come when Philip of Macedon was victorious at Chaeronea in 338. But these are the comments of a historian who has learned subsequent events. In 338 B.C. Philip's attempt at a general settlement of Greek affairs seemed to many to be no more like the end of the city-state than the Great King's settlement of fifty years before. Even Alexander's conquests, astonishing though they were, did not at first reveal what was to come. The average man, like Aeschines the orator, could not possibly have divined the changes which the next fifty years would gradually bring about. The destruction of Thebes, the reduction of Athens into subservience to Macedon and, above all, the dramatic collapse of the great Persian empire, these things he knew and they filled him with amazement;[1] but there was still no sign of any change in his own way of life or any diminution of the importance of the πόλις. Besides, though the mainland had been humiliated by Macedon, many of the Greek cities of Asia Minor welcomed Alexander as a liberator from their ancestral enemy. At first sight indeed the triumph of the Philhellene Alexander over the foreign king Darius looked like the defeat of the armies of the older Darius at Marathon, another victory for the Greek way of life. It was of course not a victory for Greek arms but for Macedonian. The Greek cities played no direct part in it and within a few years it became evident that, so far as they were concerned, the victory was a hollow one. The 'liberation of the cities' became a sorry farce when after Alexander's death his generals, fighting each other, used it as a war-cry or as a bribe. In the wake of Alexander's armies came Greeks from the mainland, conscious rather of new opportunities than of lost freedom. They could not all be successful in the race for wealth and position nor, where they mingled with barbarians, refrain from inter-marriage. But changes came slowly. The children of the mixed marriages spoke Greek and it needed two or three generations before the mixture of races became at all evident. Moreover Hellenism had the official support of Alexander, whose policy of founding cities was continued by the successors; and the universal use of the Greek language *seemed* to give some assurance that Greek notions of πολιτεία had a great future as well as a glorious past.

But what of the architect of all this? Can Alexander the Great be regarded as a political thinker? It is possible to give an affirmative answer but nearly impossible to justify it. His contemporaries had little idea of what was in his mind, and the imagination of later historians cannot give us Alexander's words, and without these it is hazardous to divine his thoughts. For we cannot judge the political thought of any man merely by his political actions, more particularly since political events have a way sometimes of nullifying the intentions of their promoter. It is especially difficult to know the plans of Alexander, whose death came upon him at an early age, when he had won world-power but had hardly begun to use it, had shown his genius for conquest and vast-scale organisation but not his ideas about the purpose of these activities.

---

[1] Aeschines, *Against Ctesiphon* 132-134, *circa* 330 B.C.

Beyond what can be inferred from his founding of many cities we hardly know anything of his views on the State, its size, constitution and membership—subjects which he could not long neglect if he had in mind to create any political organisation, whether world-wide or smaller, other than the numerous cities. Kingship was the form of government which was natural to him. He was by descent and upbringing as well as in fact a βασιλεύς not a τύραννος. He looked back to Achilles and Agamemnon not to Polycrates or Pisistratus. Whatever special position the city of Pella may have had, it was part of a kingdom; and Alexander's way of life, his πολιτεία, had never been that of the small, autonomous city-state. His country had had no share in the great legal and constitutional developments of Greece. Solon and Lycurgus meant nothing to him, still less the Greek notions of freedom and democracy. From Aristotle he learned[1] that the proper way of life for civilised men was that of the city-state, and so much of his tutor's teaching he seems to have accepted—for other people. For himself he had other ideas. If he saw himself in Aristotle's *Politics* at all, it could only have been as an absolute monarch of exceptional talent, a παμβασιλεύς and a 'law unto himself', and even then not as Aristotle intended, but as monarch of some vast area or of the world itself. Had he lived longer and actually read the writings of Aristotle, he would inevitably have seen that war and conquest do not settle questions of living and that sooner or later he himself would have to face the problems of government discussed by Aristotle. If he read Isocrates, it was not the Athenian traditionalist but rather the Pan-Hellenist that impressed him; and perhaps too the eulogist of Evagoras and of 'well-behaved' monarchy (*supra*, Chap. VII). For Alexander's actions betoken some belief in the duty of a king towards his subjects, in the obligation to do good to them (εὐεργετεῖν) and so create both goodwill among them and good-feeling towards himself. But he can hardly have pictured himself as 'an influence for good' and he parted company with Isocrates and Aristotle and the Greeks in general when he extended the conferring of benefits and the winning of goodwill to the Persians and other barbarians. Here, if we are to look for literary influences at all, he is likely to have been

---

[1] That is, in his youth at Pella. For the rest see Ehrenberg's essay on Aristotle and Alexander's empire already referred to (*Alexander and the Greeks*, ch. III).

attracted by the mixture of Greek and Oriental in the *Cyropaedia* of Xenophon. It is unlikely that he had ever read the theories of Antiphon and others who had demonstrated the brotherhood of mankind (Chap. V) or that he knew that the conception of government as a means of doing good (Democritus fr. 248, *supra*, p. 65) was also a product of the great thinking age of Protagoras and Socrates. But these ideas were by now familiar, and credit must be given him for making an attempt to put them into practice and break down the barrier between Greek (or Macedonian) and Barbarian.[1] What sort of *political* unity he thought could be made out of better relations between Greeks and Orientals it is impossible to say, but the cultural unity was to be predominantly Greek. He may in many cases have been thinking more of military security than of diffusion of culture when he established new cities, but, as we have just seen, the immediate effect was a spread of Hellenism and of the Greek language.[2]

Whatever Alexander's intentions may have been, the effect of his career was to set on foot many gradual changes in the political scene of the eastern Mediterranean. Before the close of the fourth century it was evident that the wars between the Generals would not end in victory and that there would never be any single successor to Alexander and his empire. The Ptolemies became the ruling dynasty in Egypt, the Seleucids in Syria; and lesser kingdoms were to spring up in Asia Minor. The kingdom of Macedonia was long disputed, but its power was generally ready to check any move towards separatism among the Greeks of the mainland. Here constitutional governments generally continued to function, but in some cases, notably Athens, the constitution

---

[1] It is impossible to apportion the credit with any accuracy. W. W. Tarn (*Proc. Brit. Acad.* XIX 1933, 123-166) gives the lion's share to Alexander. Histories of philosophy tend to associate the *cosmopolis* exclusively with Cynics and Stoics.

[2] In the Egypt of the Ptolemies, where the spread of Greek was due not so much to new cities, which were only two in number (Ptolemaïs and Alexandria), as to interpenetration, the native Egyptian tongue was only heard among labourers and country folk. In Syria the Hellenising policy was later intensified and met with fierce Jewish resistance, but in the Syrian cities was remarkably successful, the older Semitic foundations imitating the new Graeco-Macedonian cities. But all in all the policy failed in both Egypt and Syria. The countryside was barely touched and in the towns the Western immigrants tended to become assimilated to the East.

was violently altered so as to suit the Macedonians and their supporters. After the turn of the century (300 B.C.) there was a significant revival in the power and importance of leagues.[1] The Achaean league, reconstituted in 281, was the most powerful, but smaller states, more backward peoples and even tribes found co-operation easier than during the Spartan hegemony in the previous century. But federal ideas in general did not receive any more attention from philosophers now than they had a hundred years before (Chap. VII). To the political theorists a league of cities was still a plurality of cities, not a new kind of state. It could not make men better, as Plato would have wished. But if the word πόλις was still firmly attached to the city-state, the notion of the 'common interest' had been transferred to a larger group and the word κοινόν had from the fifth century been in common use for *league* or commonwealth. Later in the third century Antigonus Doson transformed Macedon itself into a *koinon*. The cities of the outer Hellenistic world, both the new foundations of Alexander and the Successors and the old island- and city-states, now 'liberated', these were the main centres of Hellenistic civilisation. Their relations with the local monarch varied from place to place and time to time. Some were not *within* but *beside* his territory. Some preserved the face of independence by making a treaty with him. Many had a written constitution, but this was not the result of entirely free action by the citizens; an external treaty which guarantees an internal constitution is not a mark of autonomy but of dependence.[2] The cities of Syria and Asia with their assemblies and gymnasia, their festivals and markets were preserving what they could of Hellenism, but they could not conceal their political impotence. Though some may have had armies at their disposal, they could hardly use them except to support the monarch. The complete sovran independence with power to make war and peace was theirs no more.

How far the diminution of local autonomy affected the lives and outlook of people in cities it is hard to say, but its immediate effect must have been a further decline in the religion of the

---

[1] Philip's general Hellenic League of 338 was revived in 302 but it failed to hold the Greek states together. On the league of Demetrius see Additional Note to this chapter.

[2] e.g. the διάγραμμα between Ptolemy Soter and Cyrene, on which see Additional Note at the end of this chapter.

city-state. The cult of the old gods continued, even spread, and their temples and festivals were still matters of local pride. But in many cases the links between the city and its god had been loosened and many people failed to find the social and emotional satisfaction formerly derived from the civic religion. Astrology and superstition, mystery-religions, cults of oriental deities began slowly to gain ground among the Greeks of Asia Minor, Syria, Egypt and the mainland itself. In the newer foundations especially the religious attachment to the city was apt to be weak. Even where the population was thoroughly Greek and not mixed with foreign blood, the people were less homogeneous than in an old city-state. Commercial activity had increased and it was now easier to voyage about the Mediterranean than it was in the fifth century. Trade brought not only travellers but also settlers to any city which offered or appeared to offer the prospect of a new career and of getting rich quickly. Such immigrants had a somewhat loose connection with their adopted city; they lived there, but it was not their home. They had no home; for the Greek idea of home centred not around a dwelling house, but round a city and a home-land. The Hellenistic settlers dwelt in cities but they were hardly citizens in the old sense, brought up in close dependence on a free city's religion and laws. Their city might indeed be full of temples, frequent in its festivals and not lacking in prosperity; but they had to look elsewhere for standards of conduct and education.

Against such a background we view the political thought of the new age. Philosophy was never more sought after than now; it seemed to make up for something that had been lost. But the new schools of Zeno and Epicurus appealed only to the highly-educated. Ordinary people needed something less advanced; and they found it in listening to itinerant popular philosophers, who gave them sermons rather than lectures. But φιλοσοφία was still linked in people's minds with education in general (Chap. VII), and many, who were not content with athleticism or commercialism, found here intellectual interest as well as guidance in matters of conduct. This kind of popular philosopher was not new. Its originator and most famous exponent, Diogenes of Sinope, was already an old man in the anecdotes which linked him with Alexander. And it was not primarily political; on the contrary, it denied the value of the πόλις. Yet Diogenes is credited with having written a book on πολιτεία.[1] This does not mean that he sketched an ideal constitution, only that the Cynics had a way of life, a πολιτεία and a morality of their own; but it was not rooted in the polis. It therefore appeared anarchic to its enemies, who compared it to the habits of a dog and nicknamed Diogenes κύων. The name appears to have been accepted. Diogenes the Cynic (κυνικός) deliberately set out to destroy the old order of morality as represented by the bourgeoisie of Athens and to change people's ideas about what was valuable and what was not. That is what he meant when he called himself a forger and stated his resolve 'to change the stamp of the currency'.[2] This is a new reversal of values; it differs from that of Callicles and the superman (Chap. V), but it is equally destructive of the πόλις. It was the superfluousness, not the weakness of society that caused Diogenes to wish to abolish it. He was a 'cosmopolitan', but Cynic cosmopolitanism was individualistic and dissociative and did not look to the unity of mankind.

Whatever Diogenes may have said in his lost *Politeia*, he and his successors, called Κυνικοί, had plenty of listeners when they preached the vanity of the πόλις and all its artificial νόμοι. It was 'nomos' to seek wealth. To change this convention, to convince those who had no possessions or had lost them that property was really a useless encumbrance, was a salutary and useful service. But it angered those who had property to find their sacred possessions laughed at. Much of the indignation which the early Cynics aroused among their contemporaries[3] was due to 'middle-class' prejudice; the rest was due to their own readiness to 'épater

[1] Rightly credited; but we only know of its supposed contents from attacks of its enemies at a much later date. See note at the end of Chap. XIII.

[2] παραχαράττειν τὸ νόμισμα. Note the etymological connection between νόμος and νόμισμα. Coinage is itself a convention.

[3] These attacks became progressively more violent and more abusive with accusations of cannibalism and incest. They are no more to be believed than those persons who made equally damaging attacks on the behaviour of early Christians, who excited a not dissimilar indignation, e.g. Minucius Felix, *Octavius*, ch. 28. Both Epicureans and Stoics joined in the attack in the first century B.C., the former using the Cynic connection, which Zeno was not ashamed to acknowledge, in order to bring the Stoic wise man into disrepute, the latter disputing the genuineness of Diogenes' *Politeia* and trying to dissociate themselves from Cynicism. See D. R. Dudley, *History of Cynicism* (1937), pp. 102-103, and W. Crönert, *Kolotes und Menedemos* (1906), pp. 58-65 (C. Wessely's *Studien zur Palaeographie und Papyruskunde* VI).

les bourgeois'. No less shocking was it to laugh at patriotism. This thoroughly city-state virtue was a declining force in the cities of the Hellenistic world, but things did not change so rapidly at Athens, and old-fashioned people must have been annoyed by Crates, the Theban Cynic who parodied the verses of Homer in which Odysseus longs for his homecoming and praises his native Ithaca. To Crates even a home is an encumbrance and in his parody he puts the Cynic symbol of a wanderer's haversack in place of the home-land of Ithaca. In this fragment we come as near as may be to a Cynic view of the State:

> The Wallet is a city set in a sea of humbug,
> Rich and rare, all girt about[1] and empty.
> Thither sails no fawning fool or fornicator,
> Here are thyme and scallion, figs and bread.
> Wherefore they fight not with each other nor carry arms,
> They fight not over these things nor for a handful of small
>   coin nor for fame. (Fr. 2 M)

Possessions as a cause of war, hatred of vice and luxury, these remind us of Plato's *Republic*; for Crates was no less of a puritan than Plato and the Cynic renunciation of wealth is a Socratic trait. But to do without the πόλις was unthinkable in the fifth century; it was not so difficult at the end of the fourth, when the city had so little to offer that a man could really live by. Crates, when his native city of Thebes was rebuilt about 315 B.C., refused to return to it; it meant nothing to him. 'I have no one city . . . but the whole world to live in' (Fr. 17 M). What was a paradox in the fifth century Democritus (Fr. 247, *supra* p. 66) becomes now a commonplace, not a theory but a fact. But to say 'I am at home everywhere' is only to say 'I am a stranger everywhere'; and it is worth noting that Crates and the girl who threw away riches to become his wife had a base, if not a home, to which they could return from their wanderings and that this base was Athens. For Crates at heart liked civilised life. He wrote plays, his parodies had a serious purpose and he even modelled his prose style on Plato. Athens was still the foremost literary and theatrical centre of the world; Menander and Diphilus held the comic stage. In the third century B.C. she lost her primacy in literature and science to Alexandria, but in philosophy she was destined to hold the

---

[1] The Homeric περίρρυτος should not have been altered by Stephanus and others to περίρρυπος, 'all dirty'.

field for another 900 years. To the philosophic schools of Athens therefore we now return.

At the Academy mathematical studies were still pursued, but how far Plato's methods of political training were continued we do not know. Certainly its influence declined and when it won fresh vigour under Arcesilaus about 260 B.C., it was no longer an institute of political education. We hear of two alumni of the third century Academy, the so-called liberators of Sicyon, Ecdelus and Demophanes,[1] but we can only wonder what they learned there. But there are 'Platonic', if not Academic, writings, short dialogues in the Socratic manner, which survive. Of these the *Minos* may be taken as the most significant politically; its sub-title περὶ νόμου gives an indication of its subject. It is agreed between 'Socrates' and his interlocutor that Law or Nomos must be something more than customary behaviour, something more than the decrees and decisions of the City. It should aim at the discovery of reality (τὸ ὄν); the differences between various νόμοι argue a want of success in the search, not the unreality of Law. But who shall discover this reality for us and tell us what is right (ὄρθος) law? Just as only the physician can say what are the right prescriptions (and the same with cooks and other experts), so the right prescriptions are those ordered by *kings and good men*, since they alone are experts in laws. For it is not here a question of personal rule, but of finding the best *lawgiver*. On the supposition that the oldest and most enduring is the best, the palm is awarded not to Lycurgus but to Minos of Crete, who had been educated, we are told, by Zeus himself,[2] and whose laws remained strong and became a model for the Spartan Lycurgus; one of his merits as a lawgiver was that he believed in conforming to his own laws. Of the other and more clearly spurious *Platonica* little need be said here. When they deal with political ideas, they do so in a way which is partly old-fashioned and partly even flippant, though perhaps unintentionally. If you know what is needful for the city, discussion is unnecessary; if you do not, discussion will not tell you (*Demodocus*). In the *Sisyphus* a person of that name is laughed at for taking his duties as a citizen seriously; and the dialogue, doubtless in allusion to the Sisyphus of mythology,

---

[1] On whom see M. Cary, *A History of the Greek World* 323-146 B.C. (1932), pp. 138-141.
[2] Cp. Dio. Chrys. 1 38 ff.

ends where it began; the task of finding right counsel still awaits doing.

At the Lyceum Aristotle was succeeded by Theophrastus, who was hardly less many-sided than his master. He had, too, the same bent for natural science and wrote extensively on plants and animals. His most popular and influential book *Characters* belongs to the sphere of ethics, but of ethics quite divorced from politics, of the behaviour of men according to their individual character-istics, not after the ἦθος of a city. All the same, one of Theophras-tus' characters (nr. 26) is the Oligarchic Man, the man who wants to rule, is impatient of popular control and is perpetually com-plaining about the low-class people, who hold office and power, and about the heavy burden of taxation. If Theophrastus does not also describe the democratic kind of man, that is because he was only concerned with unpleasant types, not because the idea of a Democratic Man was dead (*supra*, p. 35). On the contrary we have evidence only a little earlier than Theophrastus that it was alive and discussed. The same 'average man', Aeschines the ora-tor, whose testimony was invoked above, described the δημοτικός, but he did so in terms very unlike Plato's. He used terms both of morals and of politics and made him out to be, in contrast to the oligarchic, fair and reasonable, not extravagant and not greedy, brave, intelligent and at all times a friend of the people.[1] Theo-phrastus wrote much,[2] but of his work on political philosophy we have only the titles, e.g. On Laws, On Kingship, The Best Constitution, and Political Measures for Appropriate Occasions (πολιτικὰ πρὸς τοὺς καιρούς). These last two titles seem to show that Theophrastus, like Aristotle, looked at the political science from two aspects, one theoretical and imaginative, the other having a practical bearing on immediate problems (cp. p. 212), and that he did so more systematically than in the haphazard arrangement of Aristotle's surviving *Politics*. One citation from the latter work certainly lives up to its title. It advises 'occupying powers' to use inoffensive titles for their officials, such as the Lacedaemonian Arranger (ἁρμοστής) rather than the Athenian Overseer (ἐπίσκοπος) or Garrison (φύλαξ). The περὶ νόμων is not to be compared to Plato's *Laws*, but to Aristotle's collection of constitutions, for it was a description of the laws of different

---

[1] Aeschines, *Ctesiph.* 168-170.
[2] Some 220 titles are listed by Diogenes Laertius.

countries. He was reputed to have made a summary of the *Republic* of Plato.

It will be noted that Theophrastus is credited with writing on Kingship, the first, or among the first, of a long line of treatises περὶ βασιλείας. The subject was not of course new, but the conquests of Alexander had led to increasing practical importance of the study of Monarchy. Philosophers, while generally neglecting the federal ideas, paid much attention to the monarchical, exactly as earlier in the century, but for different reasons. Then ideas of federation were ignored as not relevant to the true πόλις, monarchical ideas accepted as consistent with it. But now monarchy was eagerly studied because only by accepting it could philosophers have access to kings and so, since personal power rested with kings, exercise a political influence. The loss of these treatises on monarchy is a gap in our knowledge of Greek political theory about 300 B.C. Some indication of what Hellenistic monarchy was like in practice and how one differed from another can be put together from inscriptions, papyri and other sources; but it is another matter to know what ideas lay behind, and how far these ideas sprang from the writings and advice of Greek philosophers from Isocrates and Plato onwards. So much having perished, we can but congratulate ourselves that at least one authentic and relevant fragment of Theophrastus' work has come to light at Oxyrhynchus.[1] The unknown writer cites as from the second book of Theophrastus on Kingship: 'And this is truly he that rules by the sceptre not by the spear as Caeneus.' He goes on to explain the allusion to Caeneus, king of the Lapithae, who set up his spear as an object of worship and was himself invulnerable in war. His rule became proverbially a rule of force, symbolised by the spear. The writer points out that even the invulnerable Caeneus was subdued by the Centaurs, the inference being that kingship ought not to rest upon force, but, as Theophrastus said, on the staff or σκῆπτρον, which from Homeric times (see Chap. I) had been the mark of legitimate rule. Later theorists inclined to ignore legitimacy and concentrate on the personal qualities of the monarch (see Chap. XIV).

It is probable that Theophrastus, though an accurate and illuminating observer, was not in the first rank as an original thinker and that the loss of his political writings, though lamentable

[1] P. Oxy. 1611, 38-97, Vol. XIII (1919).

enough, is less serious than the loss of all the works of that
'great and prolific Peripatetic',[1] Dicaearchus of Messene. He wrote
lives of philosophers, on history and geography and on literary
and musical subjects. His *Life of Greece* (Βίος Ἑλλάδος) traced its
history back to a golden age of Kronos, when earth bore fruits
unworked; this was followed by a nomadic, then an agricultural
existence. It dealt also with the pre-polis associations, clan, brotherhood and tribe. But details are lacking which would enable
us to compare it with pre-history as seen by Protagoras or Plato,
still less to know whether he was looking to the past for a form
of government and what inference he drew for πολιτική. All that
can be said is that he leaned more towards the degeneration theory
of human development than to the improvement theory,[2] and
that he ascribed much of the blame to the folly of mankind. For
he had a lively sense of human responsibility and asserted that
men caused more disasters to themselves than the so-called Acts
of God (Fr. 24 w). Dicaearchus appears to have followed Aristotle
and Theophrastus[3] in writing descriptions of the constitutions of
certain cities, notably Athens and Corinth, and some of these
were in Cicero's library. Cicero also had, when he could find it,
a copy of the Τριπολιτικός of Dicaearchus and this we need as
badly as he did, for assuredly it would be *aptus ad quod cogitamus*.[4]
But the only fragment (72 w) definitely cited as coming from the
work is an account, preserved by Athenaeus, of the Spartan system of common meals. It may be inferred from the 'three' in the
title[5] that the *Tripoliticus* contained Dicaearchus' political theory,
which later writers called εἶδος Δικαιαρχικόν, *genus Dicaearchi*.
This, according to the Byzantine bishop Photius (Fr. 71 w), was
an amalgam of the three forms of constitution, therein differing
from Plato's *Republic*, extracting the best from each of the three.
This may be set alongside the following passage from the *De Re*

---

[1] Cicero, *De Off.* II 16.

[2] See above, p. 189 n. 1.

[3] And others. There has survived (Müller, *F.H.G.* II 197 ff.), wrongly
attributed to Heraclides Ponticus of the Academy, a scrappy and worthless
epitome of one of these. There must have been a demand for this kind of
reading.

[4] Cicero, *Ad Att.* XIII 32.

[5] The word is not otherwise known and may have been coined by D.
If there was in ordinary use a word τριπολιτικός, its meaning is unknown;
it might equally well refer to three cities as to three constitutions.

Publica of Cicero, though it cannot be verified[1] that Cicero is actually reproducing Dicaearchus: (Scipio speaks) 'Of the three forms kingship is to my mind by far the best, but better still would be something balanced and harmonised out of all three best kinds of *res publica*. For it is agreed that there should be in a State a certain royal and authoritative element, a second element assigned to and dependent on the influence of leading men, and thirdly a number of matters reserved for a decision of the people according to their will. Such a constitution has firstly a considerable degree of equality, without which free peoples cannot long go on, and secondly stability (*firmitudo*), whereas those other (unmixed) forms too readily degenerate into their corresponding bad forms.'

Dicaearchus' approval of the Spartan social system and his advocacy of a mixed constitution gave him the reputation of being *par excellence* the defender of the Spartan constitution with its combination of monarchy, aristocracy (gerousia)[2] and democracy (Spartiatae). But after all, it was the Athenian in Plato's *Laws* who complimented the Spartans on having a constitution 'mixed and moderate', and its relative permanence was widely believed to be due to these qualities. What then was there in the *Tripoliticus* and why did the notion of a mixed constitution become so firmly attached to the name of Dicaearchus? Perhaps the answer is that Dicaearchus revived and even rescued certain ideas in Plato's *Laws* which had been overlaid by the *Politics* of Aristotle. For Aristotle rejected the Spartan social system, and his moderate and middle-class constitution owed nothing to Sparta or any existing model. Though he sometimes spoke of his 'polity' as *mixed* as well as *moderate*,[3] he did not really mix the elements. He was trying to do

---

[1] But it is fairly certain. Cicero was soaked in Dicaearchus and mentions him with abundant praise and tantalising frequency. D.'s books are 'in piles about him as he writes' (*Att.* II 2) and his political works as well as Plato's must have been beside him when he was compiling *De Re Pub.* I. Unfortunately, while he translates or paraphrases long passages of Plato's *Repub.* VIII, he does not expressly say that he is reproducing Dicaearchus. The above passage (I 69) is not included in Wehrli.

[2] Not, as we might expect, the ephorate, at least if Polybius (VI, chs. 10 and 11) is correctly reproducing D. The Lacedaemonian Megillus in Plato's *Laws* (IV 712 D) regarded the ephors as τυραννικοί and so did 'some people' according to Aristotle (*Pol.* II 1265 b *fin.*), while others thought them democratic, as being drawn from the people (*ibid.* and 1270 b).

[3] μίξις ὀλιγαρχίας καὶ δημοκρατίας (*Pol.* IV 1293 b).

justice to three different principles. Dicaearchus was trying to make a fourth kind of constitution by fusing together portions of the other three—a *quartum genus . . . moderatum et permixtum tribus*.[1] This was something different from the middle-class polity of Aristotle and far removed from Solon's idea of 'mixing well the constitution'.[2] And while it went even farther than Plato in praise of Sparta, its antecedents are clearly more Platonic than Aristotelian. How it came to be applied to the Roman constitution we shall see in the next chapter.

Aristoxenus the musician, also a Peripatetic by upbringing, wrote on πολιτικοὶ νόμοι in at least eight books (Fr. 45 w), but nothing is known of their contents. He corresponded with Dicaearchus on political subjects (Cic., *Att.* XIII 32), but apart from musical theory his interests seem to have been in questions of morals and the history of philosophy. He leaned towards Pythagoreanism, as was natural in a musician and a native of the Tarentum of Archytas. His hostility to Plato has already (p. 27) been noted. More closely connected with political thought, but no better represented by surviving fragments, was another and more surprising product of the Lyceum, Demetrius of Phalerum. He attended lectures of Aristotle and Theophrastus and he knew Menander and the orator Dinarchus. About 324 B.C. he began to make a political career for himself and by 317 he had received from Cassander of Macedon a commission to govern Athens. This he did for ten years and was driven out in 307 by Demetrius the Besieger. He took refuge at the Court of Ptolemy and devoted the rest of his life to writing short books on a great variety of subjects (Cic., *de Fin.* V 54). In spite of his own fondness for outlandish and extravagant clothes he made laws prohibiting various types of luxurious expenditure. Indeed, tradition tells us little about his legislative work at Athens except the anti-luxury laws. He believed in constitutional government of some kind and did not intend to rule simply as a tyrant. He made a new code of laws and employed law-guardians (νομοφύλακες) to see that they were observed. But the employment of any such constitutional safeguard was considered to be a limitation of the power of the people to make laws.[3] He also had an army of officials called

---

[1] Cicero, *de Re Pub.* I 45.
[2] Aristotle, *Politics* II 1273 b.
[3] Aristotle, *Politics* IV 1298 b *fin.*

γυναικόνομοι who were censors of morals and had the powers of a police force. He had a census taken of the inhabitants of Attica. Behind all this legislation what kind of *politeia* was Demetrius aiming at? As a pupil of the Lyceum he might be expected to follow Aristotle and he is said to have fixed the property valuation for citizenship at 1000 drachmas, which would give a wide basis such as Aristotle advised. On the other hand there was his own position;[1] and his régime was regarded as the antithesis of democracy. The watch kept on officials and the general censorship of morals suggest that here we have another Peripatetic who in political theory was more influenced by the *Laws* of Plato than the *Politics* of Aristotle.[2]

Fortune, while denying us the chance to read the works of some of the greater Peripatetics, has preserved for us some of the lesser. The uncritical acceptance of the authority of Aristotle began early to exert an unfortunate influence; but that did not at first take the form of believing the truth of his written works, rather of adding to these after his death. Various works have been preserved and handed down to us under the name of Aristotle. In them there is much copying and summarising of Aristotle and it was in accordance with the practice of the time that they should pass as his work. They are therefore less worth having than would have been the works of any of the other members of the Lyceum. But they are not, to judge by our *Politics*, pure Aristotle[3], and they show traces of the tendency, just noted, to hark back to Plato in political philosophy. For example the *Magna Moralia* or *Great Ethics* has a chapter (1 33) on Justice, which is mainly a summary of *Eth. N.* Book V. But the writer in his attempt to explain Aristotle's proportionate equality adds a comparison with Plato, *Republic* II, and the mutual exchange of wares by farmers and craftsmen. Similarly the author of *Virtues and Vices*, an ethical work of the Theophrastean type, turns aside (1251 b 30) to refer to the analogy between the good state and the good condition

[1] On which see Ferguson, *Hellenistic Athens*, p. 47, n. 3.

[2] See note at end of this chapter.

[3] It must, however, be stated that there is great difference of opinion here, especially about the *Magna Moralia* and its relation to Aristotle's other ethical works. After all, Aristotle himself may have been affected by the tendency to return to Plato. If the view expressed in the notes on Chap. XI above be correct, he may even have started it, giving advice to his successors to re-read the political works of Plato.

of mind or soul. He does not mention Plato by name, but the allusion to Platonic doctrine is clear.

Other works of the Peripatetic school include three books grouped together under the title *Oeconomica*. The first, which was in antiquity attributed to Theophrastus,[1] derives largely from Xenophon and Aristotle and is chiefly concerned with the management of women and slaves.[2] The third book, which has survived only in a Latin translation of the thirteenth century, deals with the relations of husband and wife. But the second book, clearly a separate work,[3] contains matter more relevant to our purpose. Reversing the older terminology, the author regards government as a part of οἰκονομική, rather as three parts of it; for there are: government (*a*) by a king, (*b*) by a satrap or governor, (*c*) of an independent city, as well as the control exercised by a private person over his own property. Some change in the outlook of political theorists since the death of Alexander is clearly reflected here. The differences between the forms of government are not now discussed in terms of rich and poor, few and many, or middle-class and artisans. All governments appear to him to have only one problem—how to raise money; and the three forms of government are to be distinguished chiefly by their different means of doing this. In this respect the book is more reminiscent of Xenophon's *Ways and Means* than a work of political theory, but otherwise it clearly belongs to the third not to the fourth century. It is therefore disappointing to find that the author after a short first chapter tells us no more about government as seen through Hellenistic eyes, but devotes the rest of his book to stories illustrating the different ways of raising revenue.

There has also come down to us ascribed to Aristotle a treatise on rhetoric, to which was prefixed a four-page prefatory letter, addressed to Alexander the Great and sending him the work, as if he had asked for it. It was thus called *Rhetorica ad Alexandrum*.

[1] By Philodemus in the first century B.C. See note at the end of Chap. XIII.

[2] It does, however, define both πόλις and πολιτική in a way which in contrast to Book II shows the old ideas firmly rooted and taken for granted: the art of government and the art of setting up a State are both part of πολιτική; we cannot separate them, as we can the art of playing upon from the art of constructing a musical instrument (1 1343 a). The writer regards (*ibid.*) the home as prior to the city and does not discuss Aristotle's theory of the logical priority of the πόλις (p. 214 and n.).

[3] B. A. van Groningen, *Aristote : le second livre de l'économique* (Leyden, 1933).

It is not by Aristotle; it is not even Peripatetic, but rather Iso-cratean and is plausibly assigned to the fourth-century rhetor Anaximenes of Lampsacus. It is a good example of the rhetorical way of looking at things (see Chap. VII), undertaking to teach the right things to say about political matters, and its general standpoint is that of a nervous property-owner. The purpose of legislation is summed up by saying that 'in democracies laws ought to check the Many in their designs upon the property of the rich; and in oligarchies to prevent those who share in the government from abusing their power to the detriment of the weaker and from bringing false charges against the citizens' (23). All that is commonplace enough, as is to be expected in a handbook on rhetoric. What is more relevant to our purpose, though equally non-Peripatetic, is the prefatory letter. It was written by someone who, having carefully read the treatise itself, adapted some of its contents to suit his own, very much later age.[1] He urges the king 'to embrace the philosophy of words' (11), but his attitude is not that of a rhetorician at all; he is not interested in their speeches, λόγοι, but in *the* speech, *the* Logos. He can cite maxims of rhetoric such as 'Speech with education is the guide of life' (11) but all the while he has only one λόγος, that of the king. 'For those who live in a democracy the standard of reference in all things is the Law, for those who live under the rule of a king it is Logos' (8-9). The word of 'Alexander', he goes on, 'is to his subjects what the common, or general law (κοινὸς νόμος) is to the autonomous cities'. For law is useful; it serves as a guide to many, but others need 'thy life and thy word, O king' as patterns by which to live (9). The author's background is a world in which there are in-dependent cities having their own laws[2] but where fully developed monarchical rule predominates, and his letter, though spurious as a letter, is an interesting pointer to the new ideas about monarchy. (See Chap. XIV.)

The first Peripatetics had on the whole kept to the traditional view of the city-state. But men had now good reason to doubt whether the πόλις really was both the centre and the end of man's

[1] Chronologically it does not belong here, but about the second century B.C.; but it seemed better not to detach it from the τέχνη ῥητορική where we find it. See further below p. 287.

[2] That is what he means by 'living in a democracy', simply 'not under a king', a use which points to a date about the second century. See below p. 272.

existence, the final arbiter in education and morals. Even Theophrastus had remarked 'Good men need few laws; their actions
are not determined by laws, rather do they determine the laws'.[1]
The Cynics, as we have seen, had proved to the satisfaction of
many that the πόλις was one of those many things that men can
very well do without. Now indeed they were becoming obliged
to do without it, just in that part of it which could ill be spared,
that which provided a way and a purpose in life. Men thus thrown
back on themselves were at a loss to know how to answer the
old question 'How shall a man live?' The answers of Plato and
Aristotle were too remote from the reality of world-conditions,
and new religions, astrology and wonder-working could not
satisfy every mind. We are conscious of a new approach as we
turn from the Academy and the Lyceum (Peripatos) to two new
schools started at Athens about 300 B.C.—the Stoa or Porch of
Zeno of Citium and the Garden of Epicurus.

Stoicism was from the start eclectic. It could hardly be otherwise with a structure hastily devised to meet an urgent need.[2]
The founder Zeno was a follower of Crates the famous Cynic
and in allusion to the name of that sect Zeno's work on πολιτεία
was said to have been written 'holding on to the tail of a dog'.
Certainly there is much in Stoicism that is derived from the Cynics
and much too that goes back to Antisthenes and to Socrates.
But the dogmas of the older Stoa were also closely dependent
on Stoic theology or rather on Stoic 'physics' (φυσικά); for the
Stoic realm of Nature includes both gods and men. It is ruled by
Divine Reason and, in order to live in this rational universe, men
must behave according to divine reason, that is, conformably to
nature.[3] Whatever this may mean, it implies one way of life for
all men, not a number of different ways each deriving from its
own πόλις. There can in this sense be only one πόλις for the whole
cosmos:[4] 'The much admired πολιτεία of Zeno, who founded

---

[1] As cited by Stobaeus (Flor. 3 xxxvii 20 = Fr. cvi Wimmer), but it may
be no more than an echo of Aristotle's νόμος ὢν ἑαυτῷ (Eth. N. 1128 a,
cp. Pol. 1284 a), soon to pass into the parlance of educated people—St. Paul,
To the Romans 11 14.

[2] E. R. Bevan, Stoic and Sceptic (1913), p. 32.

[3] ὁμολογουμένως τῇ φύσει, cum natura congruenter vivere.

[4] The use of the word κόσμος to denote the ordered universe as opposed
to the disorder created by men is not new; it was old even in Plato's day.
He ascribed it (Gorg. 508 A) to οἱ σοφοί, meaning doubtless Pythagoreans.

the Stoic sect, has for its general aim', says Plutarch,[1] 'that we should discontinue living in separate cities and peoples, differentiated by varying conceptions of justice, and instead regard all men as members of one city and people, having one life and one order (κόσμος), as a herd feeding together (σύννομος) is reared on a common pasture (νομός, νόμος).'

The Stoic doctrine of the cosmopolis was developed in the third century B.C. by Chrysippus, virtually a second founder of the sect: 'Just as πόλις is used in two senses—a place to live in and also the whole complex of state and citizens, so the universe is, as it were, a πόλις consisting of gods and men, the gods holding sway, the men obeying. It is possible for men and gods to have dealings with each other because both partake of Reason; this is "law by nature" (φύσει νόμος) and all other things have come into being for these objects.'[2] This collocation of the words φύσις and νόμος is not only paradoxical but a deliberate allusion to earlier controversies in political philosophy; for Chrysippus was well read in the literature of the subject.[3] But he is not using φύσις as denoting natural growth, but in the Stoic sense as covering the whole universe endowed with divine reason. To make Law dependent on Nature in this sense produced entirely different results from the physis-doctrine of certain fifth-century sophists.[4] It makes Law both divine and universal like the immortal and unageing laws of Sophocles, but with this addition that they are dependent on Reason, Intelligence, which is also divine and universal. It is not, however, essentially different from the divine law underlying the *Laws* of Plato and it lays the foundations for doctrines of Universal and Natural Law. Chrysippus again shows his sense of the continuity of political thought when he

But to the Stoics it meant also the divine governance. *S.V.F.* II 526-529 Chrysippus. See note at the end of this chapter on *The Older Stoa*.

[1] =Fr. I 262 Zeno.

[2] Fr. II 528 Chrysippus; cp. Cicero, *N.D.* II 154 (=Fr. II 1131): Est enim mundus quasi communis deorum atque hominum domus aut urbs utrorumque. Soli enim ratione utentes iure ac lege vivunt.

[3] In addition to the allusions mentioned in these pages see also Cicero, *Tusc. Disp.* I 108, where Chrysippus is called *in omni historia curiosus* and allusion is made to multiplicity of νόμοι; *supra*, Chap. III *ad fin*. The variations in laws, customs and morals contributed to the Scepticism of Pyrrho of Elis. Diog. L. IX 83-84.

[4] See generally Chaps. IV and V.

alludes (Fr. III 314) to Pindar's famous dictum about Νόμος and to Aristotle's man as πολιτικὸν ζῷον—'Nomos is king of all, of all things human and divine; it should be the authority on things noble or base, be ruler and leader; and in virtue of this it should be the norm of what is righteous and unrighteous and, as for those (human) beings that are by nature πολιτικά, it shall tell them what they must do and forbid that which they must not.'

The next step in such a theory ought to have been to show how a cosmopolis could be brought into existence with divine law as its basis. But it seems this was not part of Chrysippus' purpose; he was chiefly concerned with the individual man and with the process (οἰκείωσις, conciliatio) of bringing him into conformity with divine reason. Yet his learning was such that he must have known that the problem of relating a divine law to human existence lay always at the back of Plato's Laws. We have no such work by Chrysippus. Two centuries later Cicero, having written a 'Republic' decides (De Legibus I 15) to follow it, like Plato, with a work on 'Laws' and to base it largely on Chrysippus. But unfortunately all that he was capable of doing was to paraphrase and expand the Stoic teaching on Law. So far as the surviving portions of Cicero's De Legibus go,[1] they give us no account of a State as envisaged by Chrysippus.

For all its universality and cosmopolitanism, its inclusion even of slaves in the cosmopolis, Stoicism was very far from being a levelling influence. Stoic ethical theories produced almost the opposite effect of the physical; and if the inconsistency went unnoticed among them, that merely testifies to the ever decreasing importance of political theory as a determinant of political practice. The Stoic ideal of a perfectly wise, virtuous and capable man, though he was not conceived primarily as a πολιτικός, tends rather towards monarchical and personal rule and towards the maintenance of an upper class in society. It is not surprising to find Stoics associating themselves with the kings and courts of the Hellenistic world; it was the best way to make their influence felt. And, though it was a matter of debate among Stoics how far the wise man should devote himself to the affairs of a city, there were many among them who stood in no doubt about the matter and the products of the philosophical schools were still employ-

[1] See notes at the end of Chap. XIII.

able.[1] But strictly speaking, they only approved of monarchical rule where it was exercised by a Stoic sage. He, of course, was nowhere to be found; so they put the matter the other way round and said that only the sage was king or capable of being king; the words 'ruler' and 'king' are properly applied not to him who exercises authority over many, but to him who has the science of ruling. Equally, only the wise man can really be a lawgiver or an educator or exercise any other function of what used to be called 'political skill'.[2] Put thus, the notion is no longer paradoxical, but an appeal for a higher standard of government, which had both the backing of Plato and an acceptable meaning for the man in the street.

There was, however, an air of make-believe about much of Stoic political thought with its non-existent sage and its fictitious fraternity; the Epicureans were more realistic. Their master Epicurus had the same general aim as Zeno—to find a way of making human life more tolerable, and like Stoicism his creed appealed chiefly to the upper classes. But Epicurus diagnosed the malady differently and his suggested cure, based on the physics and to some extent also on the ethics of Democritus (Chap. IV), is totally different from the Stoic. He believed that our greatest evils are fears—fear of death and fear of living in fear of death, fear of a next world, fear of unforeseen interventions just when things are going well. The old City State and its gods had helped to allay such fears and for Democritus happiness was bound up with the πόλις. In Epicurus' day a city could but serve as a barrier against interference and so contribute to that absence of worry (ἀταραξία) which all men desire. A city also helps us to make friends and for Epicurus friendship was one of life's greatest blessings.[3] In order

---

[1] e.g. Persaeus, sent about 277 B.C. to deputise for Zeno at the court of Antigonus II, who seems to have felt the need for a trained philosopher. If this Persaeus the Stoic, actively, if unsuccessfully, employed by Macedon (ἐπιστάτης at Corinth 244 B.C.), really wrote works On Kingship, On the Lacedaemonian Constitution and seven books Against the *Laws* of Plato (Diog. L. VII 36), we should take note of the fact and realise how little after all we really know about Stoic political theory or practice.

[2] Frr. III 611, 617, 618 Chrysippus, cp. *supra*, Chap. IX (Plato and Xenophon) and further *infra*, Chap. XIV, *init*. Of course everything depended on how much or how little was implied in τὸν ἐπιστάμενον ἄρχειν and what kind of knowledge. It meant much more for Plato and the Stoics than for Xenophon.

[3] On Epicurus on φιλία, which was not for him a political notion as for some (*supra*, p. 58 n. 3), see A. J. Festugière, *Epicure et ses Dieux*, 1946, ch. III. On Lucretian developments see next chapter.

that it might serve even these limited purposes a city had to be able to secure peace within itself; its citizens must be law-abiding, agreeing with each other to refrain from wrong-doing; for 'natural justice is a token of that which is expedient with a view to not inflicting and not receiving injury.'[1] Justice is therefore 'according to nature', even though it differs from place to place and time to time, since, after all, men differ as to what is expedient. It is expedient to be just and virtuous because otherwise a pleasant life is impossible and the greatest fruit of justice is ἀταραξία.[2] On the other hand justice is not something on its own (καθ' ἑαυτό), it is not good absolutely, but only relatively, in that it contributes to our happiness and makes civilised life possible. Injustice does not contribute to our happiness; the wrong-doer is always unhappy. But its badness is also only relative; 'injustice is not an evil in itself' (K.Δ. 34). The 'naturalness' of justice is not contradicted by the notion of it as an agreement or compact not to do wrong or to suffer it.[3]

Epicurus is in agreement with Heraclitus, Democritus and Protagoras in distinguishing between the average run of men and a really intellectual élite, but he has left us no record of a social structure in which this arrangement could be achieved and maintained. He knew that in the past the progress of civilisation had been helped forward by the active work of wise kings and rulers[4] but, unless we misunderstand him through defective information, he regarded that work as completed. Certainly his answer to the Stoic question would be that the wise man will not engage in political life, since nothing is less likely to bring about that happy

---

[1] K.Δ. 31 = Diog. L. x 150. Whatever be the exact meaning of this cumbersome saying it is clear that when Seneca (*Epist.* 97, 15) said that Epicurus *dicit nihil iustum esse natura*, he was misunderstanding οὐκ ἦν τι καθ' ἑαυτὸ δικαιοσύνη, K.Δ. 33; R. Philippson, *loc. cit.* (See note at end of this chapter.) What Epicurus meant was that the φύσις of justice (K.Δ. 37) was in accordance with the φύσις of man, though it was not part of τὰ φυσικά. It is *natural* for man to be just, because it is natural for him to want to be happy.

[2] Diogenes of Oenoanda (second century A.D.), Fr. LIX 5 (William), cited by C. Diano in his *Epicuri Ethica* (1946), p. 60, Fr. 121; cp. K.Δ. 17.

[3] This too is developed by Lucretius; see next chapter.

[4] That Lucretius, like a true Roman, gives no credit to kings but only to *magistratus* and *leges* (*De Rerum Natura* v 1136-1150) is acutely observed by A. Momigliano in *Journ. Rom. Stud.* XXXI, 1941, p. 157. Still less does he give credit to heroes like Heracles (v 22 ff.).

condition of 'not being worried on account of people' (θαρρεῖν ἀπ' ἀνθρώπων). The wise man will aim at a life of tranquil obscurity and leave public life and political activity to those who really find their happiness in it—if such there be. Epicurus knew about the 'god among men' theory (p. 220) but for him such an expression had nothing to do with virtue or political power; it only meant one who had attained freedom from all fear and worry.[1]

Looking back over the political thought of the third century B.C. one cannot help being struck with its barrenness. This is of course due in part to the decline in the πόλις and in part to the loss of contemporary writings on the subject. But it is also due to the refusal or inability to relate political thinking to the material conditions in which men lived. Epicurus and Chrysippus did their best to help men to face life cheerfully, but the men whom they helped were the few, who had sufficient education to understand their message and sufficient leisure for lessons in philosophy. They either ignored, or accepted as necessary for the maintenance of their social position, many social evils. These had assuredly not grown less since the previous century (see Chap. VII, *init.*). Perhaps the conquests of Alexander had here and there brought some temporary relief to poverty; but if so, the improvement was short-lived and the number of those who were thereby enabled to 'better themselves' must have been small in comparison with those who remained below the poverty line or in slavery; and any increase in wealth would find its way into the hands of the few not the many. Certain it is that, as the third century drew to its close and the splendour of its literary and scientific achievement waned, the contrast between the 'haves' and the 'have-nots', between οἱ δυνατοί and οἱ ἀδύνατοι became more manifest, the symptoms of mental and social malaise more conspicuous—constant fighting, infanticide and depopulation, malnutrition, fall in the value of money and in wage-rates, increased contempt of manual labour and, above all, shortage of food and the lack of any means of increasing its production. Intercommunication between the different parts of the Hellenistic world, though easier than before Alexander, was still costly and difficult and transport still insufficiently organised to make it possible for famine in one part to be quickly relieved from the surplus of another—at any rate not

---

[1] *Epist.* III, Diog. L. x 135. For his followers, of course, it was Epicurus who was a god on earth. Cicero, *Tusc.* I 48 and Lucretius frequently.

without heavy expenditure by some and fat profits to others. Lack of intercommunication would also be one of the reasons why rebellions of the oppressed classes were neither so frequent nor so vigorous as one might expect; they were also quickly suppressed and agreements existed between governments of one kind or another to assist each other in stamping out revolutionary movements.

The economic conditions were not the same everywhere, but the general picture was one of discontent and smouldering revolt. Yet this, though it called forth many individual acts of helpfulness and generosity, does not seem to have had any effect on the political thinking of educated people. Still dominated by fear of mass-revolution they could think of nothing but how it might be suppressed. The masses, divided always between free and slave, had no intellectual food. There was indeed a literature of discontent but naturally little of it found its way into libraries and anthologies, the road to survival. We have, however, fragments on papyrus of the Cynic poet Cercidas, which cry aloud against the inequalities of wealth, and against the gods, who are reputed to have the power to prevent them, but do not. The longing for release from depression and poverty is seen in the 'Utopias' of Euhemerus, who imagined a three-class society in which priests were all-powerful, and of Iambulus, in whose scheme inequalities are so levelled out that all men have become equal even in ability and all share equally the products of labour, the constant fertility of the land ensuring that none need work too hard. But these needs and aspirations are not reflected in the political philosophy that we know of. Divorced from political conditions in a way which would have been unthinkable in the time of Solon, it went on its way. Even in the fourth century the political thought of Isocrates and Plato had borne some relation, however faulty, to the existing conditions. But now, as we pass from the third to the second century, we look in vain for any understanding of the plight of society. Neither the change from the older Stoics to Panaetius nor the sceptical phase at the Academy meant improved understanding of social problems and the Epicureans, though they might drive out superstitious terror, could devise no antidote to the fear of starvation.

On the other hand there were some who, without having any real interest in the lot of the oppressed classes and not basing their action on any philosophical system, had or acquired political power and used it in attempts at reform. At Sparta[1] the abortive plans of Agis IV (243 B.C.) and the more successful efforts of Cleomenes III to re-distribute large landed estates and to enfranchise helots were part of a plan to re-establish Spartan military power on the old Lycurgan model. But any proposal to divide up land (γῆς ἀναδασμός) was sure to cause alarm among owners everywhere. The reputation of another Spartan king, Nabis, at the very end of the century was blackened into that of the worst possible tyrant[2] for similar reasons. Yet in the conflict between the Achaean league and the Romans in the next century it was not the wealthy who fought the invader to the last ditch, but the mob in Corinth and other cities, who were not finally defeated till 146 B.C. But the impact of Rome on Greek political thought belongs to our next chapter.

---

[1] On these 'reforms' see K. M. T. Chrimes, *Ancient Sparta* (1949), ch. I.
[2] The dual kingship had ended with Cleomenes III (*ob.* 219 B.C.).

FURTHER NOTES AND REFERENCES

CHAPTER XII

Only the barest minimum of the changed and changing background could be indicated at the beginning and end of the above chapter. In addition to the more general histories consult F. W. Walbank, in *J.H.S* LXIV (1944), W. S. Ferguson, *Hellenistic Athens* (1911) and *Greek Imperialism* (1913) and W. W. Tarn, *Hellenistic Civilisation* (1927, 2nd ed. 1930). There is an abundant literature on Alexander culminating, as it were, in Tarn's *Alexander the Great* (2 vols., 1948) in which Appendixes 24 and 25 are especially relevant. The constitutional position, if any, of the various cities is a complicated question: see, in addition to the above-mentioned works, A. H. M. Jones, *The Greek City from Alexander to Justinian* (1940) and the literature there cited. Equally complicated and variable were the leagues and federations. See by way of example the two inscriptions referred to in the Additional Note below. Two composite works, quite different from each other, must both be mentioned—*The Hellenistic Age* (four lectures, Cambridge, 1923) and *The Greek Political Experience* (Studies in honor of W. K. Prentice, Princeton, 1941) especially Nos. VII to XII.

THE CYNICS. The place of Diogenes and the Cynics in relation to Antisthenes (Chap. VII, *fin.*) and to the development of post-Socratic morality is extremely difficult to determine in the absence of written works and the presence of nothing but anecdotes and sayings. The view is here taken that Diogenes, not Antisthenes, was the first real κυνικός (Schwartz, *Charakterköpfe* II (1909), ch. 1; D. R. Dudley, *History of Cynicism* (1937)). This has meant, rightly or wrongly, (1) associating the idea of πόνος and the hard-working king, the servant of his people, the new Heracles, so to speak, with Prodicus and Antisthenes, not with Diogenes or Crates, and (2) the rejection of any Cynic monarchy. The exact opposite is the view of R. Höistad, *Cynic Hero and Cynic King* (Uppsala, 1948) in which even the writings of Dio Chrysostom are seriously taken as evidence for Diogenes. The fragments of Diogenes and Crates are in Mullach, *Frag. Philosoph. Gr.* II, pp. 295-341 (M).

PLATONICA. The works referred to are in the fifth volume of Plato (O.C.T.). *The Minos*, being regarded by Burnet as genuine, is in the first half of the volume.

The *Rhetorica ad Alexandrum* or Τέχνη of Anaximenes with its Preface is in the first volume of Spengel, *Rhetores Graeci*, to the *pages* of which the numbers in the text refer. P. Wendland, 'Die Schriftstellerei des Anaximenes' in *Hermes* XXXIX (1904), pp. 419-443 and 499-542, ascribes various writings to A. and even supposes that the Preface too was written by him, being afterwards remodelled and brought 'up to date' by another.

THEOPHRASTUS. The lost works are known only indirectly. Cicero (*de Finibus* V 11) writes: 'Omnium fere civitatum non Graeciae solum, sed etiam barbariae ab Aristotele mores, instituta, disciplinas, *a Theophrasto leges etiam* cognovimus. Cumque uterque eorum docuisset, qualem in re publica principem esse conveniret, pluribus praeterea conscripsisset, qui optimus esset rei publicae status, hoc amplius Theophrastus: quae essent in re publica rerum inclinationes et momenta temporum, quibus esset moderandum, utcunque res postularet.'

The last words clearly point to the πρὸς τοὺς καιρούς (p. 248 above) and to a work of practical utility; but it was Dicaearchus rather than Theophrastus who had the name of being practical (Cic. *ad Att.* II 16, 3).

DICAEARCHUS. The fragments (w) are cited after F. Wehrli, *Die Schule des Aristoteles* I (1944; this series does not include Theophrastus), where the passages in Cicero and other testimonia are collected and annotated. Fragments also in Müller, *Frag. Hist. Gr.* II, 225.

DEMETRIUS OF PHALERUM. A good account in Ferguson's *Hellenistic Athens*, pp. 38-65. The writer of the article in Pauly-Wissowa (R.E. IV 2 nr. 85 col. 2817), followed by Ferguson, neglects the Platonic and magnifies the Aristotelian influence. For a list of titles of his writings see Diog. L. v 80-81. Fragments in Müller II 362, Jacoby *F. Gr. Hist.* II nr. 228, p. 956, and F. Wehrli, *Die Schule des Aristoteles* IV (1949).

THE OLDER STOA. The *Fragments of Zeno and Cleanthes* were edited with a commentary by A. C. Pearson. But the references in the text, being chiefly to Zeno and Chrysippus, are to the volumes and fragments as numbered in H. von Arnim: *Stoicorum Veterum Fragmenta* (three vols. 1903-1905, with Vol. IV Index by M. Adler, 1924). These fragments are numerous, but repetitive and often paraphrases rather than fragments proper. The anti-Stoic writings of Plutarch, so far as they have survived (M. Pohlenz, *Hermes* LXXIV 1939, and F. H. Sandbach, *Class. Quart.* XXXIV, 1940) are an important source. Plutarch was equally opposed to the strictness of the Porch and the hedonism of the Garden.

EPICURUS. Three letters, forty 'standard maxims' (Κύριαι Δόξαι), his will and various traditions are preserved in the tenth book of Diogenes Laertius. These and other *Epicurea* with commentary in Cyril Bailey, *Epicurus: the extant remains* (1926). On the Epicurean view of Justice C. Bailey (*Greek Atomists and Epicurus* (1928) pp. 510-515) is unfair to Epicurus, leaving the impression that justice was almost an evil to be avoided, unless it yielded some advantage. Far better, even if a little overstated, is R. Philippson's article 'Die Rechtsphilosophie der Epikureer' in *Archiv für Geschichte der Philosophie* N.F. XXXIII, 1910, pp. 288-337, also pp. 433-446.

CERCIDAS. Powell and Barber, *New Chapters in Greek Literature* (1921) pp. 5-7 and the second Meliamb in A. D. Knox (Loeb Library along with Herodes and Edmonds' Theophrastus, *Characters*, 1929).

EUHEMERUS. Diod. Sic. v 41-46 (Jacoby, *F. Gr. Hist.* I, p. 302).

IAMBULUS. Diod. Sic. II 55-60. The writer had ransacked a wealth of legend, travellers' tales and philosophical speculations. The inhabitants of his Islands of the Sun have double tongues for carrying on two simultaneous conversations, they use cotton and rice (?) and in writing use a script like the Indian Nāgarī; yet they also rear children communally as Plato advocated for the Guardians in the *Republic*.

ADDITIONAL NOTE TO CHAPTER XII

As we have had occasion to remark already, Greek political philosophers appear to have given little consideration to leagues or to the relations of cities to each other and to other powers. It may not therefore be out of place to append here, merely by way of sample, a brief account first of a *league* and second of a *city-constitution* in relation to a ruling monarch. Both belong to the last quarter of the fourth century B.C., to a period when the kingdoms of the Successors were still taking shape, and each is attested by an inscription of fulness and interest. It is irrelevant to our purpose that neither of these two constitutional arrangements had a long existence in practice. We can but observe, in the absence of any general discussion of the problems, how on particular occasions they were faced by Demetrius Poliorcetes and Ptolemy Soter.

The Pan-Hellenic League of Demetrius the Besieger, 303-302 B.C.

(The numbers refer to the lines of an inscription from Epidaurus, *Suppl. Epigr. Gr.*, 1925, 1 75; W. W. Tarn in *J.H.S.* XLII, 1922, pp. 198-206, M. Cary in *C.Q.* XVII, 1923, pp. 137-148, and J. A. O. Larsen in *Class. Philol.* XX, 1925, p. 315 ff. and XXI, 1926, p. 52 ff. Other references in Cary.)

This was an attempt by Demetrius to follow up the Pan-Hellenic ideas of Isocrates, Philip and Alexander and unite most of the cities and ἔθνη of Greece into a κοινόν. The controlling power was vested in a συνέδριον or council composed of representatives of the member states. These men enjoyed extended diplomatic protection (6-11) and in normal times their attendance at meetings of the council would be required only about six times in four years; the meetings were arranged to coincide with the great athletic festivals (11-14). In war (and at the time Demetrius was disputing the Macedonian monarchy with Cassander) meetings might be summoned, if thought desirable, by the chairmen (πρόεδροι) *and* the king or a representative appointed by the kings. (The plural points to Demetrius and his father Antigonus. Larsen p. 315). Hardly less important than the power to have meetings summoned was (and is) the right to choose a place of meeting. Philip's league had met at Corinth. Here the idea of holding meetings at the same time and place as the Games both solved the problem of venue and fixed the time of *normal* meetings (14-18). The most striking feature of the constitution is that the decisions of the council are binding on all member-states and that the latter have no right to call in question the acts of their accredited representatives, no right εὐθύνας λαμβάνειν on their return home. (The discovery that effective inter-state co-operation demands some sacrifice of national autonomy was made long ago) (18-21). The chairmanship of a meeting was of course a position of power and was subject to rules of procedure. Five πρόεδροι were selected by lot and could on occasion act together as a committee with the king (see above). The chairman for the day was presumably also chosen by lot. It was not allowed to have two of the five πρόεδροι

chosen from the same city or ἔθνος[1] (21-23). The duties and responsibilities of a chairman are described and a quorum of one half is laid
down. In the matter of getting subjects put on the agenda the league of
Demetrius was generous. Written notice of motion from a member
seems to be all that was required (28-32). The arrangements about
taxation or subscriptions payable by members are obscure, as are also
the powers of the king in relation to the council and various other
matters.

A Constitution for Cyrene

The text of the inscription here utilised will be found with commentary by M. Cary in *J.H.S.* XLVIII, 1928, pp. 222-238, and, with a
more complete text and some different restorations, by F. Taeger in
Hermes LXIV, 1929, pp. 432-457. Many matters of interpretation remain
uncertain, in particular whether the constitution was first drawn up
by Cyreneans and submitted to Ptolemy for approval, or emanated
first from Ptolemy, or was the result of negotiation. Ptolemy Soter
does not call himself king, so the document is earlier than 306 B.C.
when he assumed that title. Cary dates it 322-321 B.C. Certainly the
wars of the successors were not over and the constitution, like that
of Demetrius' league, contains special provisions for a time of war.

Cyrene and its accompanying territory, as defined in the document,
are all included in making up the citizen body. This gives a numerous
membership and Ptolemy could add to their number (3-5). But effective
citizenship was confined to 10,000 persons forming the πολίτευμα,
they alone being in a position πολιτεύεσθαι.

To qualify for membership it was necessary to be over thirty years
of age and to possess a certain amount of real property, wife's property
counting towards the amount. The qualification was 20 minae of
Alexandria (2000 drachmae). The figure is low, like that of Aristotle's
moderate polity. But the timocratic character of the régime is clear
and the assessors (τιμητῆρες) in charge of citizen-lists were appointed
by the elders (see below), who in turn were appointed by Ptolemy.
(Wherever property is the basis of citizenship, assessors have much
power. Cp. Aristotle, *Pol.* v 1308 a 35ff.) It is noteworthy too that certain persons are by the nature of their work ineligible for the poli-
teuma, e.g. state-physicians, athletic trainers, teachers of riding and
the use of arms. Such measures, says Taeger (p. 443), are quite under-
standable in a land dominated by land-ownership and big business.

[1] This shows (1) that there must in some cases have been more than one
representative per member-state and (2) that member-states were not always
city-states but might be ἔθνη—groups of villages or towns. Aristotle (*Pol.*
III 1285 b 32) had recognised the possibility of an ἔθνος as a political unit
under a monarch.

The Council or βουλή resembles the Athenian only in name and number (500 members). The members of it must be over fifty or at any rate over forty years of age; they hold office for two years, being elected by lot, but only a part of the council would go out of office at one time (17-20). There is no general assembly of any body larger than the ten thousand; and even the council is not so powerful as the *gerousia*, a body of 101 elders appointed in the first instance by Ptolemy for life (21). These were relieved of certain executive offices, but they had judicial and religious functions and their life-membership of a kind of standing-committee of the council meant that they had much power, so long as they did not run counter to Ptolemy. The most influential political office appears to be the στρατηγία, which was not, of course, purely military. Little is said of the nine νομοφύλακες and the five ephors. Not mentioned in the body of the text, but in a mutilated list of names of office-holders at the end are νομοθέται. Presumably their powers to make laws were limited to matters not provided for in Ptolemy's constitution (27-34). It is clear from one line (36) that the new constitution with a πολίτευμα of 10,000 replaces an older and much more narrowly oligarchic one with only one thousand. Cary sums up the character of this διάγραμμα (39) as a 'fair compromise between oligarchy and democracy' and thinks that it 'accurately reflects the see-saw of contending parties out of which it arose'. We may perhaps see in it evidence, if not for the direct influence of Aristotle's middle polity, at any rate for the fact that his *Politics* was by no means out of date when he died, as is commonly asserted. City-constitutions still mattered a very great deal to Greek city-states, even though the power of a monarch was always there too.

CHAPTER XIII

GREEK POLITICAL THOUGHT
AT ROME

Polybius was born about 200 B.C. at Megalopolis in Arcadia, a leading city of the Achaean League. He died some eighty years later. His life thus covered the period when the Romans, having subdued Hannibal, were extending their power eastwards and reducing to subjection Greece, Macedonia and Asia Minor. He belonged, like Plato, to a well-to-do family with strong political connections; but for him history, not philosophy, was the proper study for a future ruler. Like his father, Polybius played a big part in the affairs of the Achaean League and he was in some parts of his work writing history in which he himself had acted —a fact of which he is proudly conscious. After their victories of 168 B.C. the Romans removed a thousand of the leading men from Greece to Rome and kept them there for nearly seventeen years. Polybius was inevitably one of these, but he fared better than most. He made friends with Scipio Aemilianus, then a mere boy, and, as he watched his career, came to see in him the perfect ideal of a Roman. Through constant intercourse with leading Romans he learned much of their way of life and thought. He was thus doubly well equipped to write the history which he then planned.

He was not, however, primarily a political thinker, but a practical politician, who took to writing history, first, for the usual reason that the reading of it would be useful to politicians; second, because the times in which he lived offered a unique subject and a unique opportunity—universal history at a time when it was just becoming possible to write it. 'For who among men is so worthless or lazy as not to want to know how, and by subjection to what kind of πολιτεία, the whole world came under Roman dominion in less than 53 years?' [219-167 B.C.] (I 1 (5)). Yet it was no part of his view of history to judge actions by their success or failure; he was not prepared to say that Roman expansion was justified by its success: 'Conclusions drawn simply and solely from the events of a struggle are not final verdicts (αὐτοτελεῖς) as regards either victors or vanquished' (III 4). Certainly no one could complain of Polybius that he failed to relate his thinking to the world in which he lived; but it was for him a world of war and politics and great men, not a social structure undergoing an immense strain.[1] All that he saw, or what he saw most clearly, was that the Roman State had performed remarkable feats of conquest and endurance; and, like any true Greek, he said to himself that it must therefore be a remarkably fine πολιτεία. How does it work? Has it stability? How does it compare with others?

In his examination of other constitutions Polybius, looking for some degree of permanence, decides (VI 43) to exclude both Athens and Thebes, which had their brilliant periods, but could not last. Crete, too, though it won praises from earlier writers, he will not admit to be comparable or even similar to Sparta. He disregards also imaginary constitutions such as Plato's *Republic*. To admit such into a competition for the Best State would be like entering a statue for a race; we must see our models working (VI 47). So we find him looking, as so many others had done, at Sparta, not, of course, contemporary Sparta,[2] but at the so-called constitution of Lycurgus—a conception now more than ever loaded up with a mixture of legend and theory. On its internal side it appeared, as it appeared also to Dicaearchus,[3] to offer a stable and balanced constitution of kings, elders and people, capable of working well, so long as the aim of the State is to maintain its independence and preserve its property.[4] 'But if any

---

[1] Although he was well aware, for example, of the decline in population (XXXVI 17 (5)).

[2] The reforms (alluded to in Chap. XII *ad fin.*) of Agis IV and Cleomenes III professed to be a restoring of the Lycurgan system and to some extent they were, but not so the work of Nabis (*ob.* 192 B.C.), the bitter opponent of the land-owning few.

[3] Polybius does not refer to him (*supra*, p. 251 n. 2).

[4] Because *all* the Spartiatae were property-owners, unlike the Roman *populus*—a flaw in the comparison which P. does not notice. This is a view of the function of the state which property-owners naturally supported: Hanc enim ob causam, ut sua tenerentur, res publicae civitatesque constitutae sunt. Panaetius or Cicero, *de Offic.* II 73; cp. Polybius' words πρὸς τὰ σφέτερα βεβαίως διαφυλάττειν.

has greater ambitions than these, deeming it a finer and more magnificent achievement not merely to lead, but to subdue and control other nations, so that all look to him and bow at his command, then it must be allowed that the constitution of the Lacedaemonians is inadequate and inferior to that of the Romans. The facts of themselves are sufficient to prove the greater strength of the Roman system' (VI 50).

Polybius gives a detailed description of the Roman constitution at the time of the Second Punic War, especially of its military organisation; the success of the Roman expansion depended so much on it and it was all part of the Roman πολιτεία. So too was their religion; and Polybius remarks with favour how skilfully the Roman authorities used superstitious beliefs to terrify, and religious ceremonial to impress, the common people (VI 56). We need not here describe the Roman constitution, for which Polybius' account is a major source; what we have to note is his way of giving it, as it were, a theoretical justification as a mixed constitution: 'Now, as I have already remarked, there were three effective parts of the constitution; all these had been so fairly and properly put together severally and so administered by the Romans that no one even of those who lived under it could say for certain whether the whole system was aristocratic, democratic or monarchic. And this was a very natural impression to get; for whenever we fix our attention on the powers of the consuls, it appears to have been thoroughly monarchical and royal; when on those of the Senate, it was aristocratic; and if we consider the powers of the many, certainly democratic.'[1]

If Polybius had left the matter there, he would be remembered in political thought as a distant follower of Dicaearchus, an admirer of the Roman constitution, and little more, not very penetrating and not original. But he has another theory to put forward[2] and into it he must fit the Roman constitution. It is a

[1] VI 11 (11-12). The last sentence closely resembles Plato, *Laws* 712 D, which passage, it was suggested above (p. 251), was taken over by Dicaearchus.

[2] Why he does so it is hard to say. Events after 168 may have caused him to revise his estimate of Rome and its chances of future stability. But it did not require a cyclic or any other theory to enable him to reach the conclusion that nothing can go on forever (VI 57). On the questions both of Polybius' thought and of literary history here involved see F. W. Walbank in *Class. Quart.* XXXVII 1943, pp. 73-89.

theory which has its roots not in practical politics but in books. Polybius was not a learned man, but he was well-educated. He knew something of the great political literature of his country, much more of Plato than of Aristotle. The phraseology of the Porch and the Garden had crept into his (and other people's) vocabulary, but he betrays no real knowledge of Stoic doctrine and it would be a mistake to attach a label to him[1] or to expect much philosophy from him. However, his 'constitutional cycle' is part of Greek Political Thought and we must now examine it.

He assumes that history develops in such an orderly way that if the past is known, the future may be inferred (VI 3). This can be confidently applied to Greek states; but to the Roman, whose past is not so clearly known and which is a complicated affair, it is not so easy. When constitutions are not mixed, they fall into three classes, in each of which there is a good and a bad variety—a revival of the old six-fold classification in which kingship is distinguished from tyranny (μοναρχία), aristocracy from oligarchy and democracy from mob-rule (ὀχλοκρατία). The characteristics of a good democracy are: respect for gods, parents and the laws, and adherence to the majority principle, these being absent from 'ochlocracy'. This is very much the traditional idea of democracy, as for example in Isocrates, and not the 'modern' or second-century application of the word. For, when writing the history, Polybius conceives of δημοκρατία as being (1) opposed to monarchy, that is to the Macedonian or other kings as they were in his day[2], and (2) participating in a federal principle upon which leagues were built.[3] But for the moment he forgets contemporary politics and proceeds to construct a cycle of constitutional changes

---

[1] H. J. Edwards (Introd. to Paton's (Loeb) edition, Vol. 1, p. xiii) calls him a Stoic and F. W. Walbank, following others whom he mentions, calls the cyclic theory Stoic (*loc. cit.*, pp. 85 and 88). Wilamowitz (*Der Glaube der Hellenen* II 394, 1932) and E. Schwartz (*Charakterköpfe* I 75) agree with the above view. E. Kornemann, 'Zum Staatsrecht des Polybius', *Philologus* LXXXVI, 1931, on the meagre strength of Polybius' acquaintance with Panaetius (Cicero, *de Re Pub.* I 34), builds a theory of a revision of the sixth book under Panaetian influence.

[2] F. W. Walbank, *Philip V of Macedon* (1940), p. 225, n. 1.

[3] In XXXI 2 (12) he uses in this connection the phrase δημοκρατικὴ καὶ συνεδριακὴ πολιτεία in which expression δημοκρατική means 'not subject to a king' and συνεδριακή perhaps 'representative'. So J. A. O. Larsen, 'Representation and Democracy in Hellenistic Federalism'. *Classical Philology* XL, 1945, pp. 65-97. But as Professor Walbank, writing of μόναρχος, says, 'to

as follows: First, monarchy, because it comes 'naturally and not artificially'; but real kingship can only arise out of it by a process of 'construction and reform'. It degenerates into tyranny,[1] the abolition of which is followed by aristocracy. This degenerates into oligarchy, and the unjust rule of the oligarchs provokes the people to set up a democracy. But it too degenerates into lawlessness and 'ochlocracy' results.

That all this is superficially like the changes described in the eighth book of the *Republic* Polybius is well aware,[2] but he wishes to make the theory easier for modern readers, to relate it to the actual history of man, to make it truly cyclical, so that the process may begin again, and to apply it to the Roman constitution. He accordingly, like Protagoras, Plato, Epicurus and others describes the origin and development of political life.—It began with the rule of the strongest, who was sole ruler in virtue of his physical strength. Gradually this improves into a true kingship; ideas of justice and virtue, without which living together would be impossible, take root. For man is distinguished from other animals by the possession of the faculty of reason (λογισμός)[3] and he can see that certain duties are incumbent upon him in relation to his family and his fellows generally. It thus becomes expedient (συμφέρον) for him to be virtuous and just; society is based not on force or passion (θυμός), but on reason. When, however, a king seeks to raise himself above his fellow-men too much and to insist that his word is law, the *best* people rise up and depose him; and so aristocracy comes into being. They at first rule with paternal wisdom, but power and rank go to their heads too. They meet with the same end as a tyrant, and the people themselves set up a democracy. This works well while those are alive who remember the revolution which gave them freedom and equality. But in a generation or two the wealthier folk claim privilege instead of

demand complete consistency in Polybius' use of technical language is to invite disappointment', *Class. Quart.* XXXVII, 1943, p. 79.

[1] There are thus three types of one-man rule, not two only; the cyclic theory and the six-fold theory do not match.

[2] He refers (VI 5 (1)) to 'Plato and others'. In what follows about floods and famines and the recurrent efforts of the human race he is not drawing on *Laws* III, which perhaps he had not read, but on historical traditions based on facts.

[3] The Epicurean wise man, no less than the Stoic, sought to follow reason, *Κ.Δ.* 16 (D.L. X.144) and D.L. X.117. 'Duties' (τὰ καθήκοντα) and θυμός are predominantly Stoic expressions, τὸ συμφέρον rather Epicurean.

equality; in order to gain power they use bribery and so corrupt the masses that democracy gives way to rule of violence.[1] The rich are slain or exiled, their lands divided up,[2] all under the leadership of some bold and skilful champion. Things go from bad to worse and the mob 'again reduced to an uncivilised state (ἀποτεθηριωμένον) finds a master and μόναρχος' and the process begins again.

This cyclic development (πολιτειῶν ἀνακύκλωσις) is, we are repeatedly assured, part of the order of nature. This must mean two things, first that we can do nothing to stop or alter it and therefore a mixed constitution is an impossibility; second, that the Roman Constitution, as its past has been according to nature, κατὰ φύσιν, so its future will be also. We are not told at precisely what point in the cycle the Roman State stood at that time, or how such a well-mixed affair could be included at all. It had certainly not yet reached its destined mob-rule, and had long since passed king-ship. The task of writing history so as to accord with a particular theory requires a mind more subtle and less honest than that of Polybius, who ends this not very happy excursion into political philosophy as follows (VI 57): 'It hardly requires to be proved that all things are subject to change and decay; the inevitable processes of nature are enough to convince us on that point. Now there are two causes by which every kind of constitution may be brought to destruction—one external, the other arising within. There is no regular method of investigating the external causes, but there is of the internal.' [The method is to apply the theory of ἀνακύκλωσις.] According to this the future is: 'Whenever a State, having come safely through many great dangers, then reaches pre-eminence and unchallenged mastery, the result is that as prosperity becomes more and more ingrained in it, men live more expensively and vie with each other over office and other privileges more than they need.' But the greed and love of power of the rich do not of themselves produce revolution. The responsibility will rest with the people, partly because of their

[1] χειροκρατία is used here, not ὀχλοκρατία, but it is only the use of part for the whole. Riots and violence are a feature of mob-rule. Polybius is here (VI 9, fin.) again being 'bookish' in his words, consciously or not recalling even Hesiod (W.D. 262, δωροφάγοι and [169] χειροδίκαι).

[2] γῆς ἀναδασμοί; cp. Plato, Repub. VIII 566, χρεῶν τε ἀποκοπὰς καὶ γῆς ἀναδασμόν—the constant fears of property-owners and hopes of the property-less. Plutarch, Dion 37.

hostility to the over-great and partly because they are themselves being courted by the ambitious and feel that power is in their own hands. When that stage is reached the [Roman] people 'will no longer be content to obey their betters or even attain equality with them, but will want everything for themselves. When this happens, their πολιτεία will acquire that name which sounds so well—Freedom and Democracy—but which is really the worst possible—Mob-rule.'

About fifteen or twenty years junior to Polybius was the Stoic philosopher, or heretic,[1] Panaetius. He too had connections with Rome, arising out of the dealings between his native Rhodes and the new imperial power; and he too lived for a time, what time is unknown, in the circle of Scipio Aemilianus (Fr. 119).[2] Later he lived at Athens where he became head of the Stoa. If he did not die in 109 B.C., he then retired from this post. He toned down the harshness and strictness of Stoic doctrine and did not hesitate to follow the lead of the Peripatetics and especially of Plato, where he believed them to be right. So he came to be called the founder of a new or Middle Stoa. Whatever the stricter Stoics may have said at the time about his rejection of divination and of the doctrine that only virtue is needed for happiness, his rationalising reforms actually strengthened the school against the attacks of Carneades and the other Academic Sceptics. Certainly he contributed greatly to the spread of Stoicism, which he made more acceptable to educated Romans: not that he was trying to fit it to Roman ways, rather he was making it more thoroughly Greek,[3] recapturing something of the philosophical outlook of the fifth century. The wise man of the older Stoa was not expected and often not encouraged to be πολιτικός, and when in the dialogue De Legibus Cicero refers to Stoic work de magistratibus, his interlocutor is made to express surprise: 'Do you mean to say that such matters were also dealt with by the Stoics?' 'Well, no, not exactly, except by him whom I have just mentioned and later by a great and supremely learned man—Panaetius. For the Stoics, while dis-

---

[1] So Wilamowitz, Der Glaube der Hellenen II 398, but M. Pohlenz, Die Stoa (1948) I 239 denies.

[2] For the numbering of the 'fragments' see note at the end of the chapter.

[3] Pohlenz, op. cit., p. 207, 'Seine Weltanschauung ist nichts anderes als die Hellenisierung der Stoa'. But the process was not so much a rescue from an alleged Semitic outlook of Zeno, which Pohlenz exaggerates (Antikes Führertum (1934), p. 128), but rather a revival as suggested above.

coursing very cleverly about the *res publica* in theory, did not do so in relation to the needs of the people and the citizens' (48). Panaetius was practical and utilitarian in outlook and had a clear conception of the social good.

The historical basis of his political theory was two-fold, being on the one hand the tradition that great and good men laid the foundations of human civilisation, and on the other that in that process of civilisation the polis played a secondary, but by no means negligible part.—In the remote past the foundations of justice, and subsequently of law, had been laid by rulers of noble character, by *bene morati reges*, who championed the oppressed (120). Other great men, for example Themistocles, Pericles and Alexander, had done their work only because of the steady loyalty of their people (117). The welfare of the whole people should therefore be aimed at and their co-operation secured. Panaetius did not believe in the complete equality of men but, like others of the well-to-do classes, in the moral superiority of 'the better sort'; and Cicero was doing him no injustice when he bracketed him with Polybius as an admirer of the old Roman constitution (119). But the moral superiority of the Panaetian wise man differs greatly from the Stoic sage of Zeno and Chrysippus. Not only does he share with all men the natural feelings of love and loyalty, companionship and curiosity, but he is not above ambition. He may well have an urge to become a leader, an *appetitio quaedam principatus* (98). Such a feeling is not to be condemned, if it goes along with moral superiority, a sense of fitness and a feeling for beauty. This is the new Stoic sage of Panaetius, partly modelled on Scipio Aemilianus, the ideal Roman of Polybius. But Scipio was no Stoic and his famous *humanitas* was largely a piece of idealisation; the Senatorial party needed a hero to set over against the memory of Tiberius and Caius Gracchus.

The older Stoics had rejected the πόλις. Panaetius re-instated it, but only in a secondary place. There were some obvious reasons for its re-instatement: the cosmopolis as a single unit appeared unrealisable and unworkable, and separate states were not necessarily incompatible with a *communis totius generis hominum conciliatio*.[1] The historical basis of the πόλις was also valid; it had

---

[1] Cicero, *de Off.* 1 149, not included by van Straaten. Note that world-unity is here an affair of human beings, not the divine cosmos. See E. Elorduy, *Die Sozialphilosophie der Stoa* (1936), p. 217 (*Philologus*, Supptbd. XXVIII 3).

answered the human need for being together and it had later undertaken the duty of protecting property (118). These functions it could still perform and it could not therefore be regarded either as a useless encumbrance or as contrary to nature. But Panaetius did not go so far as to make the πόλις the final arbiter of right and wrong. For him, as for the older Stoics, standards of justice depended on Reason and Nature, on λόγος and φύσις. But he gave to these words a different interpretation; he brought them back from heaven to earth and rendered the whole idea of duty no longer cosmic and intangible, but immediately intelligible to Greek and Roman alike. For him 'to live according to nature' meant simply 'to live according to the resources which nature has given us'[1] (96). This provided a very much broader and freer answer to the question, How shall a man live? and allowed him to include health and strength and even a feeling for beauty in nature and in works of art among those things which make for the good life. So, except that he did not concern himself much whether life was to be lived in a πόλις or not, Panaetius comes nearer to Aristotle than to Chrysippus in his ideas of the good man and the good life.

The most notable contemporary of Panaetius was Carneades, head of the Academy, now greatly changed since Plato's day and strongly sceptical in outlook. We have no written remains and most of his work lay outside the political field. It was Carneades who shocked public opinion at Rome by following up a lecture on justice with a rebuttal of all the arguments which he had used in its favour (9).[2] It followed from this demonstration of impartiality that the Stoic doctrine of *ius naturale* was false and the source of justice was not to be found either in God or in Universal Nature, as Chrysippus had said. The only *natural* standard of conduct was self-interest. 'Either, therefore, justice is nothing, or if it be something, it is the greatest folly, since it seeks the advantage of others and so injures itself' (21). We have heard all this, one might say, before, for example from Thrasymachus; and we have heard too of the theory of the State as a compact, a *pactio inter populum et potentes*, so that justice must have originated 'not in nature, not even in the desire for it, but in weakness' (23). Thus here again (cp. p. 75) *Machtpolitik* is trying to find an explan-

---

[1] κατὰ τὰς δεδομένας ἡμῖν ὑπὸ τῆς φύσεως ἀφορμάς.
[2] The numbers refer to the sections in Cicero, *de Re Pub.* III.

ation of justice in two different directions, uncertain whether its origin lies in the desire of the strong for power or of the weak for safety. Carneades does not attempt to reverse the accepted meaning of justice so as to replace it by the 'right of the stronger', but he shows that the exercise of power within States and still more between one State and another, is always to a greater or less degree unjust. The Romans, if they wished to act justly, would have to return to their old owners all the possessions which they had won and go back to living in hovels in misery and want (21). But if they do not act justly in building themselves an empire, they act very prudently and sensibly (28). For how can it be anything but beneficial to a State to acquire territory, enrich its treasury and moreover be praised to the skies for doing it? (22). In our personal dealings, if we want to secure the profits of dishonesty, we must practise concealment; but we openly put up monuments to anyone of whom it might be said *fines imperii propagavit*, though we know well that he could only have extended Roman dominion by depriving others (24). So long then as there is no *concordia* throughout the world, but separate states, so long will one nation's profit be another's loss.—Not since the Athenians at Melos (Chap. VI) have we seen the basis of imperialism so discussed. Carneades was not condemning the Roman empire; he was simply pointing out that it had no ethical basis and this stimulated others to try and find one.

They found it, or perhaps we may say Posidonius found it,[1] in Plato. For this Stoic philosopher, historian and ethnologist, was among those who admired the Roman character and approved of Roman dominion. The right of the stronger, where his strength is in superior wisdom, intelligence and justice, was not what Thrasymachus meant; but Plato constantly re-affirmed it in that sense and Posidonius followed.[2] It could easily be made to fit the Stoic sage, who, accordingly, now appears before us in a dress designed to outshine and replace the *nova et nimis callida sapientia*[3] of a Carneades. The wise man of Posidonius is not he who is

[1] W. Nestle, *Griechische Weltanschauung* (1946), p. 156, in an article on *Politik und Moral im Altertum* reprinted from *N. Jbb. Kl. Alt.*, 1918, p. 225 ff.

[2] Seneca, *Epist.* 90, 5.

[3] If Livy (XLII 47, 9) is to be believed, the Senate in 170 B.C., even before the visits of the Greek philosophers, was divided into two camps over *honestum* and *utile*. F. W. Walbank in *Journal of Roman Studies* XXI, 1941, pp. 82-93.

clever enough to outwit those who stand in the way of Roman expansion, but he who is morally and intellectually superior, a Scipio, as Panaetius had said, or better still, that M. Marcellus who wept because he had caused the death of Archimedes and who was 'the first to prove to the Greeks that the Romans had a sense of justice' (Frr. 45, 46 M). But to discover Roman generals of high character and ability was not to disprove the thesis of Carneades that the Roman empire was built on greed and self-interest; and the sack of Corinth and the destruction of Carthage in 146 B.C. made it hard to maintain, as some did,[1] that Roman dominion was exercised for the benefit of subject peoples and therefore not unjust. It certainly does not appear that the efforts of Panaetius and Posidonius had any success in humanising Roman policy.[2]

Of those who heard Posidonius lecture on history and philosophy the most famous is M. Tullius Cicero. To the Stoic question, Shall the *sapiens* take part in politics? he, orator and consular, could have but one answer. He could derive support (*de Re Pub.* I 12) from the Seven Wise Men of antiquity, who were often practical statesmen and advisers. His outlook was thus partly that of a politician and partly that of a lawyer and only a very little that of a philosopher. Still, he was more at home with political philosophers than with metaphysical, and his two works *De Re Publica* and *De Legibus* are partly about Rome and Roman law, but in a small measure they are also a part of the history of Greek thought. They are so chiefly as source-books; but that was not Cicero's intention, for he was not writing a history of political thought. His purpose was that of the sixth book of Polybius, but in the reverse direction—to fit Greek political theory and Roman history and constitution into one frame. He was not any more successful than Polybius, because, though he was better read and more versatile, he too did not see how superficial was the resemblance between the *mixtum genus* of Dicaearchus and the Roman system of Magistrates, Senate and People. Cicero knew the Roman State from the inside: it was a vast military and judicial organisation with complicated social arrangements of tribes and

---

[1] Cicero, *de Re Pub.* III 36.

[2] But see Mason Hammond, 'Ancient Imperialism' in *Harvard Studies in Classical Philology* LXVIII, 1948, p. 150 n. 88, where reff. are given to those who think they had.

families. It depended for its working not on what the Greeks called νόμοι, but on such notions as *imperium, consilium, auctoritas*, notions not indeed foreign to Greek thought, but having little or nothing to do with constitutions of any type.[1] Personal rule, personal influence, personal dependence of the lesser folk on the great—these were the things that counted in Roman political life. Hence Roman political thought expressed itself in such terms. Cicero did not need to have read Panaetius, still less to have had in mind anything remotely resembling the Principate, in order to coin the phrase *moderator rei publicae* to express his thoroughly Roman preference for a good and prudent leader. Nor did he really need to read Greek philosophy in order to find out the advantages, especially for those who had property, of *concordia ordinum* and the rule of the 'best men'. But he found much in Greek political thought which matched well his views on Roman politics, and this made his task appear easier than it really was. While Polybius was trying to interpret the Roman system in terms of Greek philosophy, Cicero was trying to interpret Greek philosophy in terms of the Roman constitution and to show that the Roman Republic had not only a glorious history in fact, but a respectable ancestry in political theory. The ancestry was fictitious, but it explains why Cicero ransacked his library for extracts from Plato, Aristotle, Theophrastus, Dicaearchus, Panaetius, and embodied them in these books alongside copious citations from early Roman law. So when we find Scipio made to extol Monarchy, he is not thinking of the Roman kingship or indeed of any form of constitution. It is the personal authority of a man of character and influence, a combination of ἀρετή and *auctoritas*.

While Cicero was adapting the doctrines of the Middle Stoa to Roman ways of thinking, others were looking to the rival school of Epicurus. But Epicureanism had undergone no fundamental change; its adherents prided themselves on keeping intact the doctrine of their founder and when they differed from each other, as Philodemus says those who 'claimed to be Epicureans' often

---

[1] If Aristotle had been alive to ask what was τὸ κύριον in the constitution of Rome, and had been told that it was the *populus Romanus*, the answer would have been wrong. As was stated above (p. 213 n. 1) τὸ κύριον meant not theoretical sovranty but its active exercise, and that belonged to Consuls and Senate. The Athenian δῆμος could exercise *imperium*, but the Roman *populus* could not.

did,[1] they disagreed about a dogmatic tradition. It may possibly be true that at Rome the followers of Caesar counted among their number more Epicureans than the senatorial party; but it would be a mistake (even apart from the odd case of Cassius[2]) to align Epicureans and Stoics at Rome on opposite sides, either in Roman political practice or in Greek political theory. It was not until the Augustan principate that Stoicism became the accepted creed of the admirers of the old Roman constitution, and the Epicureans had no programme for any πόλις, great or small. Notwithstanding these two limitations—lack of change in Epicurean doctrine and the absence of any clear political doctrine—the two prominent Epicureans of the first century B.C. whose work has not perished, Philodemus and Lucretius, have some claim to a small place in the history of political thought.

The literary critic Philodemus of Gadara, though he kept art and morality separate and wrote exceptionally amorous epigrams, was himself a man of great learning and many parts and a strict moralist too. *Ingeniosus, eruditus, austerus, gravis, tristis* are among the epithets applied by Cicero to him. The loose morals of the Epicurean philosophers were mostly an invention of their enemies, and the prose works of Philodemus show that he regarded it as a part of the Epicurean tradition to respect orthodox morality. 'Those who agree with our philosophy', he writes (254),[3] 'consider the very same things to be good, just and right as do people in general, only differing in this that we reach those opinions not simply as a matter of feeling, but of reasoning; and we forget them much less frequently.' In a pamphlet bearing the title 'On the Good King according to Homer' he collects quotations from Homer to illustrate the virtues which distinguish good princes from bad and adds comments of his own—all very much on the lines of Isocratean and Hellenistic monarchical theory (see Chaps. VII and XIV). Elsewhere he holds political philosophy in high esteem as something in its own right not dependent on 'Sophistic' (136-137). Political ambitions, however, are a serious hindrance to peace of mind, though some people do find enjoyment in the practice of politics (236-237). Democracy offers a field for political

[1] *Adversus (Sophistas) (pap. Herc.* 1005) ed. F. Sbordone (1947), p. 81.
[2] On whose conversion to Epicureanism some two years before his share in Caesar's murder, see A. Momigliano in *J. Rom. Stud.* XXXI, 1941, pp. 149-157.
[3] See notes at the end of this chapter.

activity, but it is the least intelligent of governments (375).[1] Ideas of right and wrong, just and unjust differ from one city to another. After all, what are politicians trying to do but to set up *their* standards? (256). It is expedient for us to accept the standards of the State in which we find ourselves; if we dislike them we can move to another place[2] (259). *I* am none the less healthy because I do not take the medicine which keeps *you* fit (258). We do not despise or refuse the coins (νομίσματα) of other countries, so why should we disregard their νόμοι?

Philodemus had many interests—poetry, rhetoric, philosophy; Lucretius had only one—the plight of the human race. He followed Epicurus more closely than the literary Philodemus; but he was by far the greater original genius and poet. The *De Rerum Natura* is one of the world's greatest poems; no less than the *Aeneid* it is permeated with sympathy for suffering humanity. Life is hard in any case; for millions it is made harder by the oppression of rulers and by superstitious terrors. Lucretius himself must have felt these terrors in his early life, so warmly does he acclaim Epicurus as deliverer from them; he burns to spread the good news to others, to eradicate the false belief that the gods have created and still actively control the realm of nature, expressing their anger (which by Epicurean doctrine they cannot even feel) by thunder, earthquakes and the like. Educated Romans may have discarded such beliefs, but all the ceremonies and auguries of official religion were still being employed as part of Rome's political machinery in a way that was unknown in the Athens of Epicurus. Lucretius had therefore even more cause than his predecessor to attack superstition. Had he been more of a πολιτικός and a less faithful follower of his masters in philosophy, we might have expected him to denounce directly the practice, which Polybius had approved, of using religion as an instrument for controlling the ignorant masses. As it is, however, the *De Rerum Natura* is a poem about natural phenomena and Humanity, about τὰ φυσικά and τὰ ἀνθρώπινα, not about cities and citizens.

Yet it is perhaps just here, in his wider and deeper humanity,

[1] For hazardous applications of this passage to Philodemus' political relations to Calpurnius Piso see R. Philippson in *Hermes* LIII, 1918, p. 381 ff. The epithet ἀσύνετος had been part of the traditional abuse of democracy for 400 years. See Herod. III 81.

[2] A curious but doubtless quite unconscious echo of Plato, *Crito* 53. See above p. 128.

that Lucretius has something to add to Epicurean political philosophy. Democritus had sought to promote friendly feeling as part
of the cement which holds a city together; Epicurus had regarded
friendship as a good in itself, part of the happy life and a bond
between himself and his followers; a similar bond held together
members of the Academy in Plato's day. Lucretius goes far beyond
any of these in making φιλία a quality inherent in the human race,
distinguishing it from animals and savages. For primitive and
savage men did not possess it; it was acquired in the process of
civilisation, in which it is prior to the faculty of speech. This
means that men do *not* have any desire to do wrong to each other.
Lucretius attacks the doctrine of Callicles on its own ground of
φύσις and maintains that it is just as unnatural to hurt as to be
hurt. The agreement *nec laedere nec violari* (v 1020), μήτ' ἀδικεῖν
μήτ' ἀδικεῖσθαι, does not depend, as Lycophron (p. 78) thought,
on the weak and the strong coming together; nor is it to be regarded as an incident in history, since it represents the φύσις or
norm of the human race. It is true that many men depart from it
and we have as yet no universal *concordia*. But in the past a sufficient number of men were honest and kept their word, so that
the human race has at least survived (v 1027). Thus Lucretius by
implication rejects the account of Protagoras (p. 58), which
ascribed to divine intervention, with the gift of αἰδώς and δίκη,
the saving of primitive man from destruction. It was the warmth
of human affection that brought and kept men together in families
and cities. The Roman poet saw that it needs something more than
the 'virtuous' virtues of the Greek moralist to create *concordia*.
He would have agreed with Protagoras that the history of mankind showed a rise from savagery to civilisation, but he was also
influenced by the theory of a decline from a golden age. At any
rate the evils of modern civilisation—mass-war, disease and destruction, the concentration of money and power in the wrong
hands—compared unfavourably with the healthy existence of the
primitive hunter. Admittedly, prehistoric men lived in fear of
starvation and wild beasts and food-poisoning, but they did not
poison each other in order to inherit legacies. On the whole he
inclines to the 'progress' view, more especially since the acquisition of material comforts such as clothes, hearth and home, while
it may have weakened bodily resistance, greatly strengthened
ties of family affection, gentleness, consideration for women

and children and all those elements of φιλία which make real civilisation.

FURTHER NOTES AND REFERENCES

CHAPTER XIII

POLYBIUS. The first five books of forty have survived entire. We have very extensive extracts from the sixth book, which is the important one for political thought. What is there missing doubtless contained further details about the Roman administration. Byzantine excerptors have preserved for us a good deal of the lost books, apart from what can be inferred from Livy's use of them. They are here referred to by book and chapter (and occasionally also by section) after W. R. Paton's edition with English translation (Loeb Library, six vols., 1922-1927).

His unique opportunity: I 4, III 1. (But P. is always stopping to talk about his own work.) His own part: XII 25 h (5). The character of Scipio: XXXI 23-30. Examination of constitutions: Lycurgan VI 10 and 48-50; others VI 43-47. The Roman civil and military organisation at its most powerful: VI 11-42. Its future ὀχλοκρατία: VI 57. (Was he thinking of the Gracchi or only of what Plato wrote?) Theories of constitutions, cyclic development: short statement VI 3-4; fuller statement with application to the origin of political institutions VI 5-9 (11); Roman application VI 9 (11-14). See generally F. W. Walbank in *Class. Quart.* XXXVII, 1943, and the other literature mentioned in the footnotes above.

PANAETIUS. The numbers refer to the fragments as edited with essays and comment by M. van Straaten, *Panétius* (Amsterdam, 1946). But, since opinions differ as to what is a fragment of P., a list of corresponding references is given below. Van Straaten's collection is wisely conservative, that is to say small; for example from Cicero *de Re Publica* and *de Legibus* (on which see further below), he only includes those few passages which refer to P. by name. Max Pohlenz on the other hand draws freely, too freely, on *de Re Pub.* I for Panaetius; for much of it, I suspect, is Dicaearchus (cp. *supra*, p. 251) and a great deal of that which is common to Polybius, Panaetius and Cicero is traditional conservatism (e.g. *supra*, p. 270, n. 4). Hence Pohlenz finds far more πολιτική in Panaetius than van Straaten, on whose book he wrote in *Gnomon* XXI, 1949. See also his *Die Stoa*, 2 vols. (narrative and notes), 1948, pp. 191-207, 257-263; and Eleuterio Elorduy, *Die Sozialphilosophie der Stoa*, 1936, esp. pp. 135-155 and 207-220. On

Panaetius' ideal of moral leadership, which we get in Cicero *de Off.* I expressly based on Panaetius, *videte cum grano salis vel potius cum gutta aceti* M. Pohlenz, *Antikes Führertum* (1934), 40-55.

Frag. van S.	(Reff. to Cicero are to sections, not chapters.)
48	Cicero *de Legibus* III 14
55	„ *de Finibus* IV 97
73	Diog. L. VII 149, but it is often referred to
96	Clem. Alex. *Stromata* II 129 (ch. XXI)
98	Cicero *de Officiis* I 11-14
117	„ „ „ II 16
118	„ „ „ II 73, but see p. 270, n. 4.
119	„ *de Re Pub.* I 34
120	„ *de Off.* II 41-42

CARNEADES. The references are to the sections of the fragmentary third book of Cicero *de Re Publica*.

POSIDONIUS. Fragments 2, 3, 12, 16, 45, 46 in Müller, *Frag. Hist. Gr.* III (M) and Seneca *Epist.* XC.

CICERO. Of the *de Re Publica* in six books we have only parts and not, unfortunately, the beginning. It contains much praise of the personal rule of a good monarch and has given rise to theories, mostly German, of a Cicero who planned the Principate. The second book is chiefly about early Rome, and attempts to show that monarchy is not incompatible with a mixed constitution. The fragments of the third book show that it partly imitated, though not very closely, Plato *Repub.* I and II and described the Stoic doctrine of *divina lex*. Of the remaining three books the most considerable survival is the dream of Scipio, preserved by Macrobius. In the *de Legibus* it is clear that Cicero has in mind the Roman *ius civile* not the Platonic *Laws*. Like the *de Re Publica*, it contains many extracts from early Roman laws and frequently mentions Greek writers. Both works have been partly reconstructed from references and citations in Lactantius, St. Augustine and others; and both, as is shown above, do something to fill the gap caused by the loss of certain Greek writers. But how little they can really do for us will be evident if we stop to think what our knowledge would be of Plato's *Republic* if we had to rely on Cicero! The references to Ciceronian works are to sections not chapters.

PHILODEMUS of Gadara, who lived much of his life in Italy at the houses of L. Calpurnius Piso, died about 40 B.C. presumably at Herculaneum; excavations there yielded large quantities of papyrus remains of his work. The above remarks on his political theory are based on the περὶ τοῦ καθ᾽ Ὅμηρον ἀγαθοῦ βασιλέως ed. A. Olivieri, Teubner, 1909, on the *Rhetorica* I, ed. S. Sudhaus, Teubner, 1892, to the *pages* of which the numbers in the text refer, and on the account in Pauly-Wissowa by R. Philippson. The work known as the περὶ οἰκονομίας of Ph., in so far as it is not a paraphrase of Xenophon's *Oeconomicus* or of the pseudo-Aristotelian work which he ascribes to Theophrastus, is a statement of the Epicurean view (Metrodorus) of property as opposed to the Cynic. In W. Crönert, *Kolotes und Menedemus* (C. Wessely's *Studien zur Palaeographie und Papyruskunde* VI, 1906) there are fragments of Philodemus attacking the morality of Cynics and Stoics; they show that Ph. knew of a work on πολιτεία by Diogenes, but are no evidence as to its real content. See above, p. 245, n. 3.

LUCRETIUS. There is no means of knowing what effect the *De Rerum Natura* had on the average Roman. Few of those who could understand it stood in need of rescue from superstition. The speculations of B. Farrington, *Science and Politics in the Ancient World* (1939), are insecurely based. Lucretius was a poet, not a scientist or politician; and F. is in error in projecting into early Epicureanism the mentality of Republican Rome. And the γενναῖον ψεῦδος is irrelevant.

CHAPTER XIV

HELLENISTIC MONARCHY AGAIN

οἱ βασιλεῖς τῶν ἐθνῶν κυριεύουσιν αὐτῶν καὶ οἱ ἐξουσιάζοντες
αὐτῶν Εὐεργέται καλοῦνται (St. Luke xxii. 25).

TURNING eastwards again to a world of which Lucretius
knew little, we resume contact with Hellenistic political
thought; and that, now more than ever, means the study
of the nature, powers and duties of a king. The *Cyropaedia* of
Xenophon, so barren of thought and lacking in coherence, has
proved to be curiously prophetic of the fact that kingship, half
Greek and half Oriental, dominated the eastern Mediterranean
for the next three centuries after Alexander. As we saw in Chapter
XII, this was a world in which political philosophers, if they
wished to make their influence felt, had to seek access to a king
or write fictitious letters, addressed to famous kings of the past,
Philip or Alexander, but intended to be read by kings of their
own day. One of these we noted above (p. 254), the letter prefixed
to the *Rhetorica ad Alexandrum* of Anaximenes. The writer had
urged the importance of the king's λόγος, of his pronouncements
as to what is right and lawful. And, since men everywhere were
in fact obliged to take most of their law from kings, it became a
matter of supreme importance to know what a real king ought to
be. If he is to be the source of law, he must be a man with highly
exceptional qualities. It ought not to be possible, though it did
in fact happen, that a very ordinary person be made king merely
by appointment. This was the same dilemma as confronted Aristotle, who thought that, as the πόλις was something 'in nature',
so the πολίτης must be something as it were biologically classifi-
able (*supra*, p. 216). What now is a king? How can he be defined

and classified? The Stoics had argued that only he is king who has the virtue, goodness, ability of a king. So the search for the perfect prince (cp. Chap. IX) goes on, the search for the 'king by nature'. Many more treatises on monarchy were written than have survived.

Doubtless, however, the average man still looked at kingship in the same way as the Xenophontic Socrates:[1] real kings are those who know their job, for example 'those who can lead an army and manage affairs intelligently'.[2] This ability was rare enough and, if he found it being exercised in such a way as to add to his happiness and security, he was ready enough not merely to call such a ruler 'king', but even 'god'. Was it not in such ways as these that the gods of old had benefited the people? The people in turn had bestowed worship and honour on the gods. Similar honours, he thought, were therefore due to successful kings. He did not suppose that the king was himself immortal; but a king appeared to be able to do the things that gods do. Long ago the Epic poets had sung about the ease with which gods raise up or cast down ordinary mortals and do all manner of difficult things. Now here was a king who, having both the power and the resources, could easily do these things; the title 'god' could therefore be properly applied to him. Again, how could a king be better encouraged to use his power for the benefit of his subjects than by acclaiming him as a god? By calling him Benefactor, Saviour, god manifest, men were partly expressing gratitude, partly asking favours. From the king's point of view, too, this Ruler-cult was extremely convenient. The titles of Euergetes and Soter could not of course be won without an effort; but it was an effort well worth making, even if tradition had not already made it also a duty.[3] And the rewards were not merely ceremonial. There was security to be won in this way; for, whatever the aims and motives may have been, no better method than ruler-cult could have been devised by the most astute politician of cementing the loyalty of a heterogeneous populace and of touching the fringes of an often ill-defined dominion. Moreover,

---

[1] Xenophon, *Mem.* III 9, 10. The passage is translated near the beginning of Chap. IX above.

[2] A quotation of unknown origin in Suidas, s.v. βασιλεία.

[3] The tradition of the hard-working king. See Chap. VII, *fin.*, and note on the Cynics at the end of Chap. XII.

deification appeared to give legal sanction to a monarch's position, to make it more acceptable to Greeks in cities, and differentiate it from the old tyrannies. It took different forms in different places and it had many degrees. A king might claim to be not merely god-like, but like some particular god, Apollo or Dionysus, or to be descended from, and especially to be the son of, a great god. He might be called companion of a god and share his temple.[1] He might be somewhat vaguely identified with one of the old gods, a New[2] Dionysus or the like. Or he might neglect the gods of Classical Greece and ally or identify himself with new and Oriental deities. What mattered was not religious feeling in itself, but the belief, widely spread and encouraged, that kings were a race apart, that power and authority belonged to them as to gods, that they were the source of law and justice and all the 'political virtue' which used to belong to the πόλις. As a political device it was successful; so that it appears to have suited well both the temper of the age and its immediate needs.[3]

Little has come down to us of the political writings of the later Hellenistic age and their dates are uncertain. We begin with the so-called *Letter of Aristeas*, which perhaps belongs to the second century B.C. and may therefore not be very much later than the 'letter to Alexander'. It tells the story of the seventy-two trans-lators of the Hebrew Pentateuch into Greek and purports con-temporaneously to relate how, when these seventy-two wise Jews came to Alexandria in the reign of Ptolemy II Philadelphus (285-246 B.C.), they answered seventy-two questions on the art of ruling. The author is himself a Jew and this part of the Letter (187-294)[4] is the first piece of Greek political writing to show marked Jewish influence. It naturally therefore anticipates at many points Philo of Alexandria. But the author is more thoroughly hellenized than Philo, and the answers which the translators of the Septuagint are made to give to Ptolemy's questions are, in spite of their strict monotheism, Hellenistic rather than Jewish. Of course much of the letter is a demonstration of the superiority of Jewish religion and morality; and when the Jews said (127)

---

[1] σύνναος. A. D. Nock in *Harvard Studies in Classical Philology* XLI, 1930.

[2] νέος. A. D. Nock in *Journ. Hell. Stud.* XLVIII, 1928.

[3] Contrast the spirited protest in 322 B.C. of the orator Hypereides (*Orat.* VI 21).

[4] See first note at the end of the chapter.

that they based their teaching on the principle 'that the good life depended on the observance of things lawful', they were thinking of the Law of Moses, not of Greek ideas of τὰ νόμιμα. But they did not answer Ptolemy's questions out of the Pentateuch, but out of their knowledge of Hellenistic political theory backed by their own religion. 'Aristeas' does not approach the subject with that fiery intensity so often associated with Judaism, and we have no better example of Greek political thought of the later Hellenistic era.

The mightiest empire and the best ἀρχή are to rule over oneself. The besetting sin of princes is not greed of food or drink, like common people, but greed of territory and glory. These are desires which they must control. In the advice which follows: 'What God gives, take and keep: seek not after things unattainable' (223), there is quite a Pindaric quality. It is difficult for a king to avoid being envied for his wealth and position; he can but demonstrate that he is worthy of these gifts of God. The popularity which he enjoys depends on his virtues, the goodness, nobility and generosity which God has given him (224 f.). When Ptolemy asked (217) 'How shall we do nothing that is unworthy of ourselves?' the answer was 'Look at all times to your own reputation and exalted position and let your thoughts and your deeds conform thereto, remembering that all those over whom you rule are thinking and talking about you.' The Jewish visitors constantly emphasize a ruler's dependence on God, both for his position and for the qualities needed to maintain it, especially for his hopes of success in battle. Much indeed that a king needs can only be had as a gift from God. At the same time the king is also a copy of God and to Ptolemy's very first question (which has a familiar ring), 'How shall he maintain his kingdom unshaken to the end?' they reply, 'By imitating the continuing goodness of God. For by being long-suffering and treating men with more goodness than they deserve,[1] you will turn them from evil to repentance.' As the king imitates God, his subjects will imitate him; let them behold their king taking thought (πρόνοια) for the masses under his rule, even as 'God, that provides health, sustenance and all else in season, gives benefits to the human race' (190). The same point is frequently made: God and King are both sources of what is good. Both Ptolemy and a Greek philosopher,

---

[1] 188. Reading ἀνθρώπους ἐπιεικέστερον ⟨ἢ⟩ καθώς

who is imagined to be present,[1] express approval of the Jews'
constant references to God: the greatest glory of a king is to
worship God, not with gifts and sacrifices, but in purity of mind
(234); he should remember that he is only a man leading men
and that 'God humbles the proud and exalts the lowly and the
good' (263).

The most essential quality in a king is humanity or φιλανθρωπία
(265). This word in its general sense of kindliness and a feeling
for one's fellow-men was common in Isocrates and in the orators
of the fourth century B.C., but it had acquired a wider significance
as one of the keynotes of Hellenistic kingship. So it is not unnatural that Aristeas should make Ptolemy ask how a king can
become φιλάνθρωπος (208). The reply points to the toils and tribu-
lations of human existence: 'Bearing these in mind, O king, you
will be inclined towards pity; and God too is full of pity.' The
Greeks of the classical era had more often found their gods to be
pitiless and had not generally looked upon pity as part of our duty
to our fellow-men. In Jewish thought these ideas are not new,
but the emergence of φιλανθρωπία as a *political* idea is not primarily
due to Jewish influence. The seeds were sown by the Cynics, with
their attacks on the evils of society, and watered by Panaetius with
his strong sense of social duty (Chap. XIII). In Aristeas, however,
the two strands are united. He makes little mention of law; but
it is significant that the two references which are made to it both
illustrate φιλανθρωπία. To both the Jew and the Hellenistic Greek
of, say, 100 B.C. it seemed right and proper to regard pity for the
weak and afflicted as a duty and to count humane feeling as part
of righteousness and δικαιοσύνη, part of the justice with which
rulers and officials were expected to perform their task. 'Kings
should conform to the laws in order that *acting righteously* (δικαιο-
πραγοῦντες) they may restore the lives of men' (279). Plato[2]
would not have recognised justice and righteousness in such a
dress, so little was φιλανθρωπία then regarded as νόμος. In the
other passage (240) the king is advised, if he would avoid un-

[1] 201. Menedemus of Eretria. A clever choice; his presence is just chronologically possible and he left no writings.
[2] e.g. *Laws* XI 936 where Plato remarks that poverty and hunger are
deserving of pity only when the poor persons are well-behaved and possessed of some degree of goodness. He does, however, recognise that it is
the duty of society to prevent such persons from becoming destitute, and

lawful action, to remember that God has made it the lawgiver's aim 'to preserve the lives of men'.

In the kind of *politeia* envisaged by Aristeas there is no great gulf dividing the king from his chief subjects, none of that aura of unapproachable sanctity, which we find in some other writers and which goes back to the *Cyropaedia* of Xenophon (Chap. IX). The atmosphere of goodwill which pervades the letter of Aristeas may or may not be a true reproduction of the age of Ptolemy Philadelphus or of the time of the writer.[1] But at all events friendliness between the king and his subjects is here part of a theory of monarchy; φιλία and εὔνοια are constantly on the lips of the speakers. The king is also advised not to spend much time on foreign travel: it is the mark of a patriot king to live and die in his own land. 'The poor dislike a king who spends much time abroad and the rich [who have to accompany him] feel it a slur upon themselves, as though they had been forced to leave the country for some crime' (249). A curious question is put about foreign travel (257): How shall a king find a welcome? And the answer is that he must not be too superior, but put himself on a level with other men.[2] Humility is acceptable to God; and people like the condescension of kings. (Cp. 211.)

The last two questions and answers of the series (288-292) are worth reproducing almost in full; they epitomise the thoughts of the writer on two questions which were much discussed in his day—the title to kingship and its aims. 'What is best for the people, that a private citizen be appointed king over them or one who is king by birth?' And he answered [Neither of these but] 'that which is best by nature (φύσει).' Having pointed out that the hereditary monarch, and still more the promoted citizen, has often turned out to be extremely cruel and tyrannical, he goes on: 'Ability to rule depends on good character and good education.

---

thinks that even a moderately well-organised State will be able to do so. It therefore seems to him to follow that there can be no excuse for being a beggar; and begging becomes a crime. On the other hand beggary is inevitable in a society based on wealth (*Repub.* VIII 552).

[1] It was certainly Egyptian. F. Cumont, *L'Egypte des Astrologues* (1937), pp. 33-38; Claire Préaux, *Les Grecs en Egypte*, pp. 79-86.

[2] This appears to be the meaning in this context; but ἴσος is also 'fair', and for a king to treat all men fairly meant to treat them well. Thus ἴσος πᾶσιν (191) is 'not a matter of justice but of *humanitas*', W. Schubart, p. 12. (See note at the end of this chapter.)

You, Ptolemy, are a great king but your eminence lies not in the fame and wealth of your empire: it is that you have surpassed all men in goodness and kindness, God having given you these gifts for a longer period than other men.' The doctrine that the name of king belongs properly only to men of a particular type and not simply to the holders of an office was susceptible of many variations. Goodness and kindness were not the marks either of Plato's kingly man or of the Stoic royal sage. To the other question, What is the greatest merit in a kingdom? comes the answer, 'perpetual peace for his subjects and swift redress in his courts'[1].

There is nothing comparable to Aristeas until we come to his fellow Jew, Philo of Alexandria, but there are in Stobaeus extracts from political writings of unknown date and, in spite of the names attached to them, virtually of unknown authorship.[2] First, the excerpts from a work 'On Law and Justice' ascribed to Plato's Pythagorean friend Archytas. These are full of echoes of Plato and Aristotle and, less conspicuously, of Stoicism; they are more concerned with law than with kingship. But we must remember that we only possess what it suited an anthologist to select. There is, however, no question of the rule of law, no $\delta\eta\mu o\kappa\rho\alpha\tau\iota\alpha$ in that sense (cp. p. 255, n. 2). Law and Justice are conceived in the way to which we are now accustomed, in terms of Ruler and Subject. The author bases his community ($\kappa o\iota\nu\omega\nu\iota\alpha$) on the Unwritten Laws, which are the parents and forerunners of the written laws of men (79). In our lives Law should play the same part as harmony does in listening or in singing (82). There are two Laws: the lifeless, which is something written ($\gamma\rho\alpha\mu\mu\alpha$), the living which is king.[3] It is only in virtue of law that a king is a lawful ($\nu o\mu\iota\mu o\varsigma$) king, a ruler law-abiding, a subject free and the whole community happy (83). There are three requisites for law: (1) it shall be con-

---

[1] This means, we learn, that the ruler must have $\mu\iota\sigma o\pi o\nu\eta\rho\iota\alpha$, which military leaders (280) also require. It is 'readiness to punish evil'. W. Schubart, p. 8 n.

[2] See notes at the end of this chapter.

[3] The passage is obscure and the distinction is not strictly observed. But he does not appear to say, as Goodenough thought, that the king is 'living law'; he seems rather to be discussing king *and* law, not king as law, and drawing a distinction between the unwritten but living law, which is 'king' over us all and the written or lifeless. It is the distinction between the living spirit and the dead letter.

formable to nature (ἀκόλουθον τῇ φύσει). This will be fulfilled, if it copy the justice of nature and that, we learn (84), means 'justice in proportion', the proportionate equality of Plato and Aristotle, by which each man receives according to his worth; (2) it must be effective (δυνατός). This requires that it be both fitted for, and accepted by, those for whom it is intended; (3) it must aim at the benefit of the whole community, not either monarch or individual. In this connection, having perhaps Plato's *Laws* in mind, he thinks soil and climate are important; religion and the family are also the concern of law (84, 86). For law resides not in temple-buildings or tablets of stone but in the characters of the citizens. The whole city, like a household or a citizen army (but not like a mercenary army, which needs pay), ought to be so organised as not to require any addition from the outside. The aim of this is not to avoid foreign contacts, but to ensure the moral and spiritual self-suffi-ciency of the πόλις, an austere way of life being implanted by law. Law is also compared (87) to the sun, who in his annual course *distributes* fair shares of growth and nourishment, thus setting up a εὐνομία of the seasons. The *nome* in music, the shepherd (νομεύς) and the epithets (Nomios and even Νεμήιος) of Zeus are all drawn in for analogy, as often before. The Spartan constitution is praised for good laws and good character, for having within it monarchical, aristocratic and democratic elements, also because of its 'counterbalancing with its own parts' (85), that is to say, the various elements balancing each other's power. The author objects to the use of money-fines as a punishment; they only encourage the accumulation of riches. Loss of rights and conse-quent disgrace are far more effective (86). More clearly Hellenistic is another fragment which states the now familiar thesis that 'a true ruler ought not only to have knowledge and ability to rule well but also be φιλάνθρωπος' (218), and this is somewhat thought-lessly[1] supported by the argument that a shepherd must needs be a lover of sheep. He adds an obscure reference to the dependence of the ruler on law: the best ruler is he who is closest to the law; and that is he who does nothing for his own sake, but for the sake of those under him; even as law is not for the benefit of itself but for those under it (219).

There were at one time three other so-called Pythagorean works excerpted by Stobaeus, their authors Diotogenes, Sthenidas,

---

[1] In view of Plato, *Repub.* 343 B.

Ecphantus.[1] The first of these wrote on Religion and Monarchy. He virtually cites Pseudo-Archytas that law dwells not in buildings or inscriptions, but in the characters of the people (36), though indeed this is a commonplace, going back to Isocrates (VII 41). He can, like St. Paul, recall (80) the opening of Aratus' poem and he owes much, doubtless at many removes, to the *Cyropaedia* of Xenophon and to Plato and Aristotle. The passage is incomplete (80) in which he appears to discuss four possible bases of the state—Nature, Law, Art and Chance. But the point of it seems to be the inclusion of Nomos. For Plato (*Laws* x 888 e) mentions a theory that all things are either natural or artificial or fortuitous. Now this writer adds νόμος to φύσις, τέχνη and τύχη. and goes on to remark: 'Of those states which aim at political harmony based on character Nomos is governor and artificer', which again is like Pseudo-Archytas. In the fragments on Monarchy he also insists that a king must be just and lawful and that law is the origin of justice; but alongside this law-monarchy theory there is also absolute monarchy (ἀνυπεύθυνος) and this is what was popularly meant by the term. It is with this that the author, or at any rate the excerptor, is chiefly concerned, with the king, not as law-abiding ruler (νόμιμος ἄρχων), but as living law (νόμος ἔμψυχος) (263). The work of a ruler covers three chief spheres, the judicial, the military, and the religious. To these he adds doing good to one's subjects, for this too in accordance with the 'modern' view is part of law and justice (265). Much too is said of the usual virtues of a king, and a degree of πλεονεξία is permitted to him, as it was to 'Cyrus' in Xenophon, because he needs money for generous purposes. His superiority to others, however, must not rest on wealth, but (like that of Evagoras or Scipio) on moral qualities and fitness to rule (266). In his relations with the people over whom God has set him to rule he should aim at the harmony of a well-tuned lyre; he himself should be pleasant and easy-mannered, but make it clear, again like Cyrus, that he is not a person to be trifled with (267). In order to achieve these relations with his subjects he must be 'august, good and efficient or strict' (σεμνός, χρηστός, δεινός). His august bearing should be a copy of God's majesty; a king should not judge himself by merely human standards, but separate himself from human

---

[1] Ecphantus, like Archytas, is the name of a well-known Pythagorean. See note at the end of this chapter.

weaknesses and draw near to God. Under his 'goodness' we find not only kindness and generosity but also justice—a collocation now, since Aristeas, not surprising. 'Justice draws and holds together the community; it is the only condition of the soul that is directed towards one's neighbour. As rhythm is to movement, harmony to voice, so is justice to the community. It is the common good of rulers and ruled, so long as it contributes to the coherence of the political association' (269). The extract ends with a reference to the gods, especially to Zeus, who as 'father of gods and men' shows majesty and goodness and whose thunderbolt is a symbol of his δεινότης. Kingship is imitation of God (270).

In the short fragment of 'Sthenidas', it is particularly the wisdom of God that the king must imitate; by 'God' is meant 'the father of gods and the father of men' (271), but Zeus is expressly not named, for this god is stated to be creator of all, as well as teacher of all things good and giver of laws to all equally. 'The wise man and king, then, will be the lawful imitator and servant of God' (271). The extracts from 'Ecphantus' are much longer and, though imitation of God is still a central feature, the king of Ecphantus is a very different kind of person from the august, kindly and efficient monarch of Diotogenes. While Diotogenes spoke of the duty of aiming at a higher than human standard, Ecphantus regards the higher standards as already inherent in kingship. The mortality of his human body is a fact, but so also is his participation in the divine nature. It is all part of the common nature of cosmos; God, aiming at εὐκοσμία, a right condition of the Universe, made the King, using himself as a model (272). The king's likeness to God is such that human beings can only behold him, as it were in a bright light, so bright that it dazzles the impure and unworthy and causes them to reel and faint (273). Kingship is something unadulterated and incorruptible in which human beings can only participate in proportion to their share in the divine nature. That such a kingship is no impossibility the writer urges with some emphasis[1]—'I hold that a king on earth is capable of not falling short in any of the virtues of the king in heaven. As he himself is but a stranger and a sojourner, come among men from beyond, so also, one must suppose, his virtues are the work of God and are his through God' (274-5). It would seem to follow therefore that God has made such kings possible. In practice,

---

[1] 'Il a conscience de l'audace de son affirmation' (Delatte).

however, the writer recognises the necessity of government; the human πόλις may have arisen out of human needs (Plato, *Repub.* II) but the first and most necessary association or partnership (κοι-νωνία) is that subsisting between God and King, and neither of these *needs* anything (275). The association which we call the city or state must therefore copy that partnership, with its harmony and goodwill, and direct all its laws and government to that end. The true king will have the same goodwill for his people as God has for the world and all in it; the people will love their king as a father (278). Affection banishes terror and inspires imitation. If men would spontaneously imitate the king, as the king imi-tates God, there would be no need for him to use compulsion, or even persuasion. But, as it is, men have need of the Logos. To bring this theory of κοινωνία into line with ideas of 'classical' philosophy on community, equality and independence seems to be the aim of the last extract (278-9), but we know nothing of its context and it ends with a reference to God as the Intelligence of the Universe and to the divine understanding of the king.

Most of the writings of Philo the Jew of Alexandria have been preserved for us through the interest taken in them by the early Christian Church. He lived about the turn of the era, being al-ready over sixty when he came to Rome as leader of a mission to the emperor Gaius in A.D. 41. He wrote in Greek, which was his mother-tongue. He read his Jewish scriptures in the Septua-gint translation, of the making of which he, like Aristeas before him, tells the story. He was well read in Greek Philosophy. Yet he is less close than Aristeas to the main current of Greek poli-tical thought and much less close than another foreigner, whose relation to Greek political thought was discussed in Chap. XIII, —Cicero. It is instructive to compare these two. Philo had a greater bent for philosophy and was more studious perhaps than Cicero; and he was equally skilled in selecting what he wanted from Plato or Aristotle or Posidonius and incorporating it in his own work. He had no need to translate, but he paraphrased and sometimes adapted his material. As Cicero was always on the look-out for whatever in Greek philosophy might fit his concep-tion of Rome, her Senate and People, so Philo applies his Greek reading to the Jews and their Law. Cicero made Greek philo-sophy better known to the Romans, Philo to the Jews. But there is a fundamental difference between the Roman approach of the one and the Jewish approach of the other. The Jew began with his sacred scriptures; whatsoever in Greek philosophy confirmed or illustrated these, that was of value; whatsoever else was not inconsistent with the scriptures and in itself tending to righteousness, that too was good. But to study and interpret, allegorically or otherwise, the books of the Pentateuch, to demonstrate the superiority of the Law of Moses to any human laws, to assert the revealed truths of Jewish theology—these were Philo's chief aims. He would not have claimed for himself a place among Greek political philosophers.

Philo then looks back not to Solon for a Lawgiver, but to Moses; and for a statesman and politician to Joseph,[1] not to Pericles or Themistocles. The Greek city-state he knew only from books and its 'modern' counterpart shocked him. The word democracy, δημοκρατία, meant nothing at all to him as a form of government; it was not even opposed to monarchy (cp. p. 255, n. 2) but was merged in it to denote vaguely a peaceful régime of a people under their king.[2] Kingship, of course, he knew well, both Hellenistic and Jewish. The writers already mentioned in this chapter, Aristeas and the so-called Pythagoreans,—he knew their theories and perhaps their writings and he knew the works upon which they drew so freely. For monarchy, even divine monarchy, presented no difficulty to him. Whatever be the relation in Jewish thought between Jehovah and the Lord's Anointed 'under whose shadow we shall live among the heathen',[3] we can at least say that to Philo the notion of a special close relationship between divinity and kingly power and righteousness would be familiar. It would come easily to him to associate also law with

---

[1] About whom, however, he appears to hold two conflicting opinions. Joseph, as well as being praised for his success in managing affairs in Egypt, is selected as typical of arrogance and domination. Whatever be the solution of this puzzle, Philo was not thinking primarily of the Joseph of history. See, in addition to the works mentioned at the end of this chapter, F. H. Colson in his introduction to the sixth volume of the Loeb edition.

[2] See note at the end of this chapter.

[3] *Lamentations* IV 20. It is true that Philo finds in Moses, not in David, his best link with Greek kingship, but the above is none the less true. The particular kind of righteousness embodied in Jewish kingship (*SEDEK*) is not unlike the Platonic σωφροσύνη, containing a large element of loyalty and conformity. On this aspect of Jewish kingship see A. R. Johnson in *The Labyrinth*, pp. 76-85 (Essays ed. S. H. Hooke, 1935).

divinity and to use the Natural Law of the Stoics as equivalent
to the Law of God, the supreme Logos, and to speak in one
breath of Jewish Law and Greek Nomos. He puts into the mouth
of an ideal king the words: 'Other kings carry a staff and bear a
sceptre but my sceptre is the Book of Deuteronomy.'[1] The mixture of Greek and Jewish, with a clear allusion to Plato,[2] is well
illustrated in the following passage: 'For it has been said, not
without good reason, that states can only make progress in well-
being if either kings are philosophers or philosophers are kings.
But Moses will be found to have displayed, combined in his single
person, not only these two faculties—the kingly and the philosophical—but also three others, one of which is concerned with
law-giving, the second with the high priest's office, and the last
with prophecy. . . . For Moses, through God's providence ($\pi\rho\acute{o}$-
$\nu o\iota a$), became king and lawgiver and high priest and prophet;
and in each function he won the highest place. But why it is
fitting that they should all be combined in the same person needs
explanation. It is a king's duty to command what is right and
forbid what is wrong. But to command what should be done and
to forbid what should not be done is the peculiar function of law;
so that it follows at once that the king is a living law ($\nu\acute{o}\mu os$
$\emptyset\mu\psi\upsilon\chi os$) and the law a just king.'[3] Thus Moses is made to join
hands with the Wise Man of the Stoics; for the argumentation
recalls the very words of Chrysippus[4] and the whole fits perfectly
the conception of kingship embodying a cosmic law. It need
hardly be added that all the other typical qualities of the ideal
Hellenistic king are constantly mentioned, especially justice, piety,
humanity and respect for law. But Philo gathers ideas into his
net so widely and indiscriminately that it is no wonder that the
result is as variegated as Joseph's coat, about which he likes to
allegorise. At times he seems to view an ideal state embracing
the whole world, so that with the same quotation from Chrysippus
he can write: 'This kosmos is the Great City ($\mu\epsilon\gamma\alpha\lambda\acute{o}\pi o\lambda\iota s$) and
has but one polity and one law, which is Nature's Logos, reason
commanding what things must be done and forbidding what must
not be done' (*Joseph* 29). At other times he narrows his vision to
the Jewish people and the Mosaic constitution, hardly even re-

[1] *Special Laws* IV 164. 'Ἐπινομίς is the name here given to *Deuteronomy*.
[2] *Repub.* V 473 C D.   [3] *Moses* II 2-4, trans. F. H. Colson, Loeb edition, Vol. VI.
[4] See above p. 257 with the fragment there quoted (*S.V.F.* III 314).

membering the Dispersion of the Jews and not noticing at all the beginnings of Christianity.

.   .   .   .

If the political writings briefly surveyed in the above chapter appear to have done little more than play over the now familiar tunes of Hellenistic monarchy, what is to be said of those who wrote under the fully developed Roman Empire—Plutarch, Musonius Rufus, Aelius Aristides and the egregious Dio Chrysostom of Prusa? More than ever do they derive what they were pleased to call their political philosophy from the older literature of the subject. Plutarch could ask the old question, What is the best kind of πολιτεία? and could go on urging that it is the duty of kings to be philosophers: but there was now only one πολιτεία and it covered the known civilised world. Dio of Prusa could go on repeating and embroidering at great length the themes of the thoughtful, generous and hard-working king, or describing fictitious interviews between Diogenes and Alexander: but neither he nor any of his readers had any thought of any kingship other than that of the Roman emperors. The constant use, in coins and inscriptions as well as in literature, of all the terms and expressions of Greek monarchy applied to the Roman principate is hardly part of Greek political thought, though it is evidence of its influence and of its *Nachleben*. The more absolute the power of the Roman emperor became, the stronger became the connection between monotheism and monarchy. It appeared to be self-evident that, as there was but one supreme ruler on earth and one sun in the sky, the same must also be true of Heaven and of the whole Universe; it was felt that the virtues of a good ruler were none other than the attributes of God.[1] But such thoughts were far from the minds of those who first sought to determine 'political goodness' and to educate men to attain it, who first strove to create conditions which should save mankind from the anarchy and ὕβρις of gangsters and tyrants. Only Plato would have understood the synthesis of political and religious thought which appeared to be taking place under the Empire, and even he would not have found much that would have commanded his support. But Solon and Protagoras, who laid the foundations of political thinking, speak to us in a language which we can to-day more readily understand than that of Hellenistic monarchy or Roman

[1] Pseudo-Arist., *De Mundo* (second century A.D.?), ch. VI.

principate. And the *Republic* of Plato and the *Politics* of Aristotle, for all their narrowness of outlook and glaring faults, can still be studied with advantage alongside the works of medieval and modern masters of political science. Economics and sociology, public administration and preventive medicine, education and child-welfare—of these and many other branches of πολιτική we have a clearer understanding than the ancients and better means of dealing with their problems, but our debt to those who first set us on the paths of these discoveries is one which we freely acknowledge.

FURTHER NOTES AND REFERENCES

CHAPTER XIV

The *Letter of Aristeas*. The references are to the paragraphs in P. Wendland's (Teubner) edition, 1910.

The so-called Pythagorean fragments in Stobaeus. The references are to the *pages* in the fourth volume of the Wachsmuth-Hense edition, 1909. Questions of the date and genuineness of these citations cannot be entirely separated from questions connected with John of Stobi himself (fifth century A.D.), his methods and the manuscript-tradition of his book. I have not accepted any of these fragments as genuinely emanating from the authors, known or unknown, to whom they are ascribed, regarding whatever is Pythagorean in them as long ago absorbed by Plato. (See Erich Frank, *Platon und die sogenannten Pythagoreer* and G. C. Field, *Plato and His Contemporaries*, ch. XIII.) Armand Delatte, *Essai sur la politique pythagoricienne* (1922), thinks that the 'Archytas' pieces may be genuine fourth-century material used by Plato. On the other hand his son, Louis Delatte, dealing with Diotogenes, Sthenidas and Ecphantus in his *Les Traités de la Royauté d'Ecphante, etc.* (1942), assigns all three to the second century A.D.! Though I do not accept either thesis, the two Delatte works contain the best commentary on the text. The pseudo-Doric language, on which see L. Delatte, gives no positive clue about authorship. It may further be mentioned that also in Stobaeus Vol. IV Hense are extracts purporting to come from Hippodamus (the town-planner, *supra*, p. 63) and the law-givers Zaleucus and Charondas (*supra*, p. 195, n. 4). All are discussed in A. Delatte, *Essai*, part II, chs. V and VI.

PHILO OF ALEXANDRIA. The references are to Whitaker and Colson, Text and Translation (Loeb Series). Only a fraction of Philo's work has been here touched upon. See E. R. Goodenough, *The Politics of Philo Judaeus* (Yale Univ. Press, 1938) and ch. XII of H. A. Wolfson's *Philo, Foundations of Religious Philosophy* (two vols., Harvard Univ. Press, second printing, 1948).

A NOTE ON PHILO'S USE OF δημοκρατία.

F. H. Colson (Loeb edition, Vol. VIII, p. 437) refers to recent discussions about how this word came to be so weakened in meaning. Whatever be the details of process of change and whatever external influences may have been at work, the main thing that made such a change possible was the close association of democracy with 'fair and equal', of δημοκρατία and ἰσότης. Hellenistic monarchy never resigned its claim to embody the principle of equality, that is, proportionate equality, being fair (ἴσος) to everybody. The passage in the speech of Aspasia in Plato's *Menexenus* (238-239), which is sometimes (Goodenough, *Politics of Philo*, p. 87) adduced in this connection, is, I think, genuine Plato, but not genuine political theory. It plays with the idea that it does not matter very much what name you give to a government; the people at the top, call them kings if you will, do the ruling and the rest consent: it is only when the consent of the ruled is lacking that any real difference arises.

· · ·

W. Schubart: 'Das Hellenistische Königsideal nach Inschriften und Papyri' in *Archiv für Papyrusforschung* XII (1937); E. R. Goodenough, 'The Political Philosophy of Hellenistic Kingship' in *Yale Classical Studies* I (1928).

On the transition of these monarchical ideas into the Roman Empire see (in addition to the *Cambridge Ancient History*, etc.) Albert Wifstrand in *ΔΡΑΓΜΑ* (M. P. Nilsson *dedicatum*, 1939), p. 531 ff.; M. P. Charlesworth, 'The Virtues of a Roman Emperor' in *Proc. Brit. Acad.* XXIII (1937); and W. S. Ferguson, 'Legalized Absolutism en route from Greece to Rome' (*Amer. Historical Review* XVIII, 1912). But F., both there and in *C.A.H.*, greatly overdoes the absolutism of Hellenistic kingship. In practice of course there was much variation: see for example Paola Zancan, *Il Monarcato Ellenistico* (Padua, 1934), who stresses its 'federative' character. On monarchy and monotheism M. P. Nilsson, *Grekisk Religiositet* (Stockholm, 1946), pp. 135-140 (Eng. trans. H. J. Rose, *Greek Piety* (1948), pp. 118-122).

Greek Writers of the Roman Empire. To those mentioned may be added Herodes Atticus, under whose name there has come down to us a ten-page essay περὶ πολιτείας. It is a kind of exercise in the Isocratean manner, purporting to have been spoken about 400 B.C. So successful has the author been that E. Drerup (*Studien zur Geschichte* II 1, Paderborn, 1908) thought that the writer was a contemporary supporter of Theramenes, and H. T. Wade-Gery (*C.Q.* XXXIX, 1945) that Critias may have been the author. In any case it belies its title, like another and more famous work, which marks the end of the political thought of the Roman Empire—Dante's *De Monarchia*.

GENERAL INDEX

This General Index is primarily a list of persons, especially of authors and their works, Greek, Latin and modern, secondarily a subject index, in which respect it can be supplemented by the Index of Greek Words, which follows it. It is not an index of places or events, deities or races. Its references are to pages without distinction between the notes and the rest.

GENERAL INDEX

INDEX OF GREEK WORDS

1. References in **heavy type** (**25**) are to explanations of the word or to passages otherwise important.
2. Words which occur once only and are translated where they occur are not here listed unless they are of some importance in political terminology.
3. Words occurring only in passages cited in footnotes are not necessarily included nor words like ἀλλά (but), οὐ (not), Ἑλληνικός (Hellenic).
4. Words allied in meaning and origin are sometimes given under one heading.

ἀγαθός, οἱ ἀγαθοί, **25**, 55, 56, 66, 81, 107, 131, 285

ἀγορά, meeting-place, 15, 16

ἄγραφοι νόμοι, unwritten laws, 49-50, 64, 77; see also *Law*

ἀδικεῖν, ἀδικεῖσθαι, **72** n. 2, 76 n. 1, 79, 283

ἀδίκημα, pl. ἀδικήματα, a wrong done, injury, 72

ἀδικία, injustice, wrong-doing, 58, 64 n. 1, 144, 187

ἄδικος, unjust, 84, 91

ἀδύνατος, unable, **116**, 261

αἰδώς, **58**, 173, 283

αἰσυμνήτης, **220**

αἰσχροκέρδεια, profiteering, 202

αἰσχρός, disgraceful, immoral, 51, 94

αἰσχίων, -ον, more disgraceful, 76 n. 1

ἀκρόπολις, Acropolis, 15

ἀλήθεια, truth, 67 n. 2, 70, 71, 113

ἀλογία, lack of common-sense, 108

ἀμαθία, **83**, 189

ἀνάγκη, necessity, 49 n. 1, 113

ἀμείνων, better, 76 n.2

ἀναδασμὸς τῆς γῆς, redistribution of land, 263, 274 n. 2

ἀνακύκλωσις, **274**

ἀναρχία, anarchy, 28 n.

ἄνθρωπος, man; ἀνθρώπειος, ἀνθρώπινος, human, 109, 112 n. 1, 143, 174, 282

ἀνομία, absence of law, 22, 31, 82, 142

ἀντιλογία, ἀντιλογικοὶ λόγοι, opposing arguments, 38, and cp. Chap. IV Protagoras

ἀνυπεύθυνος, cp. εὔθυνα, **36**, 295

ἀποικία, **7**

ἀπορία, problem, 212, 216

ἀρετή, **46**, **55**, 56, 81, 94, 101, 121, 141, 172, 205, **211**, 218, 225 n. 2, 237, 280

ἀριστῆες, champions, 11, 13

ἀριστοκρατία, rule of the best men, 74, 154, 225 n. 2

ἄριστος, best (οἱ ἄριστοι), 37, 39, 224

ἁρμοστής, 'harmost', 248

ἄρχειν, ἄρχεσθαι, rule, be ruled, 6, 26, 38, 42, 63 n. 1, 66 n. 1, 107, 215, 218, 235, 295

ἀρχή, rule, 26, 102, 104, 140, 290

ἄστυ, **15**

ἀσφαλής, secure, 108

ἀταραξία, freedom from worry, 65, 259, 260

ἀτιμία, **218** n. 3

αὐτάρκεια, self-sufficiency, independence 4

αὐτοκράτωρ, controlling, 35

αὐτονομία, autonomy, 4

βάναυσος, **218**, 219, 235

βάρβαρος, βάρβαροι, foreign, not Greek, **14**, 210

βασιλεύς, king; βασιλικός, royal; βασιλεία, kingdom, 11, 19, 41

---

[1] Any association of persons of long or short duration. If X is trying to sell Y a horse, they form a κοινωνία during the time they argue about the price.